Principles of Law

Relating to International Trade

DR. NICHOLAS KOULADIS

Ph.D. (Soton), LL.M. (Wales), C.P.E. (Bristol),
Pg.Cert. in E.U. Law, Pg.Dip. in Legal Practice,
Pg.Dip. in Shipping, M.C.I.T., M.I.Ex.

Solicitor of the Supreme Court, England & Wales
Solicitor-Member, Athens Bar Association (Greece)

Senior Lecturer, Southampton Solent University
Associate Law Lecturer, The Open University
Associate Law Lecturer, Southampton City College

Minister's Adviser, The Ministry of Mercantile Marine (Greece)
Shipping Law Examiner, The Chartered Institute of Shipbrokers
International Trade Law Examiner, The Institute of Export

Springer

Library of Congress Control Number: 2005936345
ISBN-10: 0-387-30386-3 e-ISBN 0-387-30699-4
ISBN-13: 978-0387-30386-4

Printed on acid-free paper.

Printed in the United States of America.

9 8 7 6 5 4 3 2 1

springeronline.com

Principles of Law Relating to International Trade

Dedicated to

My parents, Maria and Stelios, with gratitude

My wife, Vasiliki, with love

My son, Stelios, with great expectations

TABLE OF CONTENTS

CHAPTER 1
THE ENGLISH LEGAL SYSTEM 1

CHARACTERISTICS OF ENGLISH LAW 2

THE CURRENT COURT SYSTEM 4

DOCTRINE OF JUDICIAL PRECEDENT 13

ARBITRATION 14

THE CURRENT LEGAL SYSTEM 17

CONSTITUTIONAL LAW 19

THE LAW OF PROBATE AND SUCCESSION 22

THE LAW OF PROPERTY 29

CRIMINAL LAW 32

EMPLOYMENT LAW 36

CHAPTER 2
AN OVERVIEW OF THE LEGAL PROCEDURE 41

LIMITATION PERIODS 42

CIVIL LITIGATION 44

CRIMINAL LITIGATION 49

CHAPTER 3
THE LAW OF TORTS 63

THE TORT OF TRESPASS 63

THE TORT OF CONVERSION 66

THE TORT OF NUISANCE 67

DEFAMATION 68

THE TORT OF NEGLIGENCE 68

VICARIOUS LIABILITY 70

GENERAL DEFENCES 72

CHAPTER 4
THE LAW OF CONTRACT 75

ELEMENTS OF CONTRACT 76

OTHER ELEMENTS 85

TERMS OF A CONTRACT 97

REMEDIES FOR BREACH OF CONTRACT 104

DISCHARGE OF CONTRACT 109

THE LAW GOVERNING A CONTRACT 120

CHAPTER 5
THE LAW OF AGENCY 129

CLASSIFICATION OF AGENTS 129

CREATION OF AGENCY 133

AUTHORITY 134

AGENCY OF NECESSITY 136

SUBSEQUENT AUTHORITY OR AGENCY BY RATIFICATION 137

DUTIES OF AN AGENT 139

RIGHTS OF AGENT 141

RIGHTS OF THIRD PARTIES AGAINST PRINCIPAL AND AGENT 143

TERMINATION OF AGENCY 147

E.C. LAW AND AGENCY AGREEMENTS 148

CHAPTER 6
THE LAW OF SALE OF GOODS 151

DEFINITION 151

IMPLIED TERMS 153

TRANSFER OF PROPERTY IN THE GOODS 157

RIGHT OF DISPOSAL 163

TRANSFER OF TITLE BY NON-OWNERS 168

PERFORMANCE OF THE CONTRACT 171

SELLER'S REMEDIES 174

BUYER'S REMEDIES 177

CHAPTER 7
EXEMPTION CLAUSES 179

JUDICIAL CONTROL 179

STATUTORY CONTROL 183

CHAPTER 8
COMPETITION LAW 189

FREE MOVEMENT OF GOODS IN THE E.C. 189

THE COMPETITION ACT 1998 191

RESTRICTIVE TRADING AGREEMENTS AND TREATY OF ROME 194

CHAPTER 9
INTRODUCTION TO F.O.B. AND C.I.F. SALES 201

INCOTERMS 202

F.O.B. CONTRACTS 202

C.I.F. CONTRACTS 205

CHAPTER 10
EXPORT FINANCE 213

BILLS OF EXCHANGE & CHEQUES 213

CHEQUES 223

UNIFORM CUSTOMS & PRACTICE FOR DOCUMENTARY CREDITS 226

LETTERS OF CREDIT 226

OTHER METHODS OF PAYMENT 235

CHAPTER 11
INSURANCE LAW 237

LLOYD'S AND THE MARKET 237

THE CONTRACT OF INSURANCE 240

THE INSURANCE POLICY 245

INSTITUTE CARGO CLAUSES 248

AVIATION INSURANCE 253

CHAPTER 12
CARRIAGE OF GOODS BY SEA 255

BAILMENT 256

COMMON AND PRIVATE CARRIER 257

GENERAL AVERAGE 258

CHARTER-PARTIES 261

BILLS OF LADING 265

HAGUE-VISBY RULES 1968 271

HAMBURG RULES 1978 277

CHAPTER 13
CARRIAGE OF GOODS BY ROAD 281

THE C.M.R. CONVENTION 281

ROAD HAULAGE ASSOCIATION 286

CHAPTER 14
CARRIAGE OF GOODS BY AIR 289

INTRODUCTION 289

BASIC SYSTEM OF LIABILITY 290

CARRIER'S DEFENCES 292

APPLICATION OF THE LEGAL REGIMES 293

LIST OF TABLES AND DIAGRAMS

DIAGRAM

1	CONSIDERATION	81
2	ELEMENTS OF SIMPLE CONTRACT	84
3	MISREPRESENTATION	93
4	MISTAKE	97
5	TERMS OF A CONTRACT	103
6	REMEDIES FOR BREACH OF CONTRACT	108
7	DISCHARGE OF CONTRACT	119
8	TRANSFER OF TITLE	171
9	FORM OF BILL OF EXCHANGE	214

TABLE

1	THE COURTS	5
2	EXEMPTING SECTIONS 12-15 OF THE SALE OF GOODS ACT	187
3	CONVENTIONS FOR THE CARRIAGE OF GOODS	295

TABLE OF CASES

21st Century Logistic Solutions Ltd.(In Liquidation) v. *Madysen Ltd.* [2004] 2 Lloyd's Rep.92 89

A. Siohn & Company Ltd. and Academy Garments (Wigan) Ltd. v. *R. H. Hagland & Son (Transport) Ltd.* [1976] 2 Lloyd's Rep.428 257

A.M.B. Imballaggii Plastici S.R.L. v. *Pacflex Ltd.* [1999] 2 All E.R. (Comm.) 249 133

Adamastos Shipping Co. Ltd. v. *Anglo-Saxon Petroleum Co. Ltd.* [1959] A.C.133 98

Adams v. *Lindsell* (1818) 1 B.& Ald.681 80

Adamson v. *Jarvis* (1827) 130 E.R.693 141

Agapitos v. *Agnew (The Aegeon) (No.1)* [2002] 2 Lloyd's Rep.42, C.A. 244

Alexander v. *Rayson* [1936] 1 K.B.169 88

Alfred McAlpine Construction Ltd. v. *Panatown Ltd. (No.1)* [2001] A.C.518, H.L. 182

Allcard v. *Skinner* (1887) 36 Ch.D.145 90

Allen v. *Jambo Holdings Ltd.* [1980] 1 Q.L.R.1252 45

Aluminium Industrie Vaassen BV v. *Romalpa Aluminium* [1976] 1 Lloyd's Rep.443 164

Amin Rasheed Shipping Corp. v. *Kuwait Insurance Co. (The Al Wahab)* [1984] A.C.50, H.L. 123

Antoine Kortas, Case C-319/97, [1999] 3 C.M.L.R.962, O.J. 1999 C 204, 17/07/1999 p.18 19

Appleson v. *Littlewood Ltd.* [1939] 1 All E.R.464 83

Applied Implants Technology Ltd. v. *Lufthansa Cargo AG* [2000] 2 Lloyd's Rep.46 291

Arcos Ltd. v. *Ronassen* [1933] A.C.470, H.L. 154

Argy Trading Development Co. Ltd. v. *Lapid Developments Ltd.* [1977] 1 W.L.R.444 82

Ariston SRL v. *Charly Records Ltd., The Financial Times*, 21 March, 1990 105

Armory v. *Delamirie* (1721) 1 Stra.505 66

Armour v. *Thyssen* [1990] 3 All E.R.481 166

Arsenal Football Club Plc v. *Reed (No.2)* [2003] 1 All E.R.137 13

Aruna Mills v. *Dhanrajmal Gobindram* [1968] 1 Lloyd's Rep.304 205

Ashington Piggeries v. *Christopher Hill* [1972] A.C.441, H.L. 154

Ashmore Benson Pease & Co. Ltd. v. *AV Dawson Ltd.* [1973] 2 Lloyd's Rep.21, C.A. 88

Ashton v. *Turner* [1981] Q.B.137 72

Atari Corporation v. *Electonic Boutique* [1978] 1 All E.R.1010, C.A. 160

Atkinson v. *Denby* (1862) 7 H.& N.934 89

Attorney General v. *Blake* [2000] 4 All E.R.268, H.L 108

Attorney General's Reference (No.2 of 1983) [1984] A.C.456 36

Attorney-General v. *Newspaper Publishing plc.* [1987] 3 All.E.R.532 C.A. 12

Attorney-General v. *Times Newspapers Ltd.* [1974] A.C.273 H.L 12

B. Liggett (Liverpool) Ltd. v. *Barclays Bank Ltd.* [1928] 1 K.B.48 224

B.P. Exploration v. *Hund* (1983) 2 A.C.352 118

Bainbridge v. *Firmstone* (1838) 8 A.& E.743 81

Baldry v. *Marshall* [1925] 1 K.B.260 182

Bank Melli Iran v. *Barclays Bank (Dominion Colonial & Overseas)* [1951] 2 Lloyd's Rep.367 228

Bank of England v. *Vagliano Bros.* [1891] A.C.107, H.L. 215

Banks v. *Goodfellow* (1870) L.R.5 Q.B.549 25

Bannerman v. *White* (1861) 10 C.B. N.S.844 101

Banque de l'Indochine et de Suez S.A. v. *J.H. Rayner (Mincing Lane) Ltd.* [1983] Q.B.711 233

Barclays Bank Ltd. v. *W.J. Simms Son and Cooke (Southern) Ltd.* [1979] 3 All E.R.522 225

Barnett v. *Chelsea & Kensington Hospital Management Committee* [1969] 1 Q.B.428 70

Barrett McKenzie & Co. Ltd. v. *Escada (UK) Ltd.*, [2001] E.C.C.50 150

Bartlett v. *Sidney Marcus Ltd.* [1965] 2 All E.R.753 155

Barton v. *County Natwest Ltd. The Times*, 29 July, 1999 91

Beale v. *Taylor* [1967] 3 All E.R.253 153

Beard v. *London General Omnibus Co.* [1900] 2 Q.B.530 71

Belfast Ropework Co. Ltd. v. *Bushell* [1918] 1 K.B.210 257

Bell v. *Lever Bros. Ltd.* [1932] A.C.161 .... 91, 94

Benaim & Co. v. *Debono* [1924] A.C.514 124

Bence Graphics Ltd. v. *Fasson U.K. Ltd.* [1997] 1 All E.R.979, C.A. 178

Beswick v. *Beswick* [1967] 2 All E.R.1197 181

Bettini v. *Gye* (1876) 1 Q.B.D.183 .... 101, 113

Beyene v. *Irving Trust Co. Ltd.* (1985) 762 Fed.Rep. 2d 4, U.S. Second Circuit Court of Appeals 234

Bigos v. *Bousted* [1951] 1 All E.R.92 88

Bird v. *Jones* (1845) 7 Q.B.742 64

Bird's Cigarette Manufacturing Co. Ltd. v. *Rouse* (1924) 19 Ll. L. Rep.301 258

Bishop v. *Plumley* [1991] 1 W.L.R.582 29

Bisset v. *Wilkinson* [1927] A.C.177 91

Black King Shipping Corp. v. *Massie (The Litsion Pride)* [1985] 1 Lloyd's Rep.437 243

Blower v. *Great Western Railway Co.* (1872) L.R. 7 C.P.655 258

Blyth v. *Birmingham Waterworks Co.* (1856) 11 Exch.781 33

Boardman v. *Phipps* [1967] 2 A.C.46 141

Bolivia Republic v. *Indemnity Mutual Marine Assurance Co. Ltd.* (1908) 99 L.T.394, K.B.D. 243

Bolton Partners v. *Lambert* (1889) 41 Ch.D.295 137

Bolton v. *Mahadeva* [1972] 1 W.L.R.1009 110

Bond Worth Ltd., Re. [1980] Ch.228 .... 165, 166

Borden v. *Timber Products Ltd.* [1981] Ch.25 165

Boston Deep Sea Fishing and Ice Co. Ltd. v. *Ansell* (1888) 39 Ch.D.339 87

Bowmakers Ltd. v. *Barnet Instruments Ltd.* [1945] K.B.65 89

Boys v. *Chaplin* [1971] A.C.536 127

Brace v. *Calder* [1895] 2 Q.B.253 106

Bratty v. *Attorney-General for Northern Ireland* [1963] A.C.386 H.L. 34

Brinkibon Ltd. v. *Stahag Stahl und Stahlwarenhandelsgesellschaft mbH.* [1983] 2 A.C.34 .... 80, 124

British and Foreign Marine Insurance Co Ltd. v. *Gaunt* [1921] 2 A.C.41 249

British Bank of the Middle East v. *Sun Life Assurance of Canada (U.K.) Ltd* [1983] 2 Lloyd's Rep.9 134

British Crane Hire Corporation Ltd. v. *Ipswich Plant Hire Ltd.* [1975] Q.B.303 99

British Road Services v. *A.V. Crutchley Ltd.* (1967) 1 W.L.R.835 79

Brumark, Re [2001] B.C.C.259 167

Bundesverband der Arzneimittel-Importeure EV and the Commission of the European Communities v. *Bayer AG* (Joined Cases C-2/01 P and C-3/01 P) [2004] E.T.M.R. 100 ECJ 195

Bunge & Co v. *Tradax England* [1975] 2 Lloyd's Rep.235 205

Bunge Corporation v. *Tradax Export S.A.* [1981] 2 Lloyd's Rep.1; [1981] 1 W.L.R.711 .... 100, 102

Campbell v. *Paddington Corporation* [1911] 1 K.B.869 67

Car and Universal Finance Co. v. *Caldwell* [1965] 1 Q.B.525, C.A. 170

Cargill U.K. Ltd. v. *Continental U.K. Ltd.* [1989] 2 Lloyd's Rep.290, C.A. 203, 205

Carlill v. *Carbolic Smokeball Company* [1893] 1 Q.B.256 76

Carlos Federspiel v. *Twigg* [1957] 1 Lloyd's Rep.240 161

Castle v. *Playford* (1872) 26 L.T.315 157

Catlin v. *Cyprus Finance Corp. (London) Ltd.* [1983] Q.B.759 224

Cavendish-Woodhouse Ltd. v. *Manley* (1984) 148 J.P. 299 154

Cehave NV v. *Bremer Handels GmbH (The Hansa Nord)* [1975] 3 All E.R.739 155

Cellulose Acetate Silk Co. Ltd. v. *Widnes Foundry Ltd.* [1933] A.C.20 104

Central Newbury Car Auctions Ltd. v. *Unity Finance Ltd.* [1957] 1 Q.B.371 168

Central Property Trust Ltd. v. *High Trees House Ltd.* [1947] K.B.130 82

Chaigley Farms Ltd. v. *Crawford, Kay and Grayshire Ltd.* [1996] B.C.C.957 166

Chamberlain v. *Young* [1893] 2 Q.B.206, C.A. 215

Chandler v. *Webster* [1904] 1 K.B.493 118

Channel Island Ferries Ltd. v. *Sealink U.K. Ltd.* [1987] 1 Lloyd's Rep.559 (Q.B.D. (Comm)) 115

Chapelton v. *Barry Urban District Council* [1940] 1 K.B.532 180

Chappel & Co. Ltd. v. *Nestlé Co. Ltd.* [1960] A.C.87 82

Charter v. *Sullivan* [1957] 1 All E.R.809 175

Cheese v. *Lovejoy* (1877) 2 P.D.251 26

Cheikh Boutros Selim El-Khoury v. *Ceylon Shipping Lines, Ltd., (The Madeleine)* [1967] 2 Lloyd's Rep.224 263

Chellew v. *The Royal Commission on Sugar Supply* [1922] 126 L.T.103 260

Chic Fashions (West Wales) Ltd. v. *Jone* [1968] 2 Q.B.299 65

China-Pacific SA v. *Food Corp of India (The Winson)* [1982] A.C. 939 137

Clark v. *Lindsay* (1903) 19 T.L.R.202 117

Clay v. *Yates* (1856) 1 H.& N.73 89

Clegg v. *Andersson* [2003] 2 Lloyd's Rep.32, C.A. 155

Clough Mill Ltd. v. *Martin* [1985] 1 W.L.R.111 164

Clutton v. *George Attenborough & Son* [1897] A.C.90, H.L. 215

Cochrane v. *Willis* (1865) L.R.1 Ch.App.58 96

Cockshott v. *Bennet* (1788) 2 T.R.763 88

Cole v. *Turner* (1704) 6 Mod.149 64

Collen v. *Wright* (1857) 120 E.R.847 .... 144, 146

Comber v. *Anderson* (1808) 1 Camp.523 134

Commercial Union Assurance Co. Ltd. v. *Niger Co. Ltd.* (1922) 13 Ll. L. Rep.75, H.L. 246

Commission v. *Denmark* (Case 302/86), [1988] E.C.R.4607 191

Commission v. *United Kingdom* (Case 40/82), [1982] E.C.R.2793 190

Compagnie Tunisienne de Navigation SA v. *Compagnie d'Armement Maritime SA* [1971] A.C.572, H.L. 125

Comptoir d'Achat et de Vente du Boerenbond Belge SA v. *Luis de Ridder Limitada (The Julia)* [1949] A.C.293, H.L. 210

Conegate Ltd. v. *Commissioners of Customs and Excise* (Case 121/85), [1986] E.C.R.1007 190

Consten S.A. and Grundig-Verkaufs GmbH v. *E.C. Commission* (Cases 56 and 58/64), [1966] E.C.R.299 196

Container Transport International Inc. and Reliance Group Inc. v. *Oceanus Mutual Underwriting Association (Bermuda) Ltd.* [1984] 1 Lloyd's Rep.476, C.A. 242

Cope v. *Sharpe (No.2)* [1912] 1 K.B.496, C.A. 73

Couturier v. *Hastie* (1856) 5 H.L.Cas.673 96

Cox v. *Glue* (1848) 5 C.B.533 65

Credit Industriel et Commercial v. *China Merchants Bank* [2002] 2 All E.R. (Comm.) 427 .... 233, 234

Crehan v. *Inntrepreneur Pub Co. CPC* [2004] EWCA Civ. 637 193

Cundy v. *Lindsay* (1878) 3 App.Case.459 .... 95, 169

Curtice v. *London City & Midland Bank Ltd.* [1908] 1 K.B.293 225

Curtis v. *Chemical Cleaning and Dyeing Co.* [1951] 1 K.B.805 180

Customs & Excise Commissioners v. *Hare* [1996] 2 All E.R.391. 86

Cutter v. *Powell* (1795) 6 Term R.320 .... 110, 111, 112

Czarnikow-Rionda Sugar Trading Inc. v. *Standard Bank London Ltd.* [1999] 2 Lloyd's Rep.187 230

Dakin v. *Oxley* (1864) 143 E.R.938 112

Dawsons Ltd. v. *Bonnin* [1922] 2 A.C.413, H.L. 242

De Bernardy v. *Harding* (1853) 155 E.R.1586 113

De Lasala v. *De Lasala* [1980] A.C.546 13

Dean v. *Dean* [1987] 1 F.L.R.517 C.A 12

Delfini, The [1990] 1 Lloyd's Rep.252 276

Department of Trade and Industry v. *St. Christopher Motorists Association Ltd* [1974] 1 Lloyd's Rep.17 240

Derry v. *Peek* (1889) 14 App.Cas.337 92

Deutsche Gremmophon v. *Metro* (Case 78/70), [1971] E.C.R.487 199

Deutsche Post (Case COMP/35.141), Decision 2001/354/EC, O.J. L 125, 05/05/2001 p.27 198

Diamond Alkali Export Corp. v. *Bourgeois* [1921] 3 K.B.443 229

Diana Prosperity, The (1976) 2 Lloyd's Rep.621 182

Dickinson v. *Dodds* (1876) 2 Ch.D.463 78

Dimskal Shipping Co. S.A. v. *I.T.W Federation, (The Evia Luck)* [1991] 4 All E.R.871 90

Director of Public Prosecutions v. *Channel Four Television Co. Ltd.* [1993] 2 All E.R.517 12

DMA Financial Solutions v. *BaaN U.K.* 2000 W.L.1629568 .... 75, 83

Donoghue v. *Stevenson* [1932] A.C.562 69

Dovey v. *Cory* [1907] A.C.477 87

Dunlop Pneumatic Tyre Co. Ltd. v. *New Garage & Motor Co. Ltd.* [1915] A.C.79 105

Dunlop Pneumatic Tyre Co. Ltd. v. *Selfridge & Co.* [1915] A.C.847 81

E. Clement Horst Company v. *Biddell Brothers* [1912] A.C.18, H.L. 265

E.C. Commission v. *France* (Case 232/78) [1979] E.C.R.2729 189

Eagle Star Insurance Co. Ltd. v. *Spratt* [1971] 2 Lloyd's Rep.116, C.A. 246

East West Corp. v. *DKBS 1912* [2003] 1 Lloyd's Rep.239 257

Eastern Distributers Ltd. v. *Goldring* [1957] 2 All E.R.525, C.A. 168

Edler v. *Auerbach* [1950] 1 K.B.359 89

Edwards v. *Carter* [1893] A.C.360 86

Edwards v. *Skyways Ltd.* [1964] 1 W.L.R.349 83

El Amria and El Minia [1982] 2 Lloyd's Rep.28 203

Elphick v. *Barnes* (1879-80) L.R. 5 C.P.D.321 160

Empresa Cubana Importadora de Alimentos Alimport v. *Iasmos Shipping Co. SA (The Good Friend)* [1984] 2 Lloyd's Rep.586 273

Ennstone Building Products Ltd. v. *Stanger Ltd. (No.2)* [2002] EWCA Civ. 916 121

Entores Ltd. v. *Miles Far East Corporation* [1955] 2 All E.R.493 80

Equal Opportunities Commission v. *Secretary of State for Employment* [1994] 1 W.L.R.409 194

Equitable Trust Co. of New York v. *Dawson Partners Ltd.* (1927) 27 Ll. L. Rep.49, H.L. 232

Esso Petroleum Co. Ltd. v. *Customs and Excise Commissioners* [1976] 1 W.L.R.1 .... 77, 81

Europemballage Corporation and Continental Can Company Inc. v. *Commission* (Case 6/72), [1973] E.C.R.215 199

F.W. Moore & Co Ltd. v. *Landauer & Co.* [1921] 2 K.B.519, C.A. 154

Falke v. *Fletcher* (1865) 18 C.B. (N.S.) 403 66

Feldaroll Foundry Plc. v. *Hermes Leasing (London) Ltd.* [2004] EWCA Civ. 747 184

Felthouse v. *Bindley* (1862) 11 C.B.N.S.869. 80

Fibroasa Spolka Akcyjna v. *Fairbairn Lawson Combe Barbour Ltd.* [1943] A.C.32 H.L. 118

Finance Co. Ltd. v. *Stebbing* [1989] B.C.L.C.498 87

Finlay v. *Kwik Hoo Tong* [1929] 1 K.B.400 268

Finska Cellulosaforeningen (Finnish Cellulose Union) v. *Westfield Paper Co. Ltd.* [1940] 68 Ll. L. Rep.75 181

Fisher v. *Bell* [1961] 1 Q.B.394 77

Flaminio Costa v. *ENEL* (Case 6/64), [1964] E.C.R.585 194

Foakes v. *Beer* (1884) 9 App.Cas.605 83

Ford Motor Co. v. *Armstrong* (1915) 31 T.L.R.267 105

Forder v. *Great Western Railway Co.* [1905] 2 K.B.532 .... 251, 285

Fortman Holdings Ltd. v. *Modem Holdings Ltd.* [2001] EWCA Civ. 1235 174

Foster v. *Driscoll* [1929] 1 K.B.470 88

Foulders v. *Willoughby* (1841) 8 M.& W.538 66

Franco v. *Bolton* (1797) 3 Ves.368 88

G. v. *G.* [1970] 3 All E.R.546, C.A. 129

G.J. Dawson (Clapham) Ltd. v. *H. & G. Dutfield* [1936] 2 All E.R.232 152

Gardner v. *Coutts & Co.* [1967] 3 All E.R.1064 98

Garton v. *Bristol and ExeterRailway Co.* (1861) 30 L.J.Q.B.273 258

General Accident Fire & Life Assurance Corp. Ltd. v. *Tanter (The Zephyr)* [1985] 2 Lloyd's Rep.529, C.A. 246

General Re-Insurance Corp. v. *Forsakringsaktiebolaget Fennia Patria* [1983] 2 Lloyd's Rep.287 246

Gibbons v. *Westminster Bank Ltd.* [1939] 2 K.B.882 225

Gibson v. *Manchester City Council* [1979] 1 All E.R.972 77

Gill & Duffus v. *Societe Pour l'Exportation des Sucres SA* [1985] 1 Lloyd's Rep.621 205

Ginzberg v. *Barrow Haematite Steel Co and McKellar* [1966] 1 Lloyd's Rep.343 210

Glaxo Group Ltd. v. *Dowelhurst Ltd.* [2003] EWHC 110 197

Glynn v. *Margetson & Co.* [1893] A.C.351, H.L. 264

Godley v. *Perry* [1960] 1 All E.R.36 157

Goldcorp Exchange Ltd., Re [1994] 1 All E.R.806 160

Goods of Barnes, The (1926) 43 T.L.R.71 25

Goods of Chalcraft, The [1948] P.222 25

Goole and Hull Steam Towing Co. Ltd. v. *Ocean Marine Insurance Co. Ltd.* (1927) 29 Ll. L. Rep.242, K.B.D. 244

Gore v. *Gibson* (1843) 13 M.& W.623 85

Gotha City v. *Sotheby's (No.2), The Times*, 8 October, 1998 127

Grand Champion Tankers Ltd. v. *Norpipe A/S (The Marion)* [1984] A.C.563, H.L. 273

Grant v. *Australian Knitting Mills Ltd.* [1936] A.C.85 156

Granville Oil & Chemicals Ltd. v. *Davies Turner & Co.* [2003] 2 Lloyd's Rep.356 185

Great Future International Ltd. v. *Sealand Housing Corp. (In Liquidation)* EWHC 300 92

Great Peace Shipping Ltd. v. *Tsavliris Salvage (International) Ltd.* [2003] Q.B.679, [2002] 2 All E.R. (Comm) 999 .... 13, 96

Greenwood v. *Martins Bank Ltd.* [1933] A.C.51, H.L. 223

Griffiths v. *Peter Conway Ltd.* [1939] 1 All E.R.685 156

Groom v. *Barber* [1915] 1 K.B.316 206

Group Josi Re v. *Walbrook Insurance Co. Ltd.* [1996] 1 Lloyd's Rep.345 231

Hadley v. *Baxendale* (1854) 9 Exch.341 .... 106, 175

Halki Shipping Corporation v. *Sopex Oils Ltd.* [1998] 1 Lloyd's Rep.465 16

Halsey v. *Esso Petroleum Co. Ltd.* [1961] 1 W.L.R.683 68

Harlingdon & Leinster Enterprises v. *Christopher Hull Fine Arts Ltd.* [1990] 1 All E.R.737, C.A. 154

Hart v. *O'Connor* (1985) 2 All E.R.880. 85

Hartley v. *Ponsonby* (1857) 7 E.& B.872 82

Haynes v. *Harwood* [1935] 1 K.B.146, C.A. 72

Healy v. *Howlett & Sons* [1917] 1 K.B.337 161

Hedley Byrne & Co. Ltd. v. *Heller & Partners Ltd.*, [1964] A.C.465 H.L. 93

Hely-Hutchinson v. *Brayhead Ltd.* [1968] 1 Q.B.549, 593, C.A. 136

Hendy Lennox (Industrial Engines) Ltd. v. *Grahame Puttick Ltd.* [1984] 2 Lloyd's Rep.422 .... 161, 165, 166, 167

Herman v. *Jeuchner* (1885) 15 Q.B.D.561 88

Higgins Ltd. v. *Northampton Corporation* [1927] 1 Ch.128 95

Hochster v. *De la Tour* (1853) 118 E.R.922 115

Hoenig v. *Isaacs* [1952] 2 All E.R.176 112

Hollins v. *Fowler* (1875) L.R.7 H.L.757 66

Holmes v. *Wilson* (1839) 10 A.& E.503 65

Hong Kong Fir Shipping Co. Ltd. v. *Kawasaki Kisen Kaisha Ltd.* [1962] 2 Q.B.26, C.A. 102, 263

Hooker, Re [1993] C.O.D.190 12

Hornby v. *Lacy* (1817) 6 M.& S.166 130

Hotson v. *East Berkshire Area Health Authority* [1987] 2 All E.R.909 69

Howard Marine and Dredging Co. Ltd. v. *A. Ogden & Sons (Excavations) Ltd* [1978] Q.B.574 92

Howard Perry & Co. Ltd. v. *B.R.B.* [1980] 1 W.L.R.1375 66

Hughes v. *Hall (Gillian)* [1981] R.T.R.430 154

Imperial Chemical Industries Ltd. v. *E.C. Commission (Dyestuffs)* (Case 48/69), [1972] E.C.R.619. 197

Indian Oil Corp. Ltd. v. *Greenstone Shipping Corp.* [1988] Q.B.345 165

Innes v. *Wilie* (1844) 1 Car.& Kir.257 64

Internationale Handelsgesellschaft GmbH v. *Einfuhr und Vorratsstelle fur Getreide und Futtermittel* (Case 11/70), [1970] E.C.R.1125 194

Inversiones Manria S.A. v. *Sphere Drake Insurance Co. Plc. Malvern Insurance Co. Ltd. and Niagara Fire Insurance Co. Inc, (The Dora)* 243

Ionides v. *Pacific Fire and Marine Insurance Co.* (1871) L.R. 6 Q.B. 674. 245

Ionides v. *Pender* (1873-74) L.R. 9 Q.B. 531 243

J. Evans & Sons (Portsmouth) Ltd. v. *Andrea Merzario Ltd.* [1976] 2 Lloyd's Rep.165 183

J. Lauritzen A.S. v. *Wijsmuller B.V., The Super Servant Two,* [1990] 1 Lloyd's Rep.1, C.A. 117

J.& J. Cunningham Ltd. v. *Robert A Munro & Co Ltd.* (1922) 13 Ll. L. Rep.216 205

J.H. Rayner & Co. Ltd. v. *Hambro's Bank Ltd.* [1943] K.B.37 234

Jackson v. *White and Midland Bank* [1967] 2 Lloyd's Rep.68 224

Jocelyne, The [1977] 2 Lloyd's Rep.121 262

John Crowther Group plc. v. *Carpets International plc.* [1990] B.C.L.C.460 87

Johnson v. *Midland Railway* (1849) 18 L.J.Ex.366 257

Johnson v. *Taylor Bros. & Co. Ltd.* [1920] A.C.144, H.L. 124

Jolley v. *Sutton LBC* [2000] 2 Lloyd's Rep.65, H.L. 70

Jones v. *Vernon's Pools Ltd* 83

Joseph Thorley Ltd. v. *Orchis Steamship Co. Ltd.* [1907] 1 K.B.660 264

K/S Merc-Scandia XXXXII v. *Lloyd's Underwriters (The Mercandian Continent)* [2001] 2 Lloyd's Rep.563, C.A. 244

Kay v. *Butterworth* [1945] 173 L.T.191 .... 32, 34

Kearly v. *Thomson* (1890) 24 Q.B.D.742 89

Keighley, Maxsted & Co. v. *Durant* [1901] A.C.240 137

Kelner v. *Baxter* (1866) L.R. 2 C.P.174 145

Kelsen v. *Imperial Tobacco Co.* [1957] 2 Q.B.334 65

Kent v. *Griffiths (No.3)* [2001] Q.B.36, C.A. 69

Keppel v. *Wheeler* [1927] 1 K.B. 577 140

Kiriri Cotton Co. v. *Dewani* [1960] A.C.192 89

Kirkham v. *Attenborough* [1897] 1 Q.B.201, C.A. 160

Kish v. *Taylor* [1912] A.C.604, H.L. 264

Knatchbull v. *Fearnhead* (1837) 3 My.& Cr.122 28

Korea Exchange Bank v. *Debenhams (Central Buying) Ltd.* [1979] 1 Lloyd's Rep.100 216

Kredietbank Antwerp v. *Midland Bank plc.* [1999] 1 All E.R.801 234

Kronprinsessan Margereta, The, [1921] A.C.486 209

Kuwait Airways Corp. v. *Iraqi Airways Co. (Damages)* [2004] EWHC 2603 127

Kwei Tek Chao v. *British Traders and Shippers Ltd.* [1954] 2 Q.B.459...........158, 209

Kyzuna Investments Ltd. v. *Ocean Marine Mutual Insurance Association (Europe)* [2000] 1 Lloyd's Rep.505 247

Laceys (Wholesale) Footwear Ltd. v *Bowler International Freight Ltd.* [1997] 2 Lloyd's Rep.369, C.A. 285

Laconia, The [1977] A.C.850, [1977] 1 All E.R.545 100

Lally and Weller v. *George Bird* 23 May 1980, (unreported) 185

Lampleigh v. *Brathwait* (1615) 80 E.R.255 82

Lancashire Loans Ltd. v. *Black* [1934] 1 K.B.380 90

Law & Bonar Ltd. v. *British American Tobacco Company* [1916] 2 K.B.605 211

Lazenbury Garages Ltd. v. *Wright* [1976] 2 All E.R.770, C.A. 175

Leach, Re [1988] Ch.226 28

Leaf v. *International Galleries* [1950] 2 K.B.86 96

Leclerc v. *Au Blé Vert* (Case 229/83), [1985] E.C.R.1 190

Leigh and Sillivan Ltd. v. *Aliakmon Shipping Co. Ltd. (The Aliakmon)* [1986] 2 All E.R.145, H.L. 211

L'Estrange v. *F Graucob Ltd.* [1934] 2 K.B 180

Lewis v. *Averay* [1972] 1 Q.B.232 .... 95, 170

Lewis v. *Clay* (1898) 67 L.J.Q.B.224 94

Leyland Shipping Co. v. *Norwich Union Fire Insurance Society Ltd.* [1918] A.C.350 245

Lickbarrow v. *Mason* (1793) 126 E.R.511, H.L. 266

Lidl U.K. GmbH v. *Hertford Foods Ltd.* [2001] EWCA Civ. 938 79

Light v. *Ty Europe Ltd.* [2004] 1 Lloyd's Rep.693, C.A. 148

Limpus v. *London General Omnibus Co.* (1862) 1 H.& C.526 71

Liverpool City Council v. *Irwin* [1977] A.C.239 99

Lombard North Central plc. v. *Butterworth* [1987] Q.B.527, C.A. 101

London and Northern Bank, Re (1900) 1 Ch.220 80

Louis Dreyfus Trading Ltd. v. *Reliance Trading Ltd.* [2004] 2 Lloyd's Rep.243 (QBD (Comm.)) 153

Luxor (Eastbourne) Ltd. v. *Cooper* [1941] A.C.108 99

M v. *Home Office* [1993] 3 All E.R.537 12

Mahonia Ltd. v. *J.P. Morgan Chase Bank (No.1)* [2003] 2 Lloyd's Rep.911. 232

Malas (Hamazeh) & Sons v. *British Imex Industries Ltd.* [1958] 2 Q.B.127 230

Manbre Saccharine Co. Ltd. v. *Corn Products Co Ltd.* [1919] 1 K.B.198 209

Manfield v. *Maitland* (1821) 4 B.& Ald.582. 241

Manufacture Française Des Pneumatiques Michelin v. *Commission of the European Communities* (Case T-203/01), [2004] 4 C.M.L.R.18, C.F.I. 199

Mapes v. *Jones* (1974) 232 E.G.717 92

Maple Flock Co. Ltd. v. *Universal Furniture Products (Wembley) Ltd.* [1934] 1 K.B.148, C.A. 173

Mareva Compania Naviera S.A. v. *International Bulk Carriers S.A. (The Mareva)* [1975] 2 Lloyd's Rep.509, C.A. 107

Mash & Murrell v. *Emmanuel* [1962] 1 All E.R.77 204

McCrone v. *Riding* [1938] 1 All E.R.157 33

McFadden v. *Blue Star Line* [1905] 1 K.B.697 263

Medical Defence Union v. *Department of Trade* [1979] 1 Lloyd's Rep.499 240

Merrett v. *Babb* [2001] Q.B.1174, C.A. 69

Michael Galley Footwear Ltd (In Liquidation) v. *Iaboni* [1982] 2 All E.R.200 284

Michelin, (Case COMP/E-2/36.041/PO), Decision 2002/405/EC, O.J. L 143, 31/05/2002 p.1. 198

Mihalis Angelos, The [1970] 2 Lloyd's Rep.43 C.A 100

Miramar Maritime Corp. v. *Holborn Oil Trading (The Miramar)* [1984] A.C.676 262

Mitsui & Co. Ltd. v. *Flota Mercante Grancolombiana SA (The Ciudad de Pasto and The Ciudad de Neiva)* [1989] 1 All E.R.951 164

Mizenchuk v. *Thompson and Nash Taxi and U-Drive Co.* [1948] 1 D.L.R.136 257

Modelboard v. *Outerbox Ltd.* [1993] B.C.L.C.623 166

Monarch Steamship Co. Ltd. v *A/B Karlshamns Oljefabriker* [1949] A.C.196, H.L. 276

Montrod Ltd. v. *Grundkotter Fleischvertriebs GmbH* [2002] 3 All E.R. 697 231

Moorcock, The (1889) L.R. 14 P.D.64 98

Moore & Co. v. *Landauer & Co.* [1921] 2 K.B.519 .... 110, 112

Moore v. *Lunn* (1922) 11 Ll. L. Rep.86 263

Moorgate Mercantile Co. v. *Twitchings* [1977] A.C.890, H.L. 168

Moralice (London) Ltd. v. *E.D.& F. Man* [1954] 2 Lloyd's Rep.525 233

Moran Galloway & Co. v. *Uzielli* [1905] 2 K.B.555 ... 241

Moran, Galloway & Co. v. *Uzielli* [1905] 2 K.B.555 ... 242

Morrison & Co. Ltd. v. *Shaw Savill & Albion Co. Ltd.* [1916] 2 K.B.783, C.A. ... 264

Morrison Steamship Co. Ltd. v. *Greystoke Castle (Cargo Owners)* [1947] A.C.265 ... 259

Mulox I.B.C. v. *Geels* [1994] I.R.L.R.422 ... 121

Natal Land & Colonisation Co. Ltd. v. *Pauline Colliery Syndicate* [1904] A.C.120 ... 137

National Commercial Bank (Jamaica) Ltd v. *Hew* [2003] UKPC 51 ... 90

National Employers Insurance Association Ltd. v. *Jones* [1988] 2 All E.R.425, H.L. ... 170

National Petroleum Co. v. *Owners of the Athelviscount* (1934) 48 Ll. L. Rep.164 ... 275

National Westminster Bank Plc v. *Spectrum Plus Ltd.* [2004] 3 W.L.R.503 ... 13

New Bullas Trading Ltd., Re [1994] B.C.C.36 ... 167

Newborne v. *Sensolid (Great Britain) Ltd.* [1954] 1 Q.B.45 ... 146

Newtons of Wembley Ltd. v. *Williams* [1965] 1 Q.B.560, C.A. ... 170

Norris v. *Southampton City Council, The Times*, 27 January, 1982 ... 116, 117

North & South Wales Bank v. *Macbeth* [1908] A.C.137, H.L. ... 215

North Ocean Shipping v. *Hyundai Construction, The Atlantic Baron* [1979] Q.B.705 ... 90

Northern Foods Plc. v. *Focal Foods Ltd.* [2003] 2 Lloyd's Rep.728 ... 78

Nugent v. *Smith* (1875-76) L.R. 1 C.P.D.423 ... 256, 258

NV Nederlandsche Banden Industrie Michelin v. *Commission of the European Communities* (Case 322/81), [1983] E.C.R.3461 ... 199

Ocean Tramp Tankers Corp. v. *V/O Sovfracht, The Eugenia*, [1964] 2 Q.B.226, C.A. ... 117

O'Connell v. *Jackson* [1971] 2 Lloyd's Rep.354, C.A. ... 72

Olearia Tirrena SpA v. *NV Algemeene Oliehandel (The Osterbek)* [1973] 2 Lloyd's Rep.86, C.A. ... 204

Olley v. *Marlborough Court Ltd.* [1949] 1 K.B.532 ... 180

Omnium D'Enterprises v. *Sutherland* [1919] 1 K.B.618 ... 114

Oosthoek's Uitgeversmaatschappij BV (Case 286/81), [1982] E.C.R.4575 ... 191

Oppenheimer v. *Attenborough & Son* [1908] 1 K.B.221, C.A. ... 169

Ormrod v. *Crosville Motor Service* [1953] 1 W.L.R.1120 ... 66

Oscar Chess Ltd. v. *Williams* [1957] 1 W.L.R.370 93

Owners of Cargo Laden on Makedonia v. Makedonia Owners (The Makedonia) [1962] 2 All E.R.614 263

Owners of Cargo Lately Laden on Board the Ardennes v. *Owners of the Ardennes (The Ardennes)* [1951] 1 K.B.55 267

Ozalid Group v. *African Continental Bank* [1979] 2 Lloyd's Rep.231 232

P.B. Groenveld BV v. *Produktschap voor Vee en Vlees* (Case 15/79), [1970] E.C.R.3409 190

Pacific Motor Auctions Pty Ltd. v. *Motor Credits (Hire Finance) Ltd.* [1965] 2 All E.R.105 170

Padbury v. *Holliday and Greenwood Ltd.* (1912) 28 T.L.R.494 71

Pagnan SpA v. *Tradax Ocean Transportation SA* [1987] 2 Lloyd's Rep.342 ... 115, 203

Panchaud Frères S.A. v. *Etablissements General Grain Co.* [1970] 1 Lloyd's Rep.53 208

Panorama Developments (Guildford) v. *Fidelis Furnishing Fabrics* [1971] 3 All E.R.16 135

Papayanni & Jerinica v. *Grampian Steamship Co. Ltd.* (1896) 12 T.L.R.540 260

Papera Traders Co. Ltd. v. *Hyundai Merchant Marine Co. Ltd. (The Eurasian Dream)* [2002] 1 Lloyd's Rep.719 273

Parchim, The [1918] A.C.157 211

Parke Davis & Co. v. *Probel and Centrafarm* (Case 24/67), [1968] E.C.R.55 .... 197, 199

Parker v. *Felgate* (1883) 8 P.D.171 25

Parkinson v. *Royal College of Ambulance* [1925] 2 K.B.1 88

Partridge v. *Crittenden* [1968] 2 All E.R.421 77

Payne v. *Cave* (1789) 3 Term.Rep.148 78

Peachdart Ltd., Re [1984] Ch.131 165

Pearce v. *Brooks* (1866) L.R.1 Ex.213 88

Pera Shipping Corporation v. *Petroship S.A., (The Pera)* [1984] 2 Lloyd's Rep.363 182

Petraco (Bermuda) v. *Petromed International S.A.* [1988] 2 Lloyd's Rep.357, C.A. 203

Petrograde Inc. v. *Stinnes GmbH* [1995] 1 Lloyd's Rep.142 204

Pharmaceutical Society of Great Britain v. *Boots Cash Chemists Ltd.* [1953] 1 All E.R.482 77

Pharmaceutical Society v. *Storkwain* (1986) 1 W.L.R.903 32

Pharmed Medicare Private Ltd. v. *Univar Ltd.* [2002] EWCA Civ.1569 136

Philip Alexander Securities and Futures Ltd. v. *Bamberger, The Times*, 22 July, 1996 .... 15, 16

Philippson and Others Appellants v. *Imperial Airways, Limited* [1939] A.C.332, H.L. 293

Phillips v. *Eyre* (1870-71) L.R. 6 Q.B.1 127

Pickford Ltd. v. *Celestica Ltd.* [2003] EWCA Civ. 1741 .... 78, 79, 80

Pilcher v. *Rawlins* (1872) 7 Ch.App.259 31

Pink v. *Fleming* (1890) 25 Q.B.D.396 245

Pinnel's Case (1602) 77 E.R.237. 110

Planché v. *Colburn* (1831) 131 E.R.305 113

Planché v. *Fletcher* (1779) 1 Doug. K.B.251 243

Plus Group Ltd. v. *Pyke* [2002] EWCA Civ. 370 87

Polemis, Re [1921] 3 K.B.560 70

Porter v. *Freudenberg* [1915] 1 K.B.857 88

Portland Management Ltd. v. *Harte* [1977] Q.B.306 65

Poseidon Freight Forwarding Co. Ltd. v. *Davies Turner Southern Ltd.* 2 Lloyd's Rep.388 181

Poussard v. *Spiers & Pond* (1876) 1 Q.B.D.410 .... 101, 113, 115, 116

President of India v. *Metcalfe Shipping Co. Ltd. (The Dunelmia)* [1970] 2 Q.B.289 262

Procter & Gamble Philippine Manufacturing Corp. v. *Kurt A. Becher GmbH & Co.* [1988] 2 Lloyd's Rep.21, C.A. 268

Pyrene & Co v. *Scindia Navigation Co* [1954] 2 Q.B.402 204

Quantum Corp. Inc. v. *Plane Trucking Ltd.* [2003] 1 All ER.873, C.A. 282, 286

R v. *Galbraith* [1982] 2 All E.R.1060 57

R v. *Kingston upon Hull Justices, ex parte McCan* (1991) 155 J.P.569 52

R v. *New Statesman (Editor)* (1928) 44 T.L.R.301 12

R v. *Newton* (1983) 77 C.App.R.13 .... 52, 56

R v. *Powell* (1994) 98 Cr.App.R.224 12

R v. *Samuda* (1989) 11 Cr.App.R.471 C.A 12

R v. *St. George* (1840) 9 C.& P.483 64

R v. *Wilson* [1955] 1 All E.R.744 64

R. & B. Customs Brokers Co. Ltd. v. *United Dominions Trust Ltd.* [1988] 1 All E.R.847 184

R. v. *Bird* [1985] Crim.L.R.388 36

R. v. *Burgess* (1991) 2 W.L.R.1206 34

R. v. *Caldwell* [1981] 1 All E.R.961 33

R. v. *Cunningham* [1957] 2 All E.R.412 33

R. v. *Dudley and Stephens* (1884) 14 Q.B.D.273 35

R. v. *Duffy* [1967] 1 Q.B.63 35

R. v. *Gotts* (1992) 1 All E.R.832 35

R. v. *Graham* [1982] 1 W.L.R.294 35

R. v. *Henn (Maurice Donald) (No.1)* [1979] 2 C.M.L.R.495, H.L. 190

R. v. *Howe* [1987] A.C.417 35

R. v. *Larsonneur* (1933) 24 C.A.R.74 32

R. v. *Miller* [1983] A.C.161 32

R. v. *M'Naghten* (1843) 10 Cl.& Fin.200 .... 32, 34

R. v. *Moloney* [1985] 1 All E.R.1025 33

R. v. *Pharmaceutical Society, ex parte API* (Case 266/87) [1989] E.C.R.1295 190

R. v. *Pike* [1961] Crim.L.R.547 33

R. v. *Secretary of State for Transport, ex parte Factortame* (Case C-213/89), [1990] 3 C.M.L.R.867 194

R. v. *Shivpuri* (1986) 2 W.L.R.988 33

R. v. *Simpson (Ian McDonald)* [2004] Q.B.118 13

R. v. *Spencer* [1985] Q.B.771 C.A. 14

R.E. Jones Ltd. v. *Waring & Gillow Ltd.* [1926] A.C.670, H.L. 219

R.H. Willis & Sons v. *British Car Auctions Ltd.* [1978] 1 W.L.R.438 66

Race Relations Board v. *Applin* [1975] A.C.259 34

Raffles v. *Wichelaus* (1864) 2 H.C.906 96

Rafsanjan Pistachio Producers Co-operation v. *Bank Leumi (U.K.) plc.* [1992] 1 Lloyd's Rep.513 .... 231, 232

Raiffeisen Zentralbank Osterreich AG v. *Five Star General Trading LLC (The Mount I)* [2001] 1 Lloyd's Rep.597, C.A. 122

Rakhit v. *Carty* [1990] 2 All E.R.202 C.A 13

Ramsgate Victoria Hotel Co. Ltd. v. *Montefiore* (1866) L.R. 1 Ex.109 78

Rayner v. *Rederiaktiebolaget Condor* [1895] 2 Q.B.289 66

Reardon Smith Line Ltd. v. *Black Sea & Baltic General Insurance Co. Ltd.* [1939] A.C.562, H.L. 263

Reardon Smith Line v. *Hansen Tangen* [1976] 1 W.L.R.989, H.L. 102, 154

Reference Re Amendment of the Constitution of Canada (1982) 125 D.L.R. (3rd) 1 22

Reinhart Co. v. *Joshua Hoyle & Sons Ltd.* [1961] 1 Lloyd's Rep.346 211

Rewe-Zentrale AG v. *Bundesmonopolverwaltung für Branntwein* (Case 120/78), [1979] E.C.R.649 191

Richco International Ltd. v. *Bunge & Co. Ltd. (The New Prosper)* [1991] 2 Lloyd's Rep.93 205

Rio Tinto Co. Ltd. v. *Seed Shipping Co. Ltd.* (1926) 24 Ll. L. Rep.316 264

Riverstone Meat Co. Pty Ltd. v. *Lancashire Shipping Co. Ltd. (The Muncaster Castle)* [1961] A.C.807, H.L. 273

Rolls Razor Ltd. v *Cox* [1967] 1 Q.B.552, C.A. 131

Roscorla v. *Thomas* (1842) 3 Q.B.234 81

Rose v. *Plenty* [1976] 1 W.L.R.141 71

Roselodge Ltd. (formerly Rose Diamond Products Ltd.) v. *Castle* [1966] 2 Lloyd's Rep.113 242

Ross v. *H.M. Advocate* (1991) S.L.T.564 35

Rossiter v. *Miller* (1878) 3 A.C.1124 262

Rowland v. *Divall* [1923] 2 K.B. 500 153

Rowson v. *Atlantic Transport* [1903] 2 K.B.666 263

Rudolph A Oetker v. *IFA Internationale Frachtagentur AG (The Almak)* [1985] 1 Lloyd's Rep.557 267

Russell v. *Niemann* (1864) 34 L.J. C.P.10 258

SA Hercules Chemicals NV v. *Commission* [1991] E.C.R. II-1711, C.F.I 195

Samcrete Egypt Engineers & Contractors SAE v. *Land Rover Exports Ltd.* [2001] EWCA Civ 2019 122

Saunders v. *Anglia Building Society* [1971] A.C.1004 94

Scaramanga & Co. v. *Stamp* (1879-80) L.R. 5 C.P.D.295 264

Schuler A.G. v. *Wickman Machine Tool Sales Ltd.* [1974] A.C.235, H.L. 101

Schumacher v. *Hauptzollamt Frankfurt-am Main-Ost* (Case 215/87), [1989] E.C.R.617 190

Scott v. *Avery* (1856) 5 H.L.C.811, H.L. 15

Scruttons Ltd. v. *Midland Silicones Ltd.* [1962] A.C.446 181

Seaconsar Far East Ltd. v. *Bank Markazi Jomhouri Islami Iran* [1999] 1 Lloyd's Rep.36 C.A. 232

Selectmove, Re [1995] 2 All E.R.521 83

Sewell v. *Burdick* [1884] 10 App.Cas.74, H.L. 266

Shaw v. *Commissioner of Police of the Metropolis* [1987] 1 W.L.R.1332 169

Shaw v. *Symmons* [1917] 1 K.B.799 257

Shell (U.K.) Ltd. v. *Lostock Garages Ltd.* [1976] 1 W.L.R.1187 99

Shepherd v. *Kottgen* (1877) 37 L.T.618 260

Shipton, Anderson & Co. and Harrison Bros' Arbitration, Re [1915] 3 K.B.676 116

Shipton, Anderson & Co. Ltd. v. *Weil Bros & Co. Ltd.* [1912] 1 K.B.574 173

Shirlaw v. *Southern Foundries Ltd.* [1939] 2 K.B.206, [1940] A.C.701 H.L. 98

Shogun Finance Ltd. v. *Hudson* [2004] 1 A.C.919 .... 95, 96

Sika Contracts Ltd. v. *Gill, The Times*, 27 April 1978 145

Simpson v. *John Reynolds* [1975] 2 All E.R.88 82

Sirius International Insurance Co. Ltd. v. *FAI General Insurance Ltd.* [2004] 1 All E.R.308 231

Skibsaktieselskapet Thor. Thoresens Linje v. *H. Tyrer & Co. Ltd* (1929) 35 Ll. L. Rep.163 67

Slater v. *Finning* [1996] 3 All E.R.398, H.L. 156

Societe Italo-Belge Pour le Commerce et L'Industrie SA (Antwerp) v. *Palm and Vegetable Oils (Malaysia), The Post Chaser* [1981] 2 Lloyd's Rep.695 82

Society of Lloyd's v. *Canadian Imperial Bank of Commerce* [1993] 2 Lloyd's Rep.579 230

Sopromа SpA v. *Marine & Animal By-Products Corporation* [1966] 1 Lloyd's Rep.367 .... 230, 233

Spiro v. *Lintern* [1973] 1 W.L.R.1002 136

Spracklan's Estate Re [1938] 2 All E.R.345 26

Springer v. *G.W. Rail. Co.* [1921] 1 K.B.257 137

St. Albans City Council v. *International Computers Ltd.* [1996] 4 All E.R.481, C.A. 151

Standard Chartered Bank v. *Pakistan National Shipping Corporation and Others (No.2)* [2003] 1 Lloyd's Rep.227, H.L. 92

Stanley v. *Powell* [1891] 1 Q.B.86 64

Starkey v. *Bank of England* [1903] A.C.114 144

Starmark Enterprises Ltd. v. *C.P.L. Distribution Ltd.* [2002] Ch.306 C.A. 13

Steel v. *State Line Steamship Co.* (1877-78) L.R. 3 App. Cas.72, H.L. 263

Stein, Forbes & Co. v. *County Tailoring* (1916) 115 L.T.215 175
Stilk v. *Myrick* (1809) 170 E.R.1168 82
Strang Steel & Co. v. *A. Scott & Co.* (1889) 14 A.C.601, 608 260
Suiker Unie v. *Commission* (Cases 40-48, 50, 54-56, 111, 113-114/73), [1975] E.C.R.1663 197
Sze Hai Tong Bank v. *Rambler Cycle Co. Ltd.* [1959] 2 Lloyd's Rep.114 266
Tanner v. *Tanner* [1975] 1 W.L.R.1346 88
Tarling v. *Baxter* (1827) 6 B. & C.360 158
Tate & Lyle Industries Ltd. v. *Greater London Council* [1983] 2 A.C.509 67
Tate v. *Williamson* (1866) 2 Ch.App.55 90
Taylor v. *Caldwell* (1863) 122 E.R.309 116
Tesco Plc v. *Customs and Excise Commissioners, The Times*, 16 October, 2003 82
Teutonia, The (1871-73) L.R. 4 P.C. 171 264
Texas Instruments Ltd. v. *Nason (Europe) Ltd.* [1991] 1 Lloyd's Rep.146 285
Theodorou v. Chester [1951] 1 Lloyd's Rep.204, K.B.D. 249
Thermo Engineers Ltd and Anhydro A/S v. *Ferrymasters Ltd.* [1981] 1 W.L.R.1470 282
Thomas v. *National Union of Mineworkers* [1985] 2 All E.R.1 64
Thompson W.L. Ltd. v. *Robinson (Gunmakers) Ltd.* [1955] 1 All E.R.154 175
Thornton v. *Shoe Lane Parking Ltd.* [1971] 1 Lloyd's Rep.289 77
Thyssen Inc. v. *Calypso Shipping Corp. SA* [2000] 2 Lloyd's Rep.243 273
Tinn v. *Hoffman & Co.* (1873) 29 L.T.271 79
TM Noten BV v. *Paul Charles Harding* [1990] 2 Lloyd's Rep.283 258
Torvald Klaveness A/S v. *Arni Maritime Corp., The Gregos* [1994] 1 W.L.R.1465, H.L. 101
Tournier v. *National Provincial and Union Bank of England* [1924] 1 K.B.461, C.A. 225
Transpacific Eternity SA v. *Kanematsu Corp. (The Antares III)* [2002] 1 Lloyd's Rep.233 ..... 164, 202
Transpetrol Ltd v. *Transol Olieprodukten Nederland BV* [1989] 1 Lloyd's Rep.309 204
Tribe v. *Taylor* (1875-76) L.R. 1 C.P.D.505 142
Truck & Spares Ltd. v. *Maritime Agencies (Southampton) Ltd.* [1951] 2 All E.R.982 266
Tsakiroglou & Co. Ltd. v. *Noblee and Thorl GmbH* [1962] A.C.93 117

Tuberville v. *Savage* (1969) 1 Mod.Rep.3 64

Turnbull v. *Garden* (1869) 38 L.J. Ch.331 141

Turpin v. *Bilton* (1843) 5 Man. & G.455 140

Twine v. *Bean's Express Ltd.* (1946) 62 T.L.R.458 71

Underwood Ltd. v. *Burgh Castle Brick & Cement Syndicate* [1922] 1 K.B.123, C.A. 159

United Bank Ltd. v. *Banque Nationale de Paris* [1992] 2 S.L.R.64, H. Ct. of Singapore 234

United Brands Company and United Brands Continentaal B.V. v. *Commission of the European Communities* (Case 27/76), [1978] ECR 207 193

United City Merchants (Investments) v. *Royal Bank of Canada* [1983] 1 A.C.168. 231

United States v. *Eastmount Shipping Corp.* (1974) A.M.C.1183 260

Universal Non Tariff Fire Insurance Co, Re (1874-75) L.R. 19 Eq. 485 242

Universe Tankships v. *I.T.F, (The Universe Sentinel)* [1982] 2 All E.R.67 90

Verband Sozialer Wettbewerb eV v. *Clinique Laboratoires SNC* (Case C-315/92), [1994] E.C.R. I-317 191

Viho Europe BV v. *Commission* (Case C-73/95P), [1996] E.C.R. I-5457 196

Vinden v. *Hughes* [1905] 1 K.B.795 215

Virgin/British Airways (Case IV/D-2/34.780), Decision 2000/74/EC, O.J. L 30, 04/02/2000, p.1 199

Volkswagen A.G. v. *Commission of the European Communities* (Case C-338/00), [2004] 4 C.M.L.R.7 195

Vortigern, The [1899] P.140, C.A. 263

Wachauf (Case 5/88), [1989] E.C.R.2609 194

Wagon Mound, The [1961] A.C.388 70

Wait, Re [1927] 1 Ch.606 158

Waldron-Kelly v. *British Railways Board* [1981] C.L.Y.303 185

Wallis v. *Smith* (1882) L.R. 21 Ch.D.243 105

Walsh v. *Lonsdale*, (1882) 21 Ch.D.9 32

Walter v. *James* (1871) L.R. 6 Ex.124 139

Waren Import Gesellschaft Krohn & Co. v. *Alfred C. Toepfer (The 'Vladimir Ilich')* 1 Lloyd's Rep.322 207

Warner Bros. v. *Nelson* [1936] 3 All E.R.160 107

Watford Electronics Ltd. v. *Sanderson C.F.L. Ltd.*, [2001] 1 All E.R. (Comm) 696 185

Watson v. *British Boxing Board of Control Ltd.* [2001] Q.B.1134, C.A. 72

Watson v. *Davies* [1931] 1 Ch.455 138

Waugh v. *H.B. Clifford & Sons* [1982] Ch.374 135

Webster (EJ) v. *Dickson (F) Transport* [1969] 1 Lloyd's Rep.89 257

Weir & Co. v. *Girvin & Co.* [1899] 1 Q.B.193 241

Wellcome Trust Ltd. v. *Hammad* [1998] 1 All E.R.622 C.A. 13

White v. *John Warwick & Co. Ltd.* [1953] 2 All E.R.1021 182

Whitecross Wire & Iron Co. Ltd. v. *Savill* (1822) 8 Q.B.D.653, C.A. 260

Whitworth Street Estates (Manchester) Ltd. v. *James Miller & Partners Ltd.* [1970] A.C.583, H.L. 124

Wildhandel v. *Tucker & Cross* [1975] 2 Lloyd's Rep.240 206

Williams v. *Fanshaw Porter & Hazelhurst* [2004] 2 All E.R.616, C.A. 43

Williams v. *Glasbrook Bros.* [1947] 2 All E.R.884. 13

Williams v. *Roffey Bros. and Nicholls (Contractors) Ltd.* [1990] 1 All E.R.512, C.A. 83

Wilson v. *Jones* (1866-67) L.R. 2 Ex.139 241

Wilson v. *United Counties Bank Limited* [1920] A.C.102, H.L. 224

Winkfield, The [1902] P.42 66

Winzar v. *Chief Constable of Kent*, *The Times*, 28 March 1983 32

With v. *O'Flanagan* [1936] Ch.575 91

Wood v. *Scarth* (1858) 1 F.& F.293 96

X Ltd. v. *Morgan-Grampian (Publishers) Ltd.* [1990] 2 All E.R.1 H.L. 12

Yonge v. *Toynbee* [1910] 1 K.B.215 144

Yorkshire Insurance Co. Ltd. v. *Nisbet Shipping Co. Ltd.* [1962] 2 Q.B.330 244

Young v. *Bristol Aeroplane Co. Ltd.* [1944] K.B.718 C.A. 13

Youssoupoff v. *Metro-Goldwyn-Mayer Pictures Ltd.* (1934) 50 T.L.R.581. 68

Z Ltd. v. *A-Z and AA-LL* [1982] Q.B.558, C.A. 107

PREFACE

There has been over 10 years since the first edition of 'Principles of Law Relating to Overseas Trade', and during this time I have felt that an expansion and update of the text was timely. A great deal of development happened to areas of law covered by the text, which made the publication of a new edition essential.

The title of this edition has changed slightly to 'Principles of Law Relating to International Trade', to reflect the scope of the book more accurately. However, the book's format has changed considerably in this edition. The main body of text has been maintained in similar vein to the previous book, offering a plain exposition of the relevant topics. The added footnotes now contain the appropriate authoritative references, as well as further and more detailed information on the relevant issues. It is felt that this format would be more helpful to the reader who would now be able to research further into any of the topics considered in the main text.

Law is an intellectual activity, requiring reflection, creativity, and debate. This is why even if we do not agree with all or part of them, some books have to be read just to keep the mind sharp. Therefore, the reader should focus on any ideas enshrined by the text which seem new, odd, or simply wrong, since it is not the act of reading itself that is enriching, but rather the act of developing thoughts based on that reading.

I have spent a considerable time of my life believing that there should be a single unified philosophy in law, but, as of yet, have only been able to discern a certain methodology. Law does not work by means of deducing from rules or regulations, but rather through making various hypotheses based on legal principles and values.

It is necessary, of course, to know and study these principles to help put an order to our knowledge. This, I hope, is the purpose of the present book, which is intended for those engaged in business, their professional advisers, and students.

As always, there is a 'warning' to the reader to the effect that law is not static but dynamic, and therefore it must be appreciated that this presents an insoluble problem to the author of any law text. Within the limits of the possible, every reasonable effort has been made to present the most up-to-date information available.

During the preparation of the present edition I have incurred many debts. The text was written while I was a lecturer at Southampton University and senior lecturer at Southampton Solent University and so benefited from the challenges of the students who followed the courses I have been privileged to lead. My thanks go to colleagues and former colleagues and particularly Dr. Mike Biles, Mr. Phil Purves, Mr. Jerry Stanford, Mr. Rory Addison, Ms. Paula Elliott, Mr. John Hoar, Mr. John Mathews, Dr. David Bailey, and Professor David Johnson, for their help and support.

I am under a special debt of gratitude to Mr. Maurice Jensen, solicitor, for his guidance and useful advice on legal practice matters.

I am also grateful to Mr. John Kent who, through his business ambitions and inspirations, gave me the opportunity to practise what I preach on numerous occasions. Above all, however, I should like to convey my thanks to him for being a good friend.

I would also like to acknowledge the assistance of Springer Science + Business Media for bringing the project to press despite my continued attempts to subvert their timetable.

My greatest debt goes to my wife Vasiliki and my three-year old son Stelios who encouraged and distracted me, together ensuring that I completed the book.

N.K.

CHAPTER 1

THE ENGLISH LEGAL SYSTEM

In the strict sense of the word, law is the rules of conduct imposed by a State upon its members and enforced by its Courts. Such rules of conduct constitute 'the law of the land' which enforces certain standards of behaviour among citizens within a State. This is not complete or 'the definition' of law, since the writer would consider that there is little point in defining law as a single concept; law can mean different things according to context.[1]

Inevitably legal theorists, who are mainly experts in jurisprudence,[2] have put forward a large number of theories as to the meaning of the term 'law' and its role in society.

An important point to note is that the law enforceable by the Courts must be distinguished from what is sometimes referred to as 'natural' or 'moral' law. In many cases the rules of law and morality coincide.[3] However, this is not always the case and for example, adultery, although considered by society to be a moral wrong, no punishment can be administered by the Courts.

In conclusion, it would not be correct to say that most people obey the law because it is just, or because it coincides with the view of the majority of people.[4]

Legal systems can be broadly divided into two categories:

(a) Modern Roman Law: which is derived from the ancient law of the Roman Empire.[5]

(b) English Common Law: which is a native product of Britain that has absorbed only a few rules of Roman Law and is applied in most parts of the Commonwealth and the U.S.A.

Law can be divided into two broad areas:[6]

---

1 For example the meaning would be different in the case of political, social, or religious context.

2 Which in plain English means the science of law.

3 For example the crime of murder would offend both law and morality, and the State will punish the offender.

4 Earth did not become spherical when the majority of people ceased to believe it to be flat!

5 This system of law has been adopted and today applies to most European States, South Africa, South America, certain parts of Canada, and in the State of Louisiana in the U.S.A.

6 For further distinctions between Criminal and Civil law see *infra*, p.17.

(a) **Public Law**: which governs the relations of citizens with the State and of one State with another.[7] This includes criminal law, constitutional and administrative law, and international law.

(b) **Private or Civil Law**: which is part of the law of a State which governs the relations of citizens among themselves. It includes the law of torts (civil wrongs), the law of property, and the law of contract.

English law consists of two main and complementary components:

(a) **Common Law**: which comprises of 'judicial precedents'[8] and enacted laws. It is called 'common' because it was made common to the whole of England and Wales after the Norman Conquest in 1066.[9]

(b) **Equity**: which comprises of legal principles[10] laid down in the Court of Chancery before 1873 and which intended to supplement the Common Law by 'softening' the Common Law where this was too rigid and inflexible.

CHARACTERISTICS OF ENGLISH LAW

There are some special features, which distinguish the English Legal System from other systems. These may be summed up as follows:

(1) **Absence of Codification**: In some countries most of the law has been reduced to written codes which contain the whole of the law on a particular subject. This is not the case in England.

(2) **The System of Judicial Precedent**: In English Law, a Judge is bound to apply rules of law formulated in earlier cases provided the facts of the case are sufficiently similar, and the earlier case was heard in a Court of superior, or in some cases of equal status.

---

7 What is called 'public international law'.

8 For an explanation of *judicial precedent*, see *infra*, p.13.

9 Prior to this time there was no common system of law for the whole country.

10 There are actually twelve maxims of equity which should be considered whenever an equitable remedy is sought. Very briefly these twelve equitable maxims are: (1) equity will not suffer a wrong to be without a remedy, (2) equity follows the law, (3) where there is equal equity the law must prevail, (4) where the equities are equal the first in time shall prevail, (5) he who seeks equity must do equity, (6) he who comes to equity must come with clean hands, (7) delay defeats equity, (8) equality is equity, (9) equity looks to the intent rather than the form, (10) equity looks on that as done which ought to be done, (11) equity imputes an intention to fulfil an obligation, (12) equity acts *in personam*.

(3) **The Judiciary**: Judges are independent of both Parliament and the Civil Service. Furthermore, Judges are immune from liability provided they act honestly in the belief that they are within their jurisdiction.

(4) **The Accusatorial Procedure**: In both civil and criminal cases the Court remains neutral and hears the arguments presented by each side. In countries where the inquisitorial procedure is used the Court plays a more active part, itself questioning the witnesses.

BRIEF HISTORY OF COMMON LAW

Before the Norman Conquest (1066), England was only loosely united under the Crown. Therefore, the local areas largely governed themselves and had their own systems of Courts and local laws based on ancestral customs. Following the conquest of England by William I, the Normans established:

(i) the feudal system of land tenure, whereby all persons who possessed land did so merely as tenants or sub-tenants to the Kings; and

(ii) a strong central government and a national judicial system.

In the Middle Ages, following the Norman Conquest, a form of feudal land tenure was introduced, as briefly described above, thereby establishing an efficient central government and a common law, i.e. a law common to all parts of England.

During the 1100s an attempt was made to establish a common legal system for the whole country. Royal judges[11] were sent regularly to all parts of the country to settle disputes in the King's name. Gradually these judges extended their jurisdiction to criminal matters, so laying the foundations of a common law of property and crime.

During the later Middle Ages the common law was expanded to include a law of contract and a law of torts, the latter being civil wrongs not amounting to crimes.

THE COMMON LAW COURTS

The King's Grand Council[12] originally had judicial as well as governmental functions. During the Middle Ages, however, its judicial powers gradually devolved to various subsidiary Courts.

---

[11] These judges were called 'justices in eyre'. Most disputes related to possession of land.

[12] Which was called 'Curia Regis'. Some refer to this Court as 'the King's Court'.

(i) The Courts of Assize: From 1100s onwards these Courts dealt mainly with criminal matters. They were not 'based' on any one place, but they toured the country and heard and determined the more serious criminal questions.

(ii) The Court of King's Bench: This Court separated from the King's Grand Council in the 1200s and dealt with all civil actions.

(iii) The Court of Exchequer: This Court dealt mainly with revenue matters.

(iv) The Court of Exchequer Chamber: These were Courts dealing with appeals 'in error' from the other common law courts.

BRIEF HISTORY OF EQUITY

In the 1200s all appeals against decisions of the Royal judges were made direct to the King, who was considered to be the 'fountain of justice', and was therefore the head of the judicial system. Later in the same century the Kings passed these appeals to the principal Royal official, the Lord Chancellor.

Chancellors were probably the most important members of the King's Grand Council. The early Chancellors were members of the clergy who were very concerned to order what was, as a matter of conscience, fair between the parties, rather than in accordance with narrow and technical rules of law. Consequently, the Chancellor's Court became extremely popular. Therefore, Vice-Chancellors were appointed to deal with litigation and a Court of Chancery was established in London. This Court dealt with matters where (i) the common law provided no remedy, or (ii) although a remedy was available, it was insufficient in the particular case. This led to the Court of Chancery offering remedies of its own, such as injunctions.[13]

THE CURRENT COURT SYSTEM

In the 1800s, as part of a general process of reform of the law, the Judicature Acts were passed to abolish all existing Courts and substitute a unified Court structure. These Acts dictated that (i) Equity and Common Law should be administered side by side in all Courts, and (ii) where there is any conflict between a rule of Equity and a rule of Common Law the rule of Equity shall prevail. The English Court Structure is quite complex. It has four basic levels. The House of Lords,[14] the Court of Appeal, the High Court, and the Inferior

[13] On injunctions see *infra*, p.107.

[14] More properly known as the 'Appellate Committee of the House of Lords'. Interestingly, the British Government announced in June 2003 that intends to create a new type of Supreme

Courts.[15] Unfortunately, there is no clear division into criminal and civil Courts,[16] within this structure, nor a division into first instance and appeal courts.
Table 1 below may be of some help in showing the evolution of different Courts from the Middle Ages to-date.

Before the Judicature Acts (1875)	Judicature Acts (1875)	Today
Court of Queen's Bench Court of Common Pleas Court of Exchequer	**High Court** Queen's Bench Division Common Pleas Division Exchequer Division	**High Court** Queen's Bench Division
Court of Chancery Court of Bankruptcy	**High Court** Chancery Division	**High Court** Chancery Division
Court of Probate Court of Divorce Court of Admiralty	**High Court** Probate, Divorce Division and Admiralty Division	**High Court** Family Division Admiralty Court
Court of Appeal in Chancery Court of Exchequer Chamber	**Court of Appeal**	**Court of Appeal**] Civil Division **Court of Appeal**] Criminal Division

Table 1: The Courts

What follows is a brief explanation of each one of the above mentioned Courts/Tribunals.

MAGISTRATES COURTS

There are two 'types' of such Courts, depending on their consistency:

Court, where most senior judges, who are proposed to be called 'Justices of the Supreme Court', would sit outside the House of Lords. This new Supreme Court will therefore replace the current House of Lords and the Judicial Committee of the Privy Council. The Government's suggestion has met with considerable opposition, e.g. see the Law Lords' response in *The Times*, 5 November 2003. However, the Constitutional Reform Bill was introduced in the House of Lords in February 2004 who passed a delaying amendment, which means that the Bill is referred to a select committee for further consideration before it can be introduced to the House of Commons.

[15] The Crown Court, the High Court, and the Court of Appeal, make up the 'Supreme Court of Judicature'.

[16] Although, some Courts are purely civil or criminal. For example, the County Court only deals with civil cases.

(i) Magistrates Courts that consist of between two and seven lay Justices ('Justices of the Peace'), and

(ii) Magistrates Courts which consist of a 'stipendiary' magistrate.

The difference between the two is not substantial, in so far as practice is concerned; in the former type the Court would usually consist of three lay, i.e. not legally qualified nor paid, persons, whereas in the latter the stipendiary magistrate, who is a full-time legally qualified person, would sit alone.

The Magistrate Courts' main, but not only, task nowadays, falls within their criminal jurisdiction.[17] Therefore, if a person is arrested by the Police for a criminal offence, his first appearance before a Court of Law would be in the Magistrates Court.

'Magistrates' civil jurisdiction is less important nowadays than their criminal jurisdiction. It includes, for example, the granting of gaming and liquor licences, the recovery of certain civil debts, and sometimes domestic proceedings.[18]

Appeals from the Magistrates Courts may be made to (i) the Crown Court in criminal cases, or (ii) the High Court (Divisional Court of the Queen's Bench Division) in domestic or criminal proceedings.

YOUTH COURTS

Another function within the Magistrates Courts' criminal jurisdiction would be to hear and determine cases involving children and young persons. In such a case the Magistrates are said to be sitting as a Youth Court. It must be noted, however, that Youth Courts are in practice separate Courts presided over by three specially qualified lay Magistrates to deal with young offenders. The intention is to take cases concerning children and young persons away from the publicity of the ordinary Courts and allow them to be dealt with privately by the Magistrates.[19]

COUNTY COURTS

This is the main Court for contract, tort and equity actions.[20] In addition, some County Courts are designated as 'Divorce' County Courts, and they have

---

[17] The Magistrates' Court used to be known as 'petty sessions', or referred to as the 'Court of summary jurisdiction'.

[18] 'Domestic proceedings' include adoption and matrimonial proceedings.

[19] As from April 2005 some of the Court's procedures have been amended by the provisions of the Criminal Justice Act 2003.

[20] In addition to these main actions, some County Courts have Admiralty jurisdiction.

jurisdiction in matrimonial proceedings. Therefore, most divorce proceedings take place in such County Courts. Finally, it must be noted that County Courts are not appellate Courts. Nevertheless, County Courts fulfil a very important role in England, as, in practice, deal with the majority of the country's civil litigation.

Civil claims where the amount involved is £5,000 or less[21] are allocated to the 'small claims track'. What is different under this procedure is that the parties involved, i.e. the claimant and the defendant, do not need to have legal representation, but they may instead themselves appear before the Court. Furthermore, it is usual in small claim track cases that each party has to bear its own costs, irrespectively of the outcome.

TRIBUNALS

Alongside the ordinary civil courts there exist many hundreds of tribunals dealing with a wide variety of disputes arising between the individual citizen and the State or between citizen and citizen. These can be divided into three broad categories; (i) Administrative Tribunals, (ii) Industrial Tribunals, and (iii) Domestic Tribunals.

Administrative Tribunals are public statutory bodies inferior to the ordinary Courts of law and are subject to the supervision of the Queen's Bench Division of the High Court. Examples of administrative tribunals are the Immigration Appeal Tribunal, and the Lands Tribunal.

Industrial Tribunals, which are now to be called 'employment tribunals',[22] have their own jurisdiction which is pertinent to employment matters, such as unlawful racial or sexual discrimination in employment, and unfair dismissal.

Domestic Tribunals, which are set up by private bodies for their own internal purposes. For example, the Law Society of England and Wales operates disciplinary committees thus regulating conduct in the profession of solicitors.[23]

HIGH COURT

This Court's main composition is: (i) the Lord Chancellor, who presides in the Chancery Division, (ii) the Lord Chief Justice, who presides over the Queen's

---

[21] In the case of personal injury claim the amount should not exceed £3,000.

[22] Section 1, Employment Rights (Dispute Resolution) Act 1998.

[23] It must be noted that there are other types of Courts and tribunals. Offences against the disciplinary rules of the armed forces are heard by Courts Martial. Ecclesiastical Courts, which are only concerned with matters affecting churches and consecrated ground and moral offences by clergymen. Coroner's Courts, which have existed for over eight hundred years and their function to enquire into sudden or violent deaths etc. Such Courts and tribunals are considered to be beyond the scope of this work, hence they are not considered any further.

Bench Division, (iii) the President, who presides over the Family Division, (iv) the Vice-Chancellor of the Chancery Division, and (v) a number of High Court Judges sometimes referred to as 'puisne' judges. The High Court is a superior[24] Court and it comprises three divisions:

(1) The Chancery Division

The president of this Division is the Lord Chancellor, and the vice-president is the Vice-Chancellor. In practice the Lord Chancellor never sits and the work is done by the Vice-Chancellor and a number of High Court Judges. Its jurisdiction is purely civil, and covers matters relating to trusts, bankruptcy, contentious probate, company law, and land. The Court also sits as (i) the Patents Court, and (ii) as an appellate Court to hear appeals from decisions on matters of taxation, insolvency, and land registration. This Court is concentrated mainly in London, and it is unusual to sit at any other place in England and Wales.

(2) Family Division

This consists of the President and about 17 High Court Judges. Its jurisdiction covers matters relating to non-contentious probate, matrimonial causes (divorce, separation, etc.), and adoption. The Court also sits as an appellate Court to hear appeals from decisions made by the County Court or Magistrates Court regarding a minor.

(3) The Queen's Bench Division

The president of this Court is the Lord Chief Justice, assisted by a number of High Court Judges. It is usually Queen's Bench judges who spend a certain amount of time away from London on circuit in the provinces trying High Court civil actions and Crown Court criminal cases.

Most of this Court's business is based on contract and tort actions, and most such cases are tried by the judge sitting alone. Within the Queen's Bench Division there exists two further Courts:

(i) **The Commercial Court**: this hears cases relating to banking, insurance, charter-parties, and negotiable instruments. Five High Court Judges with special knowledge and experience in commercial affairs usually sit.

(ii) **The Admiralty Court**: this tries cases relating to claims for damages, loss of life/personal injury arising out of a collision between ships, claims to the ownership of a ship, claims for loss of/damage to goods carried in a ship, claims for salvage and towage in respect of a ship, and claims for

[24] This expression together with its opposite 'inferior' are technical expressions used widely by lawyers. As a 'rule of thumb', superior Courts, such as the House of Lords, the Court of Appeal, the High Court, and the Crown Court, have unlimited jurisdiction and deal with the more important and difficult cases. Inferior Courts, such as the County and the Magistrate Courts have limited jurisdiction and hear the less important and less difficult cases.

wages by a master/crew of a ship. A High Court Judge sometimes sits with a lay nautical assessor to advise him on questions of seamanship and navigation.

CROWN COURT

The main task of this Court is to hear and determine serious criminal offences and appeals from the Magistrates Courts. Usually a High Court or a Circuit Judge sits alone in this Court. It must also be noted that this is the one of only two Courts in the English Court structure which includes, as a general rule, a jury of 12 people. One has perhaps come across the expression 'the Old Bailey', and although it is realised by most that this is a criminal Court, a misconception may be formed that it is a Court of its own. However, the explanation is quite simple; when the Crown Court sits in the City of London it is known as the Central Criminal Court (or the Old Bailey). So that in effect, the 'Old Bailey' is the Crown Court of the City of London.

THE JUDICIAL COMMITTEE OF THE PRIVY COUNCIL

This is an appellate Court and sits in London. It mainly hears appeals from Courts of the Commonwealth and Her Majesty's dominions, i.e. outside the U.K.[25] In practice, most cases are civil and are heard by three to five Lords of Appeal in Ordinary.

THE COURT OF APPEAL

This is a purely appellate Court, and consists of two divisions:

(1) The Civil Division

This hears appeals from the High Court and the County Courts. Normally cases before the Court are heard by three Lords Justices of Appeal, although it is possible that only two could sit. It seems, however, that this number depends on the importance of the case, since in more important cases a 'full Court' consisting of five Lords Justices of Appeal may sit.

(2) The Criminal Division

Normally cases before the Court are heard by one, two, or three Lords Justices of Appeal, depending on the matter to be heard.

---

[25] However, it also has ecclesiastical jurisdiction. Decisions of this Court are not strictly decisions but advice or legal opinion on points of law raised by such cases.

THE HOUSE OF LORDS

This is the final appellate Court for most cases, whether civil or criminal. Only Lords of Appeals in Ordinary, the Lord Chancellor, the Lord Chief Justice, and the Master of the Rolls are entitled to sit in this Court.

JUDGES

As reference to different type of Judges sitting at different Courts has already been made, and will be made in this chapter, it is perhaps advisable to consider at this stage the main 'Judicial Offices' that exist in the English Judicial system. In order of seniority, the main Judicial Offices are as follows:

THE LORD CHANCELLOR: Formally, 'Lord High Chancellor', is the highest judicial appointment in the English judicial system. The Lord Chancellor is the senior Judge of both the House of Lords and the Court of Appeal.[26] In law reports the title is abbreviated as 'L.C.', e.g. 'Lord Irvine L.C.'.

THE LORDS OF APPEAL IN ORDINARY: or 'the Law Lords', are judges who sit in the House of Lords. Almost all of the Lords are appointed following experience in the Court of Appeal. Reported as 'Lord' plus the surname, e.g. 'Lord Irvine'.

THE LORDS JUSTICES OF APPEAL: These are judges sitting in the Court of Appeal. They are usually appointed to this office from High Court Judges. The title is abbreviated as 'L.J.', e.g. 'Irvine L.J.'.

THE MASTER OF THE ROLLS: This is the judge responsible for the work of the Civil Division of the Court of Appeal, where he/she also presides. The name seems to have derived from the fact that he/she formally admits newly qualified solicitors to the Roll of the Court, thus enabling them to practise. The title is abbreviated as 'M.R.', e.g. 'Lord Irvine M.R.'.

---

[26] Paradoxically, this appointment to a *judicial office*, is a political one, in that the person appointed is invited to accept the office by the Prime Minister. The Lord Chancellor has a seat in the Cabinet and is usually a prominent Queen's Counsel. In truth this appointment is contradictory to the constitutional doctrine of the separation of powers. It must be noted that under the Constitutional Reform Bill introduced by the Government, the Office of the Lord Chancellor will be abolished.. Another political appointment to an important *legal office* is that of 'Attorney-General', who is similarly invited to accept the office by the Prime Minister. The Attorney-General would normally be a Queen's Counsel who has been elected a Member of Parliament, and he/she acts as a legal adviser to the Government.

THE LORD CHIEF JUSTICE: This is the senior Judge of the Queen's Bench Division of the High Court. The title is usually abbreviated as 'C.J.', e.g. 'Lord Irvine C.J.'.

THE PRESIDENT OF THE FAMILY DIVISION OF THE HIGH COURT: This is the senior Judge in that Division, and is the Judge responsible for organising the work in this Division. Usually abbreviated as 'P.', e.g. 'Irvine P.'.

THE VICE-CHANCELLOR: This is the senior Judge of the Chancery Division of the High Court. Usually abbreviated as 'V.-C.', e.g. 'Irvine V.-C.'.

THE HIGH COURT JUDGES: or 'puisne Judges', are Judges who mainly sit in the High Court in London. Sittings outside London may only be directed by the Lord Chancellor. At present there is such a 'permanent' direction of the Lord Chancellor which authorises High Court civil cases to be tried at a number of places outside London. A High Court Judge is addressed as 'Your Lordship' and the title is abbreviated as 'J.', e.g. 'Irvine J.', with plural abbreviation 'J.J.', e.g. 'Denning and Irvine J.J.'.

THE CIRCUIT JUDGES: 'Circuits' are administrative areas in England and Wales in which Judges are attached. Presently there are six circuits,[27] and Judges attached to any one of these circuits are called 'Circuit Judges'. Although there is no clear differentiation between the two classes of Judges, it is usual for High Court Judges not to only sit in civil cases of the High Court, but also in criminal ones in the Crown Court, whereas Circuit Judges may only sit in a civil case in the High Court when the Lord Chancellor requests them to do so (as an 'additional judge').[28] Circuit Judges also sit as County Court Judges in civil cases.[29] In effect, High Court Judges would seem to be senior to Circuit Judges. A Circuit Judge is addressed as 'Your Honour'.

THE JUSTICES OF THE PEACE: These normally sit at the Magistrates Court, may only sit as Judges of the Crown Court with either a High Court Judge, or a Circuit Judge. A Magistrate is addressed as 'Your Worship', or 'Sir'/'Madam'.

There are various other 'types' of Court Judges, such as Recorders, Assistant Recorders, Deputy Circuit Judges, District Judges, however, for the purposes of the present work, the above brief narrative should be adequate.

---

27 For example, a circuit Judge in London, would belong to the South-Eastern Circuit.
28 Sections 9(1) and 9(2), of the Supreme Court Act 1981.
29 Section 5(1), County Courts Act 1984.

CONTEMPT OF COURT

Although both criminal and civil contempt of Court should be distinguished, the expression 'contempt of Court' is widely and commonly used to mean both.

Despite the criticism that the distinction has received by Courts and government Committees,[30] there has been no legislation abolishing it.

CRIMINAL CONTEMPT: This is a non-arrestable offence punishable by (i) imprisonment and/or a fine, or (ii) an injunction to restrain the contempt.[31] Behaviour amounting to criminal contempt includes interrupting Court proceedings,[32] abuse of a judge's personal character,[33] using an instrument for recording sound into the Courtroom,[34] and refusing to answer questions in Court.[35]

CIVIL CONTEMPT: This is in effect disobedience to judgments/orders of the Court[36] or breach of an undertaking given to the Court. Furthermore, a civil contempt is also a criminal offence[37] punishable by (i) imprisonment and/or a fine, or (ii) an injunction against the person committing the contempt. Two things must be noted in relation to civil contempt of Court:

-the High Court has the power to impose a fine of an unlimited amount, and

-a writ of 'sequestration' may be available as an alternative remedy.[38]

Finally, government departments and ministers are subject to the law of civil contempt.[39]

---

30 See for example Sir John Donaldson M.R.'s comments in *Attorney-General* v. *Newspaper Publishing plc.* [1987] 3 All E.R.532, C.A.

31 *Attorney-General* v. *Times Newspapers Ltd.* [1974] A.C.273, H.L.

32 *R* v. *Powell* (1994) 98 Cr.App.R.224.

33 *R* v. *New Statesman (Editor)* (1928) 44 T.L.R.301.

34 *Re Hooker* [1993] C.O.D.190.

35 *R* v. *Samuda* (1989) 11 Cr.App.R.471, C.A. But see the factors that Courts would take into consideration in the case of journalists in *X Ltd.* v. *Morgan-Grampian (Publishers) Ltd.* [1990] 2 All E.R.1 H.L.

36 Proceedings for civil contempt would normally commence either by the person in whose favour the judgment/order was made or by the Attorney-General.

37 *Dean* v. *Dean* [1987] 1 F.L.R.517, C.A.

38 A writ of ***sequestration*** is a very drastic remedy whereby the property of the person's committing the contempt is placed temporarily at the disposal of certain officials (***sequestrators***) who manage the property and receive any rents and profits from it until the contempt is purged. Sequestrators cannot sell the property, and this remedy is not available in the case of criminal contempt. In practice this remedy is only used in extreme cases; *Director of Public Prosecutions* v. *Channel Four Television Co. Ltd.* [1993] 2 All E.R.517.

39 *M.* v. *Home Office* [1993] 3 All E.R.537.

DOCTRINE OF JUDICIAL PRECEDENT

This is a characteristic of the English legal system, not found in the majority of European States. In effect, this doctrine involves the application of the principles of *stare decisis*; i.e. to stand by cases already decided. In practice, this means that both Divisions of the Court of Appeal are generally bound to follow their own previous decisions and that each Court is bound to follow the decisions of a Court above it in the hierarchy. Briefly, the position in individual Courts is currently as follows:

HOUSE OF LORDS: Until 1966 the House of Lords was bound by its own decisions. However, since then,[40] the position is that decisions of the House of Lords are binding on all Courts in the country except the House itself.[41]

COURT OF APPEAL: The Court of Appeal is generally bound by decisions of the House of Lords even if it considers them to be wrong.[42] Furthermore, the Court is bound by its own previous decisions.[43]

JUDICIAL COMMITTEE OF THE PRIVY COUNCIL: The Judicial Committee is not bound by decisions of the House of Lords, or the Court of Appeal,[44] nor by its own previous decisions.

HIGH COURT: Divisional Courts of the High Court are bound by decisions of the House of Lords and Court of Appeal, and are also normally bound by their own previous decisions.[45]

---

[40] *Practice Statement* [1966] 3 All E.R.77.

[41] It must be borne in mind however, that the House of Lord is bound by decisions made by the European Court of Justice. However, the E.C.J. is not bound by its own previous decisions, since the doctrine of precedent is not in existence in most other European countries; previous decisions are only of persuasive character in these Courts. However, it is clear that the E.C.J. lacks jurisdiction to make findings of fact, and no national Court is bound by E.C.J.'s conclusions on these; *Arsenal Football Club Plc* v. *Reed (No.2)* [2003] 1 All E.R.137.

[42] *Williams* v. *Glasbrook Bros.* [1947] 2 All E.R.884.

[43] However, it must be noted, that there are exceptions to this general rule: (i) Where there are conflicting previous decisions of the Court of Appeal, the Court may choose which one to follow, see *Starmark Enterprises Ltd.* v. *C.P.L. Distribution Ltd.* [2002] Ch.306 C.A., and *Great Peace Shipping Ltd.* v. *Tsavliris Salvage (International) Ltd.* [2003] Q.B.679. (ii) Where the Court of Appeal is satisfied that its previous decision was given ***per incuriam***, i.e. by carelessness or mistake-in error, see *Young* v. *Bristol Aeroplane Co. Ltd.* [1944] K.B.718, C.A. (iii) Where a previous decision has been 'indirectly' overruled by a subsequent House of Lords decision, or the Judicial Committee of the Privy Council, *National Westminster Bank Plc* v. *Spectrum Plus Ltd.* [2004] 3 W.L.R.503. For further explanation of these issues, see *Rakhit* v. *Carty* [1990] 2 All E.R.202 C.A., *Wellcome Trust Ltd.* v. *Hammad* [1998] 1 All E.R.622 C.A., and *R.* v. *Simpson (Ian McDonald)* [2004] Q.B.118.

[44] *De Lasala* v. *De Lasala* [1980] A.C.546.

[45] Again this general rule on Divisional Courts' previous decisions is subject to similar exceptions as those previously mentioned *supra*, footnote 43. Generally, however, there is no

CROWN COURT: The Crown Court is bound by decisions of the House of Lords, the Court of Appeal and the Queen's Bench Divisional Court. However, decisions made by the Crown Court are not binding precedents and therefore there is no obligation on its part to follow its own previous decisions.

COUNTY COURTS AND MAGISTRATES' COURTS: Decisions of these Courts are rarely reported,[46] and are not binding.

A judgment would normally contain, among other things, statements of law, i.e. principles of law applicable to the case. The collection of these statements of law, which the Judge(s) in a particular case would rely to reach the decision on the facts is known as 'ratio decidendi', i.e. the reason for deciding.

Statements made by the Judge(s) which do not provide the basis of the decision are known as 'obiter dicta' or 'obiter dictum' statements. Such statements are only of persuasive nature, and therefore do not bind any inferior Court or any future cases. They are normally referred to as 'persuasive precedents', to distinguish them from 'binding precedents'.

A decision is said to have been given 'per incuriam' i.e. through lack of care, because some relevant statute or precedent was not brought before the Court. In effect this means that the decision of the Court was mistaken because of this, and in practice such decision is not a binding precedent.

The distinction between 'overruling' and 'reversing' is considerable. A decision or precedent is 'reversed' when it is altered 'on appeal'. Whereas when a judge in a different case states that the earlier case was wrongly decided, this would be 'overruling'. In addition, a decision or precedent can be 'overruled' by a statute.

ARBITRATION

Businessmen and merchants often prefer to refer disputes to arbitration, as an alternative to litigation. The arbitrator is usually chosen by the parties for his specialist knowledge in the field where the dispute lies, and therefore speed up the process. Furthermore, as most jurisdictions recognise the decisions of

difference in the application of *stare decisis* between the Civil and Criminal Divisions of the Court of Appeal; *R.* v. *Spencer* [1985] Q.B.771 C.A.

46 This should not be confused with the expression 'Courts of Record'. Whether a case is reported or not is irrelevant in so far as Courts of Record are concerned. Courts of Record are the House of Lords, the Court of Appeal, the High Court, the Crown Court, the Restrictive Practices Court, the Employment Appeal Tribunal, and the County Court. They are called 'Courts of Record' because proceedings in those Courts are kept as a permanent record in the Public Record Office.

arbitrations, the enforcement of arbitration awards is not at a significant disadvantage to judicial decisions.[47]

The law relating to arbitration is found in the Arbitration Act 1996. This maintains the basic principle of freedom to contract, so that parties to a contract may include provisions for most of the matters dealt with by arbitration, as well as in relation to its procedure.

Unless the parties have included a provision as to the number of arbitrators[48] and whether there will be a chairman or umpire,[49] only one ('sole') arbitrator would be appointed.[50]

Where the parties have agreed to an even number of arbitrators, i.e. two, four, etc., it is presumed by the Act[51] that an additional arbitrator will also be required to act as chairman.[52]

It is quite usual for arbitration clauses to be framed in such a manner that they prevent any right to Court proceedings until an arbitration award has been made.[53]

Such clauses are quite valid on merit,[54] but if a party to the agreement commences Court proceedings, contrary to the clause, then the relevant Court would have to decide whether to break the agreement on the particular circumstances.[55] There is clearly a 'presumption', however, to the effect that the

---

[47] So, for example, an arbitrator is empowered, in certain circumstances, to (i) order either/both parties to provide security for costs, s.38, Arbitration Act 1996, and (ii) dismiss the claim, respectively, s.41(3), Arbitration Act 1996.

[48] It must be noted that specialist associations publish suggested forms of arbitration clauses which deal with the appointment and number of arbitrators, e.g. the Grain and Feed Trade Association, the London Maritime Arbitrators Association.

[49] Section 15(1).

[50] Section 15(3).

[51] Section 15(2).

[52] Unless the parties agreed otherwise, the difference between a chairman and an umpire would seem to be that the former ordinarily acts as one of the other two arbitrators taking part in any voting, whereas an umpire would not ordinarily have a part in the voting. But if the two arbitrators cannot agree, then the umpire would. This distinction is drawn from the provisions of ss.20(3) and 21(4) respectively.

[53] *Scott* v. *Avery* (1856) 5 H.L.C.811, H.L., where the arbitration clause made the issuance of an award a condition precedent to the commencement of an action before the Courts.

[54] Since such clauses do not oust the jurisdiction of the Courts but only 'technicalities and strict constructions'; *per* Denning, M.R., in *Eagle Star Insurance Co. Ltd.* v. *Yuval Insurance Co. Ltd.* [1978] 1 Lloyd's Rep.357, 362.

[55] The Court will pay particular attention on whether 'the arbitration agreement is null and void, inoperative or incapable of being performed', s.9(4), Arbitration Act 1996. In the case of a 'domestic arbitration' only, the Court would additionally consider whether 'there are sufficient other reasons for not requiring the parties to abide by the arbitration agreement', s.86(2)(b). It must be noted, however, that this latter section, as well as all other sections included in Part II of the Arbitration Act 1996 are not likely to be brought into force. For the reasoning of this exclusion from enforceability, see *Philip Alexander Securities and Futures Ltd.* v. *Bamberger, The Times*, 22 July, 1996.

relevant Court will grant a 'stay' of Court proceedings, i.e. will allow the arbitration.[56]

An important point to note is that although an arbitration agreement may be made verbally or in writing, the Act would apply only to agreements in writing.[57]

It is also essential that the parties have agreed in their contract the applicable law, since the arbitrator(s) would have to 'decide the dispute (a) in accordance with the law chosen by the parties as applicable to the substance of the dispute or, (b) if the parties agree, in accordance with such other considerations as are agreed by them or determined by the tribunal'.[58]

The effect of sections 85(2)(a) and (b) of the Act is that there is a 'domestic arbitration agreement' where:

(i) the parties to the agreement are:

(a) if natural persons, i.e. individuals, residents or nationals of the U.K., and/or

(b) if legal persons, i.e. companies, incorporated or controlled/managed from the U.K.;

and

(ii) the arbitration takes place in the U.K.

All other arbitrations are non-domestic. It must be noted, however, that the distinction, for all intents and purposes, is not a material one, if at all.[59]

An award may be challenged on procedural grounds, e.g. the award being obtained by fraud. Section 68(2) of the Act contains a list of nine 'serious' irregularities upon which a party to arbitration proceedings can rely in order to challenge the award.

The arbitrator's decision is final, and under the Act a party can appeal to the Court against such decision only if it relates 'to a question of law arising out of an award made in the proceedings'.[60]

Once the award has been made by the arbitrator, it may have to be enforced[61] outside the U.K. In such as case, leave of the Court will be required before the

[56] *Halki Shipping Corporation* v. *Sopex Oils Ltd.* [1998] 1 Lloyd's Rep.465.

[57] Section 5(1). However, under s.5(2)(a) such written agreements need not be signed, thus allowing for the use of modern technology, such as e-mail. Indeed, s.5(6) defines 'anything written or in writing' as including 'its being recorded by any means'.

[58] Section 46. As to the law applicable to contracts, see *infra*, p.120.

[59] Since Part II of the Arbitration Act 1996 is not likely to be brought into force; *Philip Alexander Securities and Futures Ltd.* v. *Bamberger, The Times*, 22 July, 1996.

[60] Section 69(3).

[61] As to methods of enforcement of civil judgments, see *infra*, p.48.

relevant provisions of the New York Convention on the Recognition and Enforcement of Arbitral Awards 1958[62] are relied upon.

THE CURRENT LEGAL SYSTEM

It is important to understand the 'philosophy' enshrined by the current English legal system. In England, the law may be said to be notionally divided into Criminal law and Civil law. Criminal law is concerned with crimes committed by a person against the State, e.g. murder. Civil law, on the other hand, is concerned with wrongs done between two or more persons, e.g. personal injury.

Indeed, if one looks at the Criminal law cases, will notice that are usually reported as the Queen/King, i.e. the State, *versus* the defendant, i.e. a person. The Latin for Queen is *Regina* and for King is *Rex*, and it is normal practice to abbreviate *Regina* or *Rex* to just *R*. Thus, for example, a criminal case would be reported as *R.* v. *Smith*, followed by the year for reference purposes.

CASE REPORTING

The above is true in so far as the more serious criminal offences, known as 'indictable',[63] are concerned. Prosecutions for less serious offences, known as 'summary',[64] are normally commenced in the name of the prosecutor, e.g. *Smith* v. *Jones*.[65] Civil cases, are reported with the names of the claimant, and nowadays in practice called the claimant, i.e. a person(s), *versus* the defendant, i.e. another person(s).

So, for example, a civil case would be reported as *Smith* v. *Jones*, followed by the year. Lawyers traditionally however, pronounce this as 'Smith *and* Jones'. There are also instances where special applications may be made whereby there will be no claimant nor a defendant in the name of the case, e.g. where an application to Court is made for the interpretation of a person's will. Then, if we assume that the name of the deceased was Jones, the case would be known as *Re*

---

62 Given effect by s.66(4) of the Arbitration Act 1996.

63 Indictable offences are generally the more serious forms of crime, such as all forms of homicide, major theft, assaults inflicting bodily harm, rape. The word 'indictment' means a document which sets out in writing the 'charges' against the accused, each separate charge is called 'a count' of the indictment.

64 Summary offences are offences specifically named as being triable before the Magistrates' Court, hence all summary offences are defined by statute. They are generally the less serious forms of crime, such as minor thefts, minor assaults, road traffic offences.

65 For more information on the classification of criminal offences, see *infra*, p.49.

Jones. It is also possible to see case headings reported as *ex parte*[66] *Smith*. This indicates that *Smith* is the party on whose application the case is heard.

Finally, in the case of civil appeals, the party that appeals is called the 'appellant', and the other party the 'respondent'. It is important to note that in case reporting the appellant's name is placed first, and therefore, the name of the case on appeal may be reversed. Thus, if there is a case decision in the High Court reported as *Smith* v. *Jones*, on the defendant's (Jones) appeal to the House of Lords it will be reported as *Jones* v. *Smith*.

SOURCES OF ENGLISH LAW

The doctrine of Judicial Precedent as discussed earlier in this Chapter, applies to criminal as well as to civil law. English law may be said to mainly derive from, or be made by, five distinct ways:

i) **Acts of Parliament**: Lawyers refer to them as statutes. These are presented in a draft form to Parliament and at that stage they are called Bills. Then they are passed by Parliament (House of Commons) and the House of Lords, and then the Queen gives her assent to them.[67] In this respect this bears a similarity to Continental legal systems, since these Bills/Acts are in effect codification of the law.

ii) **Decided Cases**: The vast majority of English law is comprised of decided cases.

iii) **Delegated Legislation**: The British Parliament often passes an Act which provides a general framework, and itself gives Government Ministers the power to fill in any 'gaps' and update it. Therefore, under such Act(s) the Minister(s) may be empowered to make 'Rules', 'Orders', 'Statutory Instruments', or 'Orders in Council'. In other words, these powers of the State through its Parliament are delegated to the appropriate Minister(s).

iv) **Trade Custom**: This is a quite important source of English law, particularly where a trade is concerned. In effect, reasonable trade practices may be adopted into law, and in some cases may supersede the general rule of law in the particular trade.[68]

---

[66] In effect an *ex parte* application to the Court is an application from one litigant without notice to the other litigant parties. See further *infra*, p.44.

[67] For a brief outline of the legislation process see *infra*, p.20.

[68] For example, in general insurance law it is accepted that the normal agency law principles apply in so far as payment of the insurance premium is concerned. It is the insured as principal, and not his insurance broker, who is liable to the insurer for such payment. It is not the

v) **European Union Law**: This applies to all Member States of the Union in four distinct forms:

-*Treaties*: These are binding on all Member States.

-*Regulations*: Again these are binding on all Member States and they have 'direct effect', i.e. there is no need for any implementation or adoption by the Parliaments of the Member States. Furthermore, Regulations prevail over the national laws of Member States.

-*Directives*: These are also binding but usually leave a Member State a choice of the method by which the particular Directive will be implemented. Furthermore, they do not always apply to all Member States at the same time, since each individual State is given a particular period of time within which to implement such Directive(s).[69]

-*Decisions*: These are binding upon those to whom they are addressed whether they are Member States or persons. Furthermore, Decisions of the European Court of Justice are binding on the highest Courts in Member States.

CONSTITUTIONAL LAW

The United Kingdom is known for its unwritten constitution.[70] Indeed, one of the 'tricky' questions that one may ask a law student, is to fetch from the library a copy of the British Constitution; something that if attempted is likely to indicate lack of understanding.

No written constitution does not mean no constitution, but that it is to be found in the ordinary law of the land, i.e. statute and case law. An additional point of difference between British and Continental constitutional systems, derives from the very idea which the British legal system cultivates to its citizens; in a few words, a citizen is permitted to do anything as long as the law does not prohibit it!

But what are the reasons that the U.K. has not adopted a written constitution? Well, one of the reasons may be historical; since England was a sovereign State for many centuries, the question of adopting a written constitution on the attainment of independence did not arise.

---

insurance broker because he is an agent of the insured. However, in marine insurance the practice has been that the broker is responsible to the insurer for payment or non-payment of the premium to the insurer; s.53(1) of Marine Insurance Act 1906.

[69] *Cf. Antoine Kortas*, Case C-319/97, [1999] 3 C.M.L.R.962, O.J. 1999 C 204, 17/07/1999, p.18, where the E.C.J. held that a Directive can have direct effect.

[70] It must be noted that it is not the only country that does not have a written constitution; New Zealand and Israel are, for example, other countries with unwritten constitutions.

However, there may be other less well 'publicised' reasons why there is no written constitution in the U.K. Perhaps there is a lack of interest in political philosophy, or the constitutional 'bad' experiences of other countries, and, like anywhere else in the world, there has been a lack of enthusiasm in writing a constitution among politicians since this would restraint and impede their freedom!

INTRODUCTION

The system by which the British Parliament 'operates' is complex, but an attempt will be made here, to briefly show how legislation is introduced. Firstly, a draft of the proposed legislation is prepared and circulated by the Government as a consultative document. This is called a 'Green Paper' or a 'Bill'.[71] After consultation, the Green Paper is usually amended and in this new form is called a 'White Paper'. At this stage the White Paper is officially produced to the Parliament (House of Commons) for their consideration ('First Reading').

Following this, Parliament will debate about the White Paper, and this second stage is called 'Second Reading'.

Next, a Committee of Members of Parliament, from all political parties, will have a detailed discussion on the White Paper. This is usually called the 'Committee Stage'.

After this 'Committee Stage', follows the 'Report Stage', whereby the committee of the Members of Parliament will report their conclusions to Parliament (House of Commons).

Next, the 'Third Reading' stage is dealt with by the Parliament, which is in effect the final debate on the White Paper. In other European countries once a similar stage in the life of a proposed legislation has been reached, and there is majority agreement in Parliament, the proposed legislation proceeds to be codified. This is not the case in the U.K. however.

The White Paper or Bill as it is usually referred to, is transmitted to the other House, i.e. the House of Lords, where it has to go through five similar stages.

If there is agreement between the Lords, then the Bill or White Paper is presented to the Queen for 'Royal Assent', i.e. the Queen (the Sovereign) signs

[71] It is also possible to have a 'private member's bill', i.e. one introduced by a Member of Parliament who is not a member of the Government. If the bill receives support from the House of Commons it may be adopted by the Government and go through the normal legislative process; e.g. the Abolition of the Death penalty Act 1965, recent proposal to ban hunting with dogs, etc. There are also two other types of Bills; Local and Personal. Local authorities or other public bodies may seek to promote a private Bill in Parliament. If the Bill receives Parliamentary approval the Bill becomes an Act of Parliament. These local Bills usually deal with large construction projects connected with docks, ports, railways, tramways, waterworks etc. Personal Bills are comparatively rare and relate to private individuals; usually in respect of naturalisation, divorce, peerage, etc.

the Bill. It is at this stage that the proposed legislation will become an Act of Parliament or a statute.

SOURCES OF BRITISH CONSTITUTIONAL LAW

Although the British Constitution is unwritten, it is traceable to mostly written sources. So what follows is a brief account of these sources, whether written or not.

EUROPEAN UNION LAW: This comprises of Treaties, Regulations, Directives, and Decisions. It is submitted that these have brought about major constitutional innovation in the U.K. For example, Regulations are said to be directly applicable, i.e. are European rules applied by the Courts of all European Union countries. Thus a Regulation once introduced will apply in Britain without the need of any further enactment.[72]

COMMON LAW: This mainly consists of judicial decisions. It is sometimes referred by lawyers as the 'judge-made law'. This was recognised by many scholars and legal text writers[73] who sometimes even stated that the British constitution was a Judge-made constitution. Indeed, a Judge may have to decide what Parliament intended the law to be when it used certain words in a statute. In effect Judges when giving a so-called 'interpretation' of the law often change the law in very radical ways.

LEGISLATION: By legislation it is meant Acts of Parliament or statutes. These are a type of 'code' in as much as they codify a large part of 'judge-made law', i.e. the Common Law. In addition, Acts introduce, nowadays in particular, new laws by way of a code similar to the way most continental legal systems operate. Thus, for example, the U.K. in order to join the European Community had to introduce the European Communities Act 1972.

CONVENTIONS OF THE CONSTITUTION: These are unwritten rules of the British Constitution, which deal with various important (and unimportant) issues. For example, there is no statute or judicial decision which dictates that there must be a Prime Minister and a Cabinet! Nevertheless, by Constitutional convention this rule is of utmost importance. Other conventions include the rule that the Crown (i.e. the Queen) must assent to Bills duly passed by Parliament, and that a government defeated on a vote of confidence in the

---

72 For further sources of European Union Law see *supra*, p.19.

73 See for example, A.V. Dicey's *Introduction to the Study of the Law of the Constitution*, Roger E. Michener (editor), 1982, Liberty Fund Inc.

House of Commons would resign and advise a dissolution of Parliament. There are numerous conventions which must be observed by government, such as that all Cabinet Ministers assume responsibility for Cabinet decisions and action taken to implement these decisions. If a Minister disagrees with a decision and wishes to express dissent in public, then by Constitutional convention, he is obliged to resign first. Thus, during Mrs. Thatcher's government, her Defence Minister, Mr. M. Haseltine, had to resign from Cabinet, since he strongly disagreed and wished to make his view publicly known on a Cabinet decision for the sale of a helicopter manufacturer to an American consortium. At this stage it is important to point out that most of these Constitutional conventions are unwritten.[74] Furthermore, unlike statutes or Common Law, conventions are not subject to judicial decision or judicial review. Most of the Constitutional conventions originally evolved in order to ensure that the Monarch exercised his prerogative powers. One of the main arguments for the non-codification of these conventions is that historically in a time of constitutional crisis the Monarch's personal views ought to prevail. By codifying these conventions one would, in effect, downgrade them to being like any other statute, which would possibly result in the erosion of the Royal discretion.

CONCLUSION

It must not be thought that the British Constitution is a case of 'anything goes' since it is not written or, indeed, because it treated in this chapter in such a short manner. The above brief account is not meant to be exhaustive in any way, whatsoever. There are numerous other sources of constitutional law in Britain, such as authoritative works, and the custom of Parliament, which have not been mentioned, since they are beyond the scope of the present work. It is felt, however, that this brief introduction would serve well in as much as giving a very loose outline of the British constitutional system.

THE LAW OF PROBATE AND SUCCESSION

This part of law deals with wills, probate and administration. In practice, when somebody dies leaving little property a solicitor may not be consulted at all. It is

[74] There are some Constitutional conventions which are recorded however, e.g. in the case of the Commonwealth there used to be resolutions of Imperial Conferences wherein some Conventions were recorded or created. It must be noted that conventions are not unique to Britain and they arise even in countries which have a formal (written) constitution, as the Canadian Reference case indicates; *Reference Re Amendment of the Constitution of Canada* (1982) 125 D.L.R. (3rd) 1, Supreme Court of Canada.

usual, however, that the advice of a solicitor is sought as to the entitlement to the deceased's property and the liability of the estate tax. Quite a few people die having made a will, referred to by lawyers as 'testate', although most people die without leaving a valid will, i.e. 'intestate'. Furthermore, it may be that although they have made a will it does not for some reason deal effectively with the whole of their estate, i.e. die partially intestate. The terminology used in this area of law and its effect may be summarised as follows:

'ABSOLUTE INTEREST': This is the maximum possible benefit a person may have on any property/gift. The expression used is peculiar to the law of succession, in that one refers in the context of succession, for example, to a beneficiary X 'taking the property absolutely'.

'ADEMPTION': If a testator at the time of his death does not own the property which is the subject of a 'specific legacy' or 'specific devise' in the deceased's will, it is said that the gift is 'adeemed', i.e. it fails.

'ATTESTATION': This is, in effect, the validation of the person's making the will (testator-see below) signature.

'BENEFICIARY': Is any person to whom any part (or the whole!) of the deceased's estate is given.

'BEQUEST': This is a disposition by will of personalty, i.e. a 'legacy'.

'CONTINGENT' or 'CONTINGENT GIFT': This usually refers to gifts made and are actually granted provided some condition has been fulfilled before such gift 'vests'. For example, a gift to a child provided it attains the age of 21.

'CODICIL': In effect a minor amendment of the terms of an existing will, made by the testator.

'DEVISE': This is a gift in a will of realty, i.e. disposition of freehold land. A devise may be either:

(i) **'Specific'**, which is a gift of a particular property owned by the deceased and which is distinguished from any other property of the same kind, e.g. 'my 50 shares in X plc.', or 'my freehold property X'.

(ii) **'Residuary'**, which includes all the rest of the deceased's property.

'LAPSE': If a 'beneficiary' does not survive the 'testator', a gift under the testator's will to him/her 'lapses', i.e. the gift will fall into the 'residue' of the deceased's estate.

'LEGACY': This is a gift in a will of goods and chattels by will. It is quite important to know that legacies are divided into five categories:

(i) **'General'**, where, for example, a gift of £5,000, or a pen, is given.

(ii) **'Specific'**, where a specific gift is given, e.g. 'my Rolex watch'.

(iii) **'Demonstrative'**, where a gift is to be taken from a particular lot, e.g. £5,000 out of a specific bank account.

(iv) **'Pecuniary'**, which is a gift of money, e.g. '£5,000 payable from my X account at Y bank'.

(v) **'Residuary'**, which means what remains from the deceased's estate after all payments of inheritance and other taxes have been made and all legacies and devises have been distributed.

'LIFE INTEREST': This is a grant on a part (or the whole) of the deceased's estate to a beneficiary for as long as the beneficiary remains alive. For example 'to X for life'.

'REMAINDER': What remains of an interest on a part (or the whole) of the deceased's estate. The expression is usually appropriate where there are life interests involved, e.g. 'to X for life, remainder to Y absolutely'.

'RESIDUE' OR 'RESIDUARY ESTATE': This simply refers to what remains of the deceased's estate. For example, the residue of X's estate after payment of inheritance tax.

'TESTATOR' and 'TESTATRIX': The former means the male person who made the will, whereas the latter is the feminine of such person.

'VESTED' or 'VESTED GIFT' or 'VESTED INTEREST': This simply means a present fixed right of future enjoyment, e.g. '£500,000 to the children of X'. In this example X's children have a vested interest in the £500,000. If in this example, X has no children at the time of the testator's death, then £500,000 will be put aside from the testator's estate until X dies. In effect a vested gift is 'unconditional'.

One may notice that there is some 'overlap' with a few of the above definitions and explanations. Although for present purposes this is not important, there are specific reasons, mainly concerning taxation, which in practice make the above terminology very important. Such reasons, however, are beyond the scope of the present chapter, which only gives the broadest of outlines regarding the law of succession.

VALIDITY OF WILLS

In general, one must bear in mind that a will disposing (i) land would be governed by the law of the country in which the land is situated, and (ii) personal property must be made according to the law of the testator's domicile at his death.[75]

In so far as English law is concerned, there are three requirements for the validity of a will:[76]

(1) **CAPACITY**: The testator must, at the date of making his will, (i) be 18 years old or over, and (ii) have the necessary mental capacity.[77]

(2) **INTENTION**: The testator must, at the date of making his will, know and approve the contents of the will.[78]

(3) **FORMALITIES**: A will must be written down[79] and signed[80] by the testator[81] in the presence of at least two witnesses.[82] An important practical point, in so far as the choice of witnesses is concerned, is that the beneficiaries of a will should not attest the testator's signature. If they do, then any gifts to such witnesses disposed by the testator's will are likely to fail,[83] although the validity of the will as such would not be affected.

---

75 Although, a change of domicile after execution would not necessarily revoke a will; section 3, Wills Act 1837.

76 Note that the same requirements apply to the creation of a valid codicil.

77 For the criteria taken into consideration by the Courts see *Banks* v. *Goodfellow* (1870) L.R.5 Q.B.549. Also, sections 2 and 3 of the Mental Capacity Act 2005.

78 *Parker* v. *Felgate* (1883) 8 P.D.171.

79 Section 17 of the Administration of Justice Act 1982, does not specify a document, form, or anything else. Therefore, it might be acceptable if the will is written on a non-paper based form, e.g. in *Goods of Barnes, The* (1926) 43 T.L.R.71, the will was written on an eggshell!

80 Any mark made by the testator and intended to be a signature would be sufficient; *Goods of Chalcraft, The* [1948] P.222.

81 The Administration of Justice Act 1982, allows signature by another person provided this is done (i) at the testator's direction, and (ii) in the testator's presence.

82 The two witnesses must obviously be present at the same time the testator signs his will. However, the witnesses do not need to sign in each other's presence, nor do they need to know that the testator is signing a will or to see the testator's signature itself.

83 Section 15, Wills Act 1837 (as amended by section 1 of the Wills Act 1968).

Revocation and Alterations

A will can be revoked at any time during the testator's lifetime by the testator:

(i) making a subsequent will or codicil,[84] or

(ii) destroying the will.[85]

Furthermore, marriage[86] or divorce[87] of a testator will, by operation of law, automatically revoke his will. With regards to alterations on a will, provided these are attested, in practice initialised, by the testator and the witnesses will be valid.

Intestacy

Where a person dies without a will, or with a will which does not dispose of all his property ('partial intestacy'), then all the deceased's property, and in the case of a partial intestacy all property which the deceased failed to dispose by his will, vests in his 'personal representatives',[88] who will distribute it in accordance to the intestacy rules.

The order by which an intestate's property is distributed depends on whether there is a surviving spouse. Very briefly, the position would be as follows:

(1) **Surviving Spouse Only**: the deceased's estate passes absolutely to the surviving spouse.

(2) **Surviving Spouse and Issue**: the spouse takes all personal chattels absolutely, and £125,000 free of tax and costs, and a life interest in half of the deceased's residuary estate. The issue[89] are entitled to the other half of

---

84 Section 20, Wills Act 1837. Note that any 'writing declaring an intention to revoke' which is executed like a will is sufficient; *Re Spracklan's Estate* [1938] 2 All E.R.345, where the Court considered that a letter written by the testatrix, duly attested and sent to her bank requesting the bank to destroy her will which the bank held for safe-keeping, fulfilled the requirements for revocation of her will.

85 Section 20, Wills Act 1837. Note that it is not sufficient to throw the will in a waste-bin; *Cheese* v. *Lovejoy* (1877) 2 P.D.251. The destruction of the will may be made by the testator himself, or by someone other than the testator, but such act must be done in the testator's presence and at the testator's direction.

86 Section 18, Wills Act 1837 (as amended by the Administration of Justice Act 1982).

87 Section 18A, Wills Act 1837 (as amended by the Administration of Justice Act 1982). See further section 3, Law Reform (Succession) Act 1995.

88 For a brief explanation, see *infra*, p.27.

89 Under the Adoption Act 1976, adopted children are treated as the deceased's issue. Furthermore, it is irrelevant whether the parents of a child were or were not to married to each other; Family Law Reform Act 1987.

the deceased's residuary estate, and to the remainder interest in the half in which the spouse has a life interest.

(3) **SURVIVING SPOUSE - NO ISSUE - SURVIVING PARENTS/BROTHERS** (or their issue): again the spouse takes all personal chattels absolutely, and £200,000 free of tax and costs, and half of the deceased's residuary estate absolutely. The other half of the residuary estate passes to the intestate's parents (equally if both alive), or if they are not alive to the brothers and sisters of the whole blood,[90] or their issue.

(4) **NO SPOUSE, ISSUE, PARENTS/BROTHERS/SISTERS** (or their issue): If there are no brothers or sisters, nor any of their issue, then it the priority is as follows:

-grandparents, who share equally if both alive, otherwise

-uncles and aunts of the whole blood,[91] but if none survived deceased, then

-uncles and aunts of the half blood,[92] but if no other relatives exist, then the Crown would take the deceased's estate as *bona vacantia*.[93]

GRANTS OF REPRESENTATION

The persons who deal with a deceased's estate are called his personal representatives. Such representatives are of two kinds:

(i) 'Executor'/'Executrix', the latter being the feminine of 'Executor'. These are appointed by the testator/testatrix in his will.

(ii) 'Administrators' on intestacy, who, are usually the beneficiaries under the intestacy Rules.[94]

However, before the personal representatives can deal with the deceased's estate, they must be issued with a 'grant of representation'.[95] These are Court orders

---

[90] This expression simply means those persons who share the same parents as the deceased.

[91] This means the brothers and sisters of one of the intestate's parents.

[92] In other words, brothers and sisters of the half blood of one of the intestate's parents.

[93] See further section 46, Administration of Estates Act 1925.

[94] There is also another kind of administrators, called 'pendente lite' (translated as pending litigation), who are appointed by the Court where legal proceedings regarding the validity of the will are pending in order to look after the deceased's estate.

[95] Strictly, however, an executor's title to deal with the deceased's estate derives from the will, and therefore an executor on death has full authority to deal with or without a grant of representation.

evidencing the representative's entitlement to deal with the deceased's estate.[96] Furthermore, a grant of representation is conclusive evidence as to the terms of the will, or that the deceased died intestate. Once the grant has been received by the representatives, they should, in practice, advertise the fact in a newspaper,[97] register the grant with the various institutions,[98] collect any debts due to the deceased, and pay any debts[99] and expenses.[100]

PROVISION FOR FAMILY AND DEPENDANTS

Under a will the testator has a right to leave his estate to whomever he chooses. However, English law enables certain classes of persons to apply to the Court for provision from the deceased's estate, whether under a valid will or intestacy. This is usually done on the basis that the deceased's will or intestacy fails to make adequate financial provision for such class of persons. For a person to succeed in applying for this provision, all criteria (i), (ii), and (iii) below must be fulfilled:

(i) apply within six months[101] from the grant of representation,

(ii) be either

-the deceased's spouse, or former unmarried spouse,[102]

-a cohabitant of the deceased during the two years prior to the death,[103]

-a child of the deceased, even if unborn at the time of the death,[104]

-any person who was treated by the deceased as a child of the family, such as stepchildren,[105]

---

96 The rules followed for the grant of representation are contained in the Non-Contentious Probate Rules 1987 (as amended by the Non-Contentious Probate (Amendment) Rules 1991).

97 This should be any newspaper which circulates in the district in which the deceased's estate lies, or it could be the *London Gazette*. It must be understood that this advertising should be placed in order to protect the representatives from liability against any disappointed beneficiary or creditor; *Knatchbull* v. *Fearnhead* (1837) 3 My.& Cr.122.

98 Such as banks, insurance companies, etc.

99 For example, any outstanding mortgages of the deceased.

100 Such as funeral, and administration expenses.

101 Section 4, Inheritance (Provision for Family and Dependants) Act 1975. Note that no application can be made before the grant of representation.

102 Sections 1(1)(a) and 1(1)(b) respectively, Inheritance (Provision for Family and Dependants) Act 1975.

103 Section 1(1)(ba), inserted by s.2 of the Law Reform (Succession) Act 1995, Inheritance (Provision for Family and Dependants) Act 1975.

104 Sections 1(1)(c) and 25(1) respectively, Inheritance (Provision for Family and Dependants) Act 1975.

105 Section 1(1)(d), Inheritance (Provision for Family and Dependants) Act 1975. See also *Re Leach* [1988] Ch.226.

-a dependant person who prior to the death was, wholly or partly, maintained[106] by the deceased.[107]

(iii) be able to show that the will or intestacy has failed to make reasonable financial provision.

It is sufficient to say that there are statutory guidelines[108] which are usually taken into account by a Court when considering the merits of an application.

THE LAW OF PROPERTY

This is a particularly complicated topic and giving an extensive and detailed account of the law would be beyond the scope of this work. Instead, only a brief narrative is given on (i) real and personal property, and (ii) estates and interests in land, both sets of concepts being necessary for an introduction to the niceties involved in this field of law.

PROPERTY IN ENGLISH LAW

The word 'property' derives from the French word *propre*, which loosely means one's own. In English law there are two types of property:

(a) real property, and

(b) personal property.

In so far as land is concerned, there can only be two legal estates:

(i) fee simple absolute in possession[109] (freehold), and

(ii) term of years absolute (leasehold).[110]

---

[106] *Bishop* v. *Plumley* [1991] 1 W.L.R.582.

[107] Section 1(1)(e), Inheritance (Provision for Family and Dependants) Act 1975.

[108] Under s.3, Inheritance (Provision for Family and Dependants) Act 1975.

[109] These are technical legal terms and therefore they do not bear the ordinary English meaning. 'Fee' indicates an estate capable of passing to one's heirs on death, 'simple' means that this passing is to the general heirs (as opposed to a certain class of heirs), 'absolute' means that it is a straightforward transfer without pre-conditions attached, and 'in possession' means that the person having this estate is entitled to physical possession. There has recently been introduced a new form of tenure which enables owners of interdependent units, e.g. flats, to be owned on a virtual freehold basis. It also deals with the provision of services and upkeep of common areas. See further the Commonhold and Leasehold Reform Act 2002, and the Commonhold Regulations 2004 (S.I.2004, No.1829). Similar systems of tenure operate in Australia, and the U.S.A.

In very simple words, a freehold estate may last for an indefinite time, whereas leasehold is for a fixed period of time. The terminology used in land law is peculiar to English law. The old land law in England (the feudal system of land tenure) dictated that all land belonged to the King and all landholders were consequently tenants. Hence, the expression now used in land law to describe what in other jurisdictions would be the 'true owner' is 'tenant', even in the case of freehold above.

A person wrongfully dispossessed of his land would have a choice of:

(i) a *real action* or *action in rem* for the recovery of the land, or

(ii) a *personal action* or *action in personam* for damages against the dispossessor.

From the above terms it has been derived that property recoverable by a real action is called *realty*, i.e. freehold/leasehold interests in land, and all other property *personalty*. However, although a leasehold estate in land was originally classified as personalty, since 1926 leases are considered to be like a freehold estate and therefore treated and classified as realty.[111]

'Chattels' is the expression given to property, which is deemed personal property (personalty). Bearing this in mind, there is a further classification with regards to personalty in the English law of property:

(i) *chattels real*, i.e. any interest in land which is less than a freehold, and
(ii)*chattels personal*, i.e. moveable property.[112]

The important point to note here is that in English law, real property means in effect freehold and leasehold interests in land, and personal property means all moveable property, e.g. goods. The word 'chose' in French means a thing, and in English law all property is classified into:

(i) *choses in possession*, which includes all tangible things capable of physical possession, and

(ii) *choses in action*, which includes intangible rights that are not capable of physical possession.[113]

[110] Section 1, The Law of Property Act 1925.

[111] Law of Property Act 1925.

[112] According to section 55(1)(x) of the Administration of Estates Act 1925, personal chattels mean 'carriages, horses, stable furniture and effects (not used for business purposes), motor cars and accessories (not used for business purposes), garden effects, domestic animals, plate, plated articles, linen, china, glass, books, pictures, prints, furniture, jewellery, articles of household or personal use or ornament, musical and scientific instruments and apparatus, wines, liquors and consumable stores'.

[113] For example, if a person, X, owns a lorry, he has a chose in possession, but if he/she hires it out for six months to Y, then X has a chose in action, i.e. a right to take action after the six months to recover possession of his lorry.

Goods, for example, would be (i) choses in possession.

Real property may only be transferred (in law) by deed, even if such transfer is by way of a gift.[114]

Personal property may generally be transferred, (i) by delivery, if such property can be classified as a chose in possession, e.g. goods, or (ii) by assignment,[115] if such property is a chose in action.

It is important to understand the meaning in English law of the word 'owner'. In effect ownership of any property under English law may be said to consist of two elements: *legal* ownership and *equitable* ownership. The two may co-exist on all types of property.

An owner of a property, whether real or personal, is the person who is entitled to all *legal* rights over a particular property. This is the *legal* owner and in law is in a stronger position than the *equitable* owner.[116]

For example, let us assume that X transfers, either by will (upon his death) or *inter-vivos* (during his life), his property, whether real or personal, to Y, provided that Y promises to use it for the benefit of Z. In such situation both Y and Z would have an interest in X's property, upon X's death or the transfer of the property if *inter-vivos*. Y would become the *legal* owner, whereas Z will become the *equitable* owner or *beneficial* owner of the property.

This differentiation between the legal and equitable owner of property is very important in the law of property. The importance can be illustrated by a simple example, which may well serve best in understanding the utility of these concepts in English law.

A lease for more than three years must be created by deed[117] in order to become a legal estate[118] (i.e. leasehold, see above). If X were to prepare a written lease, but not execute it as a deed and paid Y £10,000 for letting Y's property for five years, then X would be £10,000 poorer and have no legal standing if Y wished to recover his property one week after payment by X! However, because of the law of equity and the way ownership is devised under English law, X's

---

[114] Section 52, Law of Property Act 1925.

[115] Section 136, Law of Property Act 1925.

[116] This is mainly because the legal owner can sell the property by defeating any equitable rights/interests attaching to it. This is called *overreaching* in English law, and very briefly, can only take place when the buyer of the property is a *bona-fide* purchaser of the legal estate for value without notice; *Pilcher* v. *Rawlins* (1872) 7 Ch.App.259.

[117] A contract in a deed is a contract which is in writing and satisfies the requirements of section 1 of the Law of Property (Miscellaneous Provisions) Act 1989. It must be noted that any interest in land, and the transfer of a British ship (or any share thereof) must be made in a deed. In order for a deed to be properly executed, the document must be signed, sealed and delivered. The requirement of a seal dates from when illiteracy was prevalent and a seal was used in place of a signature. However, since the introduction of s.1(1)(b) of the Law of Property (Miscellaneous Provisions) Act 1989, a seal is no longer required for an instrument to be validly executed.

[118] Section 52, The Law of Property Act 1925.

written lease would create an equitable interest[119] in Y's property. Even if X's agreement with Y for the five-year lease was merely oral, X would still be protected by equity.[120]

CRIMINAL LAW

In English law criminal liability must be established by the prosecution 'beyond all reasonable doubt'. This is called the 'legal burden' and means that all elements of a crime must be proved to have existed at the time the offence was committed.

A crime usually[121] consists of two basic elements:

(i) 'actus reus', i.e. the actual committing of a prohibited act, and

(ii) 'mens rea',[122] i.e. the guilty intent.[123]

The above burden of proof must be established by the prosecution, with certain exceptions, such as where the accused raises the defence of insanity and he therefore must prove that he falls within the *McNaghten Rules*.[124]

The *actus reus* of an offence consists of an act[125] or omission,[126] or it may consist of a 'state of affairs'.[127]

---

[119] Indeed, such a lease would be capable of being converted into a legal estate by *specific performance*.

[120] In *Walsh* v. *Lonsdale*, (1882) 21 Ch.D.9, D entered into an agreement in writing to grant to C a lease for seven years. The agreement provided for rent payable in advance, and it was not made by deed, as the law required. C became in arrears with payment of rent. The Court held that although law would not recognise the seven-year lease ever existed between the parties, in equity, however, the agreement for the lease was as good as a lease. Therefore, C was held liable to pay for the rent arrears.

[121] But not all crimes need to include the element of *mens rea*. There are some crimes which when committed give rise to 'strict liability', for example, offences under the Road Traffic Act. Invariably, but not always; *Pharmaceutical Society* v. *Storkwain* (1986) 1 W.L.R.903, most of these offences of strict liability are imposed/created by statutes.

[122] This is called the 'evidential burden'.

[123] These expressions derive from the maxim 'actus non facit reum, nisi mens sit rea', meaning that guilt does not arise from the act unless the act is done with a guilty intent.

[124] These Rules contain the requirements which form the basis for the defence of insanity and they derived from the the House of Lords case of *R.* v. *M'Naghten* (1843) 10 Cl.& Fin.200.

[125] For example, *Kay* v. *Butterworth* [1945] 173 L.T.191, where the driver of a vehicle was found guilty of driving since he had continued to drive when he knew he was feeling drowsy.

[126] *R.* v. *Miller* [1983] A.C.161; the defendant was a squatter and had fallen asleep while smoking a cigarette. He awoke to find that his bed was on fire and instead of attempting to put out the fire he moved to another room. The House of Lords held that he should bear responsibility for the result of his failure.

[127] *Winzar* v. *Chief Constable of Kent*, *The Times*, 28 March 1983; the police removed the accused from a hospital to a police car parked in the highway. The accused was charged with being found drunk in the highway. See also *R.* v. *Larsonneur* (1933) 24 C.A.R.74.

The mental element of an offence, i.e. the *mens rea*, must accompany the *actus reus*. This mental element will vary according to the offence charged, as follows:

(i) **INTENTION**: It must be clearly understood that intention is something quite distinct from motive or desire,[128] unlike what some films lead the public to believe! One could best grasp the meaning of intention by a couple of simple examples. In the case of theft it would be necessary to show that the accused intended to permanently deprive the victim of the property concerned. Murder is another offence which requires intention to kill or cause serious bodily harm on the part of the accused.[129]

(ii) **RECKLESSNESS**: This is simply the deliberate taking by the defendant of an unjustifiable risk,[130] or the defendant created an obvious risk of damage and continued with his activity not having given any thought to the existence of such risk.[131] An example of an offence requiring recklessness is manslaughter.[132]

(iii) **NEGLIGENCE**: This is a failure by the defendant to foresee the consequences of his act in circumstances where a reasonable man would have foreseen.[133] An example of an offence requiring negligence is careless driving under the Road Traffic Act.[134]

INCHOATE OFFENCES

Incomplete offences are classified into the following three varieties:

Attempts: It must be borne in mind that if a person does an act with intent to commit an offence, even if commission of the offence is impossible, he will be guilty of 'attempting to commit the offence'.[135]

---

[128] Indeed, this is, according to Lord Bridge, a 'necessity, which frequently arises, to explain to a jury that intention is something quite distinct from motive or desire'; *R.* v. *Moloney* [1985] 1 All E.R.1025.

[129] *R.* v. *Moloney* [1985] 1 All E.R.1025.

[130] This is usually referred to as 'subjective recklessness'; *R.* v. *Cunningham* [1957] 2 All E.R.412.

[131] *R.* v. *Caldwell* [1981] 1 All E.R.961.

[132] *R.* v. *Pike* [1961] Crim.L.R.547.

[133] *Blyth* v. *Birmingham Waterworks Co.* (1856) 11 Exch.781.

[134] Thus, a learner driver's driving would be considered *careless* if he/she failed to measure up to the standard of the reasonably experienced driver; *McCrone* v. *Riding* [1938] 1 All E.R.157.

[135] Thus, if a person carries some substance thinking that it is drugs but customs officers discover it and the substance turns out not to be drugs, such person would be *attempting* a crime; *R.* v. *Shivpuri* (1986) 2 W.L.R.988.

Incitement: In English law it is an offence to incite another person to commit a crime, irrespectively of whether the crime has actually been committed or not. This would include any form of influence from one person on another with a view to procure the commission of an offence, including the use of threats.[136]

Conspiracy: Statutory conspiracy would involve an agreement to do an unlawful act, and similarly to a criminal attempt, the offence would be committed irrespectively of whether the commission of the offence is impossible. There are some exceptions from liability however, where a person conspires with (i) his spouse, (ii) another person who is under the age of criminal responsibility, and (iii) an intended victim of the offence.

GENERAL DEFENCES

In criminal law there are a number of main defences.

Insanity: The general presumption and the starting point are that everyone is presumed sane. The burden of proof is on the defendant to show that he was/is insane on a balance of probabilities. In effect, the defendant must be in such a condition as not to know the nature and quality of his acts.[137] If this is established, then the verdict reached by the Court is 'not guilty by reason of insanity'. This is a complete defence and the Court in such a case has power to make guardianship, or supervision, or treatment orders.

Automatism: The 'classic' example is the situation where a person drives his car when he is stung by a wasp, and he involuntarily swerves and kills/injures another road user. This is however, a simplistic example, and in practice this is one of the much discussed and sometimes controversial defences. This is because such involuntary action may be the result of a recognised disease of the mind. However, Courts have indicated that if a defendant raises a defence based on a disease of the mind the proper defence would be insanity.[138] Obviously, automatism is not available where the state of unconsciousness is self-induced.[139]

Intoxication: This is generally not a defence to any crime, contrary to the popular belief that a drunken does not have control of himself. The only

[136] *Race Relations Board* v. *Applin* [1975] A.C.259.

[137] *R.* v. *M'Naghten* (1843) 10 Cl.& Fin.200.

[138] *Bratty* v. *Attorney-General for Northern Ireland* [1963] A.C.386 H.L.; *R.* v. *Burgess* (1991) 2 W.L.R.1206.

[139] So it cannot be raised as a defence by a driver who falls asleep at the wheel of his car and injures/kills another road user; *Kay* v. *Butterworth* [1945] 173 L.T.191.

exception to this is where the intoxication is involuntary, as for example, where the defendant's drink was 'laced' without his knowledge.[140]

Duress: If a defendant shows that he committed the offence against his will and under compulsion, i.e. involuntarily,[141] then it is said that such person has a complete defence. Most statements on what constitutes duress dwell on the need for the will of the accused to have been overborne by threats of death or serious personal injury.[142] However, this defence would not normally be available in murder[143] and treason[144] cases.

Necessity: This is similar to duress, both involving in effect a type of 'involuntary' act by the accused. The difference between the two would seem to be that duress is imposed by another human being whereas necessity is imposed by the surrounding circumstances. It has been the traditional view that English law does not recognise a defence of necessity.[145] Bear in mind, however, that necessity is very much the basis of the defences of duress and self-defence, which are clearly recognised by English law. Indeed, necessity is frequently referred to as 'duress of circumstances', as opposed to 'duress by threats'.

Self – Defence: This defence simply applies to force used to protect one's self, members of his family,[146] friends, or even a total stranger who is under attack. The main 'theme' in English law, which determines whether the defence has been established, is the question of whether the force the accused used was reasonable in the circumstances, as the accused knew them to be or honestly believed them to be. Furthermore, retreat is not necessary to precede any action

---

140 *Ross* v. *H.M. Advocate* (1991) S.L.T.564.

141 And a sober person of reasonable firmness, sharing relevant characteristics with the defendant, would have responded as the defendant did; *R.* v. *Howe* [1987] A.C.417.

142 *R.* v. *Graham* [1982] 1 W.L.R.294.

143 *R.* v. *Gotts* (1992) 1 All E.R.832.

144 *Cf. R.* v. *Purdy* (1946) 10 J. of Crim. L.182.

145 *R.* v. *Dudley and Stephens* (1884) 14 Q.B.D.273; three men and a cabin boy had been on a lifeboat without food for 20 days, their ship having been wrecked. The two men killed the cabin boy with a knife and lived off his flesh and blood for the following 4 days. On their trial for murder they alleged that the cabin boy was in the worst state and was likely to have died first, and put forward the defence of necessity, i.e. had they not lived off the boy's flesh they would probably all have died. The Court did not accept the defence of necessity. *Cf. A (Children) (Conjoined Twins: Surgical Separation), Re,* [2001] 2 W.L.R. 480 C.A., where the surgical operation on conjoined twins would result in death of one and survival of the other, was considered. The Court was of the view that the operation would not constitute murder since, *inter alia*, the three components of the doctrine of necessity were satisfied, namely that (a) the act was required to avoid inevitable and irreparable evil; (b) no more would be done than was reasonably necessary for the purpose to be achieved, and (c) the evil to be inflicted was not disproportionate to the evil avoided.

146 *R.* v. *Duffy* [1967] 1 Q.B.63.

of self-defence.[147] Indeed, in some circumstances a person may be justified in taking pre-emptive action to defend.[148]

EMPLOYMENT LAW

An employment contract is similar to any other simple contract,[149] it can be made orally and/or in writing. Furthermore, and contrary to the wide view that an employer would produce a contract for signing, no such requirement exists, and in practice, the only obligation an employer has in this respect is to, within two months of commencement of employment, give the employee a written statement containing a job description.[150]

An employer is obliged to provide as far as is possible a safe place of work and to provide safe equipment in order that the employee can carry out their duties safely.

Furthermore, an employer must take reasonable care to ensure that an employee is not exposed to unnecessary risk resulting from their employment. What constitutes reasonable will depend on the nature of the employment, and will include factors such as cost for mitigating the risk, degree of risk, seriousness of the risk. This includes such matters as adequate training, provision of safety equipment and suitable working conditions appropriate to the work being done.

Most of the employer's duties with regard to safety have been incorporated into the Health & Safety at Work Act 1974 as well as dealing with aspects of safety in the workplace they also lay out criminal penalties for failing to comply with provisions of the Act. The intention of the Act is to extend protection to all workers, and involve them in the safety process. Every employer, is now required under the Act to prepare and make available a safety policy. If an employee is injured in the workplace his employer may face a criminal prosecution from the Health & Safety Executive and possibly a civil action in the tort of negligence from the injured person.

---

[147] *R.* v. *Bird* [1985] Crim.L.R.388.

[148] It might be justifiable for a person to make and possess a petrol bomb where this is done to protect his family or property against an imminent attack; *Attorney General's Reference (No.2 of 1983)* [1984] A.C.456.

[149] These are contracts which do not require any formality, thus, they may be made orally, in writing, or indeed, in any other way. See further *infra*, p.75.

[150] Section 1, Employment Rights Act 1996. Matters that need be included are outlined in ss.1-3 of the Act.

In relation to an employee[151] being dismissed by his employer, there are three potential remedies. The Common Law claim for wrongful dismissal, and the two statutory claims of unfair dismissal, and redundancy.

THE CONTRACTUAL CLAIM: WRONGFUL DISMISSAL

This is a Common Law claim and is based on the fact that the contract has been terminated by the employer in a manner which is a breach of the contract of employment. So, when one hears of 'wrongful dismissal' should realise that this is a claim for breach of the employment contract.[152] For example, where the employer terminates a contract for an indefinite term with no notice or with inadequate notice, or if a fixed term contract is terminated before its expiry date. Most, but not all, employment contracts are for an indefinite term and terminable by either side giving the correct contractual notice. If the employer gives the proper period of notice, then no breach will have occurred and there will be no claim for wrongful dismissal whatever the reason for the termination.

In a fixed-term contract, the contract is not terminable by notice, unless it contains a 'break clause'. In the case of a fixed-term contract without a break clause, termination of the contract prior to its expiry date will be a breach of contract and the employee may claim wrongful dismissal. If there is a break clause then the employer may terminate under it and if he gives the appropriate period of notice, the employee cannot succeed in a wrongful dismissal claim.

The break clause would normally contain a notice period, and if the employer does not comply with this then he will be in breach. However, the Employment Rights Act 1996 provides some minimum requirements in relation to the length of such notice. Therefore, if the agreed notice period is shorter than the statutory minimum period, then the longer statutory period of notice must be given, since these prevail over any shorter contractual period:

(a) One week's notice after one month's continuous employment.

(b) Two weeks' notice after two years' continuous employment.

(c) If employee employed for more than two continuous years, then one additional week's notice should be added to (b) above for each year of continuous employment, up to a maximum of 12 weeks' notice.[153]

---

[151] An 'employee' is 'an individual who has entered into or works under a contract of employment'; section 230(1) of the Employment Right Acts 1996.

[152] Thus, where an employee simply resigns, he will have no claim.

[153] Section 86(1), Employment Rights Act 1996.

In the absence of an expressly agreed period of notice, there is an implied term that the employee is entitled to 'reasonable' notice. What will be a reasonable period will depend on the facts of the case. For more senior employees, a longer period may be implied.

However, the above described periods of notice should be the 'starting point' in assessing a 'reasonable' notice. In indefinite contracts, the only statutory minimum notice required to be given by an employee is one week's notice after one month's continuous employment.

It must be noted however, that there are two notable exceptions to the above general rules:

- An employee may be entitled to walk out without notice if a repudiatory breach by the employer has occurred which amounts to 'constructive dismissal'. Although the employee has not been actually dismissed by the employer he has been 'constructively dismissed' in breach of contract.[154]

- Or, on the other hand, an employer may dismiss without notice if the employee has been involved in 'gross misconduct'.[155]

Damages for wrongful dismissal are damages for breach of contract and the normal principles of contract law apply.[156] In a nutshell, the remedies would be damages, which are (i) reduced for non-mitigation of loss, and (ii) increased to take account of tax.

THE STATUTORY CLAIMS: UNFAIR DISMISSAL

A basic and protected right of any employee is the right not to be unfairly dismissed.[157] There is a three-month time limit from the date of the dismissal.[158] The employee must be below the normal retirement age in that business,[159] or, if there is no such normal retirement age, below the age of 65.

Additionally, he must have one year's continuous employment starting when that employment began and ending with the dismissal.[160] The employee needs

[154] For example, an employer's unilateral change of an employee's terms of employment would amount to such dismissal; s.95(1)(a), Employment Rights Act 1996.

[155] Section 86(6), Employment Rights Act 1996.

[156] On remedies for breach of contract, see *infra*, p.104.

[157] Section 94, Employment Rights Act 1996.

[158] Section 111, Employment Rights Act 1996.

[159] Section 109(1), Employment Rights Act 1996.

[160] Section 109(2), Employment Rights Act 1996. 'Continuous employment' is computed in accordance with ss.210-219 of the Act.

only show that he has been dismissed. In his defence, the employer must show that the principal reason for the dismissal is one of the five permitted reasons.[161]

The five potentially fair reasons are:

(a) The capability or qualifications of the employee for doing work of the kind he was employed to do.

(b) The conduct of the employee.

(c) The employee's redundancy.

(d) The employee could not continue to work in the position held without contravening some statutory enactment.

(e) Some other substantial reason justifying the dismissal of an employee holding the position which the employee held.

If the employer is able to show that the dismissal was for any one of the above fair reasons then it must be decided whether in the circumstances the employer acted reasonably in treating the particular reason as a sufficient reason for dismissing the employee.

Possible remedies for unfair dismissal, are reinstatement, re-engagement, and compensation (referred to sometimes as a 'compensation award').

It must be noted that the employee must mitigate his loss and will need to look for another job. Similarly to wrongful dismissal damages, failure to mitigate may result in a reduction of compensation payable.

THE STATUTORY CLAIMS: REDUNDANCY

The person primarily liable to pay a redundancy payment is the employer, and in most cases he would pay without dispute. In case of dispute, there is a six-month time limit,[162] and to claim a statutory redundancy payment, an employee must be below any normal retirement age in that business. If there is no such normal retirement age,[163] the employee must be below the age of 65. Furthermore, the employee must have two years' continuous employment.[164]

It should be noted that an employee may lose his entitlement if he unreasonably refuses an offer of suitable alternative employment made by his

161 Section 98(4), Employment Rights Act 1996.
162 Section 164(1), Employment Rights Act 1996.
163 Section 109(1), Employment Rights Act 1996.
164 Calculated in accordance with ss.210-219 of the Employment Rights Act 1996.

employer to take effect within four weeks of the end of the original contract.[165]

Finally, employers planning to dismiss as redundant more than 19 of their employees have a statutory obligation to consult appropriate representatives about the proposed dismissals within 90 days.[166]

[165] Section 141, Employment Rights Act 1996.

[166] Section 188(1)(1A), Trade Union and Labour Relations (Consolidation) Act 1992. Section 194 of the Act imposes criminal liability for failing to consult as prescribed.

CHAPTER 2

AN OVERVIEW OF THE LEGAL PROCEDURE

For all intends and purposes legal procedure should, as in most Continental jurisdictions, be distinguished into (i) civil, and (ii) criminal. A distinct difference in the English legal system is that, with the exception of certain classes of persons,[167] any person is entitled to represent himself before any of the Criminal or Civil Courts without anyone else legally representing him.

A brief note about the legal profession in England and Wales here would serve as a good guide to the differences of the legal systems of other Continental jurisdictions. The legal profession is divided into (i) solicitors, and (ii) barristers. The effect of the difference in so far as procedure is concerned may be summed up as follows:

-Usually litigants[168] would approach for advice and instruct a solicitor directly.

-The legal training of barristers is very much 'focused' on the law of evidence and in the development of advocacy skills.

-Solicitors have limited rights of audience in the higher Courts, although this is currently changing with a number of experienced solicitors having being granted full rights of audience in the Crown Court and higher appeal Courts.

-Usually, after a civil action or a prosecution commences the solicitor would instruct a barrister, whom he would refer to as 'Counsel', for advice on evidential points and representation of the client in Court.

-In the criminal legal system, the prosecuting authority is currently the Crown Prosecution Service (C.P.S.). The C.P.S. is independent of the police, and is the authority which decides whether a person should be prosecuted or not, depending on the evidence presented to them by the

---

167 For example, in civil procedure, limited companies must be legally represented. In criminal procedure there has been considerable criticism on this issue for prosecutions against alleged rapists. Indeed, in such cases Courts would not allow a person accused of rape to conduct cross-examination of the prosecution witness (who is normally the rape victim).

168 Except the Crown, which is advised, (i) in the case of any publicly important matters by the Attorney-General, and (ii) in the case of publicly important criminal matters by the Director of Public Prosecutions (D.P.P.).

Police. The service is headed by the Director of Public Prosecutions (D.P.P.), with Chief Crown Prosecutors and Crown Prosecutors below him. All or any of them must be barristers or solicitors of considerable standing and experience before appointment to the relevant office.

-The C.P.S. is represented by solicitors and/or barristers, depending on the seniority of the Court.

-In criminal litigation most solicitors have no rights of audience in the Crown Court or the other superior Courts, but only in the Magistrates Court.

-In civil litigation most solicitors have no rights of audience in the County Court or in the other superior Courts, but only in the Magistrates Court.

-In civil procedure, all hearings, except the actual trial, are considered to be 'interlocutory' hearings. These are more informal in that they do not usually take place in 'open Court'. Solicitors, or trainee solicitors, may appear in all these hearing to represent their clients. Or a barrister may appear in any of these hearings on his own or with a solicitor.

-The expressions K.C. (King's Counsel) and Q.C. (Queen's Counsel) refer to the seniority of barristers. Since in the U.K. the Monarch is currently the Queen, senior barristers are called Queen's Counsels (Q.C.).

-It is usual that Q.C.s are 'called to the bench', i.e. are invited to become Judges, although nowadays a considerable number of solicitors are also invited to take the appointments.

LIMITATION PERIODS

Although mention of limitation periods, i.e. the time within which the State, in the case of criminal law, or persons, in the case of civil law, may take action, will be made at the appropriate chapters, it would be useful to be given a summary of all these time limits from the outset.

CIVIL LAW

(1) An action on a simple contract must be brought within six years of the date when the cause of action accrued.[169]

[169] Section 5, Limitation Act 1980. A simple contract is one that does not require any particular formality, i.e. it may be made orally, in writing, or indeed, in any other way. See further *infra*, p.75.

(2) An action on a contract made under seal will be statute barred after twelve years from the date when the cause of action accrued.[170]

(3) Where the claim includes damages in respect of personal injuries caused by a tort, the period is three years.[171]

(4) In the case of non-personal injury actions based on negligence, where the damage is latent then it is either (i) six years from date when the cause of action accrued, or (ii) three years from date of knowledge of certain material facts about the damage.[172]

(5) For all other tort actions, excluding defamation,[173] personal injury and latent damage, it is six years.[174]

(6) In enforcing a judgment, it is six years from the date when the judgment became enforceable.[175]

(7) Loss or damage to goods while they are carried between two or more countries, is covered by different time limits, depending on whether such carriage is by sea, road, or air.[176]

Finally, section 32 of the Act states that deliberate concealment, either after the cause of action accrued and/or at the time when it accrued, of any fact relevant to the right of action of a person, would postpone the start of limitation period.[177]

CRIMINAL LAW

In so far as the more serious criminal offences, known as 'indictable',[178] are concerned, there are no statutory time-limits for commencing criminal proceedings.

---

[170] Section 8, Limitation Act 1980.

[171] From accrual of cause of action or knowledge if later; s.11, Limitation Act 1980. Note that s.11A has been added which imposes a ten year period on actions brought under the Consumer Protection Act 1987.

[172] Section 14A, Limitation Act 1980. This new section was inserted by the Latent Damage Act 1986.

[173] For defamation the time limit is one year; s.4A, Limitation Act 1980.

[174] Section 2, Limitation Act 1980.

[175] Section 24, Limitation Act 1980.

[176] For time limits under these legal regimes, see *infra*, pp.259, 285, 293, respectively.

[177] *Williams* v. *Fanshaw Porter & Hazelhurst* [2004] 2 All E.R.616, C.A.

[178] Indictable offences are generally the more serious forms of crime, such as all forms of homicide, major theft, assaults inflicting bodily harm, rape. See further page 49 for classification of criminal offences.

However, prosecutions for less serious offences, known as 'summary',[179] must be dealt with by a Magistrates' Court within six months after the alleged offence was committed.[180]

CIVIL LITIGATION

Before we outline how a civil action is usually conducted in England, it would be useful to come to grips with some expressions one might come across in the process of a case.

An expression used considerably in practice but also found in most civil litigation books and reported cases is 'interlocutory'. The word means intermediate, and may refer to (i) a hearing, (ii) an injunction, (iii) an order, or (iv) a judgment. In effect all four of these are preceded by the word 'interlocutory' and are not final.

(i) Interlocutory hearing usually refers to hearings before a Judge in Chambers, i.e. not in open Court. All solicitors, including trainee solicitors, have a right of audience in most of these hearings. As a rule, all hearings before the actual trial are called interlocutory. Indeed, all the following are usually granted at an interlocutory hearing.

(ii) An interlocutory injunction is an injunction[181] granted by the Court in order to maintain the *status quo* between the parties to a case until it is finally decided. Obviously, an interlocutory injunction will be granted at an interlocutory hearing.

(iii) An interlocutory order or sometimes referred to as an 'interim' order, is simply an order of the Court, which does not conclude a case.

(iv) Again an interlocutory judgment is a judgment given by the Court which is only intermediate and does not determine the action.

Finally, one may come across the expression 'ex parte'. This simply means that what follows after the expression has been granted after the Court/Judge heard only one-side. Thus, an interlocutory *ex parte* injunction means that it

[179] Summary offences are offences specifically named as being triable before the Magistrates' Court, hence all summary offences are defined by statute. They are generally the less serious forms of crime, such as minor thefts, minor assaults, road traffic offences. See further page 49 for classification of criminal offences.

[180] Section 127, Magistrates' Courts Act 1980.

[181] See also *infra*, p.107, on civil injunctions.

was granted after hearing one side only. Such interlocutory injunctions are usually applied for by one side only because either secrecy is required in order to restrain some action by the other party, or because of great urgency.[182]

The opposite of *ex parte* is *inter partes* and it means that, for example, an *inter partes* interlocutory hearing will be conducted with the parties concerned in the action present. Indeed, interlocutory *ex parte* injunctions only last until either the trial or some earlier event. Such event would usually be an application to the Court for an *inter partes* interlocutory hearing. It must be noted that whenever there is an application for an *inter partes* hearing, the party applying for such hearing must give notice of it to the other parties in the action at least three clear days before the Court is to deal with the application. Such applications are also referred to as 'on notice' applications. Therefore, most interlocutory hearings are, in practice, *inter partes*.

PROCEDURE

A civil action usually begins with a 'letter before action' by the solicitor to the defendant. Of course, if the solicitor is already aware that the defendant has solicitors acting for him then the letter should be addressed to the solicitors, otherwise the solicitor will be committing a breach of the Rules of Professional Conduct by writing directly to the defendant. Normally such letter would require a response within a specified period of time, failing which the solicitor should warn the defendant that proceedings will be issued without further notice.

In some cases, a party may wish to see documents held by the opponent in order to decide whether or not to take proceedings. Therefore, an application for disclosure of documents prior to the start of proceedings may be made to the other party(ies) in the first instance, and if refused then by way of an application to the Court.

There are also cases where a party may need access to another party's property to inspect certain objects, which may be vital to any subsequent proceedings. In such cases, again, an application for preservation and or inspection of the 'thing' concerned should be made to the other party(ies) concerned in the first instance, and if refused then to the Court.

When a party decides to issue proceedings, then a claim form must be completed, either with or without the 'Particulars of Claim',[183] which is sent

[182] It is noteworthy that such injunctions may, in appropriate circumstances, be granted by the Court even over the telephone without the production of any documents; *Allen* v. *Jambo Holdings Ltd.* [1980] 1 Q.L.R.1252.

[183] The primary function of the Particulars of Claim is to state concisely the facts upon which the claimant relies.

to the Court office.[184] It must be noted that the expression 'claimant' has recently replaced 'plaintiff', and therefore the person who makes the claim is described as the claimant and the person against whom it is made is the defendant.

Once the claim form has been served on the defendant, then the latter would have three ways in which to respond: (i) filing an acknowledgement of service, (ii) filing a defence, (iii) filing an admission.

(i) The time for acknowledgement of service is 14 days from service of the claim form provided Particulars of Claim were also included therein. If Particulars of Claim were not included then the defendant does not have to acknowledge service until 14 days after service of the Particulars of Claim.

(ii) The time for filing a defence is 14 days of service of the Particulars of Claim, or if the defendant has acknowledged service (as above), then 28 days of service of the Particulars of Claim.

(iii) Without going into the detail of different types of admission, if the defendant admits the claim, then he should file an appropriate form of admission (a copy of which usually accompanies the claim form) within 14 days of service of the Particulars of Claim.

Once the proceedings have been served, as above, it may be that the defendant does not respond, i.e. does not return the acknowledgement of service, or does not file a defence. If this is the case, then the claimant may apply to the Court in order to obtain 'Judgment in default' against the defendant.[185]

If a defence has been served by the defendant then the claimant may, if he wishes, to reply to the defence. Replies are not in practice used extensively since by not replying there is no presumption that the claimant admits the matters raised in the defence. However, replies are used where the defendant

---

[184] It must be noted that under E.C. Council Regulation 1348/2000, (O.J. L 160, 30/06/2000, p.37), which came into force in May 2001, service between E.C. States of judicial and extra-judicial documents in civil or commercial matters is very much harmonised and regularised. E.C. States have now set up 'transmitting agents' and 'receiving agencies' for the transmission and reception of, for example, Court proceedings. In simple terms the transmitting agency in an E.C. State will transmit the proceedings' documents to the receiving agency in another E.C. State which in turn would serve the document(s) upon the intended recipient. Such service should be effected by the receiving agency not later than one month after receipt. Upon successful service, a certificate of completion should then be sent to the transmitting agency. The subsequent Commission Decisions 2001/781/EC (O.J. L 298, 15/11/2001, p.1), 2001/781/EC (O.J. L 31, 01/02/2003, p.88), 2001/781/EC (O.J. L 60, 05/03/2003, p.3), and 2002/350/EC (O.J. L 126, 13/05/2002, p.1), have produced a list of all the 'receiving agencies' and documents which may be served.

[185] Note, however, that judgment in default would not be appropriate in all types of claim, e.g. mortgage claims, or claims for goods under a contract regulated by the Consumer Credit Act 1974.

has made a counterclaim,[186] or if the claimant wishes to allege facts in answer to the defence which were not included in the Particulars of Claim.

If a defence has been served, then the Court's part becomes more active in the action. This is the 'allocation' stage, whereby the Court will allocate the case to one of the three tracks, depending on the information the parties in the action have filed to the Court by way of an 'allocation questionnaire'.[187]

Thus, the Court will normally allocate claims (i) not exceeding £5,000 to the 'small claims' track, (ii) between £5,000 and £15,000 to the 'fast' track, and (iii) exceeding £15,000 to the 'multi-track'. It must be noted that the Court will also take into consideration the likely duration of the actual trial of the case, before allocating a case to either (ii) or (iii) above. Together with the allocation of the case, the Court at this stage is likely to give 'directions' as to how the case is to proceed to trial. These directions usually would include a timetable within which, for example, witness statements should be exchanged.[188]

Next in the procedure is the 'disclosure' stage. The main purpose of it being to enable the parties to evaluate their case in advance of the trial. In simple words, at this stage the parties have to reveal to each other the documents which have a bearing on the case. Furthermore, any party to the proceedings has a right of inspection of any disclosed documents.[189]

Next is the 'setting-down' stage, which is in effect the preparation for trial. At this stage it is usual that the parties to the action may reach some kind of settlement, or perhaps the claimant discontinues his claim.[190] Furthermore, the claimant must bear in mind that he has to prepare and file to the Court the

---

186 A counterclaim is also known as a 'Part 20' claim. In simple words, this occurs where C, the claimant, issues proceedings against D, the defendant, and the latter either wishes to (i) make a claim against C, or (ii) to pass the blame on to a third party.

187 This is a document served by the Court to all parties in the proceedings, and which should be completed and returned to the Court within 14 days. The questionnaire asks the parties, for example, whether they know what witnesses they will be calling and what facts they are witnesses to.

188 In practice, there are obvious variations on these directions. For example, in multi-track cases the Court may give directions as to the holding of a 'case management conference', whereby a review of all steps taken in the preparation of the case will be considered. It must be noted that as from July 2004, the E.C. Council Regulation 1206/2001 on co-operation between national Courts in the taking of evidence in civil and commercial proceedings (O.J. L 174, 27/06/2001, p.1) has come into force. Briefly, under this Regulation a civil Court in one E.C. State will be able to request a competent Court in another E.C. State (except Denmark) to take evidence directly in the requested State. Such requests should be executed within 90 days of receipt and in appropriate cases a video-conference or tele-conference may be requested under Article 10 of the Regulation.

189 It is obvious that only ***relevant*** documents which are or have been in a party's control must be disclosed. There are also certain documents which attract 'privilege', or documents which tend to incriminate the party who would produce them, and ***inspection*** of such documents may be withheld.

190 However, if there are other claimants then in order to discontinue a claimant would need the other claimants' consent in writing, or the permission of the Court to do so.

'trial bundle' not more than seven days and not less than three days before the start of the trial. A copy of the trial bundle should also be given to all the parties in the proceedings. If the presence of a barrister is necessary then the solicitor should instruct counsel to deal with the trial.

The penultimate stage in the civil procedure is that of the actual trial. Usually, it would be for the claimant to make an opening speech before the Court. The claimant's witnesses will then give evidence.

Next, the claimant's witnesses may be 'cross-examined' by the defendant. Following cross-examination, the claimant is given the opportunity to ask further questions of his witness.

The defence will present its evidence in exactly the same way as the claimant. After the evidence has been given, the defendant will make a closing speech followed by the claimant.

The Court will then deliver its judgment, and depending on the complexity of the case, can do so immediately, or at a later date. The general rule is that the Court will order the unsuccessful party to pay the costs of the successful party.[191]

The final stage, which it is intended to be briefly highlighted here, is that of enforcement. In simple words the winning party will have to consider with his solicitor the best method of enforcing the judgment.

This is particularly in 'money judgments' where they are not enforced by the Court automatically but the winning party should take enforcement action.

It must be remembered that in money judgments the enforcement action is considered as a 'debt' by the unsuccessful party, and the main methods of such enforcement action are as follows:

(i) **Execution**: The Court may seize and sell the debtor's goods to pay the judgment debt and associated costs.

(ii) **Charging order on land**: Simply, this is a Court order whereby a land charge is registered at H.M. Land Registry against land owned by the debtor to the amount due under the judgment.

(iii) **Garneshee order**, or to use its modern term, a **'third party debt' order**: Where money is already owed to the debtor by a third party, then the Court may order that the 'garneshee', i.e. the person who owes such money to the debtor, to pay the successful party an amount that represents the judgment debt.

[191] Bear in mind however, that this is not an inflexible rule and a Court may make a different order for costs if it considers it appropriate.

(iv) **Attachment of earnings**: This is a Court order whereby the debtor's employer is compelled to regularly deduct from the debtor's earnings, and pay them into Court towards satisfaction of the judgment debt.

(v) **Insolvency**: Depending on whether the debtor is a company or an individual, the successful party may decide to 'wind-up' the company, or 'petition for bankruptcy' of the debtor individual.

CRIMINAL LITIGATION

Criminal procedure in England and Wales differs considerably from that found in most Continental systems. A distinction that must be made clear from the outset in so far as criminal law is concerned, is that there is a presumption that the accused is innocent and it is for the prosecutor to produce evidence which shows that the accused is guilty 'beyond reasonable doubt'.[192] Up to 1967 offences in England and Wales were classified into felonies, which were the more serious offences,[193] and misdemeanours, which were the less serious ones.

CLASSIFICATION OF OFFENCES

Nowadays, offences are classified in accordance to the mode of trial:

'Indictable' offences are generally the more serious forms of crime.[194] The word 'indictment' means a document which sets out in writing the charges against the accused, each separate charge is called 'a count' of the indictment. In indictable offences the person accused of the offence is actually tried before a Judge and jury.

'Summary' offences are offences specifically named as being triable before the Magistrates' Court,[195] hence all summary offences are defined by statute.[196]

[192] In civil law no such presumption exists, and the evidential burden of proof is based 'on the balance of probabilities'.

[193] Up to 1870 some felonies, such as rape, carried a death penalty. Furthermore, if a person was convicted of a felony he was liable to forfeiture of his property.

[194] For example robbery, or murder.

[195] However, it must be noted that although the Magistrates' Court may try summarily an accused person, if it convicts such person but the Court feels that its own sentencing powers are inadequate, then, under section 38 of the Magistrates' Courts Act 1980, it has the power to send the defendant for sentence to the next sitting of the Crown Court.

[196] They are generally the less serious forms of crime, e.g. taking a conveyance, driving without insurance, harassment, careless and inconsiderate driving, etc.

There is also another class of offences which is a 'hybrid' of the two mentioned above. These are the so-called **'triable either way'** offences,[197] and as their name suggests may be tried at the Magistrates or the Crown Court, depending on the seriousness of the case, the Magistrate Court's sentencing powers to deal with it, and the circumstances in which the offence was committed.

Within the above mentioned three classifications, there is also another classification of offences, which was introduced by statute,[198] that of **'serious arrestable offences'**.[199] It must be borne in mind that the reason for this classification relates to the powers of the police to detain a suspect and to delay access to legal advice. However, this must not be confused with the powers of the police to actually arrest a person.[200] The police have such wide powers to arrest 'without a warrant' that it is nowadays exceptional that a warrant is necessary. So, for example, a constable may arrest a person if he has reasonable grounds to suspect that any non-arrestable offence has been committed or attempted, and appears to the constable that service of a 'summons' would be impracticable or inappropriate.[201]

Whether with or without a warrant, on arrest by the police a person must be cautioned as follows:

> 'You do not have to say anything. But it may harm your defence if you do not mention, when questioned, something which you later rely on in Court. Anything you do say may be given in evidence'.

As a brief reminder of the time limits applicable for prosecution of criminal offences, for indictable and most either way offences there are no statutory time-limits for commencing criminal proceedings. Prosecutions for summary offences must commence within 6 months after the alleged offence was committed.

A note should be made here about 'road traffic' offences, since the statute applicable[202] provides that a defendant may not be prosecuted unless notice/warning of intended prosecution was given to him/her, either (i) orally at the time of the offence, or (ii) in writing within 14 days of the offence.[203]

---

197 For example theft, burglary, assault occasioning actual bodily harm, dangerous driving.

198 Section 116, Police and Criminal Evidence Act 1984.

199 For example theft, burglary, robbery, taking a conveyance, assault occasioning actual bodily harm.

200 Indeed, the initial decision of whether an offence under investigation is a serious arrestable offence is taken by a police superintendent at the police station while the suspect is being held.

201 Section 25, Police and Criminal Evidence Act 1984. For example, where a person does not furnish a satisfactory address it could lead to his arrest.

202 Section 1, Road Traffic Offenders Act 1988 (as amended by the Road Traffic Act 1991).

203 However, s.2 of the same Act provides that where an accident occurs at the same time or immediately after the offence, then there is no requirement to give the defendant any notice/warning of prosecution.

PROCEDURE

The prosecution of almost all criminal offences starts in the Magistrates' Court[204] irrespectively of the type of crime committed. The method of commencement depends on the seriousness of the offence. It must be borne in mind that in the proceeding parts, 'summary procedure', as opposed to a summary offence, refers to criminal litigation procedure before the Magistrates' Court.

(a) **Non - Arrestable**: The prosecution of a non-arrestable offence may start by the 'laying of an information' which would lead to the Court considering whether to issue a 'summons'. In effect this means that either the prosecutor or just any person may submit a signed written allegation against the accused to a Magistrates' Court, who in turn may issue a summons and serve it on the accused.
An information is the charge to which the accused would plead at the Magistrates' Court when the trial commences, and it serves as a method of securing the accused's appearance before the Court. It should be noted that an information must specify one offence only, so if it is required to bring more than one charge against an accused then separate informations must be submitted to the Court.[205]
If the summons is issued by the Court, then it will contain the contents of the information initially submitted to the Court. Furthermore, a summons may cover more than one information, i.e. it may contain several charges. Next, the summons will be served on the accused, either personally or by post at his last known address. The summons will notify the accused of the time and venue of the hearing at the Magistrates' Court.

(b) **Arrestable**: After the defendant is arrested by the police, whether with or without a warrant, he is taken to the police station where he is charged and either released on bail[206] or kept in police custody.[207]

---

[204] A minor may be prosecuted and defend himself (or be represented) in criminal matters, however, for criminal liability, minors are divided into three classes: (a) It is an irrebuttable legal presumption that minors under the age of ten years are incapable of any crime. They may be restrained by the police under their Common Law powers to protect property or detained under the Children and Young Persons Act, 1969, if they are beyond the control of parents or guardians. (b) Between the ages of ten years and 14 years, the Common Law presumption that the minor was unable to have 'guilty intent' may be rebutted by showing that the minor was able to understand that the act was morally wrong. (c) Minors of 14 years and over are fully liable for crimes, however, the procedures and penalties are different to those for adults.

[205] This is important since once the trial has commenced there is no power to amend the information.

[206] Bail is administered under the Bail Act 1976, as amended by the Crime and Disorder Act 1998.

[207] Sections 47(3A) and 46(2), Police and Criminal Evidence Act 1984.

1. Summary Procedure - Summary Only Offence

On the day of the first hearing before the Magistrates' questions of legal aid and bail are usually dealt with. It is usual for the defence to request 'advance disclosure' (or 'advance information') of the prosecution case, but in practice defence solicitors usually get voluntary disclosure by the prosecutor on the day of the hearing.[208] The charge will be read to the defendant and he will ask to plead. The defendant will plead (i) 'guilty' or (ii) 'not guilty', and on conviction will be sentenced.

(i) **Guilty** - Summary Only Offence: The Court is likely to adjourn for 'pre-sentence' reports to be prepared to assist the Court in deciding the most appropriate method of dealing with the defendant.[209]
If an adjournment for pre-sentence report takes place, then the Magistrates should consider whether the defendant should be 'remanded on bail' or 'in custody' until the reports are prepared. It is normal, at this stage, for the defence to make an application for bail to the Court, and for the prosecution to indicate any objections to such bail. These pre-sentence reports are usually prepared by a probation officer or a social worker.
Once these pre-sentence reports are prepared, a copy is given to the prosecutor, the defendant, and the Magistrates.
The defence will need to have prepared and produce to the Court a completed 'means enquiry' form, which may be used by the Court if a financial penalty is being considered.
The prosecution will summarise the facts of the case[210] and present details of the defendant's background and previous convictions.
Next the defence speech in mitigation is presented to the Court. Here the objective of the defence is to ensure that a balance is maintained in that the sentence passed by the Court will be appropriate to both, the circumstances of the offence and of the defendant.
Finally the Magistrates will proceed to sentence the defendant.

(ii) **Not Guilty** - Summary Only Offence: The prosecution has no obligation

---

[208] Since in summary trials there is no obligation on the prosecution to notify the defence of its case; *R* v. *Kingston upon Hull Justices, ex parte McCan* (1991) 155 J.P.569

[209] In practice, it is an indication that the Court is not considering a custodial sentence. Indeed, there are occasions where the Court feels that a report is not necessary, i.e. where a custodial sentence is inevitable.

[210] Note that if the defendant pleads guilty but he/she still disputes some allegations made by the prosecution, which are substantial, then the Court has two 'options', either to accept the defence account, or to give the parties the opportunity of calling evidence so that the dispute may be resolved. In the latter case, where evidence is called, this is known as a 'Newton hearing', after the case of *R* v. *Newton* (1983) 77 C.App.R.13.

to provide advance information of their case to the defence.[211] In practice the defence requests such information which may be provided by the prosecution on a voluntary basis. However, the prosecution has an obligation to make available to the defence any material of relevance to the case upon which it does not intend to rely.[212] Furthermore, the prosecutor must disclose to the defence any previous undisclosed material which he considers might undermine the prosecution case, or confirm in writing that there is no such material.[213]

At this stage, i.e. following 'primary disclosure', the defendant may, if he so wishes, give a 'defence statement'. This is a written statement by the defendant whereby he outlines his main terms of his defence.[214]

If the defendant provides a defence statement, then the prosecution must disclose to the defence any previously undisclosed material which might assist the defendant's defence, as expressed in the defence statement, or confirm that there is no such material.[215]

Following all the above matters, the prosecution will make its opening speech, summarising the issues involved in the offence and the witnesses who will be called.

Next, the prosecution will call its witnesses, who will be 'examined-in-chief', i.e. asked questions initially by the prosecution, then 'cross-examined' by the defence, and 're-examined' by the prosecution (if necessary).

Next, the defence will make its opening speech, although in practice this is not always the case. Instead, the defence would call the defendant, if he wishes to give evidence, followed by any other defence witnesses. Again, these witnesses will be examined-in-chief, cross-examined by the prosecution, and if necessary re-examined by the defence.

Finally, the defence addresses the Court, making its closing speech. It must be remembered that the defence would always address the Court last.

Then, the Magistrates will consider the merits of the case, and, with the assistance of their clerk will reach a majority verdict. If the defendant is

---

211 The Magistrates' Courts (Advance Information) Rules 1985, (S.I.1985, No.601).

212 Criminal Procedure and Investigations Act 1996. This material is referred to as 'unused material'.

213 Section 3, Criminal Procedures and Investigations Act 1996. This is referred to as 'primary disclosure'. It must be noted that it is not actually the prosecution which makes the disclosure, but the 'disclosure officer', who is a policeman in charge of the investigation.

214 Sections 5 and 6, Criminal Procedure and Investigations Act 1996. This is sometimes referred to as 'defence disclosure'.

215 Section 7, Criminal Procedure and Investigations Act 1996. This is referred to as 'secondary disclosure'. Note that if no defence statement has been given, then there is no obligation on the prosecution to provide such information.

convicted, then an adjournment for pre-sentence reports may be ordered. At this stage it is normal for the defence to make an application for bail to the Court, and for the prosecution to indicate any objections to such bail. The defence will need to have prepared and produce to the Court a completed 'means enquiry' form, which may be used by the Court if a financial penalty is being considered.

Next the defence speech in mitigation is presented to the Court. Finally the Magistrates will proceed to sentence the defendant.

2. SUMMARY PROCEDURE - Either way Offence

If the offence is an either way offence, then the defence should request 'advance disclosure' from the prosecution. In fact, it is the obligation of the prosecution to notify the defence of its case.[216] This advance disclosure usually includes copies of written statements of prosecution witness and must be furnished by the prosecution before the 'mode of trial' hearing.

Then follows the 'mode of trial' enquiry which takes place at a hearing before the Magistrates' Court. The purpose of this hearing is to determine whether the case will be dealt by the Crown or the Magistrates' Court. If the defendant at this hearing he has not yet obtained advance disclosure of the prosecution case, then he is entitled to adjourn the hearing to enable disclosure to take place.

Following advance disclosure, then at the 'mode of trial' hearing the defendant will be asked to indicate whether he would plead guilty or not guilty if the case is to proceed.

If the defendant refuses to indicate a plea or indicates not guilty then the prosecutor will outline the nature of the charge and he will indicate in which Court it feels the case should be tried, i.e. the Magistrates' or the Crown Court.

The defence will then outline the nature of the charge and indicate which Court it feels is more suitable for the case to be tried.

Next, the Magistrates will announce whether they are prepared to deal with the case or whether the case should be sent to the Crown Court for trial.

(a) If they decide that the case should be tried in the Crown Court, then it is adjourned to a future date when 'committal proceedings'[217] will take place. The purpose of committal proceedings is to ensure that there is a case for the defendant to answer in the Crown Court.

---

216 The Magistrates' Court (Advance Information) Rules 1985, (S.I.1985, No.601).

217 See *infra*, p.57.

(b) If the Magistrates decide that they are prepared to deal with the case then the defendant is asked whether he consents to Magistrates' Court trial. It is also explained to the defendant that he/she is entitled to elect for trial in the Crown Court before a Judge and a jury.

The defendant then decides whether he wishes to be tried by the Magistrates' Court or by the Crown Court.

-If he asks for Crown Court trial, then he will not be asked to plead, i.e. guilty or not guilty, and the case will be adjourned to a future date for committal proceedings.

-If he consents to Magistrate's Court trial and pleads not guilty then the case will be adjourned to a future date for trial.[218]

-If he consents to Magistrates' Court trial and pleads guilty, then the procedure for summary trial, described below in '(ii) Guilty - Either Way Offence' will be followed.

(i) **Not Guilty** - Either Way Offence: Where the Magistrates are prepared to deal with the case and the defendant has pleaded not guilty, the next step is for the Court to fix a future date for trial. At this stage the Magistrates should consider whether the defendant should be 'remanded on bail' or 'in custody' until the day of the trial. It is therefore normal practice for the defence to make an application for bail to the Court, and for the prosecution to indicate any objections to such bail.

On the day of the trial, the prosecutor will address the Court, giving an outline of the case and indicating the witnesses which he intends to call.

Next, the prosecution will call evidence, either witnesses or witness statements. Witnesses will firstly be examined by the prosecutor, followed by cross-examination by the defence. If prosecution so wishes, may re-examine the witnesses.

The defence witnesses are then called, including the defendant, who must testify first. These witnesses are firstly examined by the defence, followed by cross-examination by the prosecution.

Finally, once all the evidence has been submitted by both prosecution and defence, it is the turn of the defence to make the 'closing speech' to the Court.

[218] It is important to bear in mind that similarly to the not guilty summary procedure described earlier, this not guilty plea by a defendant before the Magistrates' Court triggers off certain obligations to be fulfilled by the prosecution, under the Criminal Procedure and Investigations Act 1996. These are (i) duty to disclose any relevant 'unused material' to the defence, upon which prosecution does not intend to rely, and (ii) duty to disclose to the defence any previous undisclosed material which might undermine the prosecution case ('primary disclosure').

Then, the Magistrates decide on the outcome of the case, either immediately, or more usually after withdrawing to a room where, with the assistance of their clerk, deliberate on the case. This process may sometimes last for hours, depending on the complexities of the evidence.
The defendant will be either 'acquitted', in which case he may make an application for costs, or convicted.
If the defendant is convicted, then the Court will proceed sentence, but after hearing the 'plea in mitigation' by the defence, and adjourn if 'pre-sentence reports' need to be prepared. In effect the procedure from that point onwards is the same as in '(ii) Guilty - Either Way Offence' below.

(ii) Guilty - Either Way Offence: If the defendant actually pleads guilty then the Court is likely to adjourn for 'pre-sentence reports' to be prepared to assist the Court in deciding the most appropriate method of dealing with the defendant.[219]
If an adjournment for pre-sentence report takes place, then the Magistrates should consider whether the defendant should be 'remanded on bail' or 'in custody' until the reports are prepared. At this stage it is normal for the defence to make an application for bail to the Court, and for the prosecution to indicate any objections to such bail.
Once these pre-sentence reports are prepared, a copy is given to the prosecutor, the defendant, and the Magistrates.
Irrespectively of whether an adjournment for pre-sentence is ordered, the following procedure would be common in both cases.
The defence will need to have prepared and produce to the Court a completed 'means enquiry' form, which may be used by the Court if a financial penalty is being considered.
The prosecution will summarise the facts of the case[220] and present details of the defendant's background and previous convictions.
Next the defence speech in mitigation is presented to the Court. Here the objective of the defence is to ensure that a balance is maintained in that the sentence passed by the Court will be appropriate to both, the circumstances of the offence and of the defendant.
Magistrates will proceed to sentence him.

---

[219] In practice, it is an indication that the Court is not considering a custodial sentence. Indeed, there are occasions where the Court feels that a report is not necessary, i.e. where a custodial sentence is inevitable.

[220] Note that if the defendant pleads guilty but he still disputes some allegations made by the prosecution, which are substantial, then the Court has two 'options', either to accept the defence account, or to give the parties the opportunity of calling evidence so that the dispute may be resolved. In the latter case, where evidence is called, this is known as a 'Newton hearing', after the case of *R* v. *Newton* (1983) 77 C.App.R.13.

Committal Proceedings: As mentioned above, where the Magistrates indicate that they are not prepared to deal with the case, or that they are prepared to deal with the case but the defendant has not consented to be tried at the Magistrates' Court, then the case is adjourned to a future date for 'committal proceedings' to take place.[221]

The purpose of committal proceedings is to ensure that there is a case for the defendant to answer in the Crown Court. In effect this is a hearing before the Magistrates' Court, where prosecution evidence is outlined and put forward to the Court. It could be said that most 'paperwork', e.g. written witness statements and other documents, is produced by the prosecution for the Court's, as well as the defence's, consideration.

For example, if a witness would not produce a written statement voluntarily, the prosecution will put forward the point to the Magistrates who, if they consider that a written statement relevant to the case can be made by such witness, will issue a summons requiring him to attend the Court to give evidence which will be taken down in writing by the Clerk (or the Magistrates) in the form of a 'deposition'.[222]

Very briefly, at this prosecution stage, the prosecution will offer the defence one of are two types of committal proceedings, and the defence will subsequently have to decide, depending on the evidence, which one to have:

(a) **Without Consideration of the Evidence**: In essence this type would be appropriate where the defendant intends to plead not guilty but he accepts that the prosecution have a *prima facie* case against him. The hearing of such proceedings is usually very short, and it could be described as administrative in nature.

(b) **With Consideration of the Evidence**: This type of proceedings would be appropriate where the prosecution's case seems so weak 'on paper' that the defence consider that there is a realistic prospect of having the case dismissed by the Magistrates.[223]If the Magistrates do not commit the defendant for trial, then the accused is usually

---

[221] Please note that not all 'either way' offences are subject to committal proceedings, and there are also ways of 'bypassing' these proceedings, but these are beyond the scope of this book. Those interested in researching these 'exceptions' to the normal procedure would be referred to the various practitioner's reference works on the Crime and Disorder Act 1998, 'voluntary bills of indictment', and 'notice of transfer'.

[222] Section 5C, Magistrates' Courts Act 1980. A deposition is a statement taken on oath before a Magistrates' Clerk. Of course, if such witness fails to attend the Court's invitation, then a warrant for his arrest might be issued by the Magistrates.

[223] In such a case the defence will make a 'submission of no case to answer'; *R* v. *Galbraith* [1982] 2 All E.R.1060. Alternatively, the defence may feel that the Court could be persuaded to commit the defendant for trial on a lesser charge than the one being dealt with at this committal stage.

'discharged', as opposed to 'acquitted'. This means that the prosecution may re-charge the accused for the same or another offence and start the procedure again.

Where the defendant is committed for trial under either type of committal proceedings, a date is set for a 'plea and directions' hearing at the Crown Court.[224] Furthermore, legal aid will be dealt with at the conclusion of the committal proceedings hearing.
Finally, if the defendant is already on bail, it is usual for such bail to be extended until the Crown Court trial. However, if the defendant has been remanded in custody until committal proceedings, the defence may make a (further) bail application to the Magistrates.

3. SUMMARY PROCEDURE - Indictable Offences

A defendant who is charged with an offence triable only on indictment will appear before the Magistrates' Court only for a 'preliminary' hearing, following which he will be sent straight to the Crown Court.

The purpose of this hearing is to consider and determine (i) whether there is an indictable only offence charged, (ii) whether there are other related offences which should also be sent to the Crown Court, (iii) the grant of legal aid, (iv) the date on which the first Crown Court 'preliminary' hearing (see below) will take place, and (v) whether to remand the defendant in custody or on bail.

4. PROCEDURE IN CROWN COURT

There is a slight difference in the procedure depending on whether the defendant was actually committed for Crown Court trial following committal proceedings, or he was sent to the Crown Court for trial. The former will normally be most cases of either way offences, where committal proceedings will have taken place, whereas the latter relates to indictable only (and sometimes either way) offences where the Magistrates send the case to the Crown Court for trial.

In effect the difference is that where the case has been sent for trial to the Crown Court the first hearing will be a 'preliminary' hearing, whereas the first hearing for a defendant committed for trial at the Crown Court will be the

224 This 'plea and directions hearing' must take place either (i) within 4 weeks of committal if the defendant is in custody, or (ii) within 6 weeks of committal if the defendant is on bail; Practice Direction: Crown Court (Plea and Directions Hearings) [1995] 1 W.L.R.1318.

'plea and directions hearing'. However, there are other differences relating to disclosure, which are only outlined below.

When the case has been sent to the Crown Court, a preliminary hearing will be held whereby the Judge will have the opportunity to consult the prosecution and hear any application for bail. Furthermore, the Judge will set a date for the plea and directions hearing.

Obviously, where the case has been sent, as opposed to being committed, to the Crown Court, there would not have been any disclosure of the prosecution's case. Therefore, the prosecution would have to serve its case, and once this is done (or not done!) there would usually be another hearing whereby the Judge will review the case and confirm the plea and directions hearing date.

Apart from the above distinctive steps which apply when the case has been sent to the Crown Court, what follows is common whether the case has been committed or sent to the Crown Court.

The prosecution must give 'primary disclosure', by disclosing to the defence any previous undisclosed material which might *undermine* the prosecution case and upon which the prosecution does not intend to rely ('unused material), or confirm in writing that there is no such material.

Next, the defendant must give a defence statement to the prosecution whereby he outlines his main terms of his defence, e.g. alibi.

Following service of the defence statement the prosecution must give 'secondary disclosure', by disclosing to the defence any material which might *assist* the defendant's defence and upon which the prosecution does not intend to rely.

The plea and directions hearing would then be held, whereby the defendant is required to plead to the charge(s). If at this stage the defendant pleads guilty he may, in most cases, be sentenced at this hearing. Otherwise, on a not guilty plea, the Judge will proceed to gather information from all the parties on various matters relating to the case, and a trial date will be set.

There is a special procedure which is followed where the alleged crime is indictable. All trials on *indictment* begin with the 'arraignment'. This is a procedure whereby the accused pleads to each of the counts in the indictment. The jury at this stage is not present, and the purpose of this procedure is to clarify matters so that no inconvenience is caused, for example, by a late change of plea.

THE TRIAL: Here follows an outline of the procedure usually followed in a Crown Court trial.

As mentioned earlier, on a not guilty plea there is a full-trial which involves a jury. Indeed, a Crown Court trial would commence with the jury being sworn in, and then being informed of the charges.

Next, the prosecution will open the case, summarising the facts and the evidence, and in general an introduction of the prosecution case, and the relevant law, will be given to the jury.[225]

The prosecution witnesses will then be called and examined in chief by the prosecution. The defence will then cross-examine them, and the prosecution may re-examine them, if the prosecution feels that it has become necessary for clarification purposes.

Next, the defence will present their case, by making an opening speech.[226] Following this stage, the accused may testify but is not compelled to do, otherwise the defence witnesses will be called to be examined in chief by the defence and cross-examined by the prosecution.

At the end of the evidential stage, counsel for the prosecution will make a closing speech, followed by counsel for the defence.

The Judge will then sum up, commenting on the evidence and explaining the role of the jury and directing them to retire and consider their verdict, which must be unanimous.[227]

If the jury delivers a guilty verdict then the judge will proceed to deal with mitigation, pre-sentence reports (if appropriate), and bail.

If the verdict is not guilty the accused will be discharged.

SENTENCING: In so far as sentencing is concerned, the Criminal Justice Act 1991 (as amended by the Criminal Justice Act 1993) lays down a structured approach, in that the starting point is a fine. If a fine is not appropriate, i.e. the offence is too serious, then 'community sentence' is to be given. Again, if the offence is too serious for community sentence,[228] then a custodial sentence is imposed.[229]

---

[225] Note that under the Criminal Procedure and Investigation Act 1996, evidential matters which are to be challenged by the defence are not to be dealt with before the jury, but at a preliminary hearing before the Judge.

[226] It must be noted that it may be that the defence would not adduce any evidence and therefore may proceed to make a closing speech.

[227] The jury is allowed to ask questions on any relevant matters, and the Judge will answer them. Please note that after a certain period of time has expired (usually 2-3 hours) following the jury's retirement, the Judge may indicate that he will accept a *majority* verdict by no less than ten to two, or eleven to one. Of course, if the jury still fails to agree, then there may be a new trial before a new jury.

[228] Section 152 of the Criminal Justice Act 2003. Furthermore, such sentence should be examined against the five principal purposes of sentencing, i.e. protections of the public, punishment of the offender, reduction of crime, rehabilitation of the offender, and reparation for the victim; s.142, Criminal Justice Act 2003.

[229] The Criminal Justice Act 2003 makes significant changes to sentencing in criminal cases. For example, s.224 classifies for sentencing purposes an offence as either a specified violent offence or a specified sexual offence. A serious specified offence is one that involves death or serious personal injury, and carries a penalty of life imprisonment or ten years' custody or more.

What follows is a brief outline of the sentences available to the Crown Court.

(1) **Custodial Sentences**:[230] If the offender is aged between 18 and 21, he is detained in a young offenders institution, otherwise is sent to prison. Obviously, for offenders under the age of 18, different sentences would apply.

(2) **Suspended Sentence of Imprisonment**:[231] A term of imprisonment not exceeding 2 years may be suspended for a period of 1-2 years, unless the offender is aged between 18 and 21, where his detention cannot be suspended.

(3) **Community Sentences**: These consist of (i) Probation,[232] (ii) Community Service Orders,[233] (iii) Combination Orders,[234] (iv) Curfew Orders,[235] (v) Drug Treatment and Testing Orders,[236] and (vi) Attendance Centre Orders[237] for offenders under the age of 21.

(4) **Compensation Orders**:[238] The Crown Court may order an offender to pay an unlimited amount of compensation (subject to his means) to the victim of an offence. This order may be combined with any other sentences.

(5) **Forfeiture Orders**:[239] Any property in the offender's possession at the time of apprehension may be forfeited by the Court, provided the offender

[230] Criminal Justice Act 1991.

[231] Powers of Criminal Courts Act 1973.

[232] Section 2, Powers of Criminal Courts Act 1973. The offender is placed under the supervision of a probation officer and 'probation requirements', e.g. psychiatric treatment for alcohol dependency, are usually imposed. Please note that the offender's consent is usually required.

[233] Section 14, Powers of Criminal Courts Act 1973. This is imposed when the Court feels that the offender should be deprived of leisure time or should make reparation to community for his offending. Please note that the offender's consent is required.

[234] Section 56, Criminal Justice Act 1991. This is in effect a combination of Probation Order and Community Service Order. Please note that the offender's consent is required.

[235] Section 12, Criminal Justice Act 1991. The offender is required to stay for specified periods in specified places, e.g. to remain at his residence between the hours of 20:00 and 7:00. The offender's consent is required for this sentence.

[236] Sections 61-64, Crime and Disorder Act 1998. This is available to offenders over the age of 15, and it is an order whereby the offender is required to submit to treatment for drug dependency and may also be required to submit some tests indicating his progress. The offender's consent is required for this order to materialise.

[237] Sections 17-19, Criminal Justice Act 1982. This requires the offender to attend a specified place and take part in supervised activities. Please note that the offender's consent is not required.

[238] Section 35, Criminal Courts Act 1973.

[239] Section 43, Powers of Criminal Courts Act 1973.

was convicted for an offence which (i) is indictable, and (ii) two or more years' imprisonment has been imposed on the offender.

(6) **Confiscation Orders**:[240] Any proceeds of crime may be subject to a confiscation order by the Court. Such order may be combined with any other sentences.

(7) **Costs Orders**: A convicted offender may be ordered to pay costs to the prosecution, in addition to any other sentences.[241] If the accused is acquitted then he may be entitled to the defence costs to be paid.[242]

(8) **Deferment of Sentence**:[243] The Court may defer sentence for up to six months. In this case, the Court must specify the offender's expected conduct during the period and also the sentence likely to be imposed if he does not comply. Although it may at first seem that this is similar to a Probation Order, in practice it is only granted if the offender claims that a recent change in circumstances mean that it is unlikely he re-offends. For example, if the offender is an unemployed person convicted of theft, but he has been offered a stable job. In such a case the Court may decide to defer sentence to see how the offender reacts to the change in his circumstances, and if the offender's conduct has been favourable then, at the end of the period of deferment, a custodial sentence would not be imposed by the Court.

240 Sections 71-102, Criminal Justice Act 1988. See also s.83, Crime and Disorder Act 1998.

241 Section 18(1), Prosecution of Offences Act 1985.

242 Section 16, Prosecution of Offences Act 1985.

243 Section 1, Powers of Criminal Courts Act 1973.

CHAPTER 3

THE LAW OF TORTS

The word *tort* simply means 'a wrong', actionable at the suit of the party injured. It is interesting to note that early English law did not distinguish between crimes and civil wrongs. Therefore, in those early times if a person committed a wrong upon another, this would only come to the attention of the Courts if the peace of the community was threatened. With the political development of the Normans, the punishment of these lesser wrongs formed the basis of the early law of torts.

Perhaps at this stage it would be more beneficial if we briefly examine the differences between the law of torts and other wrongs. In the case of contract the right of action arises not by the injury of a party thereto, but on the existence of the contract. Furthermore, a person who is not party to the contract cannot generally sue for breach of it. Where a claim is in tort the parties are usually (but not necessarily) complete strangers to each other, e.g. claims arising out of road accidents or collisions at sea. Tortuous liability arises from the breach of a duty primarily fixed by law, and is redressible by an action for an unliquidated sum. Criminal offences are prosecuted and punished by the State, whereas in the main torts are not punishable. It must be realised that it is possible for a breach of contract to give rise to a concurrent cause of action in tort. For example, where X makes a contract with a taxi driver to be carried from A to B, and due to the driver's negligent driving there is a collision with another vehicle and X is injured, clearly the taxi driver has not fulfilled his contractual obligation to get X to B. There are clearly two causes of action,[244] one for breach of contract, and another one in the tort of negligence.

THE TORT OF TRESPASS

This tort makes actionable any direct interference with a person, his goods or his land. Trespass is the only tort where compensation can be claimed without proof of actual damage. The interference must be direct, it is not sufficient simply to show that the defendant's conduct resulted in an interference; e.g. striking a horse so that it throws the rider is a trespass to the horse but not to the person of the rider. Further, it is not necessary to prove that the defendant

[244] Needless to say that such circumstances may give rise to criminal liability, and the State may prosecute the taxi driver for committing an offence under road traffic legislation.

intended the trespass, unintentional trespass is actionable although the tendency is to confine the use of this tort to intentional or reckless interference. Thus, for example, throwing an item out of a window which hits a passer-by would be trespass to the person. However, if the item lands on the road and a passer-by later trips over it, this would be negligence.

TRESPASS TO THE PERSON

This could be said to be an intentional interference with the person or his liberty. This includes the following three distinct torts:

Assault: Any act which directly causes a person to immediately apprehend a contact with his or her person. Mere obstruction of a person's progress would not constitute an assault.[245] However, words or gestures may constitute[246] or negative[247] an assault.

Battery: Any act which causes direct physical contact with a person without consent. It is interesting to note that it is considered a battery to throw something at another person. The least touching of a person in anger would be a battery,[248] except where the touching is an accident,[249] i.e. involuntary and unintentional.

False Imprisonment: Any act that directly causes a person to be unwillingly confined within an area delimited by someone else. It must be noted that if the claimant has a means of escaping/avoiding such confinement, mere inconvenience to him would not amount to false imprisonment.[250]

---

[245] *Innes* v. *Wilie* (1844) 1 Car.& Kir.257; here a policeman blocked a doorway in order to prevent a C to enter into a room. It was held not to be an assault.

[246] *R* v. *Wilson* [1955] 1 All E.R.744. In this (criminal) case the Court considered that calling out by a person words such as 'get out knives' amounted to an assault. *Cf. Thomas* v. *National Union of Mineworkers* [1985] 2 All E.R.1, where the Court held that violent gestures by picketing miners at their colleagues who were working and were passing by in coaches did not amount to assault.

[247] *Tuberville* v. *Savage* (1969) 1 Mod.Rep.3. In this case C put his hand on his sword and said to D words to the effect that his intention was not to assault him, since during that day the Judges were in town ('assize') It was held that by using words to that effect C's gesture, i.e. putting his hand on his sword, which would have amounted to assault, was thereby negatived. In the criminal case of *R* v. *St. George* (1840) 9 C.& P.483, it was held that pointing a gun at a person who reasonably believes to be loaded would amount to assault.

[248] *Cole* v. *Turner* (1704) 6 Mod.149.

[249] *Stanley* v. *Powell* [1891] 1 Q.B.86; D was bird hunting and fired his gun but his shot ricocheted off a tree and injured C. It was held that this was an accident and therefore not actionable.

[250] *Bird* v. *Jones* (1845) 7 Q.B.742; D wrongfully obstructed part of a footpath to a bridge, thus preventing C from crossing it. It was held that since the restraint by D was not total, his action did not amount to false imprisonment.

It must be noted that the above three torts are also crimes. Battery, would usually be preceded by an assault. Thus, for example, threats would amount to an assault, but if actual force is applied then the tort of battery is committed.

TRESPASS TO LAND

Trespass to land covers any entering or remaining on, or directly causing any physical matter/object[251] to come into contact with land in the possession of another, without lawful justification. As with trespass to goods, this tort is committed against possession and not ownership.[252]

Thus, for example, it is a trespass to land if a person sits on a fence, or throwing rubbish to another person's land. It must be noted that no intention is necessary, as, for example, if one walks across private land mistakenly believing that he has right of way, will be committing trespass.

Finally, this type of trespass includes interference with the airspace above one's land,[253] or below the surface.[254] In some cases, the law, particularly statute law, may authorise the interference, e.g. the police have various powers of arrest and to search premises and provided that such powers are used for the purpose intended and in the manner specified in law, there will be no liability in trespass.[255]

TRESPASS TO GOODS

This consists of wrongful interference with goods which includes negligence and any other tort which results in damage to goods or to an interest in goods.[256]

It must be noted that an action of trespass to goods is founded on possession,[257] and that it is based on intentional[258] or negligent interference

---

[251] *Holmes* v. *Wilson* (1839) 10 A.& E.503; D were highway authorities and trespassed C's land in order to build some support for a sinking road. In an action for trespass they were ordered to pay full compensation to C. However, C brought a further action for trespass since D had not removed the road supports they had made earlier. Again the Court held that D were liable for placing any objects on C's land and letting them remain there.

[252] Thus a landlord cannot usually sue for trespass since the tenant would normally be the person who has possession; *Portland Management Ltd.* v. *Harte* [1977] Q.B.306.

[253] *Kelsen* v. *Imperial Tobacco Co.* [1957] 2 Q.B.334; it was held that D's sign which was projecting into C's airspace was a trespass to land. However, note that the Civil Aviation Act 1982 makes special provision for civil aircraft.

[254] *Cox* v. *Glue* (1848) 5 C.B.533.

[255] *Chic Fashions (West Wales) Ltd.* v. *Jone* [1968] 2 Q.B.299; police entered premises in the mistaken belief that there were some stolen goods kept therein. The Court held that it was a lawful search, and therefore the police did not commit trespass to the land.

[256] Section 1, Torts (Interference with Goods) Act 1977.

with the goods. For example, if one scratches the paintwork on a car.[259] Therefore, only persons in possession of the goods at the time of interference may take action.[260]

THE TORT OF CONVERSION

'Conversion' in the law of torts simply means the converting by a person to his own use of the goods of another.[261] Taking possession of another's goods would normally be trespass to goods, but also amount to conversion. Perhaps, conversion is any adverse interference with another's rights to goods. Most of the current law on the tort of conversion may be found in the Torts (Interference with Goods) Act 1977.

However, no comprehensive definition of what constitutes conversion is provided, and it seems that most cases limit their attempts in defining conversion to the particular facts under the Court's consideration at the time.[262] It could be said that conversion is a tort of strict liability, in that intention or negligence is not necessary.[263]

For example, it has been held that a shipowner's conduct whereby he refuses to give bills of lading to a shipper of goods, could amount to an act of conversion.[264]

Furthermore, a carrier/shipowner is vicariously liable[265] for the conversion of the goods by his servants or agents, e.g. the master of the vessel.[266] So, delivery of the goods by a ship's master to a person who is not the bill of lading holder, hence not entitled to them, would render the shipowner/carrier

---

257 *The Winkfield* [1902] P.42. Whereas, an action founded on interference with ownership of goods is the tort of conversion.

258 Thus a finder of lost goods does not commit trespass, unless the owner is known or may be easily found by him. The case of *Armory* v. *Delamirie* (1721) 1 Stra.505, indicates that such finder, by being in possession of the goods, has a right to sue anyone other than the owner of the goods. Also see *Hollins* v. *Fowler* (1875) L.R.7 H.L.757; *R.H. Willis & Sons* v. *British Car Auctions Ltd.* [1978] 1 W.L.R.438.

259 *Foulders* v. *Willoughby* (1841) 8 M.& W.538.

260 Note that there are exceptions to this general rule, but these are beyond the scope of the present chapter.

261 An action for conversion used to be known as 'trover', derived from the French 'trouver', to find. This was based on the idea of finding of one's goods and converting them to his own use. This notion of 'finding' was abolished by the Common Law Procedure Act 1852.

262 *Howard Perry & Co. Ltd.* v. *B.R.B.* [1980] 1 W.L.R.1375.

263 Thus, a completely innocent purchaser of goods which were stolen by the seller may find himself liable in conversion to the true owner of the goods.

264 *Falke* v. *Fletcher* (1865) 18 C.B. (N.S.) 403; *Rayner* v. *Rederiaktiebolaget Condor* [1895] 2 Q.B.289.

265 For vicarious liability see *infra*, p.70.

266 *Ormrod* v. *Crosville Motor Service* [1953] 1 W.L.R.1120.

liable in the tort of conversion. Such action will be on the basis that the carrier as bailee, i.e. person entrusted with the goods, has allowed the goods to be taken in breach of his duty to his bailor, i.e. the bill of lading holder entitled to possession of the goods.[267]

THE TORT OF NUISANCE

This tort protects the interests which people have in the use and enjoyment of their land. It can be defined as indirectly causing physical injury to land or to an interest in land where, in the light of all the circumstances, the injury or interference is held to be unreasonable.

There are two forms of Nuisance:

PUBLIC NUISANCE

This is an unlawful act or omission which covers a wide variety of forms of interference with public rights e.g. obstructing public highways (including waterways), selling impure food, keeping a disorderly house, etc. Under this type of tort it is not necessary for the claimant to have an interest in land.

Thus, for example, if the public right of navigation for river users has been interfered with, then this would amount to public nuisance.[268]

It is a crime as well as a tort, and if an individual wishes to sue in public nuisance then it must be shown that he has suffered some special damage different and in excess of the damage suffered by the public at large.[269]

PRIVATE NUISANCE

This covers the unlawful interference with a person's use or enjoyment of land e.g. noise, smell, roots undermining a wall, interference with natural rights, etc. Therefore, a difference between this and Public Nuisance is that

---

[267] Section 2, Torts (Interference with Goods) Act 1977. 'the holder of the bill of lading is entitled, or ought to be entitled, to claim that any dealing with the goods adverse to him is a conversion.', *per* Wright, J., in *Skibsaktieselskapet Thor. Thoresens Linje* v. *H. Tyrer & Co. Ltd* (1929) 35 Ll. L. Rep.163, 170.

[268] *Tate & Lyle Industries Ltd.* v. *Greater London Council* [1983] 2 A.C.509.

[269] *Campbell* v. *Paddington Corporation* [1911] 1 K.B.869; the Council erected a stand in order for Council members to view King Edward VII's funeral procession. The stand obstructed the view of C's flat. Since the stand was a public nuisance and C had suffered special damage in excess of that suffered by the public, C's action was successful.

the claimant must have an interest in the land. Furthermore, the claimant may recover for discomfort incidental to the use and enjoyment of the land.[270]

DEFAMATION

This could be said to consist of a false statement, which tends to injure a person's reputation, or causes such person to be shunned by ordinary members of society.[271] A point to note about defamation is that nowadays this is the only civil action which would be tried by a jury. Defamation may take two forms, libel and slander. The former is also a criminal offence and is actionable without proof of damage, whereas the latter is not and requires proof of actual damage. A defamatory statement is libel if it is in permanent form, for example writing, pictures, etc. If the statement is not of permanent form then it would be slander, for example spoken words.

In general, for a statement to be defamatory, it should (i) reflect on a person's ability, (ii) impute immorality or criminality, and (iii) impute insanity.[272] Finally, there is a special one-year time limit that applies to claims for defamation.[273]

THE TORT OF NEGLIGENCE

This is an all-embracing tort which protects all interests from damage caused by unreasonable behaviour. The tort of negligence occurs when a person's behaviour falls below the standard of care fixed by the law and this causes damage to another. For the claimant to succeed in an action in the tort of negligence he must show that:

i) the defendant owed him a duty of care, and
ii) the defendant was in breach of that duty, and
iii) loss or damage has been caused to the claimant by this breach.

Unlike codified law systems English law does not recognise any general duty to take care not to cause damage to others. Over the years Courts have recognised that in certain circumstances a duty of care exists, e.g. the driver of

---

270 *Halsey* v. *Esso Petroleum Co. Ltd.* [1961] 1 W.L.R.683; D were operators of an oil refinery which was located in a residential area. C sued D in private nuisance for his loss of sleep due to noise made by tanker lorries at night, and the smell which emerged from the refinery. C's claim was successful.

271 Or simply it could be said that it is a detraction from one's justified *fame*, i.e. *de*fame.

272 *Youssoupoff* v. *Metro-Goldwyn-Mayer Pictures Ltd.* (1934) 50 T.L.R.581.

273 Section 4A, Limitation Act 1980. Also, see the Defamation Act 1996.

a vehicle in respect to other road users, ship operator and crew in respect to other ships, crew, employers in respect to employees, occupiers of premises in respect to visitors and the general public. If the dispute involves a situation within the recognised categories, the duty is established by the doctrine of Precedent. In novel situations it is necessary to argue before the Court that a new duty situation should be recognised,[274] if this is not successful the action will fail.

DUTY OF CARE

The test applied by the Courts to determine whether a duty of care exists in a given situation is called the 'neighbour' test'.[275] In effect, the question asked is whether there is a sufficient proximity between the claimant and the defendant. Proximity in this context means 'reasonable foreseeability'. This is based on the premise that there is a duty to take reasonable care to avoid acts or omissions which, on the basis of reasonable foreseeability, would be likely to cause injury to 'neighbours'. A 'neighbour' in this context is anyone so closely and directly affected that his interests should receive consideration. It must be noted that the standard of care required in negligence cases is that of objectively reasonable care. It is presumed that a 'reasonable person' would take care to guard against foreseeable dangers which could cause harm and take a degree of care in keeping with the magnitude of the risk - the greater the risk the greater the care expected.

CAUSATION

The claimant must show that the defendant's conduct was a substantial factor in bringing about the injury.[276] If the claimant would have suffered the same

[274] For example, a duty by the ambulance service that an ambulance will arrive within reasonable time following an emergency call; *Kent* v. *Griffiths (No.3)* [2001] Q.B.36, C.A. Or a duty by a surveyor making a mortgage valuation report for the lender to the purchasers; *Merrett* v. *Babb* [2001] Q.B.1174, C.A.

[275] *Donoghue* v. *Stevenson* [1932] A.C.562; C's friend bought a bottle of beer manufactured by D and gave it to C, who drank most of it, but then noticed the decomposed remains of a snail in the bottom of the bottle. C became ill and sued D in negligence. D's defence was that no duty of care was owed because there was no contract, i.e. no proximity, between D and C, since the person who bought the beer was C's friend. The Court held that a duty of care is owed to any person who one can reasonably foresee will be injured by one's acts or omissions. Such persons were described by the Court as 'neighbours'. Therefore, D should have reasonably foreseen that somebody apart from the original purchaser may have consumed the beer and D was therefore held liable to C.

[276] If the claimant fails to establish, on the balance of probabilities, that the defendant's negligence was a material cause of the damage suffered, then the claimant's action would fail; *Hotson* v. *East Berkshire Area Health Authority* [1987] 2 All E.R.909.

injury despite the defendant's conduct then the claimant's claim in negligence will not succeed.[277] As a simple rule this usually requires the Court to be satisfied that but for the defendant's behaviour the loss would not have occurred. This is known as the 'but for test'.

LOSS OR DAMAGE AND REMOTENESS

Even where a cause and connection with loss can be established liability may be denied on the grounds that the loss sustained was too remote a consequence of the defendant's behaviour. The defendant's behaviour may trigger off an almost endless chain of events (the 'chain of causation') and the law will not hold the defendant liable for all the consequences caused by his wrongful behaviour.

The test applicable here would be that of 'reasonable foreseeability'. This simply means that the defendant would only be liable for the consequences of his act that a reasonable person would have foreseen.[278]

VICARIOUS LIABILITY

Individuals are personally accountable for their own torts. There are instances, however, where a person may be liable for the tortuous behaviour of another person. This is known as 'vicarious liability' and arises where the law

---

[277] *Barnett* v. *Chelsea & Kensington Hospital Management Committee* [1969] 1 Q.B.428; C went to the hospital complaining of vomiting and was sent away to see his own doctor without being given a proper examination. Shortly afterwards C died of arsenic poisoning. His widow sued the hospital management in negligence, but was unsuccessful since C would have died whatever action the hospital had taken. Therefore, the careless examination was not the cause of C's death.

[278] *The Wagon Mound* [1961] A.C.388, overruling *Re Polemis* [1921] 3 K.B.560; the owners of a wharf brought an action against the owners of the ship Wagon Mound in negligence. The ship had discharged oil in the harbour which ignited when hot metal from welding being carried on in the harbour fell onto a piece of cotton waste floating in the oil. The Court held that damage to the wharf by fouling was foreseeable, but not damage by fire, since oil on water does not normally ignite. Therefore, the ignition of the oil only occurred because the hot metal fell on to highly combustible cotton waste, which in itself was not reasonably foreseeable. *Jolley* v. *Sutton LBC* [2000] 2 Lloyd's Rep.65, H.L.; an abandoned boat in D's land caused serious injuries to C, a 14 year old boy, when he, together with another friend of his, tried to prop it up in order to repair it. C brought an action against D for damages in negligence and breach of statutory duty under the Occupiers' Liability Act 1957. D resisted the claim on the basis that although it was reasonably foreseeable that children would play on the boat and be injured, it was not foreseeable that they would prop up the boat and be injured by its falling off the prop. It was held that the 'accident' was reasonably foreseeable, since it was of the kind admitted by D as being reasonably foreseeable, albeit not of the same degree. In other words, since D could reasonably foresee, by its own admission, the risk of minor injuries to children, the wider risk would also fall within D's duty, unless it was different in kind from that which should have been foreseen.

recognises that there is a special relationship between the wrong-doer and the person liable.

The most common example of such a relationship is that between employer and employee.

An employer is vicariously liable for the tortuous acts or omissions of employees committed in the course of their employment. Therefore, as employers usually have more assets to attack than their employees and as they are usually insured against such liability it is usually the employer who is sued rather than the employee.

As a rule, an employer is vicariously liable for the torts of his employees that are committed within the course of their employment.[279]

If an employer imposes a prohibition on an employee, this may limit the scope of employment.[280] However, in some cases the employer may be liable even if the employee acts contrary to such prohibitive instructions.[281]

Employees[282] must be distinguished from 'independent contractors' for whose conduct the person for the time being employing them is not usually liable.

One of the 'tests' applicable here is that of control, i.e. was the execution of the work by a person under the control of another person or not?[283]

---

[279] *Limpus* v. *London General Omnibus Co.* (1862) 1 H.& C.526; a bus driver was speeding whilst driving D's bus and caused an accident by his negligent act. It was held that the driver's employers were vicariously liable to P for their employee's negligence. *Cf. Beard* v. *London General Omnibus Co.* [1900] 2 Q.B.530.

[280] *Twine* v. *Bean's Express Ltd.* (1946) 62 T.L.R.458; D had issued to their drivers an express prohibition not to give lifts to hitchhikers. One of D's drivers however, whilst giving a lift to a hitchhiker, contrary to his employer's instruction, caused an accident due to his negligence. The hitchhiker was injured and took action in negligence against D. It was held that the express prohibition against drivers giving lifts limited the scope of the driver's employment. Therefore, as the hitchhiker was merely a passenger being given a lift and not as such associated with the driver's employment, D were not vicariously liable to P.

[281] *Rose* v. *Plenty* [1976] 1 W.L.R.141; D was a milkman and his employers had issued an express prohibition against all milk-float drivers employing young children and paying them to help deliver the milk. D employed C, contrary to his employer's prohibition, and C was injured due to D's negligent driving. It was held that D's employer was liable to C. This was because D was acting within the scope of his employment, and engaging C was a method by which D carried out his job.

[282] An 'employee' is 'an individual who has entered into or works under a contract of employment'; section 230(1) of the Employment Right Acts 1996.

[283] *Padbury* v. *Holliday and Greenwood Ltd.* (1912) 28 T.L.R.494; D employed a subcontractor who had undertaken to place metallic window frames to a house built by D. A hammer was placed by one of the employees of the subcontractor on a window sill. There was a gale force wind during that day and it blew into the house one of the iron window frames, which in turn caused the hammer to fall from the window sill and injure C in the street below. It was held, that C's injuries were not caused by D's negligence but by an employee of D's independent contractor. Due to the complicated nature of today's business relationships, other 'tests' have been developed and apply to contracts in determining whether an employer-employee relationship exists, e.g. responsibility of National Insurance contributions, pension payment schemes, payment of salary for holidays, etc.

GENERAL DEFENCES

Once the basic requirements of any tort have been established by the claimant, the defendant may put forward a number of defences.

VOLENTI (non fit injuria) – CONSENT

In simple words, where the claimant voluntarily agrees to undertake the legal risk of harm at his own expense, for example, a boxer could not sue as a result of a broken nose suffered in the ring.[284] It must be noted however, that mere knowledge of the risk does not amount to consent, and Courts are not generally prepared to assume the existence of an agreement.[285] This is a complete defence, i.e. if successfully established by the defendant then the claimant's action fails altogether.

EX TURPI (causa non oritur actio) – ILLEGALITY

This means that Courts may deny an action to a claimant who suffered damage while participating in a criminal activity. Again, this is a complete defence.[286]

CONTRIBUTORY NEGLIGENCE

This means that the claimant's loss/damage was caused partly due to his own fault (as well as the defendant's).[287] In order to establish contributory negligence the defendant must prove that the claimant failed to take reasonable care, and this failure was a cause of the claimant's loss/damage.[288]

---

[284] However, where a duty of care by the boxing regulatory body is established, such as to take reasonable steps to minimise the risks inherent in the sport, *volenti* would be no defence; *Watson* v. *British Boxing Board of Control Ltd.* [2001] Q.B.1134, C.A.

[285] Presumably, a policeman who suffers injuries in trying to stop a car out of control, would not be considered as having consented to his injuries; *Haynes* v. *Harwood* [1935] 1 K.B.146, C.A.

[286] Thus, no duty of care is owed by the 'get away' driver of a burglary, to any of his accomplishes, whereby his negligent driving caused them injuries; *Ashton* v. *Turner* [1981] Q.B.137.

[287] Section 1(1), Law Reform (Contributory Negligence) Act 1945.

[288] *O'Connell* v. *Jackson* [1971] 2 Lloyd's Rep.354, C.A.; C's failure to wear a crash helmet in circumstances where a prudent road-user would, rendered him partly responsible for the injuries which he would not have received if he had been wearing a helmet, even though in no way to blame for the occurrence of the accident. A Court would have to be satisfied that had C worn a crash helmet, he would not have suffered the extend of his injuries.

It is interesting to note that in establishing the claimant's failure to take reasonable steps it is not necessary to show that the claimant owed the defendant a duty of care. Contributory negligence is not a complete defence, in that, if successfully pleaded, it reduces the claimant's damages, rather than extinguishes his claim.

SELF-DEFENCE

As it was seen earlier under the tort of trespass to the person (assault, and battery), it is accepted that a person may use reasonable force to defend himself and his property against unlawful force. Of course, what is reasonable will depend on the surrounding circumstances of the case. Nevertheless, this is a complete defence.

NECESSITY

This defence is usually raised when the defendant has caused loss/damage to an innocent claimant while attempting to prevent a greater loss to himself.[289]

[289] *Cope* v. *Sharpe (No.2)* [1912] 1 K.B.496, C.A.; D entered C's land and burnt some strips of heather in order to avoid a fire to spread to his land. As there was a real threat of fire, D's defence of necessity against C's claim for trespass succeeded.

CHAPTER 4

THE LAW OF CONTRACT

In English law, a contract may be defined as an agreement enforceable by the law, between two or more persons to do or abstain from doing some act or acts, their intention being to create legal relations and not merely to exchange mutual promises.

Furthermore, most contracts do not require any particular form, thus, they may be made orally, in writing, or indeed, in any other way.[290] This type of contract is called a *simple* contract. There are, however, a few contracts, which require a particular form. Some of these contracts must be (i) made by deed,[291] (ii) some in writing,[292] whereas some others must be evidenced by writing.[293]

The consequence of a type (i) contract not being in writing is that such contract is said to be void[294] in law. For example bills of sale, certain dispositions of interests in land, and most consumer credit agreements.

The consequence of a type (ii) contract not being evidenced in writing is that such contract will be unenforceable, i.e. it cannot be enforced in the Courts.

[290] *DMA Financial Solutions* v. *BaaN U.K.* 2000 W.L.1629568; among other things considered in this case, was the issue of whether a contract existed between C, a computer consultancy, and D, a software developer, whereby C would provide training to D's customers. C contended that the agreement which had been reached as a result of negotiations constituted a binding contract, whereas D argued that, in the absence of a written agreement no contract had been formed. It was held that a contract existed despite the absence of a written agreement since all relevant matters had been agreed and the parties had not negotiated on the basis that the outcome of their negotiations was to be subject to a written agreement.

[291] Such contracts are also called 'specialties'. A deed is a document which contains all the terms of the agreement, which is signed, sealed and delivered. The requirement of a seal dates from when illiteracy was prevalent and a seal was used in place of a signature. It is now clear that under section 1(1)(b) of the Law of Property (Miscellaneous Provisions) Act 1989 a seal is not required any more for an instrument to be validly executed. A contract in a deed is a contract which is in writing and satisfies the requirements of section 1 of the Law of Property (Miscellaneous Provisions) Act 1989. It must be noted that any interest in land, and the transfer of a British ship (or any share thereof) must be made in a deed.

[292] For example Bills of Exchange must be in writing under section 3(1) of the Bills of Exchange Act 1882.

[293] The only contracts nowadays that need to be evidenced in writing appear to be contracts of guarantee; Statute of Frauds 1677, as amended by the Law Reform (Enforcement of Contracts) Act 1954, and the Law of Property (Miscellaneous Provisions) Act 1989.

[294] The term 'void contract' is a contradiction in terms since the whole transaction is regarded a nullity. It means that at no time has there been a contract between the parties. Any goods or money obtained under the agreement must be returned. Where items have been resold to a third party, they may be recovered by the original owner. See further *infra*, p.83.

Examples of such contracts are marine insurance contracts, and contracts of guarantee.

Therefore, it could be seen how English contract law differs considerably on this issue, to the law of most other European countries.

Since most contracts under English law are simple contracts, this part of the work will only focus on the characteristics relevant to such contracts, making references to any other type of contract as necessary.

ELEMENTS OF CONTRACT

Following the above general definition of contract, it can be seen that in order to have a valid enforceable simple contract two main elements are needed; (i) an agreement, and (ii) intention to form/create legal relations.

(i) AGREEMENT

This may be said to consist of an offer made by one person, the offeror/offerer, and an acceptance by the person to whom the offer was made, the offeree.

OFFER

An offer is a statement to the effect that the person making it is willing to contract on the terms stated, as soon as these (terms) are accepted by the person to whom the statement is addressed. The offer may be made in writing, by words or conduct. Offers may be classified into two types:

Unilateral: This means that such an offer is made without the offeror knowing whether his offer will ever be taken up and accepted. Examples of such offers are advertisements in newspapers offering to pay a reward for lost items, or for the first person to swim the English Channel. In such a case, it is clear that the person making such an offer has no knowledge whether his offer will ever be accepted.[295]

Bilateral: In practice, the majority of offers are of this type. This means that such offer would be addressed to one or more named offeree(s), and the contract would be negotiated on a promise for a promise basis. For example, X may offer

[295] Thus, where in an advertisement a firm manufacturing carbolic smoke balls, promised to pay £100 to any person who caught influenza after using their product as directed, the Court held that this advertisement was an offer; *Carlill* v. *Carbolic Smokeball Company* [1893] 1 Q.B.256.

to sell Y 10 tons of coal for £500. When Y says 'I accept' or words to that effect, a contract is concluded. This would be an example of a bilateral offer.

An essential feature of an offer is that the offeror must intend to be bound without further negotiation, by a simple acceptance of his terms.

Thus, there is no offer where the owner of a house, in response to an enquiry from a person who wishes to buy it, states the price at which he might be prepared to sell.[296]

This is so even where the owner wishes to sell and invites offers at or about a specified price. In the latter case he is said to make an 'invitation to treat', and he is not bound to accept the highest or any other offer. He only invites offers which he may accept or reject.

Only an offer is capable of being converted into an agreement by the fact of acceptance. Anything other than an offer is termed an invitation to treat which may be defined as a statement that a person is ready to receive offers.

Price marked goods, in shop windows[297] and supermarkets, are only invitations to treat. The offer is made by the customer when he takes an item to the till for payment.[298] Therefore, his offer may be rejected.

The same applies in the case of petrol stations advertising the price at which petrol is to be sold.[299]

Likewise, advertisements in newspapers or in tradesmen's circulars, and price lists, are not effective offers, as they only attempt to induce offers.[300]

But it should not be supposed that all displays and advertisements are only invitations to treat. A notice displayed at the entrance to an automatic car-park has been held to be an offer, presumably because no further act of acceptance on the part of the proprietor is contemplated after the customer drives in.[301]

---

[296] *Gibson* v. *Manchester City Council* [1979] 1 All E.R.972.

[297] In *Fisher* v. *Bell* [1961] 1 Q.B.394, a shopkeeper displayed a flick knife for sale in his shop window, and was charged with the criminal offence of 'offering' to sell an offensive weapon. The Court held that he was not guilty of the offence since the display of the knife in the window was an invitation to treat and not an offer.

[298] In *Pharmaceutical Society of Great Britain* v. *Boots Cash Chemists Ltd.* [1953] 1 All E.R.482, the Court said that the display of goods on the shelves only constituted an invitation to treat and that when a customer placed the goods in the basket and presented them at the cash desk they were making an offer to buy at that point.

[299] *Esso Petroleum Co. Ltd.* v. *Customs and Excise Commissioners* [1976] 1 W.L.R.1.

[300] Thus, in *Partridge* v. *Crittenden* [1968] 2 All E.R.421, C placed an advertisement, offering wild birds for sale, which was an offence. It was held that the advertisement was an invitation to treat and not an offer and therefore, C was not guilty of the offence charged. The Electronic Commerce (E.C. Directive) Regulations 2002 (S.I.2002, No.2013) must also be borne in mind. The Regulations do not apply to business conducted via facsimile or telephone, but apply to any business which (1) sells goods or services to businesses or consumers on the internet or by S.M.S. or e-mail, or (2) advertises on the Internet or by S.M.S. or e-mail, or (3) stores or conveys electronic content to its customers or provides access to a communication network.

[301] *Thornton* v. *Shoe Lane Parking Ltd.* [1971] 1 Lloyd's Rep.289.

An offer does not continue indefinitely; once an offer has come to an end it is no longer capable of being accepted. In this respect, there are three ways[302] by which an offer can be revoked by the offeror:

(a) **Communication**: in order to validly revoke an offer the offeror must communicate the revocation to the other party at any time up until it has been accepted.[303] In general, the offeror is entitled to do this even if he has promised to keep the offer open for a specified time.

(b) **Lapse of time**: this occurs where an express time limit is placed on the duration of the offer, or where a reasonable time has elapsed since the offer was made.[304]

(c) **Death**: although there is no clear authority on this, it would appear that if the offeror died then the validity of an acceptance by the offeree would depend on whether the offeree has heard of the death of the offeror before purporting to accept the offer or not. If he has, then it would be clear that the offer would not be capable of acceptance, otherwise the acceptance of the offer would be valid.

ACCEPTANCE

Once an offer has been made, an agreement comes into existence when this offer is accepted. The offeree may express his assent either expressly by words, or by conduct.[305]

The essential feature of acceptance one must remember is that an acceptance must correspond with the offer. If it seeks to qualify or vary the offer, then it is ineffective as an acceptance.

302 Although depending on the circumstances of a case, Courts may find that an offer can be revoked by a subsequent offer made. See *Pickford Ltd.* v. *Celestica Ltd.* [2003] EWCA Civ. 1741.

303 *Payne* v. *Cave* (1789) 3 Term.Rep.148. An offer is validly revoked by an offeror even where the offeree obtains the information through a third party and not the offeror himself; *Dickinson* v. *Dodds* (1876) 2 Ch.D.463.

304 *Ramsgate Victoria Hotel Co. Ltd.* v. *Montefiore* (1866) L.R. 1 Ex.109; in June D offered to buy some shares in C's hotel. Although C did not reply to this offer, in November of the same year D allotted some shares to D who refused to accept them. It was held that C's delay had caused D's offer to lapse.

305 *Northern Foods Plc.* v. *Focal Foods Ltd.* [2003] 2 Lloyd's Rep.728; D sent a letter to C indicating the price for the supply food products. C wrote to D to offer a three year contract for the supply of such goods at D's stated price. The issue arose later during the performance of the contract, as to whether C's letter was an offer. It was held that C's letter was indeed an offer to purchase goods at the stated price and the offer was accepted by D's conduct in supplying such goods to C.

In other words, one could say that a qualified acceptance is no acceptance at all. This is termed a 'counter-offer',[306] and its effect is twofold; (i) it is a rejection of the original offer, and (ii) it is a fresh offer itself.[307] This principle of counter-offer is very important because of the modern commercial practice of making quotations and placing orders with terms attached, the so-called 'battle of the forms', in which each party sends the other a previously prepared form containing the terms on which he is prepared to contract.

For example, suppose a buyer who makes an offer to buy goods on the terms of his 'purchase form' and the seller purports to accept the offer on the terms of his 'sales form'. Since, in most cases the terms of the forms differ, there is no contract. All that has happened is that the seller has made a counter offer. This counter offer may be accepted by conduct if the buyer takes delivery of the goods. In that event, there will be a contract on the terms of the seller's form.[308] On the other hand, the contract would be on the buyer's terms if the original offer had come from the seller, and had been followed by a buyer's counter offer which had in turn been accepted by the conduct of the seller. Thus victory in the 'battle of the forms' normally goes to the party who fires the last shot!

It seems that the question is always whether the party seeking to rely on a particular set of terms has made it sufficiently clear to the other that when he offers to do business he does so on those terms. The terms of a contract can either be expressly agreed or if not so agreed, then those implied by law. The importance of this must not be underestimated[309]

---

306 *Tinn* v. *Hoffman & Co.* (1873) 29 L.T.271; an offer was made by the sellers for a special price on the sale of 1,200 tons of steel. The offeree responded to this offer with a request to purchase 800 tons of steel. It was held that there had been no acceptance of the original offer of sale. Instead there had been a counter-offer to purchase 800 tons, and therefore the sellers were entitled to accept or reject this new offer.

307 Thus, in *Pickford Ltd.* v. *Celestica Ltd.* [2003] EWCA Civ. 1741, C faxed an offer to D setting out a price for the removal of D's goods on a basis of £890 per vehicle load, and an estimated total price of £100,000. A couple weeks later and after C carried out a detailed survey for the removal, sent another more detailed offer to D for a fixed price of £98,760, and requested D to confirm acceptance of the contract. A few days later D sent a fax to C giving their 'confirmation' and stating that it related to C's original offer price of £890 per vehicle load, and adding that the removal cost was 'not to exceed £100,000'. C carried out the work and claimed £98,760, whereas D, relying on the original offer paid C £33,000 (i.e. on a vehicle load basis). It was held that D's 'confirmation' related to C's original offer, which, due to C's second offer had been revoked. In any event, the Court found that D's acceptance would amount to a counter-offer due to the introduction of the new term relating to the limit on cost not exceeding £100,000. This counter-offer was accepted by C's conduct.

308 *British Road Services* v. *A.V. Crutchley Ltd.* (1967) 1 W.L.R.835.

309 *Lidl U.K. GmbH* v. *Hertford Foods Ltd.* [2001] EWCA Civ. 938; C and D entered into a contract and although pre-printed terms of each were exchanged, the parties did not clearly agree whose terms should govern their agreement. C invoked a *force majeure* clause in its standard terms. The Court of Appeal found that the contract was governed by general law which did not contain a *force majeure* provision.

As a general rule, an acceptance must be communicated to the offeror. This means that it must be brought to the attention of the offeror. No 'confirmation' or anything else need follow a valid acceptance.[310]

Finally, silence does not amount to acceptance. Thus, if B sends a letter to S offering to buy certain property, and he adds in it 'if I hear no more about it in the next five days, I shall consider this property mine', there will be no contract if S simply ignores the letter.[311]

When acceptance is communicated by post, it becomes effective when the letter of acceptance is posted, that is, when the letter is in control of the Post Office, even if the letter is delayed, destroyed or lost in the post.[312]

However, the letter of acceptance must be properly posted, for example handing it to the postman to post would not suffice.[313] It must be reasonable to use the post as a means of communicating acceptance, and obviously, must not be excluded as a means of acceptance by the terms of the offer.

The postal rule does not apply to instantaneous methods of communication such as telex, facsimile and telephone, where the rule is that the contract is complete when the acceptance is received by the offeror, not when is transmitted.[314]

It should be noted that the postal rule only applies to the communication of acceptances. Offers and revocations of offers must be communicated to be effective.[315]

Although, the existence of an offer and an acceptance would usually amount to an agreement, there is a further element, which is absolutely necessary if such an agreement is to be enforceable in law, namely, consideration.

---

310 Lord Justice Dyson said that '"confirmation" is an ordinary word which is often used when an order is placed in acceptance of an offer. In my judgment it has no particular significance.'; *Pickford Ltd.* v. *Celestica Ltd.* [2003] EWCA Civ. 1741 at [22].

311 *Felthouse* v. *Bindley* (1862) 11 C.B.N.S.869.

312 *Adams* v. *Lindsell* (1818) 1 B.& Ald.681; on 2nd September D wrote to C offering to sell some cotton. On 5th September the letter arrived, after being misdirected in the post. C immediately posted an acceptance. On 9th September the letter of acceptance arrived, but meanwhile D had sold the cotton elsewhere, since D had received a reply as expected on 7th September. The Court held that the contract was completed, i.e. D's offer had been accepted by C, on the 5th September.

313 *Re London and Northern Bank* (1900) 1 Ch.220.

314 *Brinkibon Ltd.* v. *Stahag Stahl und Stahlwarenhandelsgesellschaft mbH.* [1983] 2 A.C.34; where the Court held that an acceptance by telex from England to Austria caused a contract to be made in Austria. Also see *Entores Ltd.* v. *Miles Far East Corporation* [1955] 2 All E.R.493.

315 *Henthorn* v. *Fraser* [1892] 2 Ch.27; D offered to sell some goods to C. The next morning D posted a letter to C withdrawing the offer. The letter reached C in late afternoon on the same day. In the meantime however, C had posted an acceptance to D. It was held that D's revocation was of no effect until it actually reached C. Therefore, D's offer had been validly accepted by C when the letter of acceptance had been posted by C.

CONSIDERATION

The parties to an agreement must have furnished each other with consideration. Consideration is the price for which the promise is bought.[316] It is based on the idea of reciprocity, i.e. that the person who makes a promise should not be able to enforce this promise, unless he has given something in exchange for it.

To put it in simple words, in a contract of sale of goods, both buyer and seller exchange promises: the buyer promises to pay, and the seller promises to deliver the goods. The consideration for the buyer's promise to pay, is the seller's promise to deliver the goods. The consideration for the seller's promise to deliver the goods is the buyer's promise to pay (see diagram 1 below).

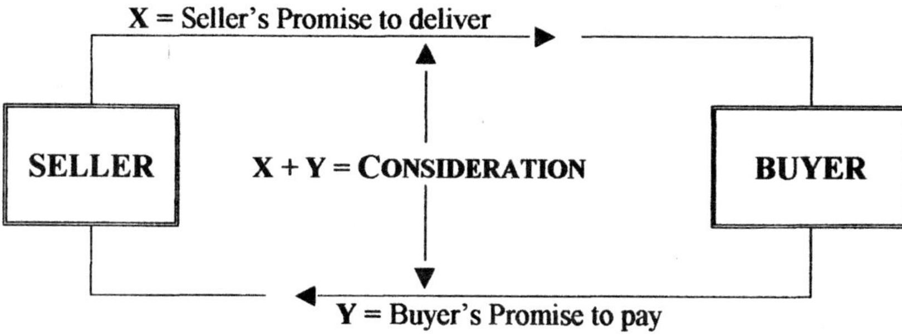

Diagram 1: Consideration

If a person makes a promise to another, and he is not to receive anything back, then this is a gratuitous promise, and such a promise, generally speaking, is not enforceable in English law. Examples of gratuitous promises are charities, gifts, etc.[317]

Past consideration is no consideration. Thus, where services are rendered voluntarily, i.e. without any promise of payment, a subsequent promise to pay for them is not supported by consideration[318] and therefore such promise is not enforceable.

---

[316] *Dunlop Pneumatic Tyre Co. Ltd.* v. *Selfridge & Co.* [1915] A.C.847.

[317] *Bainbridge* v. *Firmstone* (1838) 8 A.& E.743. Sometimes, there is difficulty in distinguishing consideration from a gift; *Esso Petroleum Co. Ltd.* v. *Customs and Excise Commissioners* [1976] 1 W.L.R.1, C offered one coin showing the face of a footballer to customers who purchased C's petrol. The majority of their Lordships thought that the coin was an offer of consideration to the customer to pay the price, whereas the minority considered the coin as a gift.

[318] *Roscorla* v. *Thomas* (1842) 3 Q.B.234; C bought a horse from D, who after the sale gave C an undertaking that the horse was not vicious. C sued D on the basis that C had broken this undertaking since the horse proved to be otherwise. It was held that the payment of the purchase price, in this case C's consideration, took place before the undertaking was given by D. Therefore, C had not furnished consideration for D's undertaking. Consideration was in the

Consideration need not be adequate to the promise, so that the requirement of consideration will be fulfilled by nominal consideration. Even a peppercorn rent could be adequate consideration.[319]

It must be noted that common law would generally consider that performance of an existing duty would not amount to consideration.[320]

Thus, where B owes S £100, and S agrees to accept £50 in full and final settlement of the debt, S may, following acceptance of the £50, sue B for the outstanding sum of £50.[321] This area of law however would seem quite unclear

past. *Cf. Lampleigh* v. *Brathwait* (1615) 80 E.R.255; D having killed a man requested C to obtain a Royal pardon. C managed to obtain it, and D then promised to pay C £100. Subsequently, however, D refused to honour his promise, and C sued him. It was held that in the circumstances D's request contained an implied term to generally pay. The subsequent promise of the £100 was to fix the amount, hence, C was entitled to the payment. See also *Simpson* v. *John Reynolds* [1975] 2 All E.R.88.

319 *Chappel & Co. Ltd.* v. *Nestlé Co. Ltd.* [1960] A.C.87; wrappers from chocolate bars were held to form part of the consideration for the sale of a music record. *Cf. Tesco Plc* v. *Customs and Excise Commissioners*, *The Times*, 16 October, 2003, where C issued vouchers to members of its loyalty scheme on basis of points awarded for purchase of goods, and it was held that members of the scheme gave no consideration for the acquisition of the vouchers.

320 Thus, in *Stilk* v. *Myrick* (1809) 170 E.R.1168, C was a seaman and during a voyage two of the crew deserted the vessel. D, the master, promised the rest of the crew to divide the wages of the two deserters between the remainder crew members if they would complete the voyage. On completion of the voyage, D refused to pay C his share. It was held that C was already contractually bound to complete the voyage and therefore did not provide any consideration for D's promise of payment. *Cf. Hartley* v. *Ponsonby* (1857) 7 E.& B.872, where nearly half of a vessel's crew deserted her, and the rest of the crew were promised payment of an extra sum of money if they would complete the voyage. C, one of the remaining crew members, was refused this payment. It was held that C was entitled to the payment on the grounds that the desertion was large enough as to make the voyage dangerous and discharge C's original contract, i.e. his contract was fundamentally different from that which he had originally entered.

321 *Pinnel's Case* (1602) 77 E.R.237. The House of Lords in *Foakes* v. *Beer* (1884) 9 App.Cas.605, reaffirmed that payment of a smaller sum in satisfaction of a larger is not good consideration. In this latter case C owed a sum of money to D, and he proposed to pay about a quarter of it in cash and the balance in instalments over a period of time, provided D would not pursue the matter and sue C. D agreed to this proposal, but when C paid the full amount, D claimed an additional sum which D claimed represented interest on the total sum of money C owed D. No consideration was found for D's promise not to sue C by the Court. The effect of this rule is, however, limited by the equitable principle of promissory estoppel. Very simply, the law of Equity may protect a person who relied upon another person's promise or representation, by not allowing the other person going back on his promise; *Central Property Trust Ltd.* v. *High Trees House Ltd.* [1947] K.B.130. Furthermore, it seems that the doctrine of promissory estoppel is a defensive doctrine; *Argy Trading Development Co. Ltd.* v. *Lapid Developments Ltd.* [1977] 1 W.L.R.444. *Societe Italo-Belge Pour le Commerce et L'Industrie SA (Antwerp)* v. *Palm and Vegetable Oils (Malaysia), The Post Chaser* [1981] 2 Lloyd's Rep.695; a sale contract provided *inter alia* that C, the sellers, were required to declare the ship to D, the buyers, 'as soon as possible after vessel's sailing'. C actually made this declaration a month after the ship had sailed. D made no protest, and requested C to hand over documentation to sub-buyers. The documents were rejected by the sub-buyers, and subsequently by D, on the basis that the clause made time of the essence, and hence C's delay in making the declaration entitled them to repudiate. C alleged that D's non-protestation combined with their subsequent request for the handing over of the documents to the sub-buyers, operated to estop D from rejecting the documents. It was held that the short time that had elapsed between the date of the representation waiving the defect, and the fact that C, the

as there are numerous cases where the line of what constitutes consideration becomes quite 'blurred'.[322]

(ii) INTENTION TO FORM/CREATE LEGAL RELATIONS

Even when the parties have reached agreement, which is supported by consideration, there could still be a non-enforceable contract because the agreement was made without any intention to effect legal relations. Thus, an agreement 'subject to contract', or 'binding in honour only', or subject to any other similar expression denying the intention of the parties' to create legal relations, will render the contract unenforceable.[323]

However, in the majority of commercial transactions there is no need to prove that the parties had such intention, as there is an automatic presumption that the agreement will be binding.[324] It is important to note that lack of intention to create or form legal relations would not make a contract a nullity *ab initio* (from the beginning), but will make such contract unenforceable. The same is also true where consideration is not present.

An 'unenforceable' contract is a valid contract but it cannot be enforced in the Courts if one of the parties refuses to carry out its terms. Items received under the contract cannot be reclaimed. Examples of unenforceable contracts are agreements for the sale of land, unless evidenced in writing, and statute-barred debts.

'Voidable' contracts are founded on a misrepresentation.[325] Also, some agreements made by minors fall into this category. The contract is in every respect a valid contract unless and until one of the parties takes steps to avoid it.

---

sellers, had not been prejudiced in reliance thereon, it was not inequitable for D, the buyers, to enforce their rights to reject the documents, and they were not liable to C for damages.

322 *Williams* v. *Roffey Bros. and Nicholls (Contractors) Ltd.* [1990] 1 All E.R.512, C.A.; the Court took the view that a promise to pay an additional sum to secure performance of an existing contract would be enforceable on the basis that a promise which ensures timely performance of an obligation confers a benefit. The danger here would be such approach to the doctrine of consideration might allow commercial blackmail, falling short of duress. *Cf. Re Selectmove* [1995] 2 All E.R.521, where an Inland Revenue inspector agreed with a company that taxes already due and owing to the Inland Revenue would be paid by the company by instalments. Following payment of some instalments, the Inland Revenue demanded the balance to be paid at once. The Court of Appeal following the House of Lords decision of *Foakes* v. *Beer* (1884) 9 App.Cas.605, held that the agreement to pay by instalments was not binding since it was not supported by consideration.

323 *Jones* v. *Vernon's Pools Ltd.* [1938] 2 All E.R.626; *Appleson* v. *Littlewood Ltd.* [1939] 1 All E.R.464. Indeed, in 'subject to contract' negotiations, the basis would seem to be that even when all terms of the contract are agreed, they do not bind the parties until they sign a formal document; *DMA Financial Solutions* v. *BaaN U.K.* 2000 W.L.1629568.

324 *Edwards* v. *Skyways Ltd.* [1964] 1 W.L.R.349.

325 See *infra*, p.91.

Anything obtained under the contract must be returned, in so far as this is possible. If goods have been resold before the contract was avoided however, the original owner will not be able to reclaim them.

The term 'void' contract is a contradiction in terms since the whole transaction is regarded a nullity. It means that at no time has there been a contract between the parties. Any goods or money obtained under the agreement must be returned. Where items have been resold to a third party, they may be recovered by the original owner. A contract may be rendered void, for example, by some forms of mistake.[326]

The importance of this terminology may become clearer with a simple practical example. If S sells goods to B under circumstances which render the sale contract void, and B re-sells them to C, then C may get no title and S can recover the goods from C, or at S's option, sue C for damages. If on the other hand, the sale contract between S and B was voidable, and B re-sold the goods to C who took them *bona fide* and before S had rescinded/avoided his contract with B, then C would get a good title and S would have a remedy only against B (i.e. no opportunity to obtain his goods back).

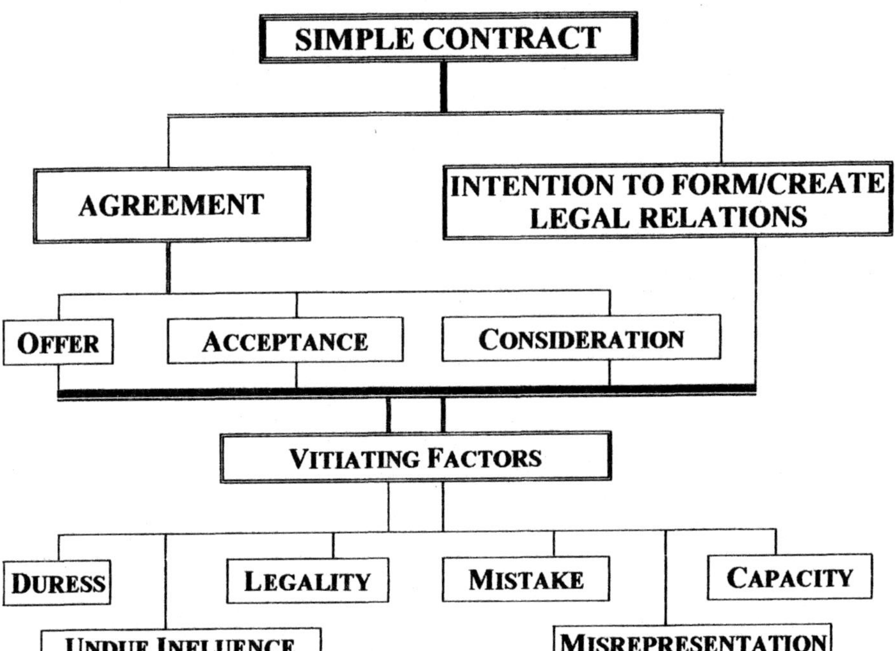

Diagram 2: Elements of Simple Contract and Vitiating Factors

[326] See *infra*, p.94.

OTHER ELEMENTS

There are certain additional elements which are necessary to be briefly considered and which may affect the validity and enforceability of a simple contract. Generally, factors which affect the validity of a contract are usually referred to as 'vitiating' factors, i.e. those which may make invalid or ineffectual an otherwise valid/effective contract.

CAPACITY

Certain persons may not be able to conclude a valid simple contract. For example, mentally disordered persons, i.e. persons suffering from any of the disorders listed in the Mental Health Act 1983.[327]

However, it must be noted that a contract would be *prima facie* valid unless the person establishes that (i) he was insane, and (ii) the other party was aware of this.[328] If 'necessary goods or services' are supplied to a person who lacks capacity to contract for the supply, he must pay a reasonable price for them.[329]

Also, a contract may be set aside by a Court if it was concluded by persons who were prevented from understanding the transaction by their drunkenness[330] and the other party to the contract was aware of this.[331]

Another type of person which may affect the validity of a simple contract is that of minors.[332] In general, it might be said that lack of capacity is a personal advantage. Therefore, a minor can recover damages from a person who refuses to perform his part of the contract. Furthermore, the parents of a minor are not liable for his contracts, unless they acted as his agent.

However, a minor would be liable if the contract concluded was one for 'necessaries', i.e. are goods suitable to the condition of life of the minor and to his actual requirements at the time of the sale and delivery.[333]

---

327 Section 1(2). Section 2(1) of the Mental Capacity Act 2005 clarifies that a person lacks capacity in relation to a matter 'if at the material time he is unable to make a decision for himself in relation to the matter because of an impairment of, or a disturbance in the functioning of, the mind or brain'. The relevant test as to the ability of an individual 'to make a decision' is contained in section 3 of the Mental Capacity Act 2005.

328 *Hart* v. *O'Connor* (1985) 2 All E.R.880.

329 'Necessary' means suitable to a person's condition in life and to his actual requirements at the time when the goods or services are supplied; s.7(2) Mental Capacity Act 2005.

330 'Where necessaries are sold and delivered to a person who by reason of … drunkenness is incompetent to contract, he must pay a reasonable price for them', s.3, Sale of Goods Act 1979 (as amended).

331 *Gore* v. *Gibson* (1843) 13 M.& W.623.

332 That is anybody who is under 18 years; s.1 Family Law Reform Act 1969.

333 Section 3(3), Sale of Goods Act 1979 (as amended). In addition, section 3 of the Minors' Contracts Act 1987, empowers the Courts to decide whether it is 'just and equitable' for any

In addition to the above types of contract, there are some contracts which may be concluded with a minor and are voidable, i.e. valid contracts which subsist unless and until avoided by the minor.[334]

A 'person' in law may be (i) a 'natural person', or (ii) a 'legal' or 'juristic' or 'artificial' person. The concept of capacity is extended to both classifications. A legal person, e.g. a corporate body, has a legal personality of its own which is civilly and criminally accountable and which is independent of the individual legal personalities of the persons making up the corporate body.[335]

The commonest form of corporate body is the Joint Stock Company. Joint Stock Companies are formed by registration[336] under the Companies Acts, and they may be either Public Limited Companies (abbreviated as 'plc') or Private Limited Companies (abbreviated as 'ltd.').[337] In brief, there is a presumption that an outsider dealing with a company, whether private or public limited one, is entitled to assume that the power of the directors to act on behalf of the company is unfettered, and so, perfectly capable of concluding a binding contract.[338]

A private limited company has full liability for all its debts owed to other parties, so in effect its liability is not limited. It is the company's shareholders whose liability is limited to the value of their shares. So, if such company

property acquired by the minor under a contract (or any property representing it) to be transferred from the minor to the other party of the contract.

[334] *Edwards* v. *Carter* [1893] A.C.360. With regard to civil litigation, a minor can sue through a 'next friend', i.e. an adult who will be liable for any costs awarded against the minor in the action, though the minor must indemnify the next friend. A minor defends a civil action through a 'guardian *ad litem*' who is not liable for costs. A minor's father is usually the next friend or guardian *ad litem*. The expression now used instead of 'next friend' and 'guardian *ad litem*' is 'litigation friend'.

[335] Although, in general, the distinction between the legal personality of a company and the legal personalities of its members holds good, the concept of corporate personality is obviously open to abuse and Courts are prepared to investigate the activities of individuals who seek to hide behind the company front or 'corporate veil' as it is sometimes called; *Customs & Excise Commissioners* v. *Hare* [1996] 2 All E.R.391.

[336] Incorporation may also be achieved by Royal Charter; this is often the case for Chartered Institutes and Universities. Other forms of corporate body are Local Authorities e.g. County Councils, Health Authorities etc. Other companies may be created by special Acts of Parliament, e.g. public utilities, etc.

[337] Since 2004, a new 'type' of company has been introduced by E.C. Council by Regulation 2157/2001 on the Statute for a European company, O.J. L 294, 10/11/2001, p.1. A European company would be known as a Societas Europea and the abbreviated title ('S.E.') should precede or follow the name of the company. Such company will be able to set up in the form of European public limited liability company, and will have to have a share capital of at least €120,000. An 'S.E.' company will be set up according to the requirement of the law of the country where it has its seat, and once registered a notice of this will have to be published in the Official Gazette of the European Communities. Most of the requirements of the country where the company has its seat will also have to be fulfilled accordingly, e.g. annual accounts. In the U.K. the Companies (Audit, Investigations and Community Enterprise) Act 2004 has also introduced the 'Community Interest Company' (C.I.C.) in s.26(1).

[338] In fact, a person dealing with a company is not even required to consult the company's memorandum or articles of association; s.35B, Companies Act 1985.

becomes insolvent, owing money to creditors, all its assets will be sold in order to satisfy those creditors' debts. However, all its shareholders (also called 'subscribers' or 'members') stand to lose is the value of their shares, irrespectively whether the sale of all company's assets proves inadequate to pay all company's creditors. The day to day running of the company is normally carried out by the directors.[339] Such directors owe a number of duties to the company, its shareholders, and employees.[340] It must be noted that in the absence of misconduct company directors have no liability.[341]

There are other types of persons who have specific powers in relation to their capacity to sue, be sued, and conclude contracts, however, these are beyond the scope of the present part.[342]

LEGALITY

Courts will not uphold an agreement which is illegal or contrary to public policy. Where the contract involves some kind of moral wrongdoing, it will generally considered to be illegal. In this connection, a Court may object to an agreement either because of a rule of common law or because it is contrary to statute.

Examples of illegal contracts are contracts to:

---

339 'Director' includes any person occupying the position of director, by whatever name called; section 741(1), Companies Act 1985.

340 Briefly, some of these duties are: (1) he should use the degree of skill reasonably expected of a person of his knowledge and experience; *Finance Co. Ltd.* v. *Stebbing* [1989] B.C.L.C.498, (2) he need not devote his continuous attention to the company business, (3) he may delegate authority to a person he trusts; *Dovey* v. *Cory* [1907] A.C.477, (4) he must act *bona fidei*; *John Crowther Group plc.* v. *Carpets International plc.* [1990] B.C.L.C.460, (5) he must not make a secret profit; *Boston Deep Sea Fishing and Ice Co. Ltd.* v. *Ansell* (1888) 39 Ch.D.339, (5) no conflict of interest should arise between him and the company; *Plus Group Ltd.* v. *Pyke* [2002] EWCA Civ. 370, (6) he must declare any personal interests; section 317 Companies Act 1985, (7) he must seek approval of shareholders if a gratuitous payment is to be made to a director; section 312 Companies Act 1985, (8) he must have regard to the interests of the company's employees; section 309 Companies Act 1985.

341 However, section 213 of the Insolvency Act 1986 (as amended) indicates that a director may be liable for 'fraudulent trading' if he continued to incur debts and trade while knowing that there is little chance of those debts being paid. Furthermore, section 214 of the same Act recognises a director's liability for 'wrongful trading' if the director failed to take reasonable steps to minimise loss to creditors of the company at a time when he knew or ought to have known that there was no reasonable prospect of the company avoiding insolvent liquidation.

342 A 'partnership' or a 'firm' as is commonly called, does not have legal personality of its own, but it can sue and be sued in its own name. Property is owned in the names of the partners and land can only be conveyed to some or all of the partners as legal owners on trust for sale for all the partners in equity. A 'club' cannot make contracts of its own; these are usually made by a member or trustee of the club on behalf of the club, other members will only be liable if they have authorised the making of the contract. 'Trade Unions' also enjoy a unique position. They cannot be treated as bodies corporate. However, they can sue and be sued in their own name, they can make contracts and own property vested in trustees.

(a) commit crimes or civil wrongs;[343]
(b) involving sexual immorality;[344]
(c) tending to promote corruption in public life;[345]
(d) of trading with an enemy in wartime;[346]
(e) directed against the welfare of a friendly foreign state;[347]
(f) prejudicial to the administration of justice.[348]

Briefly, the consequences of illegality depend on whether the contract was:

(i) illegal/unlawful on the face of it, or

(ii) lawful on the face of it.

(i) Such contracts are void and there can be no action by either party for debt, damages, or otherwise. Money paid or property transferred to the other party under the contract is usually irrecoverable.[349] However, if the claimant relies on rights other than those which are contained in the illegal contract, then relief may

[343] *Bigos* v. *Bousted* [1951] 1 All E.R.92; *Cockshott* v. *Bennet* (1788) 2 T.R.763. For example, a contract to assassinate someone, or to defraud the Inland Revenue would fall into this category; *Alexander* v. *Rayson* [1936] 1 K.B.169; C rented a flat to D, and in order to avoid tax they agreed that the money should be paid as ⅜ths for rent and ⅝ths for services. C sued D for unpaid sums for services. It was held that the agreement was made by both C and D for the purpose of defrauding the revenue authorities. Therefore, C and D were equally guilty and the contract would not be enforced.

[344] *Pearce* v. *Brooks* (1866) L.R.1 Ex.213; C let a coach out on hire to D, a prostitute, knowing that it would be used by her to ply her trade. The coach was returned in a damaged state. C was unable to recover the hire charges or for the damage as the court refused to help him enforce a contract for an immoral purpose. *Cf. Lloyd* v. *Johnson* (1798) 1 B.& P.340. An agreement to pay an allowance to a mistress was held illegal; *Franco* v. *Bolton* (1797) 3 Ves.368. But a different approach is now adopted by the Courts on domestic relations; *Tanner* v. *Tanner* [1975] 1 W.L.R.1346.

[345] Such as bribing an official; *Parkinson* v. *Royal College of Ambulance* [1925] 2 K.B.1, D was a charitable institution and Y was the secretary. Y represented, fraudulently to C, that the charity was in a position to obtain some honour, probably a knighthood, for him if he would make a suitable donation. C paid over the sum of £3,000 and said he would pay more if the honour was granted. No honour of any kind was received by C, and he brought this action to recover the money he had donated to D. It was held that the agreement was contrary to public policy and illegal, thus no relief.

[346] *Porter* v. *Freudenberg* [1915] 1 K.B.857

[347] For example, a partnership intending to import whisky into America during Prohibition; *Foster* v. *Driscoll* [1929] 1 K.B.470.

[348] Such as a contract not to prosecute a person for an offence concerning the public; *Herman* v. *Jeuchner* (1885) 15 Q.B.D.561.

[349] If a transaction is on its face manifestly illegal the Court would refuse to enforce it; *Birkett* v. *Acorn Business Machines Ltd.* [1999] 2 All E.R. (Comm.) 429, C.A.; *Ashmore Benson Pease & Co. Ltd.* v. *AV Dawson Ltd.* [1973] 2 Lloyd's Rep.21, C.A.

be available.[350] For example, if X leases his land to Z for 5 years, under an illegal contract and after the lease has expired, no payments of rent having been made, and Z does not return the land to X, then X could not recover any of the rent, since the contract was made for illegal purposes. But X could bring an action for the return of his property as owner. In other words, in such a case the right of a person to ownership is independent of the illegal contract, and therefore, such person can sue provided he does not rely on an illegal contract, that is such right does not arise from an illegal contract. So that in the above case, X can sue Z not under the illegal contract for rent, but under the fact that he/she is the owner of this land.[351] Furthermore, relief may also be available, if the claimant is not in equal wrong (*pari delicto*). If, for example, in *Parkinson* v. *Royal College of Ambulance*,[352] Y, the secretary, had oppressed C, or had used undue influence on him, in order to make him donate the £3,000, then C would have probably been entitled to recover the money.[353]

Finally, if the claimant repents, and provided that the repentance is genuine and performance is partial and not substantial, then money paid by him may be recoverable.[354]

(ii) As mentioned earlier, if both parties intended the illegal purpose, there is no action by either party, for anything. However, where one party was without knowledge of the illegal purpose, the innocent party's rights are unaffected and he may sue.[355]

DURESS

This is a common law doctrine and may be described as any unlawful actual or threatened violence to the person of the contracting party. If duress is

[350] *Edler* v. *Auerbach* [1950] 1 K.B.359.

[351] *Bowmakers Ltd.* v. *Barnet Instruments Ltd.* [1945] K.B.65.

[352] *Supra*, footnote 345. Also see *21st Century Logistic Solutions Ltd.(In Liquidation)* v. *Madysen Ltd.* [2004] 2 Lloyd's Rep.92.

[353] *Kiriri Cotton Co.* v. *Dewani* [1960] A.C.192. In *Atkinson* v. *Denby* (1862) 7 H.& N.934, C was in financial difficulties and offered to pay his creditors a certain sum in full settlement. All the creditors except D agreed to this. D said that he would only agree if C paid him £50. C paid him £50 as demanded. It was held, that C could recover this payment of £50 because he had been coerced into defrauding his creditors.

[354] *Kearly* v. *Thomson* (1890) 24 Q.B.D.742; C had a friend who was bankrupt and wished to obtain his discharge. D was likely to oppose the discharge and accordingly C paid him £40 in return of which D promised to stay away from the public examination and not oppose the discharge. D did stay away from the public examination but before an application for discharge had been made C brought an action claiming the £40. The claim failed because the illegal scheme had been substantially effected.

[355] Thus, in *Clay* v. *Yates* (1856) 1 H.& N.73, it was held that a printer who had innocently printed libellous matter could recover his charges.

proved then the contract is voidable.[356] It must be noted that although traditionally threat of violence against a party's property was not considered to be duress, in recent years the doctrine seems to become wider by encompassing what is called 'economic duress', which includes threats to break a contract.

Generally, this type of duress has been described by the Courts as pressure amounting to compulsion of the will of the victim.[357]

UNDUE INFLUENCE

This is an equitable doctrine and if proved that such influence is derived from pressure or coercion short of duress, then it renders the contract voidable. This doctrine is quite different than duress in that the burden of proof of undue influence depends on the relationship between the parties.

So, there are cases whereby due to the special relationship between the parties, a legal presumption would arise against the person exerting undue influence. Such presumption is said to arise in relationships of such trust and confidence that one of the parties to the contract or the recipient of the 'gift' is in a position to exercise undue influence over the person making the contract or 'gift'.

This includes confidential relationships such as between a person and his solicitor or financial adviser,[358], a religious leader and disciple,[359] parent and child,[360] but not between husband and wife[361] or an employee and his employer.[362]

---

356 *North Ocean Shipping* v. *Hyundai Construction, The Atlantic Baron* [1979] Q.B.705.

357 *Universe Tankships* v. *I.T.F, (The Universe Sentinel)* [1982] 2 All E.R.67; *Dimskal Shipping Co. S.A.* v. *I.T.W Federation, (The Evia Luck)* [1991] 4 All E.R.871. Both cases involved ships sailing under flags of convenience. The shipowners were threatened by the International Transport Workers Federation (I.T.F.) that unless they entered into certain agreements with I.T.F. the ships would be 'blacked'. The House of Lords in both cases held that the payments could be recovered since the contracts were obtained under 'economic pressure', i.e. blacking the ship, which is a form of duress, and were consequently voidable.

358 *Tate* v. *Williamson* (1866) 2 Ch.App.55; D had become C's financial adviser. C lived an extravagant life-style and he sold his estate to D for half its value. A year later C died and his personal representatives were successful in setting aside the sale of C's estate to D. *Cf. National Commercial Bank (Jamaica) Ltd* v. *Hew* [2003] UKPC 51.

359 *Allcard* v. *Skinner* (1887) 36 Ch.D.145; C joined a religious institution and promised to devote her property to the service of the poor. During her years in this religious order, she became a nun and gave a considerable amount of money and property to D, the Lady Superior of the Sisterhood. She later left the religious order. Although the result of C's action against D is not important due to legal 'technicalities', the Court recognised that C's gifts had been made under pressure, and hence under undue influence.

360 *Lancashire Loans Ltd.* v. *Black* [1934] 1 K.B.380; D in order to borrow money to maintain her extravagant mother's life-style, created a charge on her property. She did not receive any advice except from a solicitor who was acting for her mother and the moneylenders. The lenders brought an action against D's property. D claimed the defence of undue influence by her mother, and thereby successfully resisted the claim.

MISREPRESENTATION

The term misrepresentation refers to certain kinds of misleading statements, made before a contract is entered into, by which persons may be induced to enter into contracts. In general, in order for a representation to become a misrepresentation, the statement concerned must be:

- false
- one of fact
- addressed to the party misled
- induced the representee to enter into the contract.[363]

It must be a false statement of fact. Thus, statements of law are outside the scope of misrepresentation. Parties should not seek advice and rely on statements of the other party, on legal matters as 'ignorance of the law is no excuse'.

Also, statements of opinion are outside the scope of the doctrine of misrepresentation, unless it can be shown that the person making the statements was in a position to know and could not have reasonably held that opinion.[364]

Sales talk or puffing or what is called nowadays hype, do not come within the scope of misrepresentation. Therefore, statements like 'this is the finest or the best machine on the market' etc. would not amount to misrepresentation.

Silence in general cannot amount to misrepresentation.[365] However, where the statement was true when made but became false before the conclusion of the contract, and the party who made the statement is aware of such a change, his silence would amount to misrepresentation, as he is under a duty to disclose the change.[366] Generally, however, there is no general positive duty of one party to

---

[361] *Midland Bank* v. *Shephard* [1988] 3 All E.R.17.

[362] *Mathew* v. *Bobbins* (1980) 256 E.G.603. Nowadays, as a result of employment legislation, servants are not dominated by their masters.

[363] The misrepresentation statement does not have to be the sole inducement; *Barton* v. *County Natwest Ltd. The Times*, 29 July, 1999.

[364] *Bisset* v. *Wilkinson* [1927] A.C.177; D was selling some land and C asked whether the piece of land on sale, could support 2,000 sheep. D had no such knowledge, and he answered in the affirmative, thus stating his belief. After C bought the land, he realised that the land could not support 2,000 sheep, and sued D for misrepresentation. The Court held that as D had no personal knowledge of the facts, and as the buyer, C, knew this, there was no liability on the seller's part.

[365] *Bell* v. *Lever Bros. Ltd.* [1932] A.C.161.

[366] *With* v. *O'Flanagan* [1936] Ch.575; D, a medical practitioner, wished to sell his practice to C. C was interested and in January D represented to C that the income from the practice was making £2,000 a year. The contract was not signed until May of the same year. In the meantime, D had been ill and the practice had been run by various other doctors. In consequence the receipts fell to £5 per week, and no mention of this fact was made when the contract was entered into. C claimed rescission of the contract. It was held that C could rescind,

disclose information to the other.[367] The remedy depends on the nature of misrepresentation. There are three types of misrepresentation:

(i) Fraudulent,

(ii) Negligent, and

(iii) Innocent.

(i) Fraudulent: Fraud, in common law, means that the representor made the false representation knowing it to be false or without belief in its truth.[368] Note however, that as fraud is a serious allegation, which must be strictly substantiated, actions under this heading are not commonly brought. The misled party may sue for rescission[369] and/or damages.[370]

(ii) Negligent: Negligent misrepresentation means that the representor made the false statement without having any reasonable grounds for believing that the statement was true.[371] The Misrepresentation Act 1967 recognises only a claim for damages.[372] However, rescission may be available in appropriate cases.[373]

---

as the representation made in January was of a continuing nature and induced the contract made in May. C had a right to be informed of a change of circumstances, and D's silence amounted to a misrepresentation.

367 The only exceptions to this general rule are contracts based on the principle of utmost good faith (*uberrimae fidei*), i.e. contracts of insurance, agency contracts, and partnership agreements, where there could be said that there is a positive duty for the parties involved to disclose all material facts relating/arising from their contract.

368 *Per* Lord Herschell, in *Derry* v. *Peek* (1889) 14 App.Cas.337, 374. Here, the Plymouth, Devonport and district Tramways Company had power under a special Act of Parliament to run trams by animal power, and with the consent of the Board of Trade by mechanical or steam power. Derry and some other directors of the company issued a prospectus, inviting the public to apply for shares in it, stating that they had power to run trams by steam power, and claiming that considerable economies would result. The directors had assumed that the permission of the Board of Trade would be granted as a matter of course, but in the event the Board of Trade refused permission. Therefore, the directors were sued for fraud. The Court held that the directors were not fraudulent but honestly believed the statement in the prospectus to be true.

369 This means that in effect the contract is 'cancelled' by the Court. For a more comprehensive explanation of this remedy, see page 107 of this work.

370 *Standard Chartered Bank* v. *Pakistan National Shipping Corporation and Others (No.2)* [2003] 1 Lloyd's Rep.227, H.L. In the case of purchase of shares, such damages would be the difference between the price paid and the actual value at the date of purchase. In simple words, it is the excess which the purchaser had paid over and above the market value at the date of the representor's wrongdoing (misrepresentation); *Great Future International Ltd.* v. *Sealand Housing Corp. (In Liquidation)* [2004] EWHC 300.

371 *Howard Marine and Dredging Co. Ltd.* v. *A. Ogden & Sons (Excavations) Ltd.* [1978] Q.B.574.

372 Section 2(1), Misrepresentation Act 1967. It must be noted that a claim for damages in negligence may also be maintained under common law; *Hedley Byrne & Co. Ltd.* v. *Heller & Partners Ltd.*, [1964] A.C.465 H.L. As to the tort of negligence see *supra*, p.68.

373 *Mapes* v. *Jones* (1974) 232 E.G.717. D contracted to lease a grocer's shop to C for 21 years but in D fact did not have sufficient interest in the property himself to grant such a lease, the maximum period available to him was 18 years. As no lease was supplied as originally

(iii) Innocent: Innocent misrepresentation, under the Misrepresentation Act 1967, is where a false statement is made, but the representor had reasonable grounds to believe that the statement was true not only when he made it but also at the time the contract was entered into.[374] The misled party, may ask the Court for rescission only, but remedies under this type of misrepresentation, are left at the discretion of the Court and thus the misled party may be awarded damages instead.[375] This provision in effect caters for misrepresentations on trivial matters, as rescission may cause great hardship and inconvenience.

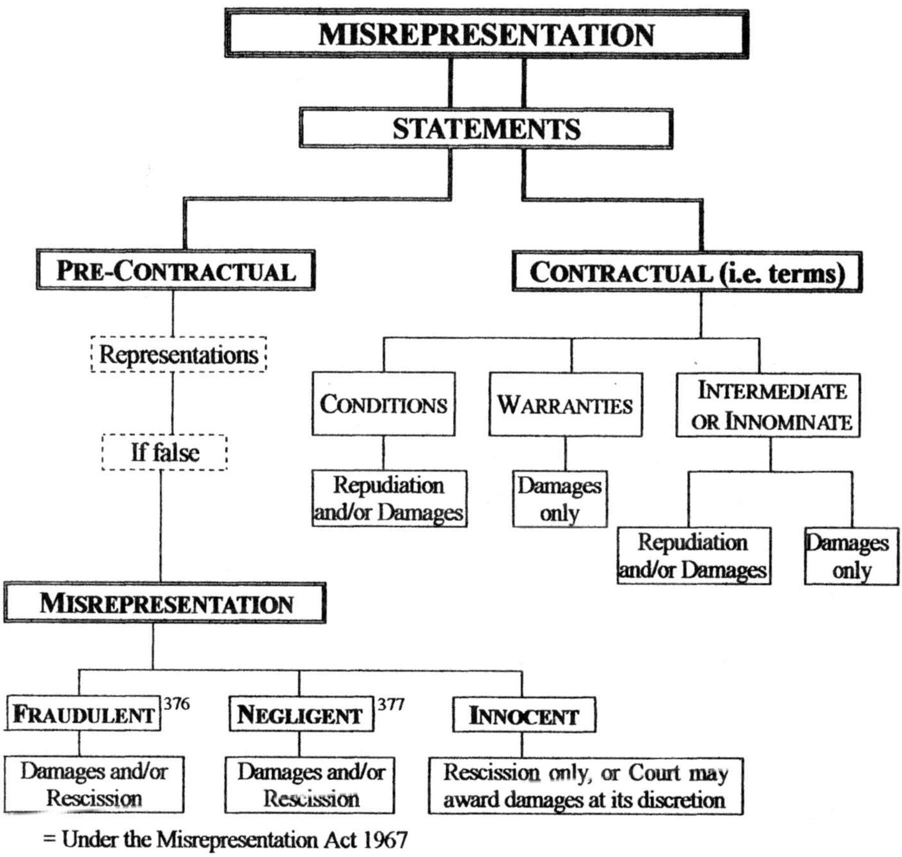

Diagram 3: Misrepresentation

promised, C shut the shop and treated the contract as repudiated. It was held, that C was entitled to rescission for misrepresentation under the Misrepresentation Act 1967.

[374] *Oscar Chess Ltd.* v. *Williams* [1957] 1 W.L.R.370.

[375] Section 2(2), Misrepresentation Act 1967.

[376] Action only available under common law, in the tort of deceit.

[377] Please note that there could also be an action in the tort of negligence under common law; *Hedley Byrne & Co. Ltd.* v. *Heller & Partners Ltd.*, [1964] A.C.465 H.L. As to the tort of negligence see *supra*, p.68.

MISTAKE

It is particularly important to distinguish between mistake and misrepresentation, since a contract affected by mistake may be void, whereas a contract affected by misrepresentation is only voidable. If S sells goods to B1 under circumstances of mistake and B1 re-sells them to B2, then B2 may get no title and S can recover the goods from B2 or sue B2 for damages. If on the other hand, the contract between S and B1 was voidable for misrepresentation, then if B1 sold the goods to B2 who took them *bona fide* before S had rescinded his contract with B1, then B2 would get a good title and S would have a remedy only against B1.

For a mistake to be operative it must be one of fact and not of law. Furthermore, errors of judgment are not mistakes in law. Thus, if B buys an article thinking it is worth £100 when in fact it is worth only £50, the contract is good and B must bear the loss if there has been no misrepresentation by the seller.[378]

Mistakes may be classified into three categories:

(a) Mistake as to the nature of the contract itself.

(b) Unilateral mistakes, i.e. made by one party only.

(c) Bilateral mistakes, i.e. where both parties make a mistake.

(a) MISTAKE AS TO THE NATURE OF THE CONTRACT: If a person signs a contract in the mistaken belief that he is signing a document of a different nature, or contents, there may be a mistake. Such person can plead *non est factum*, i.e. it is not his deed.[379]

However, in order to plead the defence of 'this is not my deed', the person who signed must prove that he made the mistake despite having taken all reasonable care, i.e. lack of negligence.[380]

---

378 *Bell* v. *Lever Bros. Ltd.* [1932] A.C.161.

379 *Lewis* v. *Clay* (1898) 67 L.J.Q.B.224; D was asked by Lord William Neville to witness a confidential document and signed in holes in blotting paper placed over the document by Neville. In fact Clay was signing two promissory notes/bills of exchange and two letters authorising C to pay the amount of the notes to Lord William Neville. The Court held that the signature of D in the circumstances had no effect. D was not bound by the bills of exchange.

380 *Saunders* v. *Anglia Building Society* [1971] A.C.1004; C, a widow aged 78 years, signed a document which Lee, her nephew's friend, told her was a deed of gift of her house to her nephew. C did not read the document but believed what Lee had told her. In fact the document was a gift of her interest in the house to Lee, who later mortgaged it to a building society. It was held that although the gift of C's interest did not confer a title on Lee, however, as the transaction intended and carried out was the same, i.e. the transfer of C's interest, and as C was negligent, by not reading it, the plea of *non est factum* was not available to her. Therefore, the document which is in fact signed must be 'fundamentally different', 'radically different', or 'totally different', in order for the plea of *non est factum* to be successful.

(b) UNILATERAL MISTAKE: This occurs where one of the parties is mistaken as to some fundamental fact concerning the contract and the other party knows, or ought to know this. If the other party does not know that as to the mistake, then this is a valid contract.[381] The cases under this classification are mainly concerned with mistakes of one party as to the identity of the other party.

Two types of mistakes with regard to identity may be put forward:

Mistakes as to the identity of the contracting party: Thus, where X contracts with Y thinking that Y is another person, Z, and if Y knows that X is under this misapprehension, then such a contract is void. Note that it is important in such a case, that X intended to deal with some other person other than Y. For example, if a person disguises his letter so as to make it appear from a respectable firm, in order to induce the other party to enter into a contract, the mistake will be as one of identity and therefore, will render the contract void.[382]

Mistakes as to the attributes of the contracting party: A good illustration of this is a case[383] C agreed to sell his car to a rogue. Before the sale took place the rogue persuaded C that he was a famous actor. He even signed a worthless cheque for £450 in the name of the famous actor concerned! Subsequently the car was sold by the rogue to D for £200. It was held that as C had effectively contracted to sell the car to the rogue he could not recover the car or damages from D, who was actually a student who had bought it from the rogue for £200. The contract was not void for unilateral mistake. When the parties

---

381 *Higgins Ltd.* v. *Northampton Corporation* [1927] 1 Ch.128; C entered into a contract with D for the erection of dwelling houses. However, in arriving at the price C made an arithmetical error. D concluded the contract, assuming that the price was correct. It was held that the contract was binding on the parties. In this case one party to the contract was mistaken, but the other party did not know, and did not ought to know of this mistake.

382 *Cundy* v. *Lindsay* (1878) 3 App.Case.459; C were linen manufacturers with a business in Belfast. Blenkarn, who was a fraudulent person, wrote to C from the address of 37 Wood Street, Cheapside, ordering a quantity of handkerchiefs but signed his letter in such a way that it appeared to come from a well-known and highly respected business called Blenkiron who were based at the address of 123 Wood Street. C knew of the existence of Blenkiron but did not know the address. Therefore, the handkerchiefs were sent to 37 Wood Street. Blenkarn then sold them to E, and was later convicted and sentenced for the fraud. C sued D in conversion claiming that the property had not passed to Blenkarn or to E, as the contract C entered into with Blenkarn was void for mistake. It was held that there was a mistake as to the party with whom C were contracting, and therefore C succeeded in their action. Therefore, C was induced to contract with Blenkarn due to the disguise, which lead C to believe that Blenkarn was Blenkiron. For a more recent case see *Shogun Finance Ltd.* v. *Hudson* [2004] 1 A.C.919, where an innocent purchaser did not acquire good title to a car he bought from a 'rogue' who in turn had obtained it fraudulently by falsifying a signature. Interestingly, all three judges in this recent case expressed the view that this area of law was in need of clarification.

383 *Lewis* v. *Averay* [1972] 1 Q.B.232.

conclude a contract *inter praesentes*, i.e. face to face, there is a presumption that each party intends to contract with the person physically present and identifiable by sight and sound. This in turn means that if one of the parties simply misrepresented himself, then this will amount to a mistake as to the attributes of that person rather than his identity.[384] Consequently, such a contract would be voidable for fraud but rarely void for mistake.

(c) **BILATERAL**: These can be further divided into **(i)** Common mistakes, and **(ii)** Mutual mistakes.

(i) **Common Mistake**: This is where both parties have made the same mistake. Thus, if B buys an article from S thinking it is worth £100 and S is also of the same opinion, when in fact it is worth only £50, the contract is good and B must bear the loss if there has been no misrepresentation by the seller.[385]

(ii) **Mutual Mistake**: This is where both parties have made a different mistake. Thus, if X offers to sell car A and Y agrees to buy, thinking X means car B, there is a bilateral mutual mistake. The test applicable in these cases, is that of the 'sense of the promise', i.e. what a reasonable man looking at the dealings of the parties would have thought that the parties were bargaining for.[386] If this 'sense of the promise' can be found by the Court then the contract will be enforced. Otherwise the contract will be void.[387]

---

384 Such a premise would suggest that contracts made over a telephone or videophone are to be treated as face to face contracts. Indeed, the House of Lords was of this view in *Shogun Finance Ltd.* v. *Hudson* [2004] 1 A.C.919.

385 *Leaf* v. *International Galleries* [1950] 2 K.B.86; C bought from D a painting for £85, after being told by D that the painting was by Constable. In fact, both C and D mistakenly believed the drawing was by Constable. Five years later C discovered that the painting was not by Constable and sued for rescission of the contract. The Court treated D's statement as a representation, and found it to be 'innocent'. Therefore, no right of rescission was available to C. Also, in *Great Peace Shipping Ltd.* v. *Tsavliris Salvage (International) Ltd.* [2002] 2 All E.R. (Comm) 999, the Court of Appeal reaffirmed that a common mistake as to the quality of the subject-matter of the contract would not avoid a contract, unless it rendered the subject-matter of the contract essentially different from the subject-matter which the parties had believed to exist. In this case, D agreed to provide a salvage service to a vessel. Consequently, D found a vessel which at the time was thought to be only 12 hours away from the stricken vessel. D agreed with C, the owners of that vessel, for the hiring of C's vessel for five days. However, a couple of hours later, D discovered that C's vessel was some 39 hours away from the stricken vessel and therefore sought to avoid the contract with C, on the basis that there had been a common mistake with regards to the distance of C's vessel from the stricken vessel. It was held, that the contract could not be avoided by D for common mistake. For the exceptions of *res extincta*, and *res sua*, to this general rule, see *Couturier* v. *Hastie* (1856) 5 H.L.Cas.673, and *Cochrane* v. *Willis* (1865) L.R.1 Ch.App.58, respectively.

386 *Wood* v. *Scarth* (1858) 1 F.& F.293.

387 *Raffles* v. *Wichelaus* (1864) 2 H.C.906; D agreed to buy some goods from C, which were to be transported on board a ship called 'Peerless'. In fact there were two ships with the same

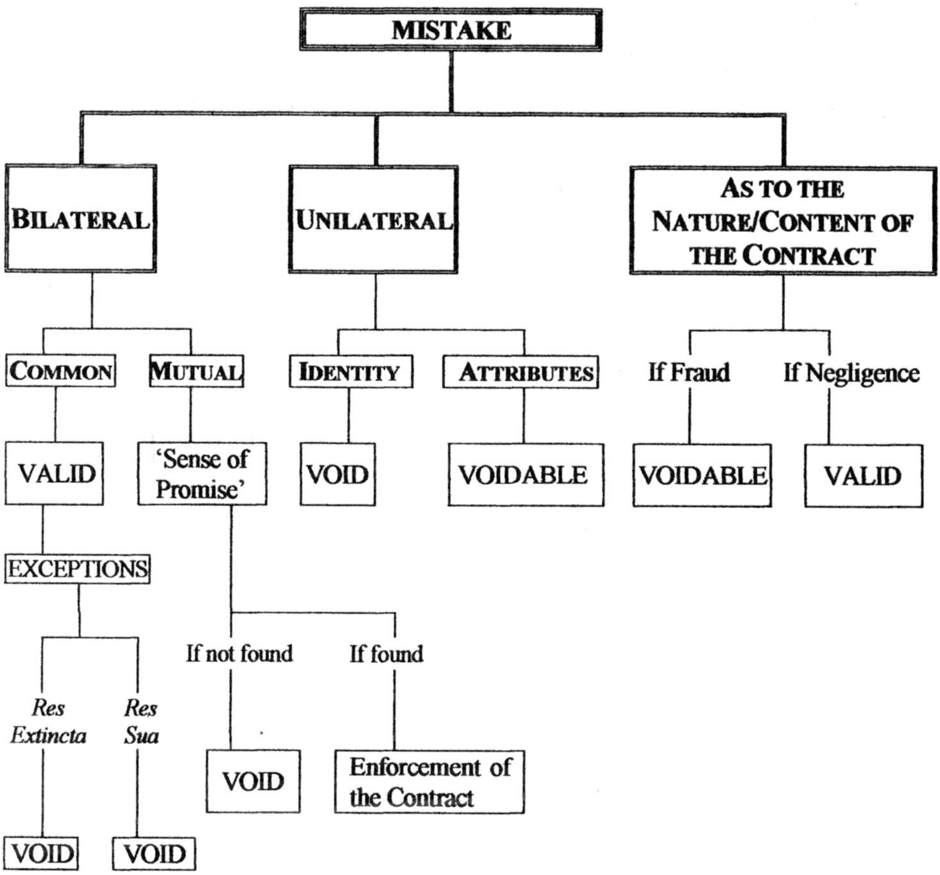

Diagram 4: Mistake

TERMS OF A CONTRACT

Once a valid contract has been made, it is necessary to see what the parties have actually contracted to do. In English law a contract may be made either orally or in writing or partly orally and partly in writing.

An easier way to understand the 'notion' of a contract term, is to realise that a term is in effect one of the promises made by one of the parties to the contract. It is what this party has agreed to do and it follows from this, that the

name sailing from the same port and carrying the same type of goods (cotton), one in October and one in December! C thought they were selling the goods on board the ship sailing in December, whereas D thought they were buying the goods on board the ship sailing in October. It was held that since this was a mistake relating to the very subject-matter of the contract, there was no contract in fact made between the parties.

total sum of all the terms from all parties is the contract in its entirety.

A contract may contain both express and implied terms. Express terms depend on the words used by the parties in reaching their agreement. Implied terms are included even though they have not been expressly stated in words.

EXPRESS

In so far as express terms are concerned, the intention of the parties is of primary importance. The ascertaining of express terms is mainly a question of fact. Problems may arise where a contract incorporates another document, e.g. subject to the rules of a trade association, or subject to some set of rules.

In such cases, the parties may not be aware of the full contents of the incorporated document, and/or there could be inconsistencies between the terms of the contract and the provisions of the incorporated document. Courts usually try to deal with such inconsistencies as best they can; and where possible put more weight on the drawn terms of the contract, as these are more likely to indicate the main intention of the parties.[388]

IMPLIED

These can be divided into (a) terms implied in fact, (b) terms implied in law, and (c) terms implied by custom or usage.

(a) Implied in fact

This is a term not expressly stated, but which the parties must have intended to include because it was 'so obvious that it goes without saying'. In other words, if while two parties were making their bargain, an officious bystander were to suggest some express provision for it in the agreement, they would suppress him with a common 'Oh, of course!'.[389]

In one case, A sold some land to B, and he undertook that if he was going to sell some adjoining land in the future, B should have 'the first refusal'. A term was held to be implied in this contract, that A would not defeat B's expectation by conveying the adjoining land to a third party by way of gift.[390]

However, Courts nowadays, are reluctant to imply a term in fact under the

[388] *Adamastos Shipping Co. Ltd.* v. *Anglo-Saxon Petroleum Co. Ltd.* [1959] A.C.133.

[389] *Shirlaw* v. *Southern Foundries Ltd.* [1939] 2 K.B.206, [1940] A.C.701 H.L. In *The Moorcock* (1889) L.R. 14 P.D.64, C contracted with D, the owners of a wharf, to have C's ship lie at D's wharf. However, C's ship was damaged because the water level fell and she touched the bottom. It was held that a term was implied in this type of contract that a wharf is safe for the use of the ships contracted to lie thereat.

[390] *Gardner* v. *Coutts & Co.* [1967] 3 All E.R.1064.

'officious bystander' test.

In other words, the Courts would not 'improve' a contract, by adding implied terms in fact.[391] This is particularly true where the parties have entered into a carefully drafted written contract containing detailed terms agreed between them.[392]

b) Implied in law

This category includes terms implied by statutes, and by common law. A person who contracts to supply services in the course of a business undertakes (impliedly) that he will carry them out with reasonable skill and care.[393] At common law such implied terms can be excluded, but nowadays the power to exclude such terms has been considerably reduced by statute. Thus a term excluding liability as to the quality of the goods, which is a term implied by the Sale of Goods Act 1979 (as amended), is invalid in a consumer sale.[394]

c) Implied by custom or usage

Customs of particular markets may be incorporated in a contract. Parties to a contract may be bound by such implied term, whether they know it or not.

The important test however, for the application of such implied term, is whether the custom is reasonable i.e. whether it is inconsistent with any express or implied terms of the contract. If it is, then it is said that the custom is unreasonable.

Where persons who are in the business of hiring machinery deal with each other on a regular basis on terms drawn up by a trade association, those terms may be implied in a transaction even though no express reference to them has been made.[395]

---

[391] *Liverpool City Council* v. *Irwin* [1977] A.C.239; in a case of a block of flats communal parts over which the tenants and the landlord have rights of access, e.g. dustbin area, or stairs, a term may be implied that the landlord would maintain these parts reasonably safe.

[392] *Shell (U.K.) Ltd.* v. *Lostock Garages Ltd.* [1976] 1 W.L.R.1187. Where an estate agent was to receive a commission 'on completion of sale', it did not mean that a term was implied to the effect that the home owner should not sell the property privately; *Luxor (Eastbourne) Ltd.* v. *Cooper* [1941] A.C.108.

[393] Section 13, Supply of Goods and Services Act 1982.

[394] Section 6, of the Unfair Contract Terms Act 1977; see *infra*, p.190.

[395] *British Crane Hire Corporation Ltd.* v. *Ipswich Plant Hire Ltd.* [1975] Q.B.303; D hired a crane from C who were the owners. The agreement was an oral one, though after the contract was made D received a printed form from C, the owners, containing conditions. One of these was that the hirer of the crane was liable to indemnify the owner against all expenses in connection with its use. Before D, the hirers, signed the form the crane sank into marshy ground, though not due to D's fault. C, the owners, were put to some cost in repairing the crane and sued D, the hirers, for an indemnity under the contract. D, the hirers, claimed that the conditions had not been incorporated in the oral contract of hire. It was held that C knew that printed conditions in similar terms to those of D, were in common use in the business. Therefore, the conditions were incorporated into the oral contract, and C's action succeeded.

EFFECT OF BREACH

Not all terms in a contract carry equal weight. Failure to perform one of the terms may have a more serious effect on the contract than failure to perform another. The identification of the terms of a contract is of great importance, because the remedies available to the parties are considerably affected.

Traditionally, terms used to be classified as conditions and warranties. A condition being a term that its breach goes to the root of the contract and therefore is capable of terminating the contract.

For example, a contract of sale may require that goods are shipped by a particular date,[396] or a charter-party may provide that the shipowner can withdraw the ship if the hire is not punctually paid.[397] Such terms have been held to be conditions.

For a term to be held to be a condition at least one of the following three requirements must be fulfilled:

-The particular term has already been classified as a condition by previous judicial decision. For example if A has entered into a charter-party with B, and the charter-party provides that the ship will be expected ready to load at a particular port, on a particular date. Such term has been held to be a condition.[398]

-The term may be a term prescribed by statute as a condition, such as the various implied terms contained in the Sales of Goods Act 1979 (as amended). This Act for example provides,[399] that it is an implied condition that the seller will have the right to sell at the time when the property is to pass to the purchaser.

-The parties have expressly or impliedly agreed that a particular term should be a condition. The word 'condition' has a number of meanings and is often used in a non-specific sense e.g. standard form 'Terms and Conditions'. If the word is

---

[396] *Bunge Corporation* v. *Tradax Export S.A.* [1981] 1 W.L.R.711; under a sale contract the buyers had an obligation to give the sellers notice that the vessel nominated for carriage of the goods was ready to load. Notice of readiness was in fact given four days late, and such failure to give notice on time was held to be a breach of a condition.

[397] *The Laconia* [1977] A.C.850, [1977] 1 All E.R.545; a vessel was chartered by C under a time charter-party which provided that hire was to be paid in advance, and that 'failing the punctual and regular payment of the hire' D were to be at liberty to withdraw the vessel from C's service. C made payment one day late, and D withdrew the vessel. It was held that the breach of the obligation to pay in advance was a condition and consequently D were entitled to withdraw the vessel from C.

[398] *The Mihalis Angelos* [1970] 2 Lloyd's Rep.43 C.A.; a clause in a charter-party provided the vessel will be 'expected ready to load' on a particular date. There was a considerable delay, and the charterers (D) repudiated the contract. It was held that the clause was a condition and therefore D were entitled to do so.

[399] In section 12(1).

expressly used,[400] the Court must be satisfied that it was intended to be used in its technical sense.[401] For example, a provision giving the buyer the right to reject goods if they did not possess a specified quality would be classified as a condition, as this would give effect to the intention of the parties.[402]

A warranty if breached entitles the innocent party to damages only. For example, the Sale of Goods Act 1979 (as amended), classifies as a warranty the implied term that the goods are free from charges in favour of third parties. In such case damages, enabling the buyer to pay off the charge, will generally be an adequate remedy. The difference between a condition and a warranty may be illustrated by contrasting the following cases:

In *Poussard* v. *Spiers & Pond*,[403] C was engaged to appear in an operetta from the start of its London run. Owing to illness, C was not available until a week after the show had opened and D, the producers, were forced to engage a substitute. D refused C's offer to take up the part. It was held that the obligation to perform from the first night was a condition of the contract. Failure to carry out this term entitled D to repudiate C's contract.

In *Bettini* v. *Gye*,[404] C, an opera singer, was engaged by D to appear in a season of concerts. C undertook to be in London at least six days before the first concert for the purpose of rehearsals. However, C arrived three days late for these rehearsals and D refused to accept C's services. It was held that the promise to appear for rehearsals was a less important term of the contract. D could claim compensation for a breach of warranty but could not repudiate C's contract.

---

[400] *Schuler A.G.* v. *Wickman Machine Tool Sales Ltd.* [1974] A.C.235, H.L.; D, entered into a distributorship agreement with C, which contained a clause purporting to make a condition that D would send its representatives to visit six U.K. manufacturers at least once in every week. D failed to make these visits a few times, and C sought to terminate the agreement for breach of the clause. It was held that this was not a condition as a single breach, however trivial would entitle the innocent party to terminate.

[401] *Lombard North Central plc.* v. *Butterworth* [1987] Q.B.527, C.A.; a contract for the lease of a computer provided that punctual payment of each instalment of hire was of the essence and that failure to make due and punctual payment entitled C to terminate the contract. D was late in paying a couple of instalments and C sought to terminate the contract and damages. It was held that the provision made prompt payment a condition. The Court clearly suggested that stipulations making time of the essence indicate a condition of the contract. *Cf. Torvald Klaveness A/S* v. *Arni Maritime Corp., The Gregos* [1994] 1 W.L.R.1465, H.L., particularly the views of Mustill, L.J. and Templeman, L.J., on whether time of a vessel's re-delivery under a time charter-party is of the essence.

[402] *Bannerman* v. *White* (1861) 10 C.B. N.S.844; C intended to buy hops from D and asked whether sulphur had been used in the cultivation of the hops, adding that if it had, he would not even bother to ask the price. D said that no sulphur had been used, though in fact it had. It was held that D's assurance that sulphur had not been used was a fundamental term of the contract, i.e. a condition.

[403] (1876) 1 Q.B.D.410.

[404] (1876) 1 Q.B.D.183.

A third category has been added to those, that of 'intermediate' or 'innominate' term. The main difference of this category, is that breach of it only justifies rescission if it leads, or amounts, to a serious failure in performance.[405]

Therefore, a term may be classified as any of the above mentioned categories depending on the particular term, its implications and construction. The contract should be examined as a whole and the intention of the parties must be determined at the time the parties entered into it. The Court will examine the terms and will have to determine what the parties intended it to function as i.e. condition, warranty or intermediate term.

Generally speaking, the Courts have expressed a preference for innominate terms rather than conditions, mainly because of the flexibility this permits them in deciding the appropriate remedy.

Therefore, the position in so far as remedies are concerned, may be summed up as follows:

i) if the term broken is a condition, the innocent party can terminate the contract usually irrespective of the degree of loss or damage flowing from the breach. In addition if loss or damage has also been caused by the breach of the term, the innocent party may claim for such loss or damage.

ii) if the term broken is a warranty, the remedy is one in damages only.

iii) if the term broken is an intermediate one the injured party can terminate the contract if the actual and prospective consequences of the breach are such as to substantially deprive him of the benefit of the whole of the consideration he bargained to receive under the contract. Otherwise, damages are only awarded.

[405] *Hong Kong Fir Shipping Co. Ltd.* v. *Kawasaki Kisen Kaisha Ltd.* [1962] 2 Q.B.26, C.A.; under a charter-party a vessel was hired for 24 months. On her first voyage, she suffered numerous break downs of machinery, mainly due to bad maintenance and incompetent and inadequate number of crew. It was subsequently estimated that the vessel would need 15 weeks of repairs to make her seaworthy. Before her repairs were successfully completed, the charterers repudiated the charter-party. The vessel's repairs were subsequently completed, she was in a seaworthy state, and there were 17 more months left of the original charter-party period. The shipowners sought damages for breach of contract. It was held that seaworthiness was not a condition of the charter-party. The delay caused by the repairs was not so great as to frustrate the commercial purpose of the charter-party. Interestingly enough, this latter statement being the test applicable in such cases, was rejected by the House of Lords in *Bunge Corporation* v. *Tradax Export S.A.* [1981] 2 Lloyd's Rep.1. *Reardon Smith Line* v. *Hansen Tangen* [1976] 1 W.L.R.989, H.L.; a ship which was going to be chartered, was described in the charter-party as Osak number 354 (this is the yard where it was built) when it was in fact Oshima number 004. In all other respects the ships were exactly the same. As this is a misdescription, i.e. usually considered to be a condition, the charterers sought to terminate the contract. The House of Lords rejected the argument and held that the description was not a condition but an innominate term and that since the injured party had not been deprived of substantially the whole benefit under the contract, the charterers were only entitled to damages.

In all the above cases, where a term has been broken, the contract is said to have been 'breached'. Therefore, a 'breach of contract' would result where any type of contractual term has been broken, irrespectively of the broken term's importance.

Furthermore, in all cases the word 'entitled' is used to indicate that the right is exercisable by the innocent/injured party at his option. Therefore, once a breach of a condition in a contract occurs, the innocent party may, at his discretion, terminate the contract. However, this innocent/injured party, may instead choose to continue with the contract, and sue for damages; or indeed not take any action to remedy the breach, which is perfectly acceptable and such party is entitled to do.

In other words, in the case of a breach of a condition the innocent party may treat such breach as a breach of warranty if he so wishes. Obviously, the opposite is not possible, i.e. a breach of warranty cannot be treated as a breach of a condition!

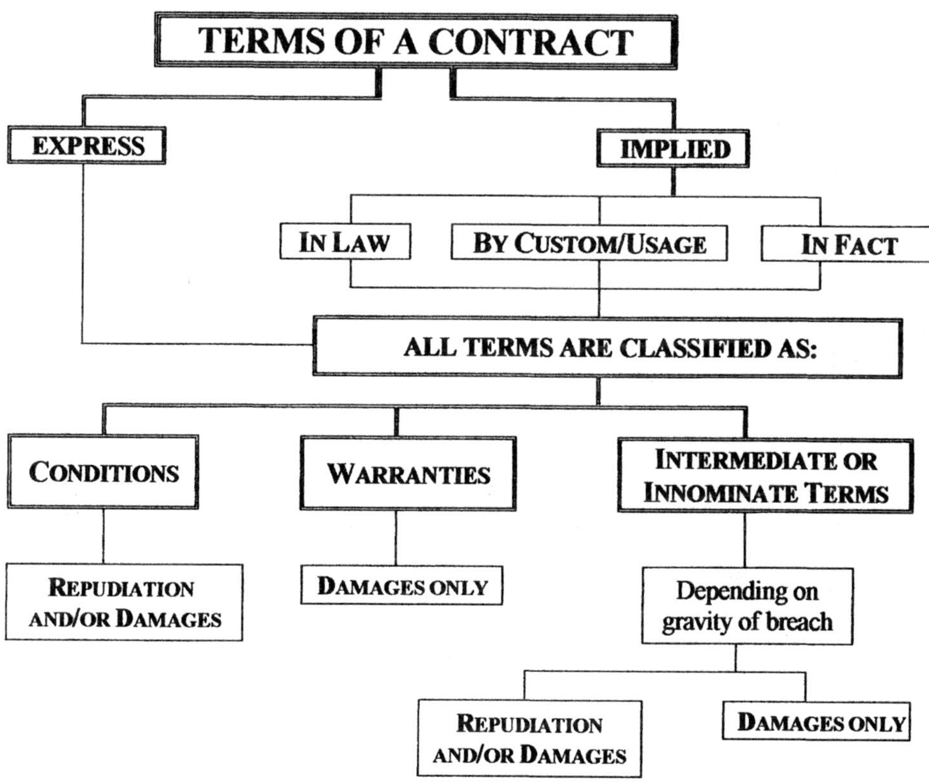

<u>Diagram 5</u>: Terms of a Contract

REMEDIES FOR BREACH OF CONTRACT

Every breach of contract will give the injured party the right to recover damages (financial compensation) under Common Law. Other remedies, such as specific performance and injunction, may be granted at the discretion of the Court as part of its equitable jurisdiction.

UNDER COMMON LAW

Apart from repudiation, i.e. termination, of the contract, which it could be viewed as the innocent party's 'self-help', the normal or usual proper remedy is that of damages.

DAMAGES

In the business world it is quite common for the parties to agree in advance the damages that will be payable in the event of a breach. These are known as 'liquidated' damages. If there is no prior agreement as to the sum to be paid, the amount of damages is said to be 'unliquidated'.

(a) Liquidated damages

It makes sense for the parties to establish at the outset of their relationship (contractual) the financial consequences of failing to live up to their bargain. Provided the parties have made a genuine attempt to estimate the likely loss, the Courts will accept the relevant figure as the damages payable. In practice, knowing the likely outcome of any legal action, the party at fault will simply pay up, without argument.

Thus, for example, liquidated damages are usually provided for, in holiday bookings, in the event of cancellation (cancellation charges notice): if cancellation is notified six weeks prior to departure the deposit is lost; if notification is made within four to six weeks of departure 30% of holiday cost is charged, etc.[406] If the Court holds that the sum is liquidated damages, it will be enforced irrespective of whether the actual loss is greater[407] or

[406] A recent investigation by the Office of Fair Trading on cancellation charges by some major tour operators during the period 1998-2001, concluded that the charges were 'a genuine estimate of the companies' losses overall'; Office of Fair Trading, *Holiday Cancellation Charges not Shown to be Unfair*, PN 46/03 24 April 2003.

[407] *Cellulose Acetate Silk Co. Ltd.* v. *Widnes Foundry Ltd.* [1933] A.C.20; D agreed to construct a building for C by a certain date. The agreement between C and D provided that C was to pay £20 for every week's delay beyond the agreed date. C were late by 30 weeks and D claimed £5,500 being their actual loss from the delay. It was held that the relevant provision in

smaller.[408] However, there is a temptation for a party with stronger bargaining power to try to impose a penalty clause, which is really designed as a threat to secure performance. Hence, if the Court decides that the clause in a contract is not for liquidated damages but it is a penalty clause, then enforcement of the penalty will not be made, but the Court will award damages on 'normal' principles. In simple words this means that damages will be awarded on an unliquidated damages basis, as if the relevant penalty clause had not been incorporated into the contract.

As a general guide, extravagant sums are in the nature of penalties. Also, where the sum provided for in the contract is payable on the occurrence of any one of several events it is probably a penalty for it is unlikely that each event can produce the same loss.[409]

(b) Unliquidated damages

The aim of unliquidated damages is to put the injured party in the position he would have been in if the contract had been carried out properly. In the main, damages are designed to compensate for loss and not to punish the defendant.[410] Contractual damages are certainly not intended to put the claimant in a better position than if the contract had been properly performed. If no loss has been suffered, the Court will only award nominal damages, i.e. a small sum to mark the fact that there had been a breach of contract. The consequences of a breach of contract may be far reaching, i.e. the breach might have caused a chain reaction of events to occur. The law must draw a line somewhere and say that damages incurred beyond a certain limit are too remote to be recovered. Damages in contract must therefore be proximate.

---

the contract was a genuine pre-estimate of loss, and C had only agreed to pay £20 a week. Therefore C were not liable for any additional sums of money claimed by D.

[408] *Dunlop Pneumatic Tyre Co. Ltd.* v. *New Garage & Motor Co. Ltd.* [1915] A.C.79.

[409] *Ariston SRL* v. *Charly Records Ltd.*, *The Financial Times*, 21 March, 1990; the Court of Appeal stated that such clauses will be construed on the principle that the sum payable for breaches should be proportionate to the extent of such breaches. By a clause C was to pay £600 for each day any of the items supplied to D were delayed. It was held that this was a penalty, because the same sum of money was payable irrespectively of whether it was a single item or any item that was delayed. *Ford Motor Co.* v. *Armstrong* (1915) 31 T.L.R.267; D agreed to pay £250 for each Ford car sold below the manufacturer's list price. Furthermore, D agreed (i) not to sell Ford cars to other dealers in the motor trade, and (ii) not to exhibit any car supplied by Ford without their permission. The Court held that the clause was a penalty, and not for liquidated damages. The same sum was payable for different kinds of breach which were not likely to produce the same loss. In addition, its size, bearing in mind that it is a 1915 case, suggested that it was not a genuine pre-estimate of loss. *Cf. Wallis* v. *Smith* (1882) L.R. 21 Ch.D.243, where a clause provided that a sum of money will be payable to C for any 'substantial breach' committed by D, and the Court of Appeal construed it as being a liquidated damages clause.

[410] In very rare cases, a Court may grant, in addition to 'normal' damages, *exemplary* damages, their purpose being to punish.

The law regarding remoteness of damage in contract is founded upon the case of *Hadley*.[411] The injured party-claimant may recover damages for:

(a) Loss which has resulted naturally and in the ordinary course of events from the defendant's breach, and

(b) the loss which, although not a natural consequence of the defendant's breach, was in the minds of the parties when the contract was made.[412]

Once breach of contract has occurred, the innocent party is under a 'duty' to mitigate (minimise) his loss. This means, that the innocent party cannot stand back and allow the loss to get worse. A seller whose goods have been rejected, for example, must attempt to get the best possible price for them elsewhere. The claimant will not be able to recover for that part of the loss, which has resulted from his failure to mitigate.[413]

IN EQUITY

So far, we have seen that the 'normal' remedy for a breach of contract is an award of damages at common law. There are some situations, however, where damages would be neither adequate nor appropriate. Equity developed other forms of relief to ensure that justice is done. It is important to understand however, that whereas common law remedies are prescribed by common law, equitable remedies are discretionary, i.e. it is up to the Court to award them.[414] Some important, of these equitable remedies, are:

[411] *Hadley* v. *Baxendale* (1854) 9 Exch.341; D unduly delayed delivery of a mill shaft to C, and so the mill was out of action for a considerable time. C had not informed D that the mill would be closed if D did not deliver it on time. It was held that C could recover damages for the delay in delivery, but not for loss of profits occasioned by closure of the mill. Therefore, there was no way that D could have foreseen that closure of the mill would be necessary as a result of the delay.

[412] *Victoria Laundry (Windsor) Ltd.* v. *Newman Industries Ltd.* [1949] 2 K.B.528; C, a company of launderers wished to expand their business and, they ordered a new boiler from D. The boiler was damaged during the course of its removal and as a result there was a five month delay in delivery C claimed (a) damages of £16 per week for the loss of profits they would have made on the planned expansion of their laundry business, and (b) damages of £262 a week for loss of profits they would have made on extremely lucrative dyeing contracts. The Court held that C were entitled to (a), but they could not recover for the especially profitable dyeing contracts of which D were ignorant.

[413] *Brace* v. *Calder* [1895] 2 Q.B.253; C was employed by D who were a partnership. This partnership was going to be dissolved, and C was offered re-engagement on the same terms by the partners, but C refused. It was held that C was entitled to nominal damages as he had failed to mitigate his loss.

[414] Indeed, in practice is wise before applying to the Court for such remedy to be able to address satisfactorily the question 'why damages are not an adequate or appropriate remedy in the circumstances?'

SPECIFIC PERFORMANCE

A decree of specific performance is an order of the Court requiring the party in breach to carry out his contractual obligations. Failure to comply with the directions of the Court lays the party in breach open to the imposition of penalties for contempt of Court.[415] However, this remedy is confined to contracts for the sale of land, and is not normally granted in the case of contracts for the sale of goods because other goods of a similar kind can be purchased and the difference assessed in money damages. If, however, there is a contract for the sale of a unique item, it would seem that as no sum of money can compensate the disappointed buyer for his lost opportunity, specific performance may be granted.[416]

INJUNCTION

This is an order of the Court requiring the party at fault not to break the contract.[417] Its main use is to enforce the negative promises that can occasionally be found in employment contracts (contracts in restraint of trade). For example, an employee may agree, not to work in a similar capacity for a rival employer during the period of his contract.[418] It should be noted that an injunction cannot be used as a 'back door' method of enforcing a contract of employment for which specific performance is not available.[419]

RESCISSION

This is a further equitable remedy for breach of contract. The rule is the same when the remedy is used for breach as it is when it is used for

415 Where imprisonment may be imposed. As to civil contempt of Court see *supra*, p.12.

416 Section 52(1), Sale of Goods Act 1979 (as amended). For obvious reasons the Act does not provide the remedy of specific performance to a disappointed seller.

417 Since this part looks at the remedies for breach of contracts, it should be noted that such injunctions are referred to as 'Final' or 'Perpetual', which means that they are granted at trial as a remedy and would usually last until a specified date or in perpetuity.

418 *Warner Bros.* v. *Nelson* [1936] 3 All E.R.160; D was the film actress Bette Davis, and had agreed not to work for anyone else during the period of her contract with C, Warner Bros. In breach of this agreement D left the U.S.A. and entered into a contract with a third party in the U.K. The Court held that C were entitled to an injunction to prevent D breaking the negative provision in the contract.

419 'Mareva' Injuctions or as they are now called 'Freezing Orders' are another equitable remedy, mostly used at the interlocutory, i.e. before trial, stage of litigation. A freezing order would restrain a party from removing its assets from the jurisdiction, i.e. England and Wales. The party applying to the Court for such order would have to show *inter alia* that there is a real risk that the other party's assets may be dissipated within, or removed from the jurisdiction; *Z Ltd.* v. *A-Z and AA-LL* [1982] Q.B.558, C.A.; *Mareva Compania Naviera S.A.* v. *International Bulk Carriers S.A. (The Mareva)* [1975] 2 Lloyd's Rep.509, C.A.

misrepresentation. In effect, rescission restores the *status quo*, i.e. it puts the parties back to the position they were in before the contract was made.

Finally, it must be noted that a type of equitable damages has been recently identified and recognised by English Courts. Such damages are based on account of profits made by the party in breach.[420]

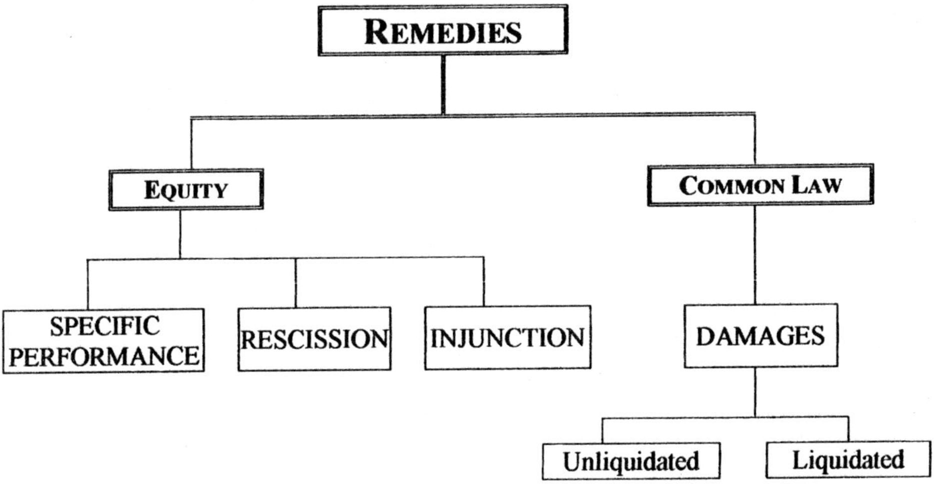

Diagram 6: Remedies for Breach of Contract

LIMITATION OF ACTIONS

It is obvious that the right to apply and obtain the above remedies does not last indefinitely. By way of reminder,[421] an action on a simple contract must be brought within six years of the date when the cause of action accrued. The cause of action, in the case of a contract, accrues at the time of the breach.

It should be noted that the Limitation Act 1980, does not discharge a contract, it merely makes the contract unenforceable in a Court of law. This means that if the defendant does not plead the statute of limitation, i.e. the Limitation Act 1980, the Court will enforce the contract.

For example, if X brings an action for money owed to him by Y under a simple contract which was performed and payment was due eight years ago,

420 *Attorney General* v. *Blake* [2000] 4 All E.R.268, H.L. It must be noted however, that an account of profits will be appropriate only in cases involving exceptional circumstances. Indeed, examples of this principle of awarding non-compensatory damages for breach of contract in commercial law are non-existent.

421 For a summary of limitation periods see *supra*, p.42.

unless Y pleads that X's action is time-barred by virtue of the Limitation Act, the Court will proceed to decide on the issue of the debt.

DISCHARGE OF CONTRACT

A contract may be discharged in four ways:

1. By agreement
2. By performance
3. By breach
4. By frustration

1) BY AGREEMENT

Obviously, a contract may be ended by agreement. Discharge by agreement may arise:

a) Out of the original agreement
The parties, for example, may have agreed from the outset that the contract should end automatically on the expiration of a fixed time. Thus, a lease of premises for a fixed term, would come within this category. Another example is a contract of employment, which can normally be brought to an end by the operation of a provision entitling either party to terminate if they wish, upon giving reasonable notice. In such cases, the agreement between employer and employee, is made at the outset, not when the notice is handed out.

b) Out of a new contract
Executory contract is a contract for goods/services to be supplied in the future, i.e. a promise for a promise. If there has been no performance and the contract is executory, then a mutual bilateral discharge will be adequate. The mutual release of the parties provides the consideration. For example, where there is a contract for sale of goods, which have not yet been supplied or paid for, but are to be supplied at a later time, and both buyer and seller agree to end the contract.
Where the contract is executed, as where it has been performed or partly performed by one party, then the other party, i.e. the party who wishes to be released, has to provide consideration for the release unless it is effected by deed.
It is important to remember that in order to have a discharge by agreement out of a new contract, it is necessary to have two elements, namely; an agreement

and a valid or effective new contract, which in turn means that consideration is required.

If consideration in the new contract is non-existent, then this is a gratuitous promise, and therefore the party giving such promise may always go back on his promise at any time and sue. Of course, if this party signs a deed then this is a contract by deed, in which case he is bound by his promise, even though there is no consideration. Immediate cash payment by the party which wants to be released would, for example, be good consideration for the other party's promise to end the contract.[422]

2) BY PERFORMANCE

A contract may be discharged by performance when both parties have performed the obligations which the contract placed upon them.

The law cases falling under this heading are instances whereby one of the parties brings an action against the other party claiming that the other party has not completed or fully completed his performance and therefore, he (the other party) is not released from his obligation, i.e. the contract cannot be discharged.

The general rule is that the manner of performance must comply exactly with the terms of the contract.

Thus, in one case, C agreed to serve on a ship sailing from Jamaica to Liverpool. He was to be paid 30 guineas on arrival to Liverpool. Some days after the ship sailed, C died. It was held that his widow could not recover anything for the work C had done before he died. C was obliged to complete the voyage before he was entitled to payment.[423]

In another case, D installed a central heating system in C's house for an agreed price of £560. The work was carried out defectively and it was estimated that it would cost £179 to put matters right. The Court of Appeal held that since D had not performed his side of the contract, he could recover nothing for the work he had done.[424]

Therefore, where there is a contract for the sale of a certain quantity of goods, and the contract provides for the goods to be packed in cases containing 30 units each, and in fact the goods are packed in cases containing 28 units each, the buyer is entitled to reject the goods, as this has been held to be a sale by 'description' under the Sale of Goods Act (as amended).[425] In other words, as

[422] *Pinnel's Case* (1602) 77 E.R.237.

[423] *Cutter* v. *Powell* (1795) 6 Term R.320.

[424] *Bolton* v. *Mahadeva* [1972] 1 W.L.R.1009.

[425] *Moore & Co.* v. *Landauer & Co.* [1921] 2 K.B.519. Such circumstances would now however be subject to s.15A of the Sale of Goods Act 1979 (as amended), and the result may be different if the breach of s.13 is considered to be 'slight'.

stated above, the manner of performance did not, in this case, comply exactly with the terms of the contract.

Unless the degree of this compliance is determined, it is not possible to decide whether the parties in a contract are freed from their obligations, and therefore, whether the contract has been discharged or not. There are some criteria which a Court would consider in order to determine whether performance must comply exactly with the terms of the contract. These are:

(i) Construction of the contract.

(ii) Whether partial performance has been accepted by one party.

(iii) Whether full performance has been prevented by one party.

(i) Construction of the contract

In this connection, a contract may be (a) divisible, (b) entire, or (c) capable of being fulfilled by substantial performance.

(a) Divisible or Severable: This means that the obligations can be split up into stages or parts. Therefore, payment can be claimed for each completed stage, unlike the above case of *Cutter* v. *Powell*,[426] where C had an entire contract, i.e. he was not entitled to payment until he had completely performed his part of the contract.

An example of a divisible contract, can be found in contracts of carriage of goods by sea where a shipowner is to be paid freight *pro-rata*, i.e. so much per ton delivered. Another example, is a contract of employment whereby payment is due every month or week, even though the contract may be for two or three years. If a contract of employment provides for payment monthly in arrears and the employee leaves in breach of contract (or justifiably dismissed), before the end of the month, he is not entitled to his agreed pay for the month. But if he works for the whole month he may be entitled to his pay. Similarly, a contract to build a house usually provides for payment to be made in three stages: after the foundations have been laid, when the roof goes on and on completion of the house.

(b) Entire: If an employer has contracted with the employee on a yearly basis, whereby the employer would have to pay his employee, say, £6,000, for a year's work, payable in the end of the year, and in fact he has paid £5,600, then performance has not been complied with, as such a contract is an entire contract, which in turn means that the contract has not been discharged. In such a case, performance must be complete and exact.

[426] (1795) 6 Term R.320.

Where C has agreed to sell D a certain quantity of canned fruit, which is to be packed in cases of 30 and on arrival it is found that half of this quantity is packed in cases of 24, D is entitled to reject the whole consignment, as this is a sale by description,[427] and this is an entire contract.[428] If the contract provided, for example, that acceptance and payment would be made only for cases arrived packed with 30 cans at destination, then D would not have been able to reject the whole consignment, but only the quantity that did not comply with this provision. Such a contract would be a divisible one.
Thus, where a shipowner contracts to transport some cargo, and freight is to be payable 'on delivery', he is entitled to the full freight, even if some of the cargo was not delivered or it was damaged.

(c) Capable of being fulfilled by substantial performance: In the example of the shipowner above, we assumed that the shipowner delivered substantially the same amount of cargo he loaded on the ship. The reason for this is that the service, i.e. the carriage of the goods, in respect of which the freight was contracted to be paid has been substantially performed.[429] If the Court considers that the claimant has substantially performed or carried out the terms of the contract, he may recover for the work he has done. The defendant can counter-claim for any defects in performance.
In *Hoenig* v. *Isaacs*,[430] the claimant agreed to decorate the defendant's flat and fit a bookcase and wardrobe for £750. On completion of the work the defendant paid £400 but he complained about faulty workmanship and refused to pay the balance of £350. The Court held that the contract had been substantially performed. The claimant was entitled to the outstanding £350, less the cost of remedying the defects, which were estimated at £55.
Thus, in the earlier mentioned case of *Cutter* v. *Powell*,[431] where the sailor died on board the vessel, the decision of the Court might have been different if, for example, he had died a couple of hours before the ship's arrival at Liverpool.
The Courts in order to decide whether a particular term must be fully performed or whether substantial performance is enough, will refer to the difference between conditions and warranties. A condition must be wholly performed whereas substantial performance of a warranty is often enough.
For example, in one case an opera singer entered into an agreement to take part in an opera starting from 28th November, and because she was taken ill

427 Under s.13, Sale of Goods Act 1979 (as amended).
428 *Moore & Co.* v. *Landauer & Co.* [1921] 2 K.B.519.
429 *Dakin* v. *Oxley* (1864) 143 E.R.938.
430 [1952] 2 All E.R.176.
431 (1795) 6 Term R.320; see *supra*, p.111, for the facts of the case.

she could not perform on that date, and therefore, the promoters entered into an agreement with another singer for the whole engagement; later, on 4th December, she presented herself and the promoters refused her services thereby treating the contract as discharged. It was held that her failure to perform as from the first night was a breach of condition, and therefore the contract was discharged.[432]

On the other hand, if in the above example, the contract was to the effect that she had to be for a rehearsal six days before the opera engagement, i.e. 22nd November, but she was taken ill and she arrived for the rehearsals on 26th November, then she would have had a successful action against the promoters, since the rehearsal clause is subsidiary to the main purposes of the contract, and this amounts to breach of warranty.[433]

(ii) Whether partial performance has been accepted by one party

Note that there must be a genuine exercise of the buyer's choice. Thus, if S agrees to deliver 50 bottles of whisky to B and delivers 40 only, then B may exercise his right to reject the whole consignment. But if B accepts delivery of 40 bottles, then he must pay for them at the contract rate.[434]

(iii) Whether full performance has been prevented by one party

This covers cases where X is prevented by Y, both being parties to a contract, from further performance. In such cases, Y is liable to an action based on *quantum meruit* (as much as he has earned) for the value of work done up to the time when performance was prevented.

Thus, where A made B his agent for the purpose of advertising and selling tickets for a Royal event, on a 10% commission to be made from the sale of the tickets, and B prepared all the advertising leaflets etc. but before he had sold any tickets, A withdrew B's authority to sell the tickets, and therefore, B was prevented from earning any commission, it was held that B could sue A on *quantum meruit* and his action be successful.[435]

In another case,[436] the claimant agreed to write a book on 'Costume and Ancient Armour', on completion of which he was to receive £100. After he had done the necessary research and written part of the book, the publishers abandoned the project. The claimant was entitled to a part payment representing the work done.

---

432 *Poussard* v. *Spiers & Pond* (1876) 1 Q.B.D.410.

433 *Bettini* v. *Gye* (1876) 1 Q.B.D.183.

434 Section 30(1), Sale of Goods Act 1979 (as amended).

435 *De Bernardy* v. *Harding* (1853) 155 E.R.1586.

436 *Planché* v. *Colburn* (1831) 131 E.R.305.

3) BY BREACH

There are several forms of breach of contract. In general, they may be classified as follows:

a) Failure to perform the contract
For example, if a seller fails to deliver goods by the appointed time or where, although delivered, they are not up to standard as to quality or quantity. In such cases it is likely that the breach will be a breach of a condition, and if the innocent/injured party chooses he/she may throw up the contract and treat the contract as discharged.[437]

b) Express repudiation
This occurs where one party states that he will not perform his part of the contract. For example, where A appoints B as his agent, and the appointment is to start being effective in one month's time; after 4 days A states to B that will not require B's services.[438]

c) Some action by one party making performance impossible
An example is where C hires his ship to D for a period of one year and agrees to pay X a commission on the hire received during the charter period. If C sells the ship free of all liability to another person, then C's action would amount to a repudiation of the agreement C had with D and X, and entitles D and X to damages.[439]
In the cases of (b) and (c) above, we have what is called an 'anticipatory breach'. This is a breach which takes place before the time for performance has arrived.

In other words this covers cases where a party states in advance that he does not intend to carry out, fully or partially, his side of the contract or puts himself in a position whereby he will be unable to perform. In such circumstances the aggrieved party may sue at once for damages.

Alternatively, he can wait for the time for performance to arrive and see whether the other party is prepared to carry out the contract. However, it must be noted that if this option is taken, there is a risk that the contract may become discharged e.g. by frustration, or illegality etc.

---

[437] The right of the innocent/injured party to claim damages for the breach remains available in such cases. Of course, it is possible for the innocent/injured party in such cases to accept the defective performance of the contract by the other party, and continue with the contract, but instead claim damages only. Such acceptance is frequently referred to as a 'waiver' or 'affirmation'. Both expressions mean the same thing; the innocent/injured party has waived his right to be treated as discharged from his further obligations, or the innocent/injured party has affirmed the contract.

[438] *Hochster* v. *De la Tour* (1853) 118 E.R.922.

[439] *Omnium D'Enterprises* v. *Sutherland* [1919] 1 K.B.618.

Not every breach entitles the innocent party to treat the contract as discharged. It must be shown that the breach affects a vital part of the contract, i.e. that it is a breach of condition[440] rather than a breach of warranty, or that the other party had no intention of performing his contract.[441]

4) BY FRUSTRATION

In general, for an event to frustrate a contract, it must:

i) occur after the contract is made, and

ii) not be something which is foreseeable,[442] and

iii) not be caused by the act or fault of the party claiming not to be liable for breach of contract, and

iv) make it illegal to carry out the contract or impossible to carry out the contract or renders performance of the contract radically different from that which was contemplated at the time the contract was made.

In order to examine the doctrine of frustration, it is desirable to classify contracts into two main categories, **(a)** contracts for personal service, and **(b)** other contracts.

(a) Contracts for personal service, may be discharged by:

[440] *Poussard* v. *Spiers & Pond* (1876) 1 Q.B.D.410.

[441] *Hochster* v. *De la Tour* (1853) 118 E.R.922; D agreed to engage C's services for a period of three months commencing 1st June. A couple of weeks later, and before performance of the service contract commenced, i.e. before 1st June, D notified C that C's services would not be needed. C sued D for breach of contract in May, and D alleged that C could not start such action before 1st June, i.e. the time for performance of the contract was reached. It was held that C was entitled to commence an action for damages before 1st June.

[442] *Force majeure* clauses in commercial contracts have the effect of entitling the parties to be discharged from further performance, should one or more of the events described in the clause occur. It must be noted that where such clauses purport to apply the doctrine of frustration on the contract, they would be subject to the doctrine's requirements; *Channel Island Ferries Ltd.* v. *Sealink U.K. Ltd.* [1987] 1 Lloyd's Rep.559 (Q.B.D. (Comm)). In this case C and D agreed to a joint venture agreement, whereby they would use their ships to provide a ferry service on the Channel Island route. The agreement contained a broad *force majeure* clause which included strikes. The crews of D's vessels promptly took industrial action and organised sit- ins. C sued D for breach of contract, and D sought to rely on the strike as *force majeure*. It was held that the strikes had not come about for reasons beyond D's control, hence, not within the *force majeure* provision. For a successfully invoked *force majeure* clause, see *Pagnan SpA* v. *Tradax Ocean Transportation SA* [1987] 2 Lloyd's Rep.342.

i) Death: Thus, where A contracted to play the piano at a concert and died before the date of performance, the contract was frustrated, i.e. discharged by frustration.

ii) Incapacity: Incapacity must affect the contract in a fundamental manner, as temporary incapacity is not enough. For example, in one case[443] an opera singer entered into an agreement to take part in an opera starting from 28th November, and because she was taken ill she could not perform on that date, and therefore, the promoters entered into an agreement with another singer for the whole engagement; later, on 4th December, she presented herself and the promoters refused her services thereby treating the contract as discharged. It was held that her failure to perform as from the first night was a breach of condition. Therefore, this affected the contract in a fundamental manner.

The doctrine of frustration only applies where there is no fault by either party,[444] otherwise we must approach such a problem differently.

(b)Other contracts, may be frustrated where there is:

i) Government interference, i.e. requisitioning of goods under emergency powers. Thus, in *Re Shipton, Anderson & Co. and Harrison Bros' Arbitration*,[445] a quantity of wheat was bought from a seller's warehouse. Before delivery and transfer of property occurred however, the Government using its emergency powers in times of war, requisitioned the wheat. As delivery of the wheat could not be made the seller was not in breach of the sale contract.

ii) Destruction of the subject-matter. Thus, in *Taylor* v. *Caldwell*,[446] the claimant hired a music hall for a series of concerts. However, after making the agreement and before the date of the first performance, the hall was destroyed by fire. It was held, that the contract was discharged and parties released from their obligations.

---

443 *Poussard* v. *Spiers & Pond* (1876) 1 Q.B.D.410.

444 *Norris* v. *Southampton City Council*, *The Times*, 27 January, 1982; C was a cleaner and he was convicted of assault and reckless driving and was sentenced to a term of imprisonment. His employers, D, dismissed him, and he claimed that his dismissal was unfair. The Tribunal held that the contract of employment was frustrated and that C was not dismissed and therefore not entitled to compensation. However, the Employment Appeal Tribunal added that frustration could only arise where there was no fault by either party. The impossibility of further performance was brought by Norris's fault.

445 [1915] 3 K.B.676.

446 (1863) 122 E.R.309.

iii) Non-occurrence of an event. In such cases, the contract must be substantially affected. Thus, in *Krell* v. *Henry*,[447] D hired a room overlooking the route of Edward VII's coronation procession. The procession was cancelled owing to the King's serious illness. Although it would have been possible to come and sit in the room, the main purpose of the contract, to view the procession, had been destroyed. Held, that contract had been frustrated.

iv) Commercial purpose of the contract has been defeated (although performance possible). *Krell* v. *Henry* above may be contrasted with *Tsakiroglou & Co. Ltd.* v. *Noblee*[448] where C, the sellers, agreed to deliver the goods to D, the buyers, in Hamburg. The sellers, C, failed to deliver, and their defence to D's claim was that the contract had been frustrated due to the closure of the Suez Canal. Held, that this was not sufficient to render the contract frustrated. In other words, mere inconvenience and extra expense would not be sufficient grounds for the doctrine of frustration to operate.

The doctrine of frustration will not apply where the parties have made provisions in the contract. Thus, in *Clark* v. *Lindsay*,[449] the contracts provided that if the coronation procession of Edward VII was postponed the tickets would be valid for the day on which it did take place or that the parties should get their money back with a deduction for the room owner's expenses. Therefore, the cancellation of the procession did not render the contracts frustrated.

The doctrine of frustration will not apply, where the frustrating event is self-induced.[450] Furthermore, it seems that frustration is not generally applicable to leases and contracts for the sale of land. The reason is probably that the property continues to exist or survives the frustrating event. However, it might be said that the lease of cliff land would be frustrated if the land slipped into the sea. Judicial opinion has been divided upon the issue of whether leases and contracts for the sale of land can be frustrated.[451]

---

[447] [1903] 2 K.B.740.

[448] *Tsakiroglou & Co. Ltd.* v. *Noblee and Thorl GmbH* [1962] A.C.93.

[449] *Clark* v. *Lindsay* (1903) 19 T.L.R.202.

[450] *Norris* v. *Southampton City Council*, *The Times*, 27 January, 1982. See also, *Ocean Tramp Tankers Corp.* v. *V/O Sovfracht, The Eugenia*, [1964] 2 Q.B.226, C.A. In *J. Lauritzen A.S.* v. *Wijsmuller B.V., The Super Servant Two*, [1990] 1 Lloyd's Rep.1, C.A., the existence of a choice between two vessels was provided in the contract but D did not exercise it when one of the two vessels was lost, and subsequently claimed frustration. It was held that since D had elected not to make the alternative vessel available to C, the contract was not frustrated.

[451] *Cricklewood Property and Investment Trust Ltd.* v. *Leighton's Investment Trust Ltd.* [1945] A.C. 221; C leased some land to D for a period of 99 years and with the proviso that (i) D were going to build some shops within the period of the first 12 months, and (ii) ground rent would only be assessed and commence being payable upon notification by C relating to the of the building of the shops. Once D obtained notification, C (the lessors) claimed payment of the

Before the Law Reform (Frustrated Contracts) Act 1943 became law, money due and not paid could be claimed and money paid before the frustrating event was not recoverable.[452] However, after 1943, i.e. the Law Reform (Frustrated Contracts) Act, money paid is recoverable, and money payable ceases to be payable. Furthermore, the Act provides that the parties may recover expenses in connection with the contract, or retain the relevant sum from money received. It is also possible to recover on a *quantum meruit*, in respect of part performance before the frustrating event, provided the other party, received 'a valuable benefit'.[453] In real terms the way this compensation is awarded, is twofold:

a) the Court will consider the actual value of the valuable benefit;

b) the 'just' sum which will include expenses.

The Act states that the provision of valuable benefit will apply each part of a divisible contract, as if each were a separate contract.

---

ground rents. D (the lessees) repudiated liability on the ground that the obligation to pay rent had been discharged by frustration, because of the war-time restrictions placed by the Government on building, which had made it impossible to erect the shops. It was held, that even if the doctrine of frustration could apply to a lease, the circumstances did not justify such application; the lease had not been determined by frustration, and the liability for rent continued. *Hillingdon Estates Co.* v. *Stonefield Estates Ltd.* [1952] Ch. 627; in 1938, C entered into a contract for the sale of certain lands to D, the purchasers. In 1948, the City Council made a compulsory purchase order affecting one piece of land. A few weeks later notices were served by the City Council on the sellers and purchasers. D, the purchasers, alleged that they were discharged by frustration, on or before the date of the service of the notices, from liability to perform any of the agreements on their part contained in the contract and became entitled to recover from C, the sellers, a sum representing interest on the purchase price of the affected piece of land. D, the sellers, counter-claimed for specific performance of the contract. Held, the contract had not been frustrated, since the compulsory purchase order duly affected D, the sellers, in so far as they were given notice of it, and, if they chose to enforce the contract, they were under no obligation to do anything except to convey the property subject to, among other things, the compulsory purchase order. The reason for the Court's finding although it might seem odd at first sight, is very sound in so far as principles of land law are concerned. When there is a contract by S to sell land to B at a certain price, in English law B becomes the owner in equity of the land, subject, of course, to his obligation to perform his part of the contract by paying the purchase money. From the moment the contract is entered into S holds the legal estate as trustee for B, the purchaser.

[452] Thus, in *Chandler* v. *Webster* [1904] 1 K.B.493, D agreed to let C have a room for the purpose of viewing the coronation procession, for £141 15s. The contract provided that the money be payable immediately. The procession did not take place and C, who had paid £100 on account, left the balance unpaid. Furthermore, C sued to recover the £100 and D counter-claimed for £41 15s. It was held that C's action failed and D's counter-claim succeeded because the obligation to pay the rent had fallen due before the frustrating event. This was a very strict rule, and a distinction was drawn on such matters by the House of Lords in *Fibroasa Spolka Akcyjna* v. *Fairbairn Lawson Combe Barbour Ltd.* [1943] A.C.32; advance payments could be recovered only where there was a total failure of consideration.

[453] *B.P. Exploration* v. *Hund* (1983) 2 A.C.352.

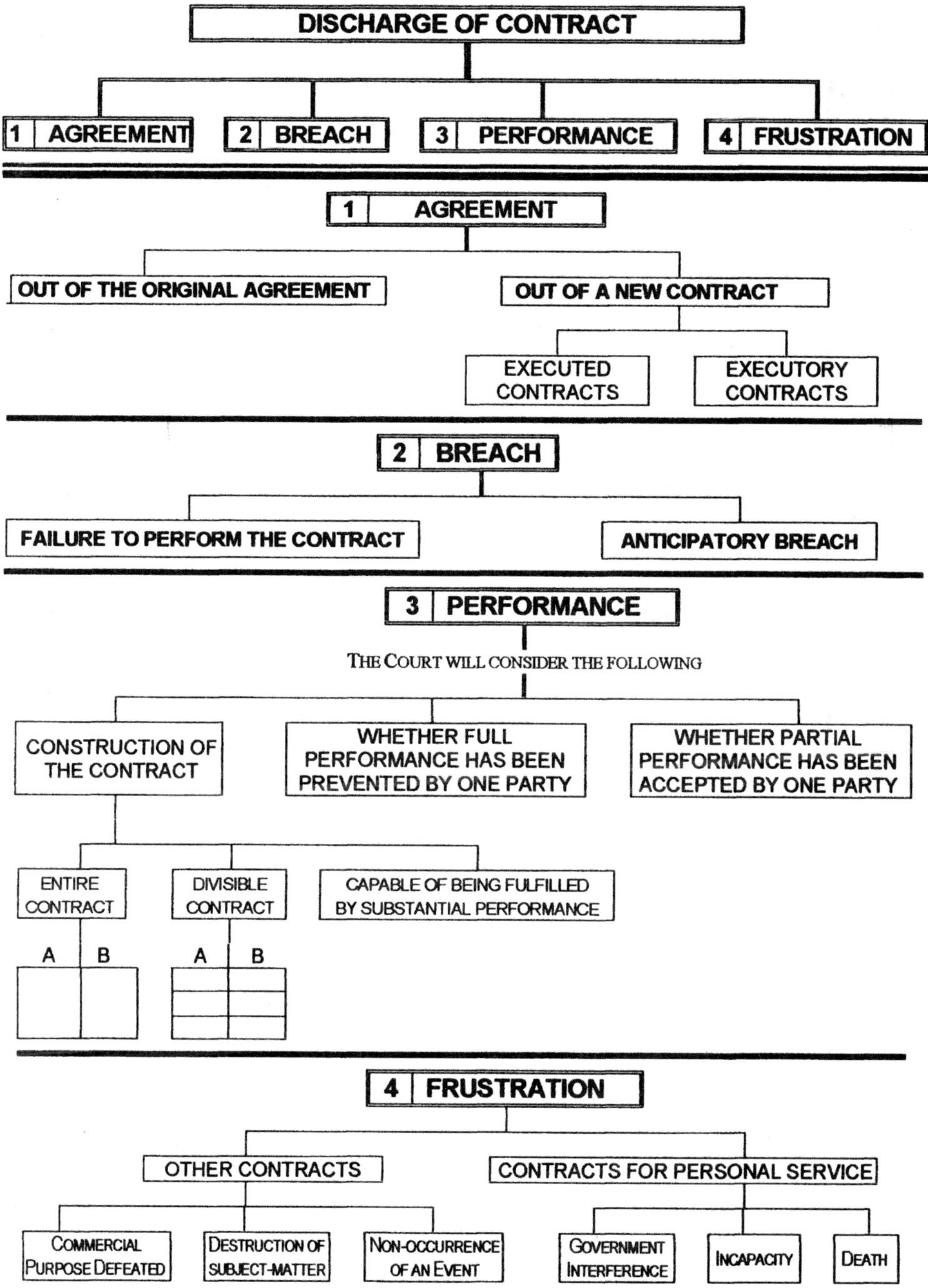

Diagram 7: Discharge of Contract

The Law Governing a Contract

It is of great importance for the parties to know what law governs the contract that they have made, because the law for example, of sale and agency differs from country to country. Even where it is clear that the applicable law is that of another country, the contents of that law still have to be proved to the judge in the ordinary way by expert witnesses or some other admissible evidence. It is often very difficult to decide whether a particular contract is to be governed by the law of one country or that of another. For example, a contract to work for a French employer in France may be made in England; is French or English law to apply? If the contract states clearly that one or other of the conflicting systems is to prevail, this will be *prima facie* evidence that the system mentioned is to govern the contract; but if no such clause is included, the Court will endeavour to ascertain the intention of the parties, and effect will be given to that intention as far as possible.

The law intended by the parties is often referred to as 'the proper law of the contract'. This must not be confused with the expression 'forum', which refers to the place where jurisdiction would be exercised in a particular case. For example, where a Japanese person is sued in England on a contract made in Italy which provides that German law would apply, the forum/place is England, whereas the applicable/proper law would be that of Germany. In very simple words, in the circumstances of this example, an English Court will hear the case, and will apply German law to resolve the contract dispute.

What follows is a brief explanation of the Rome Convention 1980 and the Common Law principles, which determine the applicable law in a contract. For completeness, some references are also made to the 1986 Hague Convention on the law applicable to Contracts for the International Sale of Goods (hereinafter referred to as 'the 1986 Hague Convention').

The Contracts (Applicable Law) Act 1990

The Contracts (Applicable Law) Act 1990 has brought into force the 1980 Rome Convention on the Law Applicable to Contractual Obligations, and came into force in April 1991. This is the legislation covering questions of 'applicable law' to govern a contract or 'proper law' as it is best known in the U.K. The Convention applies to contractual obligations in any situation involving a choice between the laws of different countries. Therefore, it applies to any contract with an international flavour not just those which have an E.C. connection.

> 'A contract shall be governed by the law chosen by the parties. The choice must be express or demonstrated with reasonable certainty by the terms of the contract or the circumstances of the case. By their

choice the parties can select the law applicable to the whole or a part only of a contract.'

Thus, it is clear from the above quoted Article 3(1) that where the intention of the parties is clearly expressed generally no difficulty will arise,[454] but where no definite expression of intention is made it is necessary to presume intention from the attendant circumstances. There are a number of important exclusions to the application of the Convention:

1)Certain obligations arising under bills of exchange, cheques and other negotiable instruments;

2)Arbitration agreements[455] and agreements on the choice of Court, i.e. jurisdiction clauses;

3)It does not cover trusts, matrimonial matters and questions on capacity.

4)It does not apply to contracts of insurance which cover risks situated in the territories of member states of the E.C., although it does apply to contracts of re-insurance.

If no law has been expressly or impliedly chosen by the parties, Article 4(1) provides that 'the contract shall be governed by the law of the country with which it is most closely connected'.[456]

The Convention lays down some rebuttable presumptions in order to determine this close connection between the contract and the country. This is presumed by Article 4(2) as the law of the country of the party making the 'characteristic performance'.[457] In a contract of sale, this will most probably be the seller's country.[458]

---

[454] Almost identical provision can be found in Art.7(1) of the 1986 Hague Convention. Similarly, the freedom to chose the applicable law is retained in the Electronic Commerce (E.C. Directive) Regulations 2002 (S.I.2002, No.2013).

[455] It must be noted that arbitration agreements are considered as separate agreements within a contract. For arbitration, see *supra*, p.14.

[456] This contrasts with Art.8(1) main 'test' under the 1986 Hague Convention, which refers to 'the law of the State where the seller has his place of business at the time of conclusion of the contract'. However, a similar 'test' applies under Art.14(1) which defines 'the relevant place of business' as being the one 'which has the closest relationship to the contract and its performance'.

[457] *Ennstone Building Products Ltd.* v. *Stanger Ltd. (No.2)* [2002] EWCA Civ. 916; the presumption of Article 4(2) was not overridden where two English companies concluded a contract in Scotland, the contract was to be performed in Scotland, and a breach of the contract occurred in Scotland. Thus, English law was the appropriate law to apply to such contract, since it was closely connected with England.

[458] In an employment contract the law applicable has been held to be that of the State where the employee principally works; *Mulox* I.B.C. v. *Geels* [1994] I.R.L.R.422. The performance

Where the parties have agreed on the law of contract, but a subsequent assignment/transfer of the benefit of the contract takes place, i.e. the contract is assigned/transferred by one party of the contract to a third party, then such agreement of assignment/transfer is likely to be governed by the law of the contract to be transferred.[459]

The Convention also provides that, in the case of a contract for the carriage of goods, 'if the country in which, at the time the contract is concluded, the carrier has his principal place of business is also the country in which the place of loading or the place of discharge or the principal place of business of the consignor is situated, it shall be presumed that the contract is most closely connected with that country'. In other words there is a rebuttable presumption that if, for example, X has to effect the performance which is characteristic of his contract with Y, then the law of the state where X's place of business is situated will apply. However, Article 5(5) states that the presumptions laid down by the Convention should not be applied if 'it appears from the circumstances as a whole that the contract is more closely connected with another country'.[460]

Since, in broad terms, the Convention continues to recognise the right of the parties to choose the applicable law, it is likely to be even more important than before to ensure that the appropriate governing law is clearly spelt out in the contract.

UNDER COMMON LAW

It should be noted that in determining the proper law of a contract made before April 1991, i.e. before the Act came into force, or contracts which are not

which is characteristic in a guarantee contract is the duty to pay; *Samcrete Egypt Engineers & Contractors SAE* v. *Land Rover Exports Ltd.* [2001] EWCA Civ 2019, where C and X entered into a distributorship agreement subject to English law and Court jurisdiction, but only after C was provided with a guarantee from D, who were the parent company of X. The guarantee did not include a choice of law clause, and stated that any payments due to C will be made in England. A dispute arose between C and D, and consequently, C commenced legal proceedings under the guarantee contract, in England. The question arose as to whether the characteristic performance of the guarantee contract was to be made in Egypt, where D had its seat, or England, where C had its seat. There was sufficient evidence of connection to England, including the fact that the payment under the guarantee was to be made in England, and that the distributorship agreement made England the country most closely connected to the contract of guarantee.

459 *Raiffeisen Zentralbank Osterreich AG* v. *Five Star General Trading LLC (The Mount I)* [2001] 1 Lloyd's Rep.597, C.A.; D contended that an assignment of an insurance policy was invalid since under the Rome Convention the notice of assignment involved a transfer of property and as the claim was a proprietary one, it was governed by French law (*lex situs*). It was held that the assignment was an assignment of a contractual obligation and as such, in English law, the Rome Convention should apply. Further, that since the insurers and the insured had agreed for their insurance contract to be governed by English law, the assignment should also be governed by English law.

460 Articles 8(3) and 18 of the 1986 Hague Convention contain very similar provisions.

covered by the Act, the rules of Common Law would be applicable. In the absence of contrary evidence it is presumed that the parties intend the contract to be governed by the law of the country of performance.

The Courts tend to apply as the relevant test of the applicable proper law: 'With which system of law has the contract its closest and most real connection?' As mentioned above, the basic rule is that the applicable law is that stated in the agreement between the parties or, where no such express agreement exists, it may be possible for the court to infer the law intended from the circumstances of the case. The following points should be noted:

- The proper law is to be decided by reference to a system of law and not to a particular country.
- The proper law is ascertained in relation to the situation at the time the contract is made.
- It is possible for different aspects of the contract to be decided by reference to different legal systems. This is called *depecage*.[461]

THE LAW INTENDED BY THE PARTIES

The parties may choose any law that they wish, even if the contract has no connection with it.[462] However, this choice must be exercised for a *bona fide* purpose and not merely to avoid statutory control. For instance, the mandatory provisions of the Unfair Contract Terms Act 1977 cannot be contracted out of by the parties.[463]

CLOSE CONNECTION

The following factors are considered by the Court when deciding this issue:

1) The form of the contract.
2) The place where the contract was concluded.
3) The place where the contract is to be performed.
4) The parties' place of residence and business.

---

[461] This is also recognised by Art.7(1) of the 1986 Hague Convention, which recognises that the parties' choice of applicable law 'may be limited to a part of the contract'.

[462] *Amin Rasheed Shipping Corp.* v. *Kuwait Insurance Co. (The Al Wahab)* [1984] A.C.50, H.L.

[463] See *infra*, p.186.

5) The place where an arbitration is to be held.

6) The personality of the parties.

1) The form of the contract

Generally speaking, the form of the contract carries as little weight as the language which the parties have used, especially as English is the recognised language of commerce. The same is also true about the currency of payment. Nevertheless, these factors taken together usually do provide a clue as to the ascertainment of the law of the closest connection.[464]

2) The place where the contract was concluded

This is a factor of considerable importance, particularly so when the contract has to be performed in the same place, or under the same jurisdiction. As it usually is the case in international trade, a contract is concluded between two parties who are not present in the same country. In this case, note that the contract is supposed to have been concluded at the place where its acceptance is effected.[465]

3) The place where the contract is to be performed

This is a very important factor in deciding which is the law governing a contract. It would appear that it is more weighty a factor than the place where the contract was concluded, therefore, great importance should be attached to it.[466]

4) The parties' place of residence and business

The capacity of the parties to a contract is in general governed by the law of their domicile at the time when the contract was made. A person's domicile is

---

[464] *Whitworth Street Estates (Manchester) Ltd.* v. *James Miller & Partners Ltd.* [1970] A.C.583, H.L.; the parties entered into a standard form agreement published by the Royal Institute of British Architects (R.I.B.A.). A dispute arose, and the House of Lords held, *inter alia*, that the use of the English R.I.B.A. form contract indicated an intention that English law was the proper law of the agreement.

[465] Thus, if X in Paris receives a shipment order from Y in Japan on C.I.F. Tokyo terms and X accepts this order, the likely governing law of the contract will be French, as it is to be performed in France by delivery of the goods on board a ship sailing for the agreed port of destination; *Johnson* v. *Taylor Bros. & Co. Ltd.* [1920] A.C.144, H.L. *Brinkibon Ltd.* v. *Stahag Stahl und Stahlwarenhandelsgesellschaft mbH.* [1983] 2 A.C.34; the Court held that an acceptance by telex from England to Austria caused a contract to be made in Austria, i.e. where the contract was concluded.

[466] Thus, in *Benaim & Co.* v. *Debono* [1924] A.C.514, an offer by X in Gibraltar to sell on F.O.B. terms to Y in Malta was made and accepted. Y rejected the goods and the question arose as to whether the law of Gibraltar or Malta applied to the contract. It was held that although the posting of the acceptance letter took place in Malta and therefore the contract was concluded in Malta, the place of performance was Gibraltar since the goods were shipped F.O.B. Gibraltar. Thus, the applicable law was that of Gibraltar.

the country in which he has his permanent home. Domicile must be distinguished from nationality, which is the political relation that exists between an individual and the State to which he owes allegiance. In order to make the distinction clearer, domicile determines civil rights and obligation, e.g. right of marriage and succession, whereas nationality determines public rights and obligations, e.g. the right to vote or to hold political office.
Finally, it must be noted, that there is one exception to the rule relating to the capacity of the parties, in an ordinary mercantile contract. In particular, capacity in the case of such contracts is governed by the law of the country where the contract is made.

5) The place where an arbitration is to be held
This is another factor, which only gives an indication of the intended governing law. It is quite a weighty indication, as it infers that the parties intend to submit the contract to the law of the place of arbitration.[467]

SOME ADDITIONAL RULES APPLICABLE TO FOREIGN CONTRACTS

The following is a more detailed account of the main rules for determining conflicts between English and foreign law in the English Courts:

1) A contract otherwise valid cannot be enforced in England if its enforcement is opposed to an English rule of procedure. For example, the English Limitation Act 1980 will apply to foreign contracts sued upon in the English Courts. If X, an Englishman, in France, enters into an oral contract with B, a Frenchman, and the contract is one which by English law must be evidenced in writing, it is unenforceable in the English Courts, even if French law requires no written evidence.
   The principle is that the procedure and the rules of evidence to be applied are those in force in the country in which the litigation occurs.

2) The form of the contract is in general governed by the law of the country in which the contract is made. Obviously, this rule is not applicable where the parties intend the contract to operate in and be subject to the law of some other country.

---

[467] *Compagnie Tunisienne de Navigation SA* v. *Compagnie d'Armement Maritime SA* [1971] A.C.572, H.L.; the charter-party had an English arbitration clause, but a choice of law clause in terms that the contract should be 'governed by the law of the flag of the vessel carrying the goods'. Another clause stated that the ship was to be 'governed or controlled or chartered by French shipowners'. Therefore, it appears that the parties anticipated that ships flying French flags would be employed. In fact, shipments were mad on a number of ships flying differing flags. It was held that the two clauses pointed to a choice of French law.

3) The validity and construction of a contract is governed by the law of the country to which the parties intended to submit themselves. In connection to this, it should be noted that the sections relating to the avoidance of liability for negligence, unreasonable indemnity clauses, etc. of the Unfair Contract Terms Act 1977[468] will not operate as part of the proper law, where the proper law of a contract is the law of any part of the U.K. only by choice of the parties (and apart from that choice would be the law of some country outside the U.K.).
   In other words, where two parties, say an Italian and an American, have entered into a contract in New York, and the place of performance is to be the U.S.A., under normal circumstances, the law of the U.S.A. will govern such a contract. If, however, the contract provides that the proper law is to be that of the U.K., then the U.K. law will be the proper law (by choice) and the sections of the Unfair Contract Terms Act 1977 relating to the avoidance of liability for negligence, unreasonable indemnity clauses, etc. will not be applicable. The remaining sections of the Act, of course, will be applicable.

4) Discharge of contract is governed by the proper law. Foreign law will not receive judicial notice by the English Courts, but must be proved by an expert witness. Note that under the European Communities Act 1972, judicial notice is to be taken of the Treaties referred to in the Act, and of any decision or expression of opinion, by the European Court of Justice.

APPLICABLE LAW, *FORUM*, AND RECOGNITION OF JUDGMENTS

An English Court dealing with a civil case that may involve a foreign element must determine three issues:

1. Whether an English Court is the appropriate place to hear a case (*forum*).

2. Which law governs the dispute.

3. Will an English court recognise and enforce judgements made by a foreign Court.

In many cases an English Court will seek connecting factors to decide what law governs any particular situation. For example, where a tort was committed, or where a contract was to be performed, or where a marriage took place, or the law of the place where a property is situated.

---

[468] See *infra*, p.189.

Torts

Under common law with regards to torts committed in England the Courts applied English law, even in situations where the parties involved were not British or where the connection with England was limited (e.g. a libel written in Switzerland but published in England). This was the principle of 'double actionability'.[469] This rule required that the tortuous act must be actionable in both (a) England, and (b) the country where the tort was committed. These conditions of common law have been modified by Part 3 of the Private International Law (Miscellaneous Provisions) Act 1995, which amends the applicable law to that of *lex loci delicti*, i.e. the law of the place where the tort was committed.[470] In particular, where the tort occurs in different countries the applicable law (i) in respect of personal injury or death is that of the country where the individual was when he sustained the injury, (ii) in respect of damage to property is that of the place where the property was when damaged, and (iii) in respect of all other cases is the law of the country in which the most significant element of those events occurred.[471]

Property

Property located outside the E.C. is dealt with in a fairly straightforward manner. English Courts have no right to try cases to determine title to a property, or right of possession, regardless of the nationality of the parties to the proceedings. Torts relating to the property, i.e. trespass may be tried in England subject to the restrictions above.

Within the E.C. exclusive jurisdiction of the Courts lies in the country where the property is located.

The Law of the Person

This used to be fairly straightforward, the English Court would exercise jurisdiction over a wide range of persons in circumstances that many other courts would not recognise. English Courts had jurisdiction over anyone who was in the country who was served a writ at that time. The dispute may not necessarily be anyway connected with anything in England at all, the presence of the person in the country was sufficient.

However the Brussels Convention on Jurisdiction and Enforcement of Judgments in Civil and Commercial Matters 1968, which deals with the jurisdiction of Courts within the E.C., states that a Court has jurisdiction in the country of domicile of the defendant. This also applies to corporations or partnerships.

---

[469] *Phillips* v. *Eyre* (1870-71) L.R. 6 Q.B.1; *Boys* v. *Chaplin* [1971] A.C.536. See also *Gotha City* v. *Sotheby's (No.2)*, *The Times*, 8 October, 1998.

[470] *Kuwait Airways Corp.* v. *Iraqi Airways Co. (Damages)* [2004] EWHC 2603.

[471] Section 11, Private International Law (Miscellaneous Provisions) Act 1995.

For defendants outside the E.C. the issue is more complex. Under normal circumstances if the defendant in a civil case is outside the U.K. then the Court has no jurisdiction. However under certain circumstances the High Court may give the claimant permission to serve a writ out of jurisdiction if they can prove that they have a good arguable case and that it falls under one or more heads. The High Court has to be satisfied that England is the 'forum' in which the case can be suitably tried. The burden of proof to establish this lies with the claimant.

Recognition & Enforcement of Foreign Judgments

Just as the English Courts have to decide to test which law applies in a case, similarly there is the problem of deciding if judgements in a foreign Court that may involve an English element will be enforced.

For judgements rendered in a foreign Court outside the E.C. and the Commonwealth[472] the situation is governed by the Foreign Judgements (Reciprocal Enforcement's) Act 1933. This provides for judgements to be enforced in English Courts, providing that the Court was jurisdictionally competent to render a judgement the defendant must have been resident in that country.

E.C. member States, must recognise judgements given by the Courts of other members. This is now regulated by the European 'Judgments Regulation'.[473] Therefore, all civil and commercial matters are governed by the European Judgment Regulation[474] unless they involve:

- -taxation
- -customs
- -social security
- -bankruptcy or insolvency
- -matrimonial
- -wills and succession
- -arbitration

[472] Judgments obtained by Commonwealth countries are enforced by the application of the Administration of Justice Act 1920.

[473] Council Regulation (E.C.) No. 44/2001 of 22nd December 2000 on Jurisdiction and the Recognition and Enforcement of Judgments in Civil and Commercial Matters. The Regulation applies to all judgments after 1st March 2002, and applies to all E.C. member States except Denmark. The important part to note is that under Article 23(1) of the Judgments Regulation the parties are free to choose which Court will have jurisdiction and this jurisdiction will be exclusive unless the parties have agreed otherwise.

[474] As supplemented by the Civil Jurisdiction and Judgments Order 2001.

CHAPTER 5

THE LAW OF AGENCY

An agent is a person employed by a principal to make contracts on his behalf with third parties. An employee who makes contracts on behalf of his employer is acting as an agent. A shop assistant, for example, is in this category. A person who wishes to sell shares will usually employ the services of a stockbroker to arrange the sale for him. Agents are given a number of names, the most common being 'broker', 'representative', or 'factor'. The ordinary rules of contract apply to the contract of agency. Therefore, three rules must be considered, in so far as capacity is concerned:

1) The third party must have capacity to contract in order that the contract which the agent makes with him on behalf of the principal may be enforceable. In other words, the ordinary rules concerning capacity are applicable.

2) The agent must have capacity to contract if his contract with the principal is to be enforceable; otherwise agent and principal may not be able to enforce the rights and duties arising under the contract of agency. Thus, if a minor appoints a person his agent, the contract of agency will be unenforceable.

3) However, a person who lacks legal capacity to make a contract does not lose that incapacity by employment of an agent. Thus, a minor who has merely a restricted capacity to contract as a principal, may be appointed to act as agent for any purpose for a principal who has full contractual capacity; but a minor cannot, by appointing another person to contract for him as agent, overcome his own lack of capacity to make certain contracts.[475]

CLASSIFICATION OF AGENTS

There are various classifications of agents. For example, they may be divided according to the degree of authority which they possess:

1) **UNIVERSAL AGENTS**: who have unrestricted authority (such agents are rarely met with in practice). The principal is bound by all acts having legal

[475] *G.* v. *G.* [1970] 3 All E.R.546, C.A.

significance done on his behalf by his universal agent. This power/authority which this kind of agents enjoy, is called a 'power of attorney'.

2) **Special Agents**: who are appointed only for a specific purpose or occasion to which their authority is restricted, or in respect of a matter not within the ordinary course of their business or profession. If a special agent does anything outside his authority, the principal is not necessarily bound by it; and a third party is not entitled to assume that the agent has unlimited powers, but should make due enquiry as to the extent of his authority. Thus, an estate agent may be appointed to sell a house; once a buyer has been found and the contracts have been exchanged the agent is rewarded and the authority lapses.

3) **General Agents**: who are appointed to do anything within the authority given to them by the principal in all transactions, or in all transactions relating to a specified trade or matter. (Many of the agencies created in international trade are of this type).

Another classification depends upon the agent's liability:

1) Agents who are not, as a rule, personally liable to their principals in respect of contracts entered into by them on behalf of their principals.

2) ***Del Credere* Agent**: which is one that is answerable to his principal for due payment by third parties to whom he has sold goods on behalf of his principal.[476] He is liable only if the third party cannot pay. He is not liable, if, say, the third party refuses to take delivery. He guarantees that payment will be made by the other party (third party) with whom he has contracted on behalf of the principal. A *del credere* agent is paid an extra commission to compensate him for the extra risk undertaken as surety. In other words, the liability of such an agent to the principal, as a surety for the buyer, is limited to cases where there is an ascertained amount or certain sum due as a debt from the buyer to the principal, and the buyer fails to pay, either through insolvency or some other event that makes it impossible to recover payment.

3) **Confirming House**: which is mainly involved in overseas trade and arises where an exporter in this country on receiving an order from a customer abroad obtains confirmation from some third person either in the buyer's country or here. This third person, as confirming agent, assumes liability to the supplying exporter, if the buyer fails to perform the contract.

Agents may also be classified according to their functions, for example:

[476] *Hornby* v. *Lacy* (1817) 6 M.& S.166.

1) **FACTORS OR 'MERCANTILE AGENTS'**: A factor is a mercantile agent, or 'a person having in the customary course of his business as such agent authority either to sell goods, or to consign goods for the purpose of sale, or to buy goods, or to raise money on the security of goods, or to consign goods for the purpose of sale, or to buy goods, or to raise money on the security of goods'.[477] The essential feature of a factor is that he holds stock, not as a mere bailee like a carrier, but as a mercantile agent for the purpose of sale. In short, a factor is a mercantile agent to whom goods are consigned for sale by the principal. Furthermore, he is authorised to sell in his own name. From the above definition the following points arise:

   (a) Mercantile Agent: An agent is a factor if, and only if, it is in the customary course of his business as such agent (i) to sell goods, or (ii) to consign goods for sale, or (iii) to buy goods, or (iv) to raise money on the security of goods. Therefore, a person will normally be considered a factor, or become a factor, if any of the above four requirements is satisfied.

   (b) Customary course of business: This does not mean that a person has to be normally in business as a factor, nor a known kind of commercial agent. For example, a man who normally sells second-hand furniture which he has previously bought on his own account, becomes a factor if he undertakes to sell a bedroom suite for a principal.

   (c) He must be authorised to sell the goods in his own name without saying he is an agent. Thus, in *Rolls Razor* v. *Cox*,[478] X was a self-employed door to door salesman of washing machines. Y was a company that supplied him with stock and a van. Y went into liquidation owing to X money for commission on goods sold. X wished to keep Y's goods until he was paid in full rather than prove in the liquidation. X alleged he could do this by exercising a factor's right of general lien. X needed to do this because Y did not owe him money on the goods in his hands but on goods already sold. It was held that he (X) was not a factor and not entitled to a factor's lien.

2) **BROKERS**: These differ from factors in being agents who buy or sell goods on behalf of their principals but without handling the actual goods. They are agents for both the buyer and the seller, bringing together parties in opposite situations to their mutual satisfaction in return for a commission called brokerage.

---

[477] Section 1(1), Factors Act 1889.

[478] *Rolls Razor Ltd.* v *Cox* [1967] 1 Q.B.552, C.A.

3) Bankers

4) Forwarding Agents

5) Servants

6) Estate Agents

7) Wife, Housekeeper, etc.

Distributors

One of the options open to an exporter, when considering securing a steady flow of export orders, is the conclusion of a distribution agreement with an importer abroad. This, would effectively, assist the exporter in achieving intensive exports by establishing a permanent marketing organisation overseas, whose duty would be to create and maintain a demand for the goods in question.

Frequently, one hears the expressions 'sole' or 'exclusive' being used, in connection to rights of representation by agents and distributors. However, there is no clear meaning attached to these terms, and therefore, it is preferable for the parties to make sure that in their agreement they clarify the rights which they intend the distributor to have. Alternatively, it would appear that the following meaning may be attributed to the terms 'sole' and 'exclusive':

(a) Both terms imply that the supplier shall not be entitled to appoint another distributor or agent, in the case of agency, for the allotted territory.

(b) If the representation is 'sole', the supplier or principal himself may undertake sales in the allotted territory on his own account without any liability.

(c) If the representation is 'exclusive', the supplier or principal is not allowed himself to compete with the distributor or representative in the allotted territory. This interpretation is supported by the definition of the word 'exclusive' found in the Copyright, Designs and Patents Act 1988, where the term 'exclusive licence' is defined.[479]

Sole distribution agreements usually provide that the supplier/seller, grants the distributor/buyer sole trading rights within a particular territory with respect to goods of a specified kind while the distributor/buyer may undertake to rely on the supplier/seller as the sole source of supply whenever he requires to buy

[479] Section 92(1) of the Copyright, Designs and Patents Act 1988, defines an 'exclusive licence' as one '...authorising the licensee to the exclusion of all other persons, including the person granting the licence...'.

goods of the specified kind. Where such a contract is concluded between X, a manufacturer of computers in the U.K., and Y, an Indian importer, X is not entitled to appoint another distributor for his computers in India, nor, if that is the intention of the parties, is Y at liberty to buy competitive makes of computers in the U.K.

It must be noted that the sole distributor is not an agent of the British manufacturer or merchant.[480] Unlike an agent, the sole distributor does not act on behalf of the British supplier/seller and is not accountable to him for the profits derived from the resale of the goods in his own territory. Furthermore, the profit of the sole distributor is normally the difference between the buying and selling price whereas the profit of the agent is usually the commission which he earns when concluding a sales contract on behalf of his principal, or when the principal concludes a sales contract with a customer introduced by the agent.

The sole distribution agreement differs from an exclusive agency agreement also in another aspect; the contracts which are concluded within the distributorship framework are proper contracts of sale by which the foreign merchant (the distributor) buys in his own name and when he resells the goods in his territory no contractual bond is normally established between the re-purchaser and the British supplier/seller. A sole distribution agreement might further be concluded between an exporter in the U.K. and a manufacturer or wholesaler also in the U.K. In this case the exporter, who is sometimes referred to as 'export distributor', is granted the exclusive right of distributing the manufacturer's goods abroad, either anywhere or in a specified market. Two types of export distribution agreements are in use and the contract should make it clear which type is intended: (i) under some export distribution agreements the distributor undertakes to place annually orders of a fixed amount with the manufacturer, and (ii) under other agreements he merely undertakes to place such orders if and when he receives them from his customers abroad.

Finally, note that care should be taken in drafting a sole/exclusive distributorship agreement so that its terms do not infringe the provisions of Article 81 of the E.C. Treaty of Rome.[481]

CREATION OF AGENCY

In this connection the following points should be noted:

1) Agents may be appointed either expressly or impliedly. Agency may be implied from the particular relationship of two persons.

---

[480] A distributor would not normally be considered as a 'commercial agent'; *A.M.B. Imballaggii Plastici S.R.L.* v. *Pacflex Ltd.* [1999] 2 All E.R. (Comm.) 249.

[481] *Infra*, pp.199-202.

2) Persons who allow a person to act as their agent must have authority to appoint him. Therefore, a person without authority himself cannot make representations as to the authority of others.[482] In other words, assume that you are an employee in a life insurance firm, and the branch manager says 'you now have authority to effect any shipping contracts on behalf of the firm'. You enter into a contract with someone on behalf of the firm to, say, build a ship. If the branch manager had no authority to bind the firm on matters concerning shipbuilding, (as the company is a life insurance company) then you have no authority to bind the firm either, in respect of shipbuilding.

AUTHORITY

In this respect, we are concerned with actual authority and ostensible (apparent) authority.

1) ACTUAL AUTHORITY

This may arise as follows:

a) **ACTUAL AUTHORITY by express agreement**: This means that the agent is entitled to exercise the powers actually given to him under the contract of agency, and will bind the principal by the exercise of those powers.

b) **ACTUAL AUTHORITY by implication**: The Courts would be prepared to imply powers arising out of a contract of agency, when these powers are ordinarily or necessarily incidental to the performance of his express authority.[483] In other words, Courts will look at the task undertaken by the

[482] Thus, in *British Bank of the Middle East* v. *Sun Life Assurance of Canada (U.K.) Ltd.*. [1983] 2 Lloyd's Rep.9, the House of Lords decided that X, a manager of Sun Life, had no authority to bind the company to a transaction concerning life assurance and mortgage protection with Y. The fact that Z, a branch manager, who was X's senior, had held him out as having authority did not affect the decision because Z, the branch manager, had no authority to bind Sun Life in the matters concerned. All matters relating to life assurance and mortgage protection had to be referred to head office.

[483] Thus, in *Comber* v. *Anderson* (1808) 1 Camp.523, X instructed his agent, an insurance broker, to insure a cargo of corn, but gave no specific instructions as to the type of policy or with whom it was to be effected. The broker effected a policy with a company which used an exception clause excluding liability for the loss of cargo by the stranding of the ship. The ship stranded and there was a loss for which X could not recover under the policy. The question arose as to whether the agent was liable as having no authority to effect such a policy. It was held, that since the agent was given a discretion, authority to make the sort of policy he had made was implied. There was no suggestion of fraud and the agent was free to elect as between insurers.

agent under the agency agreement and will infer some additional authority arising in the course of the performance of the agency agreement. This authority is implied and dependent on the actual task undertaken.

c) **ACTUAL AUTHORITY derived from customary/usual authority**: Where the agent is one of a class of agents, e.g. estate agent, factor, solicitor,[484] etc. his actual authority may be extended to cover the powers which an agent of his class normally possesses.[485] This means that Courts will look at the usual or customary authority, which an agent of the particular type enjoys. For example, if you ask a person to find a three bedroom house and buy it for you for a certain price, and in the process of finding a suitable house, and entering into a contract, with a house owner, he also enters into a contract with a chartered surveyor, you cannot say to him that he had no such authority. His authority is actual implied. Contrast this with the hypothesis that this person is a house buying agent. Then his authority would be customary. Another example is a stockbroker who acts according to the customs of the stock exchange.

If the agent is found in breach of his authority, then this is a breach of warranty, so that the principal is still bound by the contract with the third party, but he can claim damages from the agent. Also the agent, in such a case would not be entitled to any remuneration or commission.
If the third party does not know of the agent's lack or withdrawal of authority, the contract binds the principal. If the third party knows of the agent's lack of authority he does not obtain a contract with the principal, but with the agent.

2) APPARENT OR OSTENSIBLE AUTHORITY (OR AGENCY BY ESTOPPEL)

This arises where the principal holds out a person as his agent for the purpose of making a contract with a third party, the third party relies on that fact. It could be said that ostensible or apparent is the 'authority of an agent as it

---

[484] A solicitor has normally usual authority by his client to compromise a claim. Thus, in *Waugh* v. *H.B. Clifford & Sons* [1982] Ch.374, the claimant sued D, a firm of builders, for damages for negligence in building a house. Z, who was D's solicitor, agreed with the claimant's solicitor that D should purchase the house. D however, did not wish this compromise but their solicitor did not know this at the time that he made it. The claimant asked the Court to grant a decree for specific performance, i.e. to force D to buy the house, and he succeeded in this action.

[485] Thus, in *Panorama Developments (Guildford)* v. *Fidelis Furnishing Fabrics* [1971] 3 All E.R.16, the Court held that a modern company secretary was not a mere clerk and must be regarded as having authority to sign contracts connected with the administrative side of the company's affairs, and thus binds the company. In this case, the secretary bound the company when he ordered taxis, some of which were used to take customers of the firm to the airport, but some of which he used for his own purposes.

appears to others'.[486] A wife living with her husband and managing his household is presumed to have authority from her husband to pledge his credit for necessaries for the household.[487]

In other words, if a servant, such as an employee, has made purchases on his employer's behalf and the goods have been paid for by the employer, there will be implied an agency for future similar transactions with the same tradespeople;[488] for, if a person has so acted as to lead others to suppose that a certain person is his agent, he will be 'estopped' from denying the agency. This is known as 'agency by estoppel'.

If a principal gives his agent a certain authority, and later imposes a limitation upon it without notifying third parties who have dealt or are likely to deal with the agent on the faith of his original authority, such third parties can hold the principal bound by acts which are within the original apparent authority, though outside the scope of the limited actual authority. Therefore, it is quite clear that an employer who dismisses an employee dealing with third parties, or a principal who withdraws all or some of his agent's authority to deal with third parties, should notify this withdrawal to all third parties who had previous dealings with the agent, otherwise the principal would find himself bound by any contracts his agent entered on his behalf with such third parties.

AGENCY OF NECESSITY

This type of agency arises without agreement. An agent of necessity is a person who, in an emergency, acquires, by operation of law, presumed authority to act as an agent. The master of a ship may mortgage the ship and/or the cargo in order to pay for repairs or other expenditure necessary to successfully complete the voyage. Where the ship's master mortgages the ship, he is an agent of necessity for the shipowner and, in the case of cargo, for the cargo owner. If the

[486] Per Lord Denning, M.R., in *Hely-Hutchinson* v. *Brayhead Ltd.* [1968] 1 Q.B.549, 593, C.A.

[487] Thus, in *Spiro* v. *Lintern* [1973] 1 W.L.R.1002, D owned a house which he was considering selling. He agreed with E, his wife, that she would find a purchaser for the property. However, he did not authorise her to enter into any contract. E, his wife, however, made a contract with C to sell the house, and D, knowing of this, allowed C to have repairs carried out to the house and also to have work done in the garden. In this action for specific performance by C, it was held that as D knew that C was acting on the assumption that E had authority, he (D) was under a duty to tell him she (E) had no authority, and as D had not done so, he was estopped from denying her (E) authority to enter into the contract. Thus, C's action succeeded.

[488] *Pharmed Medicare Private Ltd.* v. *Univar Ltd.* [2002] EWCA Civ.1569; one of D's employees placed an order for the supply of a substantial quantity of medical preparations to C. The supply contract was for a duration of ten months. D's employee had previously ordered such goods from C, albeit of smaller amounts. However, as prices of medical preparations fell, D attempted to avoid the contract by suggesting that the employee lacked authority to conclude contracts of such magnitude. It was held that D was bound by the contract.

cargo is perishable, the ship's master can presumably sell it if it is going bad.[489] Generally, it must be reasonable for the carrier/master to have acted in the particular way. In addition, he must have acted in a *bona fide* manner, i.e. having regard to the interests of all parties concerned.[490]

SUBSEQUENT AUTHORITY OR AGENCY BY RATIFICATION

If an unauthorised person contracts as an agent, the principal for whom he intended to contract may afterwards expressly ratify or adopt the contract, and thus be bound by it. Such ratification is retrospective.

The principal may alternatively make an implied ratification by his conduct. For example, if the agent makes an unauthorised contract to buy goods, and his principal receives the goods and fails to return them or uses them, he has ratified his agent's contract by implication of law.[491]

The following rules govern whether ratification can be valid:

1) The agent must contract expressly as an agent for a principal who must be named or so described as to make it possible for the third party to identify him. Thus an undisclosed principal cannot ratify.[492]

2) An agent cannot contract on behalf of a company prior to its registration. A company cannot by ratification obtain the benefit of a contract purporting to have been made on its behalf before the company came into existence.[493] In other words, as a general rule, if a principal is to make a valid ratification of a contract purporting to have been made on his behalf, he must have been in existence at the time of the making of the contract.

3) A void contract cannot be ratified. Thus, if A enters into a contract with T, on behalf of P, his principal, for the improvement of U.S.A.'s balance of payment, when A knows that P is only a financial adviser, such a contract is void. This is because of the fact that this contract is beyond the reasonable

---

489 A carrier may, as an agent of necessity, sell perishable goods entrusted to him for carriage, when a transport strike renders a sale necessary to avoid deterioration of the goods through delay in delivery, and when it is not reasonably possible to obtain the owner's instructions in time to prevent the goods from becoming worthless; *Springer* v. *G.W. Rail. Co.* [1921] 1 K.B.257.

490 *China-Pacific SA* v. *Food Corp of India (The Winson)* [1982] A.C. 939 H.L.

491 Thus, in *Bolton Partners* v. *Lambert* (1889) 41 Ch.D.295, D made an offer to X, the managing director of the company (C). X accepted the offer on C's behalf, although he had no authority to do so. D then gave C notice that he withdrew the offer. C, the company, subsequently ratified X's unauthorised acceptance. It was held that as the ratification dated back to the time of the acceptance, the withdrawal of the offer was inoperative.

492 *Keighley, Maxsted & Co.* v. *Durant* [1901] A.C.240.

493 *Natal Land & Colonisation Co. Ltd.* v. *Pauline Colliery Syndicate* [1904] A.C.120.

means and power of P, in so far as P's capabilities are concerned. Therefore, P cannot ratify such a contract. A voidable contract can be ratified but the principal becomes liable for the fraud or misrepresentation of the agent. For example, if A, acting without authority, sells P's house and represents that the drains are in good order when they are not, and P later ratifies the contract, P becomes liable to the buyer. Remedies in such a case will depend on whether there was innocent misrepresentation, negligent misrepresentation, or fraudulent misrepresentation. Therefore, if innocent, the remedy would be rescission; if negligent, then the principal may be sued for damages; and if fraudulent, then the principal may be sued for damages or rescind the contract (rescission). It should be borne in mind, that the agent would be liable in damages to the third party for negligence, or fraud at common law, not under the Misrepresentation Act 1967.

4) Ratification must be based on full knowledge of the material facts. Thus, if the agent tells his principal that he sold his principal's house for £36,000, when he has only sold for £35,000, the principal can cancel the ratification.

5) Ratification must be of the whole contract. The Court will not allow ratification of the beneficial parts only.

6) Ratification can only be retrospective. Ratification is retrospective in its operation, which means that it relates back to the time when the contract was concluded by the agent as if the agent had the authority at the time of conclusion. This means that, for example, a principal cannot say to his agent in advance, 'I will ratify all your future contracts'.

EXCEPTIONS TO RETROSPECTIVENESS

(a) Since ratification is retrospective in its operation, if an agent accepts an offer by a third party 'subject to ratification' by his principal, the third party is not bound by this acceptance until ratification actually takes place. Note, however, that in such a case we do not have a valid acceptance because acceptance must be unconditional.[494] This situation is the only exception where ratification does not relate back to the original acceptance. In short, this rule does not apply where the third party who is dealing with the agent, knows that he is dealing with an agent who requires the ratification of his principal.[495]

---

494 *Supra*, p.79.

495 Thus, in *Watson* v. *Davies* [1931] 1 Ch.455, X and Y entered into negotiations, for the sale of X's building to Y's institution. As nothing was agreed on the negotiations, X wrote to Y stating a price of £6,500 for the building. The board of Y's institution met later on and authorised certain members of the board to accept X's offer, if they thought the building was

(b) The rule of retrospectiveness does not apply if it would cause excessive hardship to the third party.[496]

(c) Ratification must be within a reasonable time, and before the time fixed for performance has expired.

DUTIES OF AN AGENT

AGENT MUST PERFORM HIS DUTIES IN PERSON

This is based on the legal precedent 'a delegate cannot delegate' ('*delegatus non potest delegare*'). The principal, of course, can give his agent the authority to delegate, or may ratify his agent's delegation.

Delegation is allowed in certain cases:

a) Where delegation of authority is authorised by custom. Thus, if it is the practice of solicitors to employ town agents in matters of litigation, then this delegation is allowed by custom.

b) In cases of emergency, as where the agent is ill.

c) Where the appointment is necessary for properly carrying out the work.

d) Where the appointment involves the sub-agent to purely ministerial acts, e.g. the signing of a document.

---

suitable for the institution's purposes. These members of the board agreed on 11th January to buy the building 'subject to ratification of the full board'. A couple of days later, the full board met and ratified the agreement. In the morning of that day however, X send a telegraph, which was put forward to the full board at the time of the meeting, wherein he (X) stated that the building was not for sale. The board nevertheless, ratified the agreement of 11th January, purporting acceptance of X's offer. It was held that the ratification was ineffective, as an acceptance by an agent subject to ratification by his principal is a nullity until ratification, and being a conditional acceptance, is not binding on X. Furthermore, since X revoked the offer before ratification took place, he was not bound by it.

[496] Thus, in *Walter* v. *James* (1871) L.R. 6 Ex.124, A was acting on behalf of P, and he induced T to accept £60 in full discharge of a liability P had to T. Before the money was paid, P withdrew A's authority, but A nevertheless, paid T. When T discovered that the payment had been made without authority, he agreed to return the money to A. T then sued P for the money, and at this stage P purported to ratify A's payment, hoping to prevent T from succeeding on the grounds that the money had already been paid by his agent, A, and that T had handed it back voluntarily. It was held that ratification was not possible here because, if it was allowed, T would lose his action and would suffer undue hardship.

OBEDIENCE TO INSTRUCTIONS

Where an agent has specific instructions he must follow them.[497] This rule is subject to the exception of illegality, i.e. an agent who has specific instructions may not follow them if they are unlawful.

ORDINARY SKILL AND DILIGENCE

It seems that both gratuitous and paid agents may be required to exercise the same degree of care and skill whether they act gratuitously or for reward. However, the matter is still unclear and it may be that an unpaid agent will only be required to show the care that he would exercise in his own affairs.

The basic rule or principle is that a person is bound to use such skill as he claims to possess, or such as may be expected of him or may be implied from his position. For example, a solicitor must use all the skill, which is expected of a member of that profession.[498]

AGENT MUST NOT ACCEPT A BRIBE NOR MAKE ANY SECRET PROFITS

A secret profit is a financial advantage over what the agent is entitled to in contract. There need not be conspiracy to defraud.

Furthermore, the principal in such a case may have all or some of the following rights:

i) To dismiss the agent without notice

ii) To refuse the agent his remuneration or commission, in respect of the transaction, and he may recover any commission which he has paid. If the agent can prove that he acted honestly in any matter, he will not forfeit his remuneration in respect of that matter.

iii) To recover the bribe either from the agent if he has received it, or from the third party if it has not been paid but only promised.

iv) To sue the third party for damages. This is independent of whether he has recovered the amount of the bribe.

---

497 Thus, in *Turpin* v. *Bilton* (1843) 5 Man.& G.455, D was an insurance broker and C asked him to insure his vessel. D failed to carry out C's instruction, and the ship was lost. It was held that D was liable.

498 Thus in *Keppel* v. *Wheeler* [1927] 1 K.B. 577, X employed Y to sell his house. An offer made by N was received and X accepted it 'subject to contract'. A few days later a higher offer for the property was made by Z to Y, but this was not communicated to X, and the written contract between X and N was duly signed. It was held that Y was liable to X for the difference between the two offers.

v) Repudiate the whole transaction, whether or not the offer of the bribe did, in fact, influence the agent or not.

It is notable that the Courts will not enquire into the motives of the party giving the bribe, and there is an irrebuttable presumption that the agent was influenced by the bribe. The rules relating to secret profits and bribes apply to an agent who is not receiving payment.[499]

NO CONFLICT OF INTEREST BETWEEN PRINCIPAL AND AGENT

The agent must keep his principal duly informed with everything relating to the agency. Furthermore, he must not use his position for his personal benefit to the detriment of his principal. It is not necessary to show intentional wrongdoing by the agent, and the mere appearance of conflict of interest might suffice. Consequently, an agent may not contract, as principal, with his own principal, through himself as agent. Thus, if A is employed by P as an agent to sell some property, and he purports to sell it to T, but in reality buys it himself, without informing P, A cannot enforce the contract against P.[500]

RIGHTS OF AGENT

There are three main remedies/rights open to an agent, enforceable against his principal.

1) AN INDEMNITY

The agent may in the course of his duty incur liabilities or make payments of money for the principal, and he has a right to be indemnified against such liabilities and to recover any money paid.[501] The indemnity extends to three main items:

---

[499] Thus, in *Turnbull* v. *Garden* (1869) 38 L.J. Ch.331, an agent who was employed without payment to buy clothing for the principal's son received certain discounts from the seller. The agent tried to charge his principal the full price. It was held, that the principal was only required to pay the agent the sum charged by the seller of his son's outfit. The agent could not make a secret profit out of the transaction.

[500] *Boardman* v. *Phipps* [1967] 2 A.C.46.

[501] The agent must, of course, have acted within his authority; *Adamson* v. *Jarvis* (1827) 130 E.R.693, where a principal instructed an auctioneer to sell goods at auction. The agent (auctioneer) did so, however the principal did not own the goods and as a result the auctioneer had to pay damages. It was held that he (the auctioneer) was entitled to an indemnity from his principal for the damages.

a) Expenses reasonably incurred in the course of employment.

b) Any legal liability for acts or omissions properly authorised.

c) Even illegal acts, if the agent was unaware of their illegality.

2) LIEN

This is a special right under which the agent may retain the principal's goods which are in the agent's lawful possession where the principal has not satisfied his liabilities to the agent. If for example, the agent is owed money by his principal in respect of either remuneration or indemnity he may exercise a lien on any of his principal's goods until the debt is paid. In general, there is no power to sell the goods. Liens may be of two kinds:

(a) A General Lien: Under this category, the agent may retain goods of the principal even though the principal does not owe the agent money in respect of those goods, but in respect of other goods the agent has dealt with. However, note that the law does not favour general liens.

(b) A Particular Lien: This is a right to retain possession of goods which form part of the transaction in respect of which payment is due. This type is favoured by the law. If the agent surrenders possession of the goods, loses his lien. Furthermore, he must not have waived his right to lien. Finally, such right may be excluded or modified by agreement.

3) REMUNERATION

The following principles seem to apply:

i) An agent will be entitled to the agreed commission only in respect of a transaction which he was employed to bring about. The test is, whether the agent has substantially done what he was employed to do.[502]

ii) The agent must have been the effective cause of the event which he was employed to bring about.[503]

[502] Thus, in *Rimmer* v. *Knowles* (1874) 30 LTNS 496, the owner of an estate agreed to pay an agent £50 commission if he found a purchaser for the estate. The agent found someone who was prepared to take a lease for 999 years with an option to complete in 20 years. It was held that the agent was entitled to commission.

[503] Thus, in *Tribe* v. *Taylor* (1875-76) L.R. 1 C.P.D.505, the agent was employed to introduce someone to P who could provide capital in the form of a loan for his business. Although the agent was entitled to commission for effecting this transaction, it was held that he was not entitled to further commission when that person entered into partnership with P and provided further capital.

iii)The terms of the contract should determine precisely when the right to compensation arises. Thus remuneration may be payable even if the principal receives no benefit.

4) Stoppage in Transit

The lien exercised by an agent, as mentioned above, is only a possessory right and is lost when the goods lawfully pass out of the agent's possession. In order the agent to bring the goods into his possession and thus exercise his right of lien, he could exercise the right of stoppage in transit.[504]

Rights of Third Parties against Principal and Agent

Once there is a contract between the principal and the third party the agent normally drops out of the transaction and is no longer liable on it. However, the relationship between principal and third party is in part dependent upon whether the principal was disclosed or not by the agent, and also on whether a principal did actually exist at the time the contract was made. A disclosed principal is one whose existence has been made known to the third party at the time of the contract. He may be named or unnamed. An undisclosed principal is one whose existence the third party is unaware at the time of making the contract.

1) Principal Disclosed

If the principal is disclosed at the time the contract is entered into, and he actually exists, then in the absence of any express statement to the contrary, the contract is with the principal and not with the agent, who is not, therefore, personally liable to the third party. But to this rule there are the following exceptions:

a) Where an agent signs a bill of exchange or cheque without making clear that he is signing on behalf of a named principal.

b) Where the agent undertakes personal liability, or the third party has insisted that the agent also accepts liability before he makes the contract. If the agent has agreed to this, he will be liable along with the principal.

c) Where the agent is liable by custom; e.g. where a broker effects a contract of marine insurance for a principal the broker is liable to the underwriter for the premium.

---

[504] See also 'stoppage in transit', *infra*, p.177.

d) Where the agent enters into a deed on behalf of the principal, it is the agent who must sue and be sued. In other words only the parties to the deed may incur rights and liabilities in respect of the contract.

Where the agent lacks authority

Where an agent exceeds his authority he is liable to the third party for 'breach of warranty of authority', if:

a) the third party does not know of the lack of authority; and

b) the third party suffers loss as a result of his lack of knowledge.

The agent's liability is strict and does not depend upon his fraud or misrepresentation.[505] Furthermore, where the agent enters into a contract and acts in all respects *bona fide*, without notice that his authority has been terminated he will nevertheless be liable for impliedly warranting that his authority still exists.[506] In addition it may be said that an agent's liability in tort, i.e. independently of contract, when acting outside authority is threefold:

a) If he knowingly acts outside his authority he is liable in the tort of deceit.

b) If he acts negligently he may be liable in the tort of negligence.

c) Even if he acts honestly (*bona fide*) he will still be liable for breach of 'implied warranty of authority'.[507]

2) UNNAMED PRINCIPAL

Where an agent enters into a contract on behalf of an undisclosed principal he may or may not be personally liable according to the circumstances. If the agent

[505] Thus, in *Starkey* v. *Bank of England* [1903] A.C.114, X was a firm of stockbrokers. Y and the claimant were two trustees who held stocks in trust for others. X received authority to sell the stock under a power of attorney purporting to be signed by both Y and the claimant, but in fact the claimant's signature was forged. X sold the stock and send the proceeds to Y who paid them into his private account. Y died 18 months later, and on discovering what had happened the claimant brought an action against the Bank for replacement of the stock, and the Bank brought in X as liable to indemnify them. It was held that the claimant succeeded against the Bank, and the Bank in turn succeeded against X for an indemnity, because X had impliedly warranted his authority to the Bank.

[506] Thus, in *Yonge* v. *Toynbee* [1910] 1 K.B.215, X wanted to sue Y for libel. Y instructed Z, a firm of solicitors, to act for him in the matter. Before the action commenced Y was certified as being of unsound mind. However Z, Y's solicitors, not knowing of this, entered appearances in the action. X's solicitors now asked that all proceedings be struck out, and that Z, who acted for Y after his insanity, should be personally liable to pay for X's cost, because they (Z) had acted without authority. It was held that Z had impliedly warranted that they had authority to act when they had not, and that they (Z) were personally liable for X's costs.

[507] *Collen* v. *Wright* (1857) 120 E.R.847.

clearly contracts merely as an agent, but without naming his principal, and the third party fully realises that he is contracting with some person unknown, the agent will not be personally liable except in the cases enumerated above.

In other words once again the agent is not personally liable, provided he contracts as an agent. But if the agent does not make it clear that he is contracting as an agent only, he may incur liability under the rule which follows.

3) Principal Concealed (existence of principal is concealed)

Suppose an agent contracts with a third party on behalf of his principal but does not inform the third party that he is an agent and appears himself a principal, then the doctrine of the undisclosed principal applies. In such a case the third party may, on discovering the existence of the true principal, elect to hold either the principal or the agent liable, provided the contract is within the agent's authority.[508] Such choice by the third party, must, however, be exercised within a reasonable time of discovering the real principal, and therefore when the third party has obtained judgment against one party (principal or agent) he cannot afterwards proceed against the other for his right of action is exhausted. Election of this choice is deemed to have been made by any act showing an unequivocal intention of holding only one party liable. On default by the third party the principal or the agent may sue him. Furthermore, if the undisclosed principal intervenes and brings an action against the third party then the agent cannot sue, or must discontinue any action he has begun. Finally, where there is actual misrepresentation by the agent, the undisclosed principal will not be able to intervene. If the third party asks the agent, 'are you selling for a principal?' and the agent replies in the negative, the contract with the agent can be rescinded for misrepresentation and the undisclosed principal cannot intervene.

4) Where Principal is Non-Existent

Where a person has entered into a contract purporting to be acting on behalf of a principal who has never existed, he is personally liable on the contract.[509] The

---

[508] Thus, in *Sika Contracts Ltd.* v. *Gill, The Times*, 27 April 1978, X, a Chartered Civil Engineer, made a contract with Y, a building company, on behalf of Z, the owners of certain property. X did not mention to Y the name of the owners (Z) or that he (X) was acting on their (Z) behalf, until after the contract was concluded. He (X) had signed the contract and his (X) letters as 'B.L. Gill BE, MICE - Chartered Civil Engineer'. The question arose as to whether he (X) was personally liable on the contract and it was held that he was. Therefore, he (X) was personally liable to Y upon the contract.

[509] *Kelner* v. *Baxter* (1866) L.R. 2 C.P.174; D, who was one of the promoters of P, a company, before the actual formation of P, entered into a contract on the company's behalf. Once P, was formed, it ratified the contract. Later, however, it (P) became insolvent, and D, who had

principle established by cases has received statutory support in the European Communities Act 1972, which states:

> 'Where a contract purports to be made by a company or by a person as agent for a company, at a time when the company has not been formed, then subject to any agreement to the contrary the contract shall have effect as a contract entered into by the person purporting to act for the company or as agent for it, and he shall be personally liable on the contract accordingly.'[510]

As it has been mentioned, where an agent purports to contract as such without authority, or in excess of his authority, his acts may usually be ratified by the principal. But if they are not ratified, although the agent cannot be sued as principal, he can be sued, by a third party for damages for a breach of an implied warranty of authority, even if the agent *bona fide* believed himself to have authority. This is based on the premise that a person contracting as agent for another is deemed to warrant his authority.[511] Furthermore, a person, acting for a company, prior its incorporation is not merely liable for breach of warranty of authority to a third party, but is personally liable, to the third party, on the contract, i.e. the contract in such a case is between the agent and the third party. In concluding, one must remember that where a person acting for a company prior to incorporation is not merely liable for breach of warranty of authority, but is personally liable on the contract with the third party.

AUTHORITY OF THE AGENT TO RECEIVE PAYMENT

If a third party pays money to an agent and the agent has no authority to collect it, then the third party will get a good discharge only if the agent has apparent/ostensible authority to receive payment. For example, in the course of employment where the agent is a cashier in a bank or a salesman in a shop or a rent collector, then he would have apparent authority to receive payment. However, note that authority to sell is not necessarily an authority to receive payment.

---

contracted as its agent, was sued upon the contract. It was held, that D was liable. The purported ratification by the company (P) was ineffective because at the time when the contract between D and the third party was made, the company (P) did not exist. In a similar case, *Newborne* v. *Sensolid (Great Britain) Ltd.* [1954] 1 Q.B.45, C was in the process of forming a company called Newborne Ltd., and he entered into a contract with D, signing as 'Newborne Ltd.'. D repudiated the contract and it was held that D was entitled to do so because the signature purported to be that of the company itself (Newborn Ltd.) which was not yet in existence and technically could not be contracted.

510 Section 9(2).

511 *Collen* v. *Wright* (1857) 120 E.R.847.

TERMINATION OF AGENCY

The contract of agency, between the agent and the principal may be terminated in the following ways:

1) BY MUTUAL AGREEMENT

2) EXPIRATION OF TIME

If an agency is created for a definite period, then on the expiration of that period the agency will be terminated. Account, however, may be settled even after the termination of the agency.

3) PERFORMANCE OF CONTRACT/DESTRUCTION OF SUBJECT MATTER

If, for example, an agent is employed to sell a horse, the contract of agency is at an end when the horse is sold. Likewise, the agency would terminate if the horse died before the sale.

4) BY FRUSTRATION

This may arise either by impossibility of performance, or by supervening illegality. Thus, where the subject-matter of the agency is destroyed, as where an agent is employed to sell a house and the house is destroyed by fire, the agency is destroyed. Likewise, an agency is terminated by illegality, where the agency involves dealings with enemy aliens.[512]

5) DEATH OR INSANITY OF PRINCIPAL OR AGENT

The authority of the agent is, *ipso facto*, terminated by the death of the principal. Obviously the death of the agent will terminate the contract of agency, since it is one of personal service.

If an agent contracts after the principal is dead, he will be liable for breach of warranty of authority even if he believed the principal to be still alive. Similarly, supervening mental disorder, whether of the principal or of the agent, will terminate the agency.[513]

---

[512] For further information on the doctrine of frustration, see *supra*, p.115.

[513] *Yonge* v. *Toynbee* [1910] 1 K.B.215.

6) Bankruptcy or Liquidation

The bankruptcy of the principal terminates the agent's authority. The bankruptcy of the agent, however, does not necessarily terminate the agency.

7) Revocation or Renunciation

The principal may terminate the agent's authority at any time. No special formalities are required for such termination, but notice of such intention must be given to the agent within the period of notice specified in the contract, and if there is no such provision, then such period will have to be reasonable. However, the agent's apparent authority continues until third parties with whom he has had dealings are notified of the agent's lack of authority. Renunciation by the agent terminates the agency, but if it is in breach of the contract an action for damages lies at the suit of the principal.

E.C. Law and Agency Agreements

As from 1st January 1994, European Council Directive 86/653 has been effective in the U.K.[514] The Directive provides a regulatory framework on agency agreements, and it covers matters such as the way in which agents are to be remunerated, the way in which an agency can be terminated, etc. In effect this Directive is set to protect commercial agents. The Directive contains provisions concerning the duties of agent and principal which cannot be excluded.

What follows is a brief consideration of the more central areas covered by the Directive.

Regulation 2(1) defines commercial agents. The definition refers to the commercial agent as a 'self employed intermediary who has continuing authority to negotiate and conclude transactions for the sale or the purchase of goods on behalf of another person'.[515]

[514] Council Directive of 18 December 1986 on the Co-ordination of the Laws of the Member State relating to Self-Employed Commercial Agents (86/653/EEC, O.J. 1986 No. L 2/382/17). This came into effect in the U.K. by the Commercial Agents (Council Directive) Regulations 1993, (S.I.1993, No.3053), as amended by the Commercial Agents (Council Directive) (Amendment) Regulations 1993, (S.I.1993, No.3173), and the Commercial Agents (Council Directive) (Amendment) Regulations 1998, (S.I.1998, No.2868).

[515] The rights and obligations under the Regulations were only intended to arise under a contractual relationship. Therefore, the Regulations do not cover sub-agency. *Light* v. *Ty Europe Ltd.* [2004] 1 Lloyd's Rep.693, C.A., where it was held that a self-employed su-agent was not contractually bound to the principal, and thus not entitled to compensation under Regulation 17.

Regulation 3 imposes certain duties on the commercial agent. In particular the agent must:

(1) look after his principal's interest;

(2) to act 'dutifully and in good faith';

(3) to make proper efforts to negotiate such business as he is entrusted by his principal;

(4) to communicate all information to his principal and to comply with reasonable instructions

Regulation 4 deals with the duties of the principal towards his agent and that includes the principal's duties to:

(1) to provide to the agent all documentation and information necessary for the performance of the agency agreement;

(2) to notify the agent as soon as it is anticipated that the volume of business will be considerably lower than the agent could normally have anticipated;

(3) to inform the agent of his acceptance, refusal and any non-execution of the business the agent has arranged.

Regulation 5 effectively prohibits waiver by the parties of regulations 3 and 4 above.

Regulation 6 provides that the agent is entitled to customary remuneration on a reasonable basis if there is no agreement as to remuneration.

Under regulation 7(1) the agent is entitled to remuneration during the period covered by the agency contract where the transaction has been concluded as a result of his action or, where a transaction is concluded with a third party previously acquired as a customer, for such kind of transactions.

Regulation 8 is significant because the agent is entitled to commission on commercial transactions concluded, even after the agency is terminated, if either:

-the transaction is mainly attributable to his efforts during the period covered by the contract and if the transaction was entered into within a reasonable period after that contract terminated, or

-if the transaction was concluded with a third party previously acquired by the agent as a customer for transactions of the same kind.

Regulation 13(1) provides that the commercial agent and principal shall each be entitled to receive from the other a signed written contract if this is requested.

Regulation 14 provides that an agency, for a fixed period which continues to be performed by both parties after that period has lapsed, shall be deemed to be converted into an agency contract with an indefinite period.

Regulation 15(1) provides that where an agency contract is concluded for an indefinite period either party may terminate it by notice. Periods of notice are prescribed.[516] However, the parties are not permitted to agree a shorter period of notice.

Regulation 17 deals with the entitlement of a commercial agent to indemnity or compensation[517] on the termination of his agency contract.

Regulations 17(6) and (7) suggest that an agent is entitled to compensation for damage he suffers as a result of the termination of his relationship with his principal.[518] It is further provided that compensation is payable to an agent who terminates his own contract by reason of ill health or age or who dies.

Regulation 18 provides for the exclusion of payment of indemnity or compensation under Regulation 17 in certain instances, for example, where the agent himself has terminated his contract.

Regulation 19 provides that a party may not derogate from Regulations 17 and 18 to the detriment of the commercial agency before the contract expires.

---

[516] Regulation 15(2), one month in the first year, two months in the second year, and three months in the subsequent years.

[517] The difference between a compensation and an indemnification in law is quite considerable. The former is not based on damages but on the loss to the agent of the value of the agency as at the date of termination. An example of such system is France, where the established practice is to give two years' loss of average past commission as compensation, calculated on gross commission without deductions. Indemnification, on the other hand is payable on the basis of anticipated future economic loss. Member States have a choice as to which system to adopt.

[518] *Douglas King* v. *T. Tunnock Limited* [2001] E.C.C.6; the claimant agent had worked exclusively, since 1962, for the defendant. The claimant was paid a commission on sales which varied between 7% and 11% of the value of each order. In 1994 the defendant closed down its business and terminated its relationship with the claimant. No payment was made in lieu of notice, nor was any compensation paid. There was no written agreement covering the agency. The Court considered that on the facts it was clear that there was considerable goodwill in the claimant's business, and consequently it was reasonable to expect that the claimant was entitled to expect a capital sum representing at least his total earnings for the last two years of the agency, plus a payment in lieu of notice. *Cf. Barrett McKenzie & Co. Ltd.* v. *Escada (UK) Ltd.*, [2001] E.C.C.50, where the High Court took a different view on the matter of agent's compensation. It rejected the two year 'rule' and suggested that compensation should be based on the agency's value as a going business, taking into account the costs involved in earning the commission. The greater such costs, the less valuable such agency would be, with less compensation payable.

CHAPTER 6

THE LAW OF SALE OF GOODS

The law relating to the sale of goods is to be found in the Sale of Goods Act 1979 (as amended by the Sale and Supply of Goods Act 1994 and the Sale of Goods (Amendment) Act 1994). This Act provides a framework for the relationship between the buyer and seller. However, it would be wrong to think that the Act governs every aspect of a sale of goods contract. Many of the general principles of contract law still apply.

Therefore, a contract for the sale of goods, just like any other contract, must possess all the essential elements. The rules relating to the requirements of offer and acceptance, intention, consideration, etc., are largely unaffected by the Act.

DEFINITION

A contract for the sale of goods is defined in section 2(1) of the Act as:

> 'A contract by which the seller transfers or agrees to transfer the property in goods to the buyer for a money consideration, called the price'.

A closer examination of this definition would be necessary, as it will assist you in distinguishing a contract for the sale of goods from other similar kinds of contracts. The definition covers an actual sale and an agreement to sell at some future time. The essence of the transaction is the transfer of property in the goods from the seller to the buyer. Property in this context means ownership of the goods and not physical possession. Goods include all tangible items of personal property such as food, clothes and furniture. Land and money are excluded from the definition.[519] The provisions of the Act only apply to those transactions which fall within the above definition.

---

[519] Section 61(1). *St. Albans City Council* v. *International Computers Ltd.* [1996] 4 All E.R.481, C.A.; C purchased a computer software system from D for the purpose of managing the collection of the Community Charge (a local tax). The system failed and C claimed breach of the statutory implied under s.14 (merchantable quality-now satisfactory quality). One of the questions was whether computer software was 'goods' within s.61. Although the case was decided on the effectiveness of the exemption of liability clause, the Court stated *obiter* that (i) computer disks were 'goods' but a computer program was not, and (ii) where disks were sold with software written on them such software would be part of the disk and hence 'goods'.

CAPACITY (s.3)

To enter into a binding sale of goods contract is governed by the general law of contract, which has already been considered earlier on.[520]

FORMATION OF THE CONTRACT (s.4)

It is not necessary to observe complex formalities to create a contract for the sale of goods. It may be in writing or by word of mouth, or partly in writing and partly by word of mouth, or even implied from the conduct of the parties.

PRICE (s.2(1))

The consideration for the goods must be money, (i.e. price) although a part-exchange deal in which goods are exchanged for other goods plus money will be covered by the Act because some money has changed hands.[521] Section 8 of the Act deals with this, and states in this connection:

'(1) The price in a contract of sale may be fixed by the contract or may be left to be fixed in manner thereby agreed or may be determined by the course of dealing between the parties.

(2) Where the price is not determined in accordance with the foregoing provisions the buyer must pay a reasonable price.'[522]

PAYMENT (ss.27-28)

The price is such a fundamental part of the transaction that it will normally be fixed by the contract. However, it may be ascertained by the course of dealing between the parties or the contract may provide a mechanism for fixing the price e.g. by arbitration. The parties may make their own agreement as to the time of payment.[523] The seller may insist on payment in advance of delivery or, he may

---

[520] See *supra*, p.85.

[521] *G.J. Dawson (Clapham) Ltd.* v. *H. & G. Dutfield* [1936] 2 All E.R.232.

[522] What is a reasonable price is a question of fact; s.8(3).

[523] The effect of the Late Payment of Commercial Debts (Interest) Act 1998, must be borne in mind when it comes to late payment. Unless the contract provides for a substantial alternative remedy for late payment, there is a term implied to most commercial supply of goods or services contracts. The Act gives the right to claim statutory interest at 8% above the Bank of England dealing rate on all unpaid debts. Statutory interest may be claimed from the day after the agreed due date for payment, but if no date has been agreed, the Act imposes a credit period

be prepared to extend a period of credit. In the absence of such express agreement, payment is due when the goods are delivered.

IMPLIED TERMS

Although the parties are generally free to agree between themselves the details of their contract, the Act automatically includes a number of conditions and warranties in every contract for the sale of goods. These are known as the implied terms and they can be found in sections 12-15.

The following is a brief account of each of these implied terms.

TITLE (s.12)

There is an implied term[524] on the part of the seller that in the case of a sale he has a right to sell the goods, and in the case of an agreement to sell he will have the right to sell when the property is to pass. If the seller cannot pass good title, i.e. rights of ownership, to the buyer, he will be liable for breach of condition.[525]

DESCRIPTION (s.13)

Where there is a contract for the sale of goods by description, there is an implied term that the goods will correspond with the description.[526] If the buyer does not see the goods before he buys them, e.g. from a mail order catalogue, there has clearly been a sale by description. Even where the buyer has seen the goods and, perhaps, selected them himself, it may still be a sale by description, provided he has relied to some extent on a description.[527] The description of the goods may

---

of 30 days after which the interest is payable. More complicated rules apply to advance payments. The Act gives effect to the European Council Directive 2000/35/EC, on combating late payment in commercial transactions, O.J. L 200, 08/08/2000, p.35.

[524] This term is a condition; s.12(5A). Furthermore, the same section implies three warranties in subsections 12(2), 12(4), and 12(5). *Louis Dreyfus Trading Ltd.* v. *Reliance Trading Ltd.* [2004] 2 Lloyd's Rep.243 (QBD (Comm.)).

[525] Thus, in *Rowland* v. *Divall* [1923] 2 K.B. 500, C bought a car from D for £334 and used it for four months. It was later found that D had bought the car from someone who had stolen it and it had to be returned to the true owner. C sued D to recover the full purchase price that he had paid. It was held that D was in breach of section 12. C had paid £334 to become the owner of the car. Since he had not received what he had contracted for, there was a total failure of consideration entitling him to a full refund.

[526] This term is a condition; s.13(1A).

[527] Thus, in *Beale* v. *Taylor* [1967] 3 All E.R.253, D advertised a car for sale as a 1961 Triumph Herald. C inspected the car before he bought it. He (C) later discovered that the

cover such matters as size, quantity, weight, ingredients, origin or even how they are to be packed. The slightest departure from the specifications would usually entitle the buyer to reject the goods for breach of a condition of the contract.[528]

A seller may however, successfully attempt to exclude the sale from being one by description by including such phrases as 'bought as seen' or 'sold as seen' in the contract.[529]

QUALITY AND SUITABILITY (s.14)

Section 14 starts by stating that there are no implied terms as to quality or fitness for a particular purpose except as provided by sections 14 and 15. This preserves the idea of *caveat emptor* (let the buyer beware).

Section 14 provides two terms[530] which are implied only where the seller sells goods in the course of a business, and not to sales by private individuals. So if one buys something privately, and it is defective or unsuitable, there can be no complaint under section 14.

These two terms are the following:

---

vehicle consisted of a rear half of a 1961 Herald which had been welded to the front half of an earlier model. It was held that C was entitled to damages for breach of section 13 even though he had seen and inspected the car. He (C) had relied to some extent on the description contained in the advertisement. In *Harlingdon & Leinster Enterprises* v. *Christopher Hull Fine Arts Ltd.* [1990] 1 All E.R.737, C.A., both parties were art dealers. D stated to C that they had a painting by Munter for sale. D also made clear to C that they were not experts on the particular painter. C relying on their own judgment bought the painting. Subsequently, C discovered that the painting was a forgery and worth a great deal less. It was held, by a majority, that as the sellers, D, denied expert knowledge, the buyers, D, could not have relied upon the description given, thus not a sale by description. Therefore, reliance is an absolute requirement for a sale of goods to be considered as a sale by description. *Cf. Ashington Piggeries* v. *Christopher Hill* [1972] A.C.441, H.L., where the majority of their Lordships thought that the key to s.13 was identification rather than reliance. Indeed, the subsequent case of *Reardon Smith Line* v. *Hansen Tangen* [1976] 1 W.L.R.989, H.L., seems to reinforce and support this view, i.e. that words which identify an essential part of the description of the goods should be considered.

[528] *F.W. Moore & Co Ltd.* v. *Landauer & Co.* [1921] 2 K.B.519, C.A.; where a contract for the sale of 3,000 tins of canned fruit stipulated that the consignment would be packed in cases, each containing 30 tins. In fact about half of the consignment was packed in cases, each containing 24 tins. The buyer rejected the whole consignment. It was held the stipulation as to the number of tins per case was part of the description. *Arcos Ltd.* v. *Ronassen* [1933] A.C.470, H.L.; a sale contract for wooden staves stipulated that the staves should be half an inch thick. Most of the staves exceeded this thickness, although they were suitable for the purpose they were purchased. It was held that the staves did not correspond with the contract description.

[529] *Cf. Hughes* v. *Hall (Gillian)* [1981] R.T.R.430; *Cavendish-Woodhouse Ltd.* v. *Manley* (1984) 148 J.P. 299. It also seems that a seller may also exclude reliance on s.13 by disclaiming expertise; *Harlingdon & Leinster Enterprises* v. *Christopher Hull Fine Arts Ltd.* [1990] 1 All E.R.737, C.A., described in footnote 527, *supra*.

[530] Both these implied terms are classified as conditions; s.14(6).

Satisfactory Quality (s.14(2))

Before 1995 the Act implied a condition of 'merchantable quality'. In order to bring the terminology more in line with current trading conditions, 'merchantable quality' was replaced[531] by 'satisfactory quality'. Where the seller sells goods in the course of a business there is an implied term[532] that the goods supplied under the contract are of satisfactory quality. This means that a brand new washing machine should wash one's clothes properly, or new shoes should not fall apart on their first outing, or a meat pie bought for one's lunch should not make him ill. The goods do not have to measure up to an absolute standard of quality. If you buy goods second-hand or very cheaply, you cannot expect perfection.[533]

Satisfactory quality is defined in section 14(2A) as being the standard a reasonable person would regard as satisfactory, taking into account the description of the goods, the price, and all other relevant circumstances.[534]

In addition, it includes things such factors as safety and durability, appearance, finish and freedom from minor defects.[535]

Thus, in one case,[536] C ordered a new yacht from D. At the time of delivery D realised and informed C that the keel was substantially heavier than the manufacturer's standard specification prescribed. C nevertheless sailed the yacht for a few days, before returning it for modification. Following a few months' of correspondence between the parties in relation to the overweight keel, its consequences and available remedies, D informed C that the extra weight might endanger the rig and recommended that some lead weight will have to be removed from the yacht's keel. A month later C rejected the yacht and claimed the purchase price and damages for breach of contract. It was held that the yacht was not of satisfactory quality in the circumstances, so that C was entitled to the claimed purchase price and damages.

---

[531] Section 1 of the Sale and Supply of goods Act 1994 inserted a new s.14(2) in the 1979 Act.

[532] This implied term is classified as a condition; s.14(6).

[533] *Bartlett* v. *Sidney Marcus Ltd.* [1965] 2 All E.R.753; C bought a second-hand car from D who was a car dealer. C was warned that the clutch was defective and he agreed to a reduction in the price of the car to take account of this. The defect turned out to be more serious and, therefore, more costly to repair, than C expected. C claimed that D was in breach of s.14(2) ('merchantable' quality as it then was). It was held that in all the circumstances there was no breach of s.14(2), and the car met with the standard required by the section ('merchantable' quality).

[534] In *Cehave NV* v. *Bremer Handels GmbH (The Hansa Nord)* [1975] 3 All E.R.739, it was held that citrus pulp pellets which had deteriorated in transit but which were still usable for the purpose for which such pellets were normally used, namely, for animal feed, were not contrary to the requirement of s.14(2) ('merchantable' quality).

[535] Section 14(2B).

[536] *Clegg* v. *Andersson* [2003] 2 Lloyd's Rep.32, C.A.

The buyer can lose his right to complain in two situations:

(i) where the seller specifically points out that the goods are faulty; and

(ii) where he (the buyer) decides to check the goods, but fails to spot an obvious defect.

Fitness for a particular purpose (s.14(3))

Where the seller sells goods in the course of a business and the buyer, expressly or by implication, makes known to the seller any particular purpose for which the goods are being bought, there is an implied term[537] that the goods supplied under the contract are reasonably fit for that purpose.

For example, if the buyer specifies that requires shoes suitable for running a marathon in, the shoes must be suitable for this purpose.

Furthermore, where the buyer purchases goods with only one normal purpose, he makes his purpose known by implication. In other words, food must be fit for eating and clothes fit for wearing.[538]

If the buyer has any special requirements these must be made known to the seller.[539] The only exception to this rule is where the circumstances show that the buyer does not rely, or that it is unreasonable for him to rely, on the seller's skill and judgment. Reliance will normally be assumed from the fact that the buyer has taken his custom to that particular shop/agent/merchant.

However, if a buyer asks for an item under its brand name or lays down detailed specifications as to what he wants, he will find it difficult to show that he has relied on the seller's skill and judgment.

[537] This implied term is classified as a condition; s.14(6).

[538] Thus, in *Grant* v. *Australian Knitting Mills Ltd.* [1936] A.C.85, C bought a pair of woollen underpants from a shop. The manufacturers neglected to remove properly a chemical which was used in the manufacturing process. Consequently C developed a skin rash which turned into dermatitis. It was held that the underpants were not, ***inter alia***, reasonably fit for the purpose. Although C had not specifically stated the purpose for which he required the underpants, it was clear by implication that he intended to wear them.

[539] Thus, in *Griffiths* v. *Peter Conway Ltd.* [1939] 1 All E.R.685, the buyer had a Harris tweed coat specially made for her by the seller. The coat caused her to contract dermatitis. It was held that since the coat would have caused no harm to normal skin and the seller could not have known of the buyer's sensitivity, there was no breach of the implied condition of fitness of purpose. Otherwise, if the seller is unaware of any peculiar use for the goods, his obligation is no more than to supply goods which are fit for their normal purpose; *Slater* v. *Finning* [1996] 3 All E.R.398, H.L.

SAMPLE (s.15)

A contract of sale is a contract of sale by sample where there is an express or implied term to that effect in the contract. In the case of a contract for sale by sample there is an implied term:[540]

(a) that the bulk will correspond with the sample in quality;

(b) that the goods will be free from any defect rendering their quality unsatisfactory which would not be apparent on reasonable examination of the sample.[541]

EFFECT OF ss.13-15 BREACH IN NON-CONSUMER SALES

It must be noted that in non-consumer sale contracts, the buyer would not be able to reject the goods for any breach under sections 13-15 if the breach is slight. A slight breach would mean a breach which, in the particular circumstances, would render such rejection of the goods unreasonable.[542]

TRANSFER OF PROPERTY IN THE GOODS

The essence of a contract for the sale of goods is the transfer of property (ownership) in goods from the seller to the buyer. The determination of when property passed from seller to buyer will determine when the risk of loss or damage to the goods passes, and in practice who should affect insurance cover. According to section 20(1) of the Act, unless the parties have agreed otherwise, risk follows property.[543]

---

[540] This implied term is classified as a condition; s.15(3).

[541] Thus, in *Godley* v. *Perry* [1960] 1 All E.R.36, C, a six-year old boy bought a plastic toy catapult from a newsagent's shop run by Perry, the first defendant. The catapult broke while in use and C lost an eye. C sued Perry for breach of the implied conditions in s.14. Perry had bought the catapults by sample from a wholesaler. He (Perry) had tested the sample catapult by pulling back the elastic, but no defect had been revealed. Perry now brought the wholesaler into the action claiming a breach of the conditions in s.15. The wholesaler had bought the catapults by sample from an importer who had obtained the catapults from Hong Kong. The wholesaler brought the importer into the action alleging a similar breach of s.15. It was held, that C could recover damages from Perry, the first defendant, for breach of s.14, as the catapult was not, *inter alia*, fit for the purpose for which it had been bought. Furthermore, Perry, the first defendant, could recover damages from the wholesaler who in turn could recover damages from the importer, as in both cases because there had been a breach of s.15 which was implied in the relevant contracts.

[542] Section 15A. Such breaches would therefore be treated as breaches of warranty.

[543] Irrespectively of whether delivery has been made to the buyer; *Castle* v. *Playford* (1872) 26 L.T.315, under a contract for the carriage of goods to the U.K., it was agreed that the buyer would take the risk upon receipt of the bills of lading, but payment was to be on delivery. The

The rules relating to the transfer of ownership depend on whether the goods are classified as specific goods or unascertained goods.

SPECIFIC GOODS

These are 'goods identified and agreed on at the time a contract of sale is made'.[544] This includes contracts such as purchasing groceries from a supermarket or buying a coat from a market trader. In other words if at the time that the contract is made, it is possible to point out the particular goods upon which the parties have agreed, then those goods are specific. Contracts to supply a certain amount out of a specified bulk are not contracts to supply specific goods, as it is not possible to say what part of the bulk will be given.[545]

The general rule is that property in specific goods passes when the parties intend it to pass and to ascertain the intention of the parties 'regard shall be had to the terms of the contract, the conduct of the parties and the circumstances of the case'.[546] Furthermore, in a C.I.F. contract the intention of the parties would be that passing of property is conditional. If the buyer rejects them upon examination property in the goods reverts to the seller.[547]

If the parties do not indicate, expressly or impliedly, when they want ownership to pass, s.18 of the Act, sets out various rules to ascertain their presumed intention.

Rule 1: This provides that 'where there is an unconditional contract for the sale of specific goods in a deliverable state, the property in the goods passes to the buyer when the contract is made, it is immaterial whether the time of payment or the time of delivery, or both, be postponed'.

This means that the buyer can become the owner of goods even though he has not paid for them yet and they are still in the seller's possession.[548]

---

bill of lading was received but the ship was subsequently lost. It was held that the property passed upon receipt of the bills of lading. However, where there is a consumer sale, the Sale and Supply of Goods to Consumers Regulations 2002, (S.I.2002, No.3045), which implement Directive 1999/44/E.C. on Certain Aspects of the Sale of Consumer Goods and Associated Guarantees (O.J. L 171, 07/07/1999, p.12), add to s.20 of the Sale of Goods Act 1979, subsection (4) which states that risk of loss or damage does not pass to the consumer until actual delivery of goods takes place.

544 'Specific goods' includes an undivided share, specified as a fraction or percentage, of goods identified and agreed on as aforesaid; section 61.

545 Thus, in *Re Wait* [1927] 1 Ch.606, was held that a contract to sell 500 tons of wheat out of a bulk of 1,000 tons was not a contract for the sale of specific goods.

546 Section 16(2).

547 *Kwei Tek Chao* v. *British Traders and Shippers Ltd.* [1954] 2 Q.B.459.

548 Thus, in *Tarling* v. *Baxter* (1827) 6 B. & C.360, a haystack was sold but before the buyer had taken it away, it was burned down. It was held that the buyer was still liable to pay the price because he became the owner of the haystack when the contract was made, and it was immaterial that no delivery of the goods had been made.

Furthermore, 'unconditional contract' relates to whether the transfer of property in the goods is subject to some contingency. If such contingency is stipulated in the contract then Rule 1 would not apply.[549]

Rule 2: This provides that 'where there is a contract for the sale of specific goods and the seller is bound to do something to the goods for the purpose of putting them into a deliverable state, the property does not pass until the thing is done and the buyer, has notice that it has been done'.

This means that where the seller agrees to alter the goods in some way for the buyer, ownership will pass when the alterations are completed and the buyer has been informed.

Rule 3: This provides that 'where there is a contract for the sale of specific goods in a deliverable state but the seller is bound to weigh, measure, test or do some other act or thing with reference to the goods for the purpose of ascertaining the price, the property does not pass until the thing is done and the buyer has notice that it has been done'.

If, for example, you agree to buy a particular bag of potatoes, at a price of 10 pence a pound/kilo, you will not become the owner of the potatoes until the seller has weighed the bag and informed you of the price payable. If, however, it is agreed that the buyer will do the weighing, measuring or testing, ownership of the goods will pass in accordance with Rule 1 above, i.e. when the contract is made.

Rule 4: This provides that 'when goods are delivered to the buyer on approval or on sale or return .... the property in the goods passes to the buyer:

(a) when he signifies his approval or acceptance to the seller or does any other act adopting the transaction;

(b) if he does not signify his approval or acceptance to the seller but retains the goods without giving notice of rejection, then, if a time has been fixed for the return of the goods, on the expiration of that time, and, if no time has been fixed, on the expiration of a reasonable time'.

[549] *Underwood Ltd.* v. *Burgh Castle Brick & Cement Syndicate* [1922] 1 K.B.123, C.A.; there was a sale contract of a 30 tonne engine. The engine had to be removed from its concrete bed, dismantled and loaded on rail. During loading the engine was damaged. It was held that Rule 1 of s.18, was not applicable because when the contract was made the engine was not in a deliverable state. Therefore, the property in the goods did not pass at time of contract, and consequently, the sellers had not discharged all their obligations at the time the damage occurred.

Property in goods delivered on approval, will pass under part (a) of this rule either when the buyer informs the seller that he wishes to buy them or he 'adopts' the transaction,[550] for example, by re-selling the goods.[551]

Part (b) of the rule may be best understood by an example. A seller hands a horse over to a prospective buyer on approval for eight days. Unfortunately, the horse dies on the third day. Ownership of the horse would not have passed to the buyer and, therefore, the seller would have to bear the loss.[552]

UNASCERTAINED GOODS

There is no definition in the Act, but it could be said that any goods which are not specific, i.e. cannot be identified and agreed on at the time the contract of sale is made, are necessarily unascertained. Unascertained goods can fall into two categories:

(i) Unascertained goods out of a specified bulk, e.g. 500 tons of wheat from a cargo of 1,000 tons.

(ii) Purely generic ascertained goods, e.g. a Ford Focus car.

One point should be stressed here; it is possible for goods to cease to be unascertained, and to become ascertained by a process of exhaustion.[553]

In the case of a sale of unascertained goods, the general rule is that the property passes to the buyer only when the goods have been ascertained.[554] If the parties then fail to mention when they intend ownership to pass, section 18 provides for the application of Rule 5.

Rule 5: '(1) where there is a contract for the sale of unascertained or future goods by description, and goods of that description and in a deliverable state are unconditionally appropriated to the contract, either by the seller with the assent of the buyer or by the buyer with the assent of the seller, the property in the

---

[550] *Kirkham* v. *Attenborough* [1897] 1 Q.B.201, C.A.; X took some jewellery from C on a sale or return basis. However, X pledged the jewellery to D. C claimed that the jewellery was still his property. It was held that pledging the goods was an 'act adopting the transaction' under Rule 4(a) of s.18, and so property had passed to D.

[551] *Atari Corporation* v. *Electonic Boutique* [1978] 1 All E.R.1010, C.A.

[552] *Elphick* v. *Barnes* (1879-80) L.R. 5 C.P.D.321.

[553] Section 18, Rule 5(3).

[554] Section 16. *Re Goldcorp Exchange Ltd.* [1994] 1 All E.R.806; Goldcorp sold to buyers gold bullion on the basis that the gold will be stored and insured by Goldcorp. The buyers were issued with certificates representing their purchases. No gold was actually set aside, and Goldcorp became insolvent. It was held that property in the gold had not passed to the buyers because the gold had not been ascertained.

goods then passes to the buyer; and the assent may be express or implied and may be given either before or after the appropriation is made'.

This rule only applies where there is a sale by description. Goods are 'unconditionally appropriated' to the contract, when they have been irrevocably identified[555] as the goods which are the subject of the contract. In simpler terms this is usually when the goods are separated from the bulk and earmarked for a particular buyer.[556] Under Rule 5(2) of the Act, delivery to a carrier will amount to an 'appropriation'.[557]

SECTION 20A

As mentioned above, a purchaser of unascertained goods which form part of a bulk cannot acquire the property in the goods until they have been ascertained, which will frequently not happen until the goods are delivered, even though the buyer may have paid for the goods and received a document giving a right to delivery.

If the seller becomes insolvent before delivery of the goods, both the goods and the price may pass to the receiver or liquidator for the benefit of the seller's creditors. Although this law had the logical basis that a person cannot own goods which have not yet been ascertained, its result did not accord with normal commercial expectations and it was widely regarded as unfair. Consequently, the Law Commission's proposals to deal with this problem were adopted and the 1979 Act was amended accordingly.[558]

---

555 *Carlos Federspiel* v. *Twigg* [1957] 1 Lloyd's Rep.240; D agreed to sell bicycles to C. After the bicycles were manufactured, packaged and labelled with C's name, D became bankrupt. It was held that usually, but not necessarily, the appropriating act is the last act to be performed by the seller. The goods were not 'unconditionally appropriated' to C's contract under Rule 5 of s.18. The acts of crating and labelling could be regarded merely as aspects of the internal administration of the seller's business.

556 *Hendy Lennox (Industrial Engines) Ltd.* v. *Grahame Puttick Ltd.* [1984] 2 Lloyd's Rep.422; where the seller sent an invoice to the buyer showing the serial number of engines to be delivered. It was held that the engines had been 'unconditionally appropriated' to buyer's contract. Having sent the invoice identifying the particular items to be delivered to the buyer, the seller could no longer substitute them for other goods without the buyer's consent.

557 Provided the buyer's goods can be clearly identified; *Healy* v. *Howlett & Sons* [1917] 1 K.B.337, where C agreed to sell 20 boxes of fish to D. He despatched 190 boxes by rail for delivery to various customers but the boxes were not labelled for particular customers. Employees of the railway company were entrusted with the task of allocating the correct number of boxes to each destination. Due to a delay, the fish deteriorated before twenty boxes could be set aside for D. D refused to take delivery and C sued for the price. It was held that the property in the goods had not passed to C because C's boxes had not been appropriated to the contract. Indeed, a way to look at this would be to suppose that only 20 boxes had become bad; would it be impossible to say which of the various buyers would have been bound to take the 20 bad boxes?

558 The Commission's solution was to the effect that the buyer in such a situation should be able to become the owner, not of any particular goods, but of proportionate part of the bulk, and

Perhaps it is best at this place to give a working example of the particular provisions of the Act in relation to unascertained goods forming part of an identified bulk.

If a buyer were to buy just '1,000 tonnes of wheat forming part of the cargo of the ship *Nicholas*', this would clearly be a contract for the sale of unascertained goods, and would mean that the general provision of s.16, i.e. no property will pass until the goods are ascertained, should be followed.

Under s.20A, there are now three conditions, which must be fulfilled in order for such buyer to be protected if the seller becomes insolvent:

(i) The contract must be one for the sale of a specified quantity of goods. For example, 100 tonnes, or 100 litres.[559]

(ii) The goods must be sold from an identified bulk source. Although a contract to sell '1,000 tonnes of grain' is a contract for unascertained goods and s.20A would not apply, if after the contract is made the parties agree that the buyer's goods should be supplied from the cargo on board a named ship or a particular warehouse, then s.20A would apply.

(iii) The buyer must have paid part or the whole of the price.

Once the above three conditions have been fulfilled one must, of course, consider whether there is anything in the agreement which excludes the application of s.20A. For example, parties may have agreed that the buyer would not own any part of the bulk until full payment has been received. If there are no such exclusions in the sale contract, only then can one consider s.20A further.

It must be borne in mind that the effect of s.20A is to make such buyer owner of a share of the bulk. This share is determined by s.20A(3), which indicates that the undivided share of a buyer in bulk at any time shall be such share as the quantity of goods paid for, and due to the buyer out of the bulk, bears to the quantity of goods in the bulk at that time. This clearly means that the size of the buyer's share of the bulk may vary according to the quantity of the bulk at any one time.

Let us now consider the following situations:

that the buyer's share would correspond to the quantity bought and paid for. See 'Sale of Goods Forming Part of a Bulk'-Law Commission No.215.

[559] But note that it does not apply to contracts to sell a share/proportion of the goods forming part of a specified bulk, such as 'half the wheat in my warehouse' or '10% of wheat on board the ship *Nicholas*'. In such cases the buyer becomes a tenant in common of the bulk (at common law) without the need for the application of s.20A. Furthermore, s.61 (as amended) states that 'specific goods' also include 'an undivided share, specified as a fraction or percentage of goods identified and agreed on'.

The aggregate of the shares of buyers in a bulk exceed the whole of the bulk: Section 20A(4) deals with this by stating that each buyer's share would be reduced proportionately. So, for example, if S agrees to sell to each, B1, B2, B3 and B4, 5,000 tonnes of grain from silo No.1 thought to contain 20,000 tonnes but in fact only contains 16,000 tonnes, then instead of each buyer being entitled to 5,000 of the whole 16,000 tonnes (i.e. $5/16^{ths}$), each buyer's share of the bulk will be reduced proportionately to 4,000 of the whole 16,000 tonnes (i.e. $4/16^{ths}$).

One or more of the buyers take delivery of the quantity of goods due to him/them under the contract: If we take the same example, as above, where S agrees to sell 5,000 tonnes of grain to B1, B2, B3 and B4 from silo No.1 thought to contain 20,000 tonnes but in fact only contains 16,000 tonnes. It was determined that instead of each buyer being entitled to $5/16^{ths}$ of the whole, each buyer's share of the bulk will be reduced proportionately to $4/16^{ths}$ (i.e. $1/4^{th}$) of the whole bulk.

However, let us assume now that B1 takes delivery of 5,000 tonnes of grain, i.e. more than his s.20A(3) share, in the circumstances. In such a case the shares of B2, B3 and B4 would be reduced further to 11,000 tonnes divided by three. It must be noted that B1 would be entitled to do this, since s.20B(1) states that each co-owner is deemed to consent to any delivery to another co-owner of goods due to him/her under the contract and to any removal, dealing with, delivery etc. in the bulk by any other co-owner.

So, in these circumstances what are the other buyers' (B2, B3 and B4) remedies under the Act?

Section 20B(3)(a) indicates that they cannot recover any part of the goods nor can they recover compensation from B1. Furthermore, s.20B(3)(c) provides that all these rules do not affect 'the rights of any buyer under his contract'. This means that B2, B3 and B4 remain entitled, as against the seller, to delivery of the quantities due to them under their contracts.

These provisions, and the effect of 'first come, first served' where co-owners take delivery out of the bulk should in practice always be borne in mind.

RIGHT OF DISPOSAL (s.19) [*ROMALPA* CLAUSES]

In the business world sellers are expected to do business on credit terms. If ownership of the goods passes to the buyer before he pays for them and he subsequently becomes bankrupt, or, in the case of a company, goes into liquidation, the seller will be treated as an ordinary trade creditor. As such, the seller is unlikely to recover what he is owed.[560] He can protect himself from these considerable risks, by stating that the property in the goods shall not pass to the buyer until the contract price has been paid.

The inclusion of such a reservation of title clause in the contract of sale will enable a seller to retrieve his goods and re-sell them if the buyer goes bankrupt or into receivership or liquidation before paying for them.

It is important to note that s.19 only applies to 'specific' and 'ascertained' goods. It provides that where the seller has reserved the right of disposal of the goods until some condition is fulfilled, ownership of the goods will not pass to the buyer until that condition is met.[561]

However, the position becomes much more complicated where (i) the buyer has re-sold the goods, and/or (ii) where the buyer has mixed them with other goods during a manufacturing process and then sold the manufactured product.

The seller may be able to protect himself in relation to (i) above by including, a carefully worded clause in the contract, allowing him to trace the goods and claim the proceeds of sale.[562] These terms are known as *Romalpa* clauses, after the name of the case[563] in which they achieved prominence. This

---

[560] The order for distribution of assets in insolvency requires the assets to be used to meet the costs of insolvency and the claims of preferential creditors and Inland Revenue, social security contributions, and of secured creditors before those of unsecured creditors. No creditor can be paid unless the claims of all the creditors in prior classes have been met in full. If there is not enough to pay in full a class then they all receive a rateable proportion of the sum due. Companies can create floating charges which cover all their property and any property acquired after creation of the charge. Unsecured creditors rank after preferential creditors, mortgagees and floating charge holders.

[561] This s.19(1) highlights the importance of s.17(1), in the case of specific or ascertained goods, where property will pass when the parties intend it to pass. Where bills of lading are issued under an F.O.B. or F.A.S. contract, and are marked 'to the order' of the seller, the intention of the parties, in the absence of any other provisions, would be that no property would pass to the buyer/holder of the bill of lading until other conditions, such as payment, have been satisfied; *Transpacific Eternity SA* v. *Kanematsu Corp. (The Antares III)* [2002] 1 Lloyd's Rep.233. Similarly, s.19(2) suggests that where the bill of lading makes the goods deliverable to the order of the seller or his agent, then the seller is assumed to have reserved the right of disposal; *Mitsui & Co. Ltd.* v. *Flota Mercante Grancolombiana SA (The Ciudad de Pasto and The Ciudad de Neiva)* [1989] 1 All E.R.951, C.A., cartons of prawns were sold on F.O.B. terms and shipped under bills of lading to the sellers' order. By the terms of the sale contract 80% of the price was paid in advance. Before the balance was paid, the prawns were damaged. The issue in this case was whether the property had passed to the buyer. It was held that by virtue of s.19(2) SGA, property had not passed. This was because the seller *prima facie* had reserved the right of disposal where the goods were, by the bill of lading, deliverable to the sellers' order. Thus, property could not pass until payment of the balance was made.

[562] *Clough Mill Ltd.* v. *Martin* [1985] 1 W.L.R.111; C sold yarn to Heatherdale to make into fabrics. The contract included a 'simple clause' which provided that property in the yarn remained with the seller until it was paid for or resold. C claimed to be entitled to the unused yarn at the time Heatherdale went into receivership. It was held that the plain words of the 'simple clause' were effective and C was entitled to the unused yarn.

[563] ***Aluminium Industrie Vaassen BV*** v. ***Romalpa Aluminium*** [1976] 1 Lloyd's Rep.443; C, sold aluminium foil to D. A clause in the contract provided that (1) ownership of the foil would not pass to D until it was paid for; (2) if the foil became mixed with other items during a

is the case which started the development of this area of law and pointed at the problems which retention clauses might cause in cases involving insolvency.[564]

Reservation of title clauses can be classified into various 'types':

'SIMPLE' CLAUSE: Which retains title to the goods supplied until the price for those goods is paid.[565] Such clauses are generally effective and do not create a charge.[566] It is important, however, that the clause retains legal title since it has been held that a clause which retained 'equitable and beneficial ownership' of goods allowed the legal title to pass to the buyer subject to the grant back to the seller of an equitable charge, which was void unless registered.[567]

Such reservation of title clause will generally require the buyer to store the seller's goods separately from other goods so they remain identifiable. The result of this would be that if the buyer fails to comply with this provision and goods are mixed with other similar goods, and cannot be identified, the seller may be able to claim a part of the 'mixture' equivalent to the amount of his goods which went into it.[568]

---

manufacturing process, C would become the owner of the finished product and property would not pass until D had paid for the foil; (3) unmixed foil and finished products should be stored separately; (4) D was authorised to sell the finished product on condition that C was entitled to the proceeds of the sale. D became insolvent and a receiver was appointed. The Court held that C was entitled to recover a quantity of unmixed foil and the proceeds of re-sale of some unmixed foil. Therefore, D was accountable to C for the foil and the proceeds of its sale and C could trace the proceeds into the hands of the receiver. It must be noted that as far as the tracing of the proceeds of sale is concerned, such proceeds were actually held in a separate account and so were identifiable. Furthermore, D conceded during the proceedings that a relationship of fiduciary nature between the parties existed.

564 *Borden* v. *Timber Products Ltd.* [1981] Ch.25; a seller supplied resin, and his title was extinguished when the resin was used to manufacture chipboard. In *Re Peachdart Ltd.* [1984] Ch.131, a seller supplied leather to be made into handbags. The contract provided, *inter alia*, that the property in the leather and any handbags made with it would remain with the seller until the price for the leather was paid, and that a fiduciary relationship existed for the purposes of any proceeds of sale of the handbags. It was held that as this clause created a charge on the manufactured handbags it would be void due to lack of registration.

565 *Hendy Lennox (Industrial Engines) Ltd.* v. *Grahame Puttick Ltd.* [1984] 2 Lloyd's Rep.422; where diesel engines were supplied by the seller on a 30 day credit. The buyer went into receivership with three engines on their premises which were fitted to the generator sets. The seller was able to recover one of these engines which was unsold under a simple reservation of title clause.

566 *Clough Mill Ltd.* v. *Martin* [1985] 1 W.L.R.111.

567 *Re Bond Worth Ltd.* [1980] Ch.228; fibre was supplied to Bond Worth on terms that until the price was paid equitable and beneficial ownership of the fibre, any products made from the fibre and any proceeds of re-sale, would remain with the suppliers. It was held that these terms created a charge over the buyer's assets and such a charge should be registered under the Companies Act. Hence the terms were void for want of registration.

568 *Indian Oil Corp. Ltd.* v. *Greenstone Shipping Corp.* [1988] Q.B.345.

'CURRENT ACCOUNT' OR 'ALL MONIES' CLAUSE: This would retain title to goods supplied until their price and other debts are paid. For example, a provision to the effect that property in the goods shall not pass until the buyer has paid all sums due to the seller on any account.

As an example, let us assume that X supplies some goods to Y under contracts which include a 'simple' reservation of title clause and which requires payment at the end of the month following delivery. X supplies 10 widgets in October and a further 10 in November. At the end of November Y pays for the goods delivered in October but in December Y becomes insolvent without paying for the December goods. It is then discovered that all 10 widgets delivered in December have been re-sold, but 8 of the 10 October widgets are still held in stock. Ordinarily, in such a case, X would have no claim to the widgets since they became the property of the buyer at the end of October when Y paid for them. To resolve this type of problem a current account clause may provide that, for example, 'widgets supplied by X remain X's property until you have paid all sums due to us on any account'. Such clause would therefore prevent title in the 10 October widgets passing to Y.[569]

'PRODUCTS' CLAUSE: Products manufactured using the goods are to be seller's property until the buyer has paid for the goods and used in the manufacture of new products.

The effectiveness of such clauses is doubtful where the manufacturing process results in the seller's goods being irreversibly incorporated into a new product,[570] or losing their identity.[571] This is because such clause would attempt to claim title to such manufactured products, which will give the seller no more than a charge[572] over the manufactured products to secure the sums owed to him.

'PROCEEDS OF SALE' CLAUSE: Courts are unlikely to uphold a seller's claim to an interest in proceeds of the buyer's re-sale. This is because a clause which makes an express claim to proceeds of re-sale is likely to be regarded as an

[569] In the Scottish case of *Armour* v. *Thyssen* [1990] 3 All E.R.481, it was held that a current account clause was effective, and therefore it seems that such a clause does not create a charge. *Cf.* Professor Diamond's suggestions in *A Review of Security Interests in Property*, H.M.S.O., 1989, Ch.17.

[570] It seems that if the manufacturing process is reversible and the goods can be detached from the manufactured product without any damage being caused, the seller can claim that he successfully retained title in them; *Hendy Lennox (Industrial Engines) Ltd.* v. *Grahame Puttick Ltd.* [1984] 2 Lloyd's Rep.422, which involved the removal of engines.

[571] *Borden* v. *Timber Products Ltd.* [1981] Ch.25. Perhaps another factor is whether the nature of the goods was fundamentally changed; *Modelboard* v. *Outerbox Ltd.* [1993] B.C.L.C.623, card used in the manufacture of cardboard boxes; *Chaigley Farms Ltd.* v. *Crawford, Kay and Grayshire Ltd.* [1996] B.C.C.957, animal carcasses skinned at an abattoir.

[572] Which would be void unless registered; *Re Bond Worth Ltd.* [1980] Ch.228.

assignment of future book-debts or a charge on the proceeds of re-sale, which will require registration as a charge.

CONCLUSION

For the purpose of the topic under consideration, the main points on *Romalpa* clauses are summarised below:

- A retention of title claim will only succeed if the assets claimed by the seller are his property under the terms of the clause.

- If seller's goods are affixed to other property but can be detached without damaging either item, they will not lose their identity and the seller can normally recover them.

- A retention of title clause will often require the buyer to store the seller's goods separately from his own. If the buyer fails to comply and mixes the goods with other goods so as to prevent their identification as seller's property, it is likely that the seller should be able to recover his share from the mixture.

- In order to succeed against a receiver a seller must establish a proprietary claim to the proceeds of sale. He must therefore show that the goods were sold by the buyer on his behalf and the proceeds of sale were received by the buyer in a fiduciary capacity.

- Although there is now an extensive body of case law in this area, it seems that its development was made on a piecemeal basis. It remains difficult to predict whether a particular clause will effectively protect a seller.[573]

- It seems that notwithstanding the *Romalpa* case, Courts are reluctant to recognise that a retention of title clause gives rise to a fiduciary relationship so as to give sellers a proprietary claim to proceeds of sale.

[573] Indeed, this area of law has been characterised by Courts as 'a maze if not a minefield'; per Staughton J., in *Hendy Lennox (Industrial Engines) Ltd.* v. *Grahame Puttick Ltd.* [1984] 2 Lloyd's Rep.422, 428. See also the current difficulties with the practice of attempting to create a fixed charge on a company's book debts in *Re Brumark* [2001] B.C.C.259. *Cf. Re New Bullas Trading Ltd.* [1994] B.C.C.36. It would now seem that for a fixed charge over book debts to be effective, the chargee must retain control not only of the debts but also of their proceeds.

TRANSFER OF TITLE BY NON-OWNERS (s.21)

As a general rule, a buyer cannot acquire ownership from someone who himself has neither ownership nor the owner's authority to sell. This rule derives from the legal rule which states that 'no one can give what he has not got' (*nemo dat quod non habet*), and it is known as the *nemo dat* rule. The rule is incorporated in section 21 of the Sale of Goods Act 1979 (as amended):

> ' ... where goods are sold by a person who is not their owner, and who does not sell them under the authority or with the consent of the owner, the buyer acquires no better title to the goods than the seller had ... '

In these circumstances, the buyer will be required to return the goods to their true owner. The buyer's only remedy is to sue the person who sold him the item for breach of section 12. In most of these cases, however, the seller is a rogue who disappears before the buyer can take action against him. The unsuspecting buyer is left to bear the full brunt of the rogue's misdeeds. It is not surprising, therefore, that exceptions to the 'no one can give what he has not got' rule have developed. These exceptions are as follows:

ESTOPPEL (s.21)

If the true owner by his conduct allows the innocent buyer to believe that the seller has the right to sell the goods,[574] ownership of the goods will pass to the buyer because the true owner will be prevented (estopped) from denying that the seller had the right to sell.[575]

---

[574] *Central Newbury Car Auctions Ltd.* v. *Unity Finance Ltd.* [1957] 1 Q.B.371; X offered to buy a car on hire-purchase from C, a car-dealer. X filled in a proposal form and was able to get possession of the car and its registration document from C. The hire-purchase company refused to finance the transaction since X gave a false address. Eventually, X managed to sell the car to a car dealer who sold the car to a second hire-purchase company and the fraud was discovered. C claimed the car from the second hire-purchase company (under the *nemo dat* rule), and D claimed that C were estopped by their conduct from denying that X had authority to sell. Their conduct being giving X the car and its registration document. It was held (by majority) that no estoppel arose since the giving of possession of the goods was not enough, and the car's registration document was not a document of title. *Moorgate Mercantile Co.* v. *Twitchings* [1977] A.C.890, H.L.; X took a car on hire-purchase and C, the hire-purchase company, failed to register the agreement with Hire Purchase Information Ltd. (H.P.I.). This was a scheme whereby a register is kept and which hire-purchase companies use to check if a car actually belongs to another hire-purchase company and not the seller. Nearly all car dealers used this service. X offered the car to D, a car-dealer, who bought the car after checking the H.P.I. register. C sued D under the *nemo dat* rule (for conversion), and D claimed that C was estopped because C owed a duty of care to car-dealers to register all hire-purchase agreement and this had been breached (i.e. they were negligent). It was held (by majority) that as H.P.I. was a voluntary scheme no duty of care was owed by C.

[575] Thus, in *Eastern Distributers Ltd.* v. *Goldring* [1957] 2 All E.R.525, C.A., X was the owner of a van. He wanted to buy a car form Y, a dealer, but he (X) could not raise enough money for

AGENCY (s.21(2))

The law of agency applies to contracts for the sale of goods. The Factors Act 1889 is also a statute which regulates the position where the goods are dealt with by an agent. An agent who sells his principal's goods in accordance with the principal's instructions passes a good title to the buyer because he is selling the goods with the authority and consent of the owner.

The buyer may even acquire a good title to the goods where the agent has exceeded his actual authority, provided the agent is acting within the scope of his apparent or ostensible authority and the buyer is unaware of the agent's lack of authority.[576] Section 21(2) enables the apparent owner of goods to dispose of them as if he was their true owner.

SALE BY A PERSON WITH A VOIDABLE TITLE (s.23)

A person may obtain possession of goods under a contract which is void, e.g. for mistake. A void contract is, in fact, no contract at all. A buyer in these circumstances does not acquire title to the goods and, therefore, cannot pass good title on to anyone else. The original owner will be able to maintain an action in tort to recover the goods or their value from a third party who bought them in good faith.[577] A person may also acquire goods under a contract which

a deposit. X and Y then devised a scheme to generate the necessary finance. Y would pretend that he owned the van; he would then sell the van and the car to a finance company, who would let both vehicles out on hire purchase to X. The proceeds of the sale of the van would raise sufficient money to finance the required hire purchased deposits. Unfortunately, the finance company accepted the proposal for the van but turned the car down. Unknown to X, Y proceeded to sell the van to the finance company. It was held that the finance company had become the owner of the van, because the original owner (X) by his conduct had allowed the buyers (the finance company) to believe that the seller (Y) had a right to sell the goods. *Shaw* v. *Commissioner of Police of the Metropolis* [1987] 1 W.L.R.1332, N was approached by X who told him that he had a buyer for N's car. N gave X possession of the car, together with the signed car's registration document, having also signed a disclaimer of legal responsibility for the car. X gave N a post-date cheque. C, a car-dealer, agreed to buy the car from X, and gave him a banker's draft. X failed to cash the bankers' draft and the fraud was discovered. C claimed that N was estopped by his conduct from denying that X had authority to sell the car, and N claimed ownership (under the *nemo dat* rule). It was held that N's conduct amounted to a representation that X was the owner of the car. However, as in this case there was no 'sale' (as provided by s.21) between X and C but only an agreement to sell, since the bankers' draft was never cashed, no property in the car ever passed to C. For ostensible authority, see ***supra***, p.135.

576 *Oppenheimer* v. *Attenborough & Son* [1908] 1 K.B.221, C.A.; a diamond broker got possession of some diamonds by the claimant dealer, under the pretence of showing them to customers. Instead, the broker sold the diamonds, and the claimant claimed ***inter alia***, that title could not have passed to the buyer under s.2 of the Factors Act 1889 because the buyer thought that he was dealing with the owner of the diamonds, not an agent, therefore the sale was not in the 'ordinary course of business' as required by s.2. It was held that 'ordinary course of business' meant 'within business hours, at a proper place of business and in other respects in the ordinary way in which a mercantile agent would act', therefore, title could pass to the buyer under s.2.

577 *Cundy* v. *Lindsay* (1878) 3 App.Case.459.

is voidable, e.g. misrepresentation. In this case, the contract is valid unless and until it is avoided. Section 23 provides that where goods are re-sold before the contract has been avoided, the buyer acquires a good title to them provided he buys them in good faith and without notice of the seller's defect of title.[578] If the original owner acts quickly to rescind the contract and then the goods are re-sold, the seller may be prevented from passing a good title to a purchaser.

SALE BY A SELLER IN POSSESSION OF THE GOODS (s.24)

Where a seller sells goods but remains in possession of them, or any documents of title relating to them, any re-sale to a second buyer, who actually takes physical delivery of the goods or the documents of title, will pass a good title to the second buyer.[579] The disappointed first buyer may sue the seller for non-delivery of the goods.

RE-SALE BY BUYER IN POSSESSION OF GOODS-with seller's consent (s.25)

Where a person who has bought or agreed to buy goods obtains possession of the goods with the consent of the seller,[580] any re-sale to a person who takes the goods in good faith and without notice of the rights of the original seller, has the same effect as if the person making the delivery or transfer were a mercantile agent in possession of the goods with the consent of the owner.[581]

---

[578] *Lewis* v. *Averay* [1972] 1 Q.B.232. But how can a seller avoid the contract after he has parted with his goods and the buyer cannot be found? In *Car and Universal Finance Co.* v. *Caldwell* [1965] 1 Q.B.525, C.A., a rogue purchased D's car with a cheque, which was later dishonoured. As soon as the defendant discovered the fraud notified the police and the A.A. (Automobile Association), and attempted, unsuccessfully, to find the rogue. The car was subsequently sold by the rogue to a car-dealer and the car ended into the hands of the claimants. D claimed title to the car. It was held *inter alia*, that although the general rule is that an intention to rescind must be communicated to the other party, on the facts to the rogue, where that party deliberately makes it impossible to communicate an intention to rescind, it would be allowed for the innocent party to use other methods, such as giving notice of the fraud to the police and the A.A., thus effectively rescinding the contract.

[579] *Pacific Motor Auctions Pty Ltd.* v. *Motor Credits (Hire Finance) Ltd.* [1965] 2 All E.R.105.

[580] *National Employers Insurance Association Ltd.* v. *Jones* [1988] 2 All E.R.425, H.L.; a stolen car was sold to X, who then re-sold it to Y, who re-sold it to D. C, the original owner's insurers, claimed the car but D alleged that he had obtained title under s.9 of the Factors Act. This was based on the suggestion that s.9 provided that consent to the buyer in possession must be given by the seller, and not necessarily by original owner. Consequently, Y, who sold the car to D, obtained possession with the consent of X, the seller, and so the sale to D was protected by s.9 of the Factors Act 1889. This was rejected by the Court, which suggested that under s.2 of the Factors Act a mercantile agent can only divest the original owner of title to goods if he was entrusted with the goods by that owner. This was not the case here, since the original owner of the car did not entrust her car to the thief.

[581] In *Newtons of Wembley Ltd.* v. *Williams* [1965] 1 Q.B.560, C.A., C sold a car to a rogue, who paid for it by a cheque which was later dishonoured. C took immediate steps to rescind his

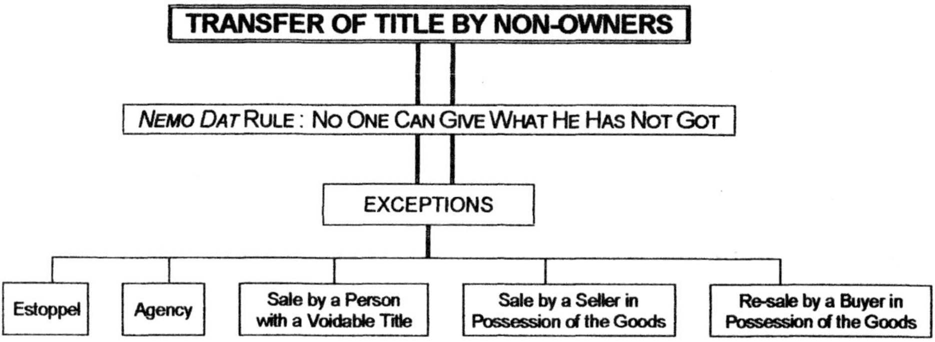

Diagram 8: Transfer of Title

PERFORMANCE OF THE CONTRACT

It is the duty of the seller to deliver the goods and the buyer's duty to accept and pay for them. The parties are free to make their own arrangements about the time and place of delivery and payment.

The Act sets out the obligations of the seller and buyer, when they have not dealt with these matters specifically in their agreement. Section 28 provides that 'Unless otherwise agreed, delivery of the goods and payment of the price are concurrent conditions'. This means that the seller can hold on to the goods until the buyer has paid for them.

DELIVERY

Delivery in the context of the Act means the voluntary transfer of possession from one person to another. The delivery may consist of:

1) physically handing over the goods;

2) handing over the means of control of the goods, e.g. the keys to the premises where they are stored;

3) transferring documents of title; or

contract with the rogue, by informing the police. Some time later, the rogue re-sold the car in a well-established street market in used cars. Y, the buyer then sold the car to another person D. It was held that D acquired a good title to the car. When the rogue sold the car at the market, he was a buyer in possession with the owner's (C) consent and he acted in the same way as a mercantile agent would have done. He (the rogue) passed a good title to the purchaser (Y) who in turn passed title to D.

4) where the goods are in possession of a third party, an acknowledgement by the third party that he is holding the goods on behalf of the buyer.

PLACE OF DELIVERY

In the absence of any agreement to the contrary, the place of delivery is the seller's place of business; it is up to the buyer to come and collect the goods.[582] If, however, the seller agrees to send the goods and engages a carrier for this purpose, section 32(1) provides that delivery to the carrier is deemed to be delivery to the buyer. The seller must make the best possible contract with the carrier on behalf of the buyer to ensure the safe arrival of the goods.

TIME OF DELIVERY

The parties may have fixed a delivery date. Failure to make delivery by that date is a breach of condition, which entitles the buyer to repudiate the contract and sue for non-delivery. Where the seller agrees to send the goods and no time for sending them has been agreed, he must despatch them within a reasonable time.[583] A demand for delivery by the buyer or an offer of delivery by the seller will not be valid unless made at a reasonable hour. What is reasonable is a question of fact. If the seller is ready and willing to deliver the goods and he requests the buyer to take delivery, but the buyer does not comply with the request within a reasonable time, then the buyer will be liable for any resulting loss and a reasonable charge for the care and custody of the goods.

DELIVERY OF THE WRONG QUANTITY

If the seller delivers a smaller quantity than ordered, the buyer may reject the consignment, but if he decides to accept the goods, he must pay for them at the contract rate.[584] If the seller sends a larger quantity than agreed, the buyer has the following choices:[585]

[582] However, where the goods are specific goods and at the time of the contract the seller and buyer are aware of the goods' location, then such location will be deemed to be the place of delivery; s.29(2).
[583] Section 29(3).
[584] Section 30(1).
[585] Section 30(2). It must be noted however, that s.30(2A) further provides that in non-consumer contracts, where the quantity of goods delivered is either less or larger than that contracted for, the buyer may not reject the reject the goods if the shortfall or excess is so slight it would be unreasonable to do so.

1) he may accept the goods he ordered and reject the rest, or
2) he may reject the lot, or
3) he may accept the whole consignment, paying for the extra goods at the contract rate.

If the seller delivers the contract goods but they are mixed with other goods, which have not been ordered, the buyer may either accept the contract goods and reject the rest, or reject the whole lot.[586]

DELIVERY BY INSTALMENTS

Unless otherwise agreed, the buyer is not bound to accept delivery by instalments.[587] The parties may, of course, agree that the goods are to be delivered in stated instalments.

A breach of contract may occur in respect of one or more instalments, e.g., the seller may deliver goods which are not fit for the purpose or the buyer may refuse to take delivery of an instalment. Clearly, the injured party will be able to sue for damages, but the question then arises whether he is also entitled to repudiate the contract.

The answer depends on whether the contract is *indivisible (entire)* or *severable (divisible)*. A contract is usually treated as being severable if each instalment is to be separately paid for.[588]

1) Indivisible Contracts: A breach of condition in respect of the first instalment will entitle the injured party to repudiate the whole contract. Breaches of condition in relation to the second and subsequent instalments must be treated as breaches of warranty for which the only remedy is an action in damages.

2) Severable Contracts: Whether a breach in relation to one or more instalment will entitle the injured party to repudiate the whole contract, depends 'on the terms of the contract and the circumstances of the case'.

If the contract is silent on the matter, the Courts apply two main tests; (a) the size of the breach in relation to the whole contract, and (b) the likelihood that the breach will be repeated.[589]

---

586 Thus, in *Shipton, Anderson & Co. Ltd.* v. *Weil Bros & Co. Ltd.* [1912] 1 K.B.574, X agreed to deliver 4,950 tons of wheat. They in fact delivered 4,950 tons 55lb. It was held that the difference was so trifling that it did not entitle the buyers to reject the whole consignment.

587 Section 31(1).

588 Depending on the particular circumstances, such breach may be severable; s.31(2).

589 Thus, in *Maple Flock Co. Ltd.* v. *Universal Furniture Products (Wembley) Ltd.* [1934] 1 K.B.148, C.A., the claimants agreed to sell and deliver 100 tons of flock by instalments. The first 15 instalments were satisfactory but the 16th was not up to the required standard. The defendants, buyers, then took delivery of 4 more satisfactory loads before refusing further

Indeed, similar tests appear to be applied by the Courts on non-sale of goods contracts involving instalment payments.[590]

ACCEPTANCE

The buyer is bound to accept the goods which the seller delivers in accordance with the contract.[591] Acceptance is deemed to have taken place when:

1) the buyer tells the seller that he has accepted the goods; or
2) he does anything to the goods which is inconsistent with the ownership of the seller (e.g. he re-sells them); or
3) he retains the goods after the lapse of a reasonable time without telling the seller that he has rejected them.

Finally, if the buyer exercises his right to reject the goods for breach of a condition, he must inform the seller of his refusal to accept them but he is not obliged to return them to the seller.[592]

SELLER'S REMEDIES

Two types of remedies are open to the seller.[593] He can pursue (a) *personal remedies* against the buyer himself and (b) *real remedies* against the goods. The former are actions the unpaid seller can take against the buyer, whereas the latter relate to seller's exercisable rights over the goods.

(a) PERSONAL REMEDIES

The seller can sue the buyer for the contract price or for damages for non-acceptance.

---

deliveries. It was held that the defendants were not entitled to repudiate the contract. The defective flock constituted a small proportion of the total quantity delivered and there was little likelihood of the breach being repeated. Thus, breach was severable and the contract as a whole stood. It also seems that in a severable contract involving a number of instalments, if the breaches occur at the beginning, i.e. the first instalments, then it is more likely that the breach will be repeated.

[590] *Fortman Holdings Ltd.* v. *Modem Holdings Ltd.* [2001] EWCA Civ. 1235; purchase of company shares by instalment payments.

[591] Section 27.

[592] Section 36.

[593] It would seem that under both available remedies interest may be claimed, s.54; see the effect of the Late Payment of Commercial Debts (Interest) Act 1998, *supra,* footnote 523.

(i) ***Action for the price*** (s.49): The seller can bring an action for the contract price in two situations:

(1) where the property in the goods has passed to the buyer,[594] or

(2) where the buyer has failed to pay by a specified date,[595] irrespective of whether ownership has passed to the buyer.

(ii) ***Damages for non-acceptance*** (s.50): If the property in the goods has not passed and the buyer will not accept the goods, the seller can sue for non-acceptance. The measure of damages is the estimated loss directly and naturally resulting in the ordinary course of events from the buyer's breach of contract.[596] If the buyer wrongfully refuses to accept and pay for the goods, the seller is expected to mitigate his loss and sell them elsewhere for the best possible price.

Section 50(3) provides guidance as to the measure of damages where there is an available market for the goods.[597] If the market price is less than the contract price, the seller can recover the difference by way of damages. Where the market price is the same or even higher than the contract price, the seller will be entitled to nominal damages only. The market price is calculated at the time when the goods ought to have been accepted.[598]

Where there is no available market, the seller's damages will be based on the first part of the *Hadley*[599] principle, i.e. damages directly and naturally resulting, in the ordinary course of events from the buyer's

[594] The buyer cannot sue for the price under this section, even where the failure of property to pass was the fault of the buyer; *Stein, Forbes & Co.* v. *County Tailoring* (1916) 115 L.T.215.

[595] Payment against documents upon the arrival of the ship carrying the goods would not be give the right for the seller to sue under this part, since the date of payment is not specified; *Stein, Forbes & Co.* v. *County Tailoring* (1916) 115 L.T.215.

[596] Section 50(2).

[597] The notion of available market is not as clear as it first appears. Section 50(3) provides only a *prima facie* rule, and it does not apply where it is unjust to do so; *Thompson W.L. Ltd.* v. *Robinson (Gunmakers) Ltd.* [1955] 1 All E.R.154, D ordered a new Vanguard car from C, a car dealer, but then D refused to accept it. C argued that he was only liable to pay nominal damages, since the contract price and the market price were the same. It was held that there was no 'available market' for Vanguard cars because supply exceeded demand and, therefore, s.50(3) did not apply. There would not be an available market unless the price of goods is fixed by supply and demand; *Charter* v. *Sullivan* [1957] 1 All E.R.809, D refused to accept a new Hillman Minx car which he had ordered from a dealer. In contrast to the previous case, the demand for this kind of cars exceeded supply and the dealer would have no difficulty in finding another buyer. It was held that the dealer was entitled to nominal damages only. D's breach would not affect the total number of cars that he (the dealer) would sell over a period of time. Furthermore, there would not be an available market where the goods involved are unique; *Lazenbury Garages Ltd.* v. *Wright* [1976] 2 All E.R.770, C.A., the Court held, ***inter alia***, that a second hand car was unique, and therefore there was no available market.

[598] Section 50(3).

[599] *Hadley* v. *Baxendale* (1854) 9 Exch.341.

breach.[600] If costs incurred by the seller, necessary in order to mitigate the loss, then such costs, e.g. for modifying the goods, storage costs, advertising costs, etc., may be recovered.[601]

(b) Real Remedies

The unpaid seller has three possible remedies in respect of the goods even though the property in the goods has passed to the buyer:

(i) **Lien** (ss.41-43): A lien is a right to retain possession of goods until the contract price has been paid. It does not give the right to the possessor to re-sell the goods. Liens are available in any of the following circumstances:

(a) where the goods have been sold without any mention of credit;

(b) where the goods have been sold on credit but the period of credit has expired;

(c) where the buyer becomes insolvent.

The seller will lose his right of lien if the price is paid or tendered or the buyer obtains possession of the goods. The seller cannot exercise this right to retain the goods if he has handed the goods to a carrier for transportation to the buyer without reserving the right of disposal of the goods or where he has given up the right.

(ii) **Stoppage in Transit** (ss.44-46): This is the right of the seller to stop goods in transit to the buyer, regain possession of them and retain them until payment has been received. The seller can exercise his right to stoppage in transit in only one situation: where the buyer has become insolvent.

(iii) **Right of re-sale** (ss.47-48): The rights of lien and stoppage in transit by themselves do not give the seller any right to re-sell the goods. He is allowed, however, to re-sell the goods in the following circumstances:

(a) where the goods are of a perishable nature;

(b) where the seller gives notice to the buyer of his intention to re-sell and the buyer does not pay or tender the price within a reasonable time;

---

[600] Section 50(2).

[601] By way of special damages; s.54. The section also provides for the recovery of interest; *infra*, footnote 523.

(c) where the seller expressly reserves the right of re-sale in the event of the buyer defaulting.

The seller can exercise the right of re-sale and also recover damages for any loss sustained by the buyer's breach of contract. The original contract of sale is rescinded and the new buyer acquires a good title to the goods as against the original buyer.

BUYER'S REMEDIES

Various remedies are available to the buyer, where the seller is in breach of contract.[602]

(a) REJECTION OF THE GOODS (s.11)

The buyer may repudiate the contract and reject the goods where the seller is in breach of a condition of the contract. Most of the implied terms contained in sections 12-15 are conditions, so if the goods are not of merchantable quality or fit for a particular purpose, the buyer is entitled to reject them. This right will be lost as soon as the goods have been accepted; the buyer must treat the breach of condition as a breach of warranty which limits his remedy to a claim for damages.

(b) AN ACTION FOR DAMAGES

The following actions for damages may be taken by the buyer:

(i) **Non-Delivery** (s.51): The buyer can sue for non-delivery when the seller wrongfully neglects or refuses to deliver the goods. The measure of

[602] The Sale and Supply of Goods to Consumers Regulations 2002, (S.I.2002, No.3045), which implement Directive 1999/44/E.C. on Certain Aspects of the Sale of Consumer Goods and Associated Guarantees (O.J. L 171, 07/07/1999, p.12), by Regulation 5 inserts 'Part 5A - Additional Rights of Buyer in Consumer Cases' in the Sale of Goods Act 1979. Part 5A contains new sections (48A-F) which apply to consumer sales, and add a considerable array of remedies. For example, any breach of the implied or express terms of the sale contract would entitle the consumer/buyer to require the seller to repair or replace the goods (s.48B(1)), or if these remedies are refused, then the consumer/buyer can request a price reduction or return the goods (s.48C(1)). Furthermore, the seller should respond to a consumer/buyer's repair or replace request within reasonable time (s.48B(2)(a)). Presumably, if the seller does not respond within reasonable time, then this could be taken as constructive refusal, and the consumer/buyer should be able to use s.48C(1), i.e. reduce the price, or return the goods. Goods returned within six months of delivery are presumed defective (s.48A(3)).

damages is the estimated loss directly and naturally resulting in the ordinary course of events from the seller's breach of contract. Where there is an available market for the goods, the measure of damages is usually the difference between the contract price and the higher price of obtaining similar goods elsewhere. If the buyer has paid in advance and the goods are not delivered, he can recover the amount paid because there has been a total failure of consideration.[603]

(ii) Breach of Warranty (s.53): The buyer can sue for damages under section 53 in the following circumstances:

(a) where the seller is in breach of warranty;

(b) where the seller is in breach of a condition, but the buyer has chosen to carry on with the contract and claim damages instead;

(c) where the seller is in breach of a condition, but the buyer has lost the right to reject the goods, because he has accepted them.

The measure of damages is the estimated loss directly and naturally resulting from the breach.[604] This is the difference in value between the goods actually delivered and goods fulfilling the warranty.

(c) SPECIFIC PERFORMANCE (s.52)

The buyer may sue for specific performance but only in cases where the goods are specific or ascertained and where monetary damages would not be an adequate remedy. Therefore, a Court is unlikely to make such an order if similar goods are available elsewhere.

---

[603] Section 54, Sale of Goods Act 1979 (as amended); see the effect of the Late Payment of Commercial Debts (Interest) Act 1998, *supra*, footnote 523.

[604] *Bence Graphics Ltd.* v. *Fasson U.K. Ltd.* [1997] 1 All E.R.979, C.A.; over a number of years D, the buyers, purchased vinyl film to make into special labels used in cargo containers. C, the sellers were aware that D would be selling the signs on to their customers. It was a term of the contract that the film would survive in good condition for five years. D, the buyers, used the film to make those signs which they sold, however, it turned out that the film would not last very long because of a latent defect which caused the signs to fade in sunlight and become unreadable. However, D, the buyers, had received no complaints from any sub-buyers. D claimed damages for breach of warranty. It was held that s.53(3) provided a prima facie rule only. The loss could have been greater than the purchase price, e.g. if all sub-buyers had sued the buyers, or nil, e.g. if all sub-buyers had suffered no loss. In this case D, the buyers, were awarded damages only for the remainder of the film which they could not use.

CHAPTER 7

EXEMPTION CLAUSES

Exemption clauses are a common feature of business contracts. They are express terms which seek to exclude or limit the liability that might belong to one party in the event of a breach of contract. Such clauses are perfectly fair where they are the result of free negotiations between equals, but, all too often, they are imposed on a weaker party by a stronger party. This abuse of freedom of contract was most commonly practised against consumers. The Courts attempted to deal with the problem, but the common law ultimately proved unequal to the ingenuity of those who sought the protection of the exemption.

Over the years, Parliament stepped in to control the use of unfair exemption clauses in particular kinds of contracts and now the overwhelming majority of these clauses are covered by the provisions of the Unfair Contract Terms Act 1977.

Statutory control of exemption clauses has been grafted on to the pre-existing common law rules. It is still necessary, therefore, to examine the attitude of the Courts to these clauses first, and afterwards consider how Parliament has dealt with the problem.

A. JUDICIAL CONTROL

The judges based their attack on exemption clauses on two main fronts, namely, incorporation and interpretation.

INCORPORATION

The person wishing to rely on an exclusion clause must show that it formed part of the contract. In this connection the following rules must be remembered:

(i) Signed Documents
Where the exemption clause is contained in a document which has been signed, it will automatically form part of the contract. The signer is presumed to have read and understood the significance of all the terms contained in the

document.[605] Note that this general rule will not apply where the signer can plead *non est factum*, i.e. 'this is not my deed', or if the other party has misrepresented the terms of the agreement.[606]

(ii) Unsigned Documents

The exemption clause may be contained in an unsigned document such as a ticket or a notice. The clause will only form part of the contract if two conditions are met. First, the document must be regarded by a reasonable man as contractual in nature and as such likely to contain exemption clauses.[607] Even if the document may be regarded as contractual, the person seeking to rely on the exemption clause must show that reasonable steps have been taken either before the contract was made or at the time the contract was made to give notice of the clause to the other contracting party.[608]

(iii) Previous Course of Dealings

An exclusion clause may be binding even though it has not been included in the contract in question, if a previous course of dealings between the parties on the

---

[605] *L'Estrange* v. *F Graucob Ltd.* [1934] 2 K.B. 394; X bought an automatic cigarette vending machine for use in her cafe. X signed a 'sales agreement' which provided that 'any express or implied condition, statement or warranty, statutory or otherwise, not stated herein is hereby excluded'. She did not read this document and was completely unaware of the sweeping exclusion clause hidden in the small print. The machine did not work properly but it was held that X was still bound to pay for it because by signing the agreement and in the absence of fraud, X had effectively signed her rights away.

[606] Thus in *Curtis* v. *Chemical Cleaning and Dyeing Co.* [1951] 1 K.B.805, X took a wedding dress to be cleaned by Y. She signed a piece of paper headed 'Receipt' after being told by the assistant that it exempted the cleaners from liability for damage to beads and sequins. The 'Receipt' in fact contained a clause excluding liability 'for any damage howsoever arising'. When the dress was returned it was badly stained. It was held that the cleaners (Y) could not escape liability for damage to the material of the dress by relying on the exemption clause because its scope had been misrepresented by Y's assistant.

[607] Thus, in *Chapelton* v. *Barry Urban District Council* [1940] 1 K.B.532, X took a deck chair from a stack near which was a notice which gave the price of hire at so much per session of so many hours and requested the public to obtain tickets from the chair attendant and retain them for inspection. He obtained a ticket which he put into his pocket without reading. Each ticket contained a clause exempting the Council from liability for 'any accident or damage arising from the hire of the chair'. X was injured when the chair he sat on collapsed. He successfully sued the Council. The court held that a reasonable man would assume that the ticket was a mere receipt and not a contractual document which might contain conditions. The Council had not succeeded in incorporating the exemption into their contract with X. Furthermore, the Court held that the ticket was a mere receipt for the hire charge.

[608] Thus, in *Olley* v. *Marlborough Court Ltd.* [1949] 1 K.B.532, X booked in for a week's stay at Y's hotel. There was a notice in the bedroom, which stated that 'the proprietors will not hold themselves responsible for articles lost or stolen unless handed to the manager for safe custody'. A stranger gained access to X's room and stole some of his belongings. The court held that Y were liable since X saw the notice only after the contract had been concluded at the reception desk. The exclusion clause could not protect Y because it had not been incorporated into the contract with X.

basis of such terms can be established.[609] This principle has been accepted more readily in commercial contracts than in consumer transactions.[610]

(iv) Privity of Contract

According to the doctrine of privity of contract a person who is not a party to a contract can neither benefit from the contract nor be made liable under it.

So while a duly incorporated exemption clause may protect a party to a contract it will not protect his servants or agents. They are strangers to the contract and so cannot take advantage of an exclusion or limitation clause,[611] nor can they sue (in their own name) on such a contract to which they are not a party.[612]

---

[609] Thus, in *J. Spurling* v. *Bradshaw* [1956] 1 Lloyd's Rep.392, D delivered 8 barrels of orange juice to C who were warehousemen. A few days later D received a document from C which acknowledged receipt of the barrels. It also contained a clause exempting D from liability for loss or damage 'occasioned by the negligence, wrongful act or default' caused by themselves, their employees or agents. When D collected the barrels some were empty, and some contained dirty water. D refused to pay the storage charges and was sued by C. Although D did not receive the document containing the exclusion clause until after the conclusion of the contract, the clause had been incorporated into the contract as a result of a regular course of dealings between the parties over the years. D had received similar documents on previous occasions and he was now bound by the terms contained in them. *Cf. Poseidon Freight Forwarding Co. Ltd.* v. *Davies Turner Southern Ltd.* 2 Lloyd's Rep.388, C and D were freight forwarders. In 1992 D misdelivered two consignments shipped by C and was liable for the loss unless it could be shown that the contract between C and D incorporated the British International Freight Association (B.I.F.A.) Standard Trading Conditions 1989 edition. D argued that the terms were incorporated either initially by means of documents transmitted to C by D or by a course of dealing. Seven documents and 69 faxes were received by C before 1992 and although the documents bore the B.I.F.A. terms on the back, none of the faxes did, although many stated that they did. It was held that reasonable notice of the BIFA terms was not given to C. The terms were only actually sent regarding eastbound shipments and therefore C was entitled to assume that the terms did not apply to westbound shipments.

[610] *Finska Cellulosaforeningen (Finnish Cellulose Union)* v. *Westfield Paper Co. Ltd.* [1940] 68 Ll. L. Rep.75; a C.I.F. seller tendered a bill of lading to the buyer which contained the words 'all conditions and exceptions as per charter-party'. It was held that the seller was not obliged to tender the charter-party since there had been a long standing course of dealing between the parties on the terms of the standard form of charter-party, which was known to the buyer.

[611] Thus, in *Scruttons Ltd.* v. *Midland Silicones Ltd.* [1962] A.C.446, X, a shipping firm, agreed to ship a drum of chemicals belonging to Y from N. York to London. The contract of carriage limited the liability of the carrier, i.e. X, for damage to £179 per package. The drum was damaged by the negligence of Z, a firm of stevedores, who had been engaged by X (the carrier) to unload the ship. Y sued Z in tort for the full extent of the damage, which amounted to £593. Z claimed the protection of the limitation clause. It was held that as Z were not parties to the contract of carriage (between X and Y), Y's action succeeded. The Court in this case said that a way in which the benefit of an exemption could be made available to a third party, such as the firm of stevedores, by fulfilling the following four conditions: (a) A contract of carriage must specifically state that the stevedore is intended to be protected by the exemption clause; (b) the carrier must make it clear that he is contracting both on his own behalf and as agent for the stevedores; (c) the carrier has authority from the stevedore to act in this way, and (d) there is some consideration moving from the stevedore.

[612] This doctrine of privity gave rise to injustice; *Beswick* v. *Beswick* [1967] 2 All E.R.1197. This was particularly so, where a third party was a beneficiary of a contract, but if there was a breach of such contract, only the parties which concluded it could sue in their own name.

Interpretation

Where a clause is duly incorporated into a contract, the Courts will proceed to examine the words used to see if the clause covers the breach and loss which has actually occurred. The main rules of interpretation used by the Courts[613] are as follows:

(i) Strict Interpretation

An exemption clause will be effective only if it expressly covers the kind of liability which has in fact arisen. A clause, for example, which excludes liability for a breach of warranty will not provide protection against liability for a breach of condition.[614]

(ii) *Contra Proferentem*

If there is any ambiguity or doubt as to the meaning of an exemption clause the court will construe it *contra proferentem*, i.e. against the party who inserted it in the contract. Very clear words must be used before a party will be held exempt from liability in negligence.[615]

Hence, such a third party was considerably disadvantaged. However, by s.1 of the Contracts (Rights of Third Parties) Act 1999, a third party may now sue to enforce a contractual term if the contract expressly states that he can, or if the contract confers a benefit upon him. Nevertheless, difficulties still exist in this area, in circumstances where the person who suffers loss is not a party to the contract he may have difficulties pursuing a claim; see *Alfred McAlpine Construction Ltd.* v. *Panatown Ltd. (No.1)* [2001] A.C.518, H.L.

613 When attempting to interpret a contractual provision, a Court must 'place itself in the same factual matrix as that on which the parties were. All of these opinions seem to me implicitly to recognise that, in the search for the relevant background, there may be facts, which form part of the circumstances in which the parties contract in which one, or both, may take no particular interest, their minds being addressed to or concentrated on other facts, so that if asked they would assert that they did not have these facts in the forefront of their mind, but that will not prevent those facts from forming part of an objective setting in which the contract is to be construed', per Wilberforce, L.J., *The Diana Prosperity* (1976) 2 Lloyd's Rep.621, 625.

614 Thus, in *Baldry* v. *Marshall* [1925] 1 K.B.260, X asked Y, who were car dealers, to supply a car that would be suitable for touring purposes. Y recommended a Bugatti, which X bought. The written contract excluded Y's liability for any 'guarantee or warranty, statutory or otherwise'. The car turned out to be unsuitable for X's purposes, so he rejected it and sued to recover what he had paid. It was held that the requirement that the car be suitable for touring was a condition. Since the clause did not exclude liability for breach of a condition, X was not bound by it.

615 Thus, in *White* v. *John Warwick & Co. Ltd.* [1953] 2 All E.R.1021, C hired a cycle from D. The written hire agreement stated that 'Nothing in this agreement shall render the owners liable for any personal injury'. While C was riding the cycle, the saddle tilted forward and he was injured. D might have been liable in tort (for negligence) as well as in contract. It was held that the ambiguous wording of the exclusion clause would effectively protect D from their strict contractual liability, but it would not exempt them from liability in negligence. See also *Pera Shipping Corporation* v. *Petroship S.A., (The Pera)* [1984] 2 Lloyd's Rep.363, where a clause D had introduced relating to the time to bring a claim D was held to be ambiguous and hence D could not rely to avoid C's claim.

(iii) Repugnancy

Under this rule, a court can strike out an exemption clause which is inconsistent with or repugnant to the main purpose of the contract.[616]

B. Statutory Control

At first, Parliament intervened on a piecemeal basis to control the use of exemption clauses in specific types of contract. However, the introduction and enactment of the Unfair Contact Terms Act 1977 changed this by laying down rules of general application to most contracts.

Unfair Contract Terms Act 1977

a) The title of the Act is misleading in two respects: (i) it affects the law of tort as well as contract law because it covers non-contractual notices and signs, and (ii) it does not deal with all unfair terms in contracts, only unfair exemption of liability clauses.

b) Most of the provisions of the Act apply only to 'business liability', i.e. liability for things done in the course of business or from the occupation of premises used for business purposes. A business includes a profession and the activities of any government department or local or public authority.

c) The Act does not apply to international supply contracts (section 26) and sections 2-4 do not apply to certain contracts listed in Schedule 1, which includes:

   i) contracts of insurance;
   ii) contracts in relation to land;
   iii) contracts of marine salvage;
   iv) contracts for the carriage of goods by ship;
   v) contracts of affreightment (i.e. charter-parties).[617]

[616] Thus, in *J. Evans & Sons (Portsmouth) Ltd.* v. *Andrea Merzario Ltd.* [1976] 2 Lloyd's Rep.165, C had imported machines from Italy for many years and for this purpose C used the services of D, who were forwarding agents. When D changed over to containers C was orally promised to be stowed below deck. On one occasion C's container was stored on deck and it was lost overboard. It was held that D could not rely on an exemption clause contained in the standard conditions of the forwarding trade, on which the parties had contracted, because it was repugnant to the oral promise that had been given.

[617] As to charter-parties, see *infra*, p.261.

d) The Act affords the greatest protection to consumers; under section 12(1) a person 'deals as a consumer' if:

   i) he neither makes the contract in the course of a business nor holds himself out as doing so,[618] and

   ii) the other party does make the contract in the course of a business, and

   iii) if it involves a contract for the supply of goods that are of a type ordinarily supplied for private use or consumption.[619]

e) Exemption clauses are regulated by the Act in two ways. They are either rendered void and completely ineffective or they are made subject to a test of reasonableness. Although the application of the 'reasonableness test' is a matter for the court to decide in the light of all the circumstances of a particular case, the Act lays down some guiding principles for the judges.

Reasonableness

The following simple rules applicable to reasonableness should be noted:

a) Reasonableness must be judged in the case of a contractual term in the light of circumstances at the time when the contract was made and in the case of a non-contractual notice or sign, when the liability arose.

b) It is up to the person who claims that a term or notice is reasonable to show that it is.

---

618 It would seem that the expression 'person' in this context may include a legal entity, e.g. a limited company; *R. & B. Customs Brokers Co. Ltd.* v. *United Dominions Trust Ltd* [1988] 1 All E.R.847, where the purchase of a car by a limited company for use by the company's directors was treated as a consumer transaction on the basis that such transaction was not a regular one within the business of the company. More recently, in *Feldaroll Foundry Plc.* v. *Hermes Leasing (London) Ltd.* [2004] EWCA Civ. 747, the Court of Appeal stated that the words 'deals as a consumer' in the 1977 Act, was consistent with the wider meaning which the Court gave to the words 'seller in the course of a business' in the Sale of Goods Act 1979. The fact that C, the buyer, was a public company and in *R.& B. Customs Brokers* case involved a one man private company was insufficient to distinguish the present case on the facts. A declaration made by the car's driver in the agreement that the car was to be used for business purposes was also irrelevant, as it was not directed to the capacity in which C, the buyer, was dealing. *Cf.* Regulation 3(1) of Unfair Terms in Consumer Contracts Regulations 1999, (S.I.1999, No.2083), see *infra*, p.188.

619 Regulation 14(2), of the Sale and Supply of Goods to Consumers Regulations 2002, (S.I.2002, No.3045), implementing Directive 1999/44/E.C. on Certain Aspects of the Sale of Consumer Goods and Associated Guarantees (O.J. No. L 171, 07/07/1999, p.12), amends this definition of 'dealing as consumer' by providing that where the consumer/party dealing as consumer is an individual the requirement that the contract involves the supply of goods ordinarily supplied for private use or consumption can be ignored.

c) Where the exemption clause appears in any kind of contract under which goods are supplied, its reasonableness may be judged according to the criteria contained in Schedule 2, which are as follows:

(i) The bargaining strengths of the parties relative to each other and the availability of alternative supplies. A monopoly supplier, for example, will find it difficult to justify a wide exclusion clause.[620]

(ii) Whether the customer received an inducement to agree to the term. The supplier may have offered the customer a choice, such as lower price but subject to an exemption clause or a higher price without the exemption. Provided a real choice is available, the supplier will probably be able to show that the exemption clause was reasonable.

(iii) Whether the customer knew or ought reasonably to have known of the existence and extent of the term. If the customer goes into the contract with his eyes wide open, he may have to accept the exemption clause.[621]

(iv) Where the term excludes or restricts any relevant liability if some condition is not complied with, whether it was reasonable at the time of the contract to expect that compliance with that condition would be practicable. A supplier, for example, may limit his liability to defects which are brought to his attention within a certain time, e.g. three days. The Court will consider whether compliance with such a time limit is practicable.[622]

(v) Whether the goods were manufactured, processed or adapted to the special order of the customer. An exemption clause may well be reasonable if the customer has insisted on the supplier complying with detailed specifications.

---

[620] Thus, in *Waldron-Kelly* v. *British Railways Board* [1981] C.L.Y.303, C placed a suitcase in the care of B.R. at Stockport railway station for delivery to Haverford West railway station. B.R.'s General Conditions of Carriage limited their liability for non-delivery to an amount assessed by reference to the weight of the goods. The suitcase disappeared and C claimed £320.32 as the full value of the suitcase. B.R. sought to rely on their conditions which limited their liability to £27. It was held that B.R. could not rely on the exemption clause because it did not satisfy the requirement of reasonableness. C was awarded £320.32.

[621] *Granville Oil & Chemicals Ltd.* v. *Davies Turner & Co.* [2003] 2 Lloyd's Rep.356; *Watford Electronics Ltd.* v. *Sanderson C.F.L. Ltd.*, [2001] 1 All E.R. (Comm) 696.

[622] Thus, in *Lally and Weller* v. *George Bird* 23 May 1980, (unreported), C agreed to undertake a house removal for D for £100.80. The contract contained exemption clauses which limited C's liability for losses or breakages to £10 per article and excluded all liability unless claims were made within three days. It was held that these clauses were unreasonable. *Stewart Gill Ltd.* v. *Horatio Myer & Co. Ltd.* [1992] 1 Q.B.600; a clause in a sale contract provided *inter alia* that 'The customer shall not be entitled to withhold any amount due to the company under the contract by reason of .... set off counterclaim allegation of incorrect or defective goods', was held to be ineffective.

The reasonableness of exemption clauses in contracts other than for the sale or supply of goods must be judged without the benefit of the above criteria. The following is a short description of the more important sections of the Unfair Contract Terms Act 1977:

Section 2 - Exemption of liability for negligence
Under section 2(1) no one acting in the course of a business can exclude or restrict his liability in negligence for death or personal injury by means of a term in a contract or by way of a notice. Liability in negligence for any other kind of loss or damage can be excluded provided the term or notice satisfies the 'reasonableness test'.

Section 3 - Exemption of liability for breach of contract
This section applies to two types of contract:

i) where the other party deals as a consumer; and

ii) where the business uses its own written standard terms of business.

In both cases, the business cannot exclude or limit liability for breach of contract, non-performance of the contract or different performance of the contract unless the exemption clause satisfies the requirement of reasonableness.[623]

Section 4 - Unreasonable indemnity clauses
An indemnity clause is a term in a contract between two parties, X and Y, in which Y agrees to indemnify X for any liability that X may be under. X may incur liability in respect of a third party, Z, in which case Y must compensate X for any claim which is made by Z against X. For example a builder, may get the owner of a house to agree to indemnify him for any injury or damage that his work on the house might cause to third parties. So if the builder negligently demolishes a wall and injures a next door neighbour, the builder can call on the house owner to make good any award of damages. In some cases, Y is required to indemnify X in respect of a liability that X may be under to Y himself. Such an indemnity clause has the same effect as an exclusion clause. Under s.4 indemnity clauses in contracts where one of the parties deals as a consumer are unenforceable unless they satisfy the requirement of reasonableness.

Section 5 - Guarantees of consumer goods
At one time, it was common practice for guarantees given with goods to contain a clause exempting the manufacturer from liability in negligence if the product

[623] Contractual terms seeking to exclude or restrict liability for misrepresentation are dealt with by s.3 of the Misrepresentation Act 1967. The section provides that such clauses are ineffective unless they satisfy the requirement of reasonableness outlined in s.11(1) of the Unfair Contract Terms Act 1977.

proved defective. Under section 5 a manufacturer or distributor cannot exclude or restrict his liability in negligence for loss arising from defects in goods ordinarily supplied for private use or consumption by means of a term or notice contained in a guarantee.[624]

Section 6 - Exemption of implied terms in sale and hire purchase contracts
The original Sale of Goods Act 1893 gave the parties complete freedom to exclude the implied terms contained in sections 12-15. Retailers often used the opportunity to deprive consumers of their rights by getting customers to sign an order form, which included an exemption clause hidden in the small print or by displaying suitably worded notices at the point of sale.
This however, was identified as a major defect of the original Act and proposals for the amendment of this provision were made by the Law Commission. The changes were effected by the Supply of Goods Act 1973 and Sale of Goods Act 1979.

Section 7 - Exemption of implied terms in other supply of goods contracts
Terms as to title, description, satisfactory quality, fitness for purpose and sample are included in contracts for supply of goods by way of hire, exchange or work and materials contracts by virtue of the Supply of Goods and Services Act 1982.

The main provisions of the Unfair Contract Terms Act 1977 in relation to the exclusion of statutory (Sale of Goods Act) implied terms may be summarised as follows:

EXEMPTION OF IMPLIED TERMS IN CONTRACTS FOR THE SALE OF GOODS		
IMPLIED TERMS	CONSUMER TRANSACTION	NON-CONSUMER TRANSACTION
Title	Void	Void
Description	Void	Subject to reasonableness test
Quality & Suitability	Void	Subject to reasonableness test
Sample	Void	Subject to reasonableness test

Table 2: Exempting sections 12-15 of the Sale of Goods Act

624 In relation to consumer guarantees, Regulation 15, of the Sale and Supply of Goods to Consumers Regulations 2002, (S.I.2002, No.3045), provides that where goods are supplied with a consumer guarantee, such guarantee would take effect as a contractual obligation.

UNFAIR TERMS IN CONSUMER CONTRACTS REGULATIONS 1999[625]

The Regulations apply to all terms in a contract between a seller/supplier who acts in the course of a business and a consumer.[626] Very briefly, the Regulations hold as unfair any contractual term that (i) has not been individually negotiated, and (ii) creates a significant imbalance to the detriment of the consumer.[627]

Schedule 2 of the Regulations includes a non-exhaustive list of terms, which may be regarded as unfair:

- excluding/limiting liability in the event of death or personal injury to the consumer

- one-sided penalties against the consumer, e.g. non-refundable deposits

- one-sided privileges, e.g. provision for unilateral alteration of contract terms

- limiting the consumer's recovery rights for non-performance by the non-consumer.

In assessing unfair terms all the relevant circumstances to the conclusion of the contract would also be taken into account.

These Regulations extend the rights of consumers, who can now have a right to contest a contract that they consider to be unfair. In addition, it is now required that contracts are written in 'plain intelligible language', with the wording clearly readable.[628]

---

625 S.I.1999, No.2083. These Regulations implement Council Directive 93/13/EEC on Unfair Terms in Consumer Contracts (O.J. No. L 95, 21/04/1993, p.29).

626 Regulation 3(1) defines a 'consumer' as any natural person who is acting for purposes which are outside his trade, business or profession.

627 Regulation 5(1).

628 Regulation 7(1). Note that guidelines for the language used in contracts involving consumers have been issued by the National Consumer Council (N.C.C.).

CHAPTER 8

COMPETITION LAW

FREE MOVEMENT OF GOODS IN THE E.C.

The European Community since its inception has set up four principles; (a) the free movement of goods, (b) persons, (c) services and (d) capital.

The purpose of the free movement of goods principle is to promote efficiency in production by removing barriers to trade between member states. This principle together with the E.C. competition law provisions/policies constitute the essential element for the creation of a true common market.

Articles 28-31 of the E.C. Treaty (formerly Articles 30-36) form the framework of the legal regime for the free movement of goods, and deal with import and export restrictions on the free flow of goods around the common market, and so are very relevant to competition.

ARTICLE 28

This prohibits between member states measures which impose total or partial restraint on imports, such as rules requiring import licenses. A quantitative restriction or quota is a national measure which restrains the volume or amount of imports or exports, by placing direct or indirect limits on the physical actual quantity of goods/commodities/products/raw materials that may enter or leave a country. Article 28 (formerly Article 30) in effect prohibits the re-introduction of such restrictions or other measures having an equivalent effect to quantitative restrictions. However, this prohibition under the Article is sometimes violated by member states, thus resulting in litigation in the European Court; e.g. in 1978 France imposed an embargo on sheep-meat from the U.K.[629]

According to Directive 70/50,[630] 'measures' means 'laws, regulations, administrative provisions, administrative practices, and all instruments issuing from a public authority including recommendations'. However, the concept of 'measures having an equivalent effect' is not confined to legislation, regulations or administrative practices within the ambit of national authorities. It also includes rules enacted by agencies such as professional bodies where

[629] *E.C. Commission* v. *France* (Case 232/78) [1979] E.C.R.2729.

[630] Directive 70/50, [1970] O.J. L13/29.

these agencies exercise special powers.[631] Article 29 (formerly Article 34) contains similar provisions to Article 28 which apply[632] to the export of goods. Finally, it should be noted that Articles 28 and 29 are not an absolute prohibition, since Article 30 (formerly Article 36) provides derogation.

ARTICLE 30

This sets out circumstances in which such controls may be permitted, e.g. because of public security reasons. In particular this Article in setting out the various exceptions states:

> 'The provisions of Articles 28 and 29 shall not preclude prohibitions or restrictions on imports, exports or goods in transit justified on grounds of public morality, public policy or public security; the protection of health and life of humans, animals or plants; the protection of national treasures possessing artistic, historic or archaeological value; or the protection of industrial and commercial property.
> Such prohibitions or restrictions shall not, however, constitute a means of arbitrary discrimination or a disguised restriction on trade between Member States.'

In summarising therefore, one could conclude that there are four exceptions by which a member state may impose quantitative restrictions:

1) In order to protect public morality,[633] public policy,[634] or public security.
2) For the purpose of protecting the health of life of humans, animals or plants;[635]
3) In order to protect the artistic, historic or archaeological treasures.

---

[631] *R.* v. *Pharmaceutical Society, ex parte API* (Case 266/87) [1989] E.C.R.1295.

[632] But do not have an identical effect to that of Article 28; *P.B. Groenveld BV* v. *Produktschap voor Vee en Vlees* (Case 15/79), [1970] E.C.R.3409.

[633] Thus, for example a restriction imposed by the U.K. on the imports of pornographic materials was considered by the European Court justified, in *R.* v. *Henn (Maurice Donald) (No.1)* [1979] 2 C.M.L.R.495, H.L., since the materials could not legitimately be manufactured within the U.K. On similar lines was the decision of E.C.J. in *Conegate Ltd.* v. *Commissioners of Customs and Excise* (Case 121/85), [1986] E.C.R.1007, which involved the import of life-size inflatable dolls in the U.K.

[634] Public policy is generally interpreted strictly; *Leclerc* v. *Au Blé Vert* (Case 229/83), [1985] E.C.R.1, where an attempt by the French government to fix minimum fuel prices according to French refinery costs on the basis of public policy was rejected.

[635] *Commission* v. *United Kingdom* (Case 40/82), [1982] E.C.R.2793; an unsuccessful attempt by the U.K. to ban all imports of poultry on the basis of preventing the spread of a desease which affected poultry. See also *Schumacher* v. *Hauptzollamt Frankfurt-am Main-Ost* (Case 215/87), [1989] E.C.R.617.

4) The protection of industrial or commercial property. This would include copyright, patents and other intellectual property rights.

Although the above four exceptions are those derived from Article 36, it would appear that the European Court has derived a number of other exceptions in the *Cassis de Dijon Case*.[636] In this case the German authorities imposed a restriction on the sale of fruit liqueurs which contained less than 25% alcohol. Cassis contained 15%, and the E.C.J. held that this restriction was prohibited under Article 30, i.e. a measure having equivalent effect to an import quota. In reaching its decision the Court considered that a Member State may impose some types of 'mandatory requirements' on the free movement of goods, such as fairness of commercial transactions, the objective of this would be the protection of consumers from misrepresentations etc.;[637] or the protection of the environment.[638]

THE COMPETITION ACT 1998

This Act has been in force since 1st March 2000, and replaced or amended a number of U.K. Acts.[639] The Office of Fair Trading[640] is the person who applies and enforces the provisions of the Act in order to ensure that the competition process is unhindered by anti-competitive activity.

The Act introduces two prohibitions:

(1) Agreements which prevent, restrict or distort competition and which may affect trade within the U.K. (Chapter I prohibition), and

[636] *Rewe-Zentrale AG* v. *Bundesmonopolverwaltung für Branntwein* (Case 120/78), [1979] E.C.R.649.

[637] The E.C.J. has found that laws introduced by one country preventing particular advertising/sale promotion methods, such as offering free gifts to buyers of goods (encyclopaedias), were in breach of Article 28; *Oosthoek's Uitgeversmaatschappij BV* (Case 286/81), [1982] E.C.R.4575. Similarly, laws introduced by one country preventing the use of the name 'Clinique' on the basis of protecting consumers being misled by the medical properties associated with the word 'clinique' were found to be in breach of Article 28; *Verband Sozialer Wettbewerb eV* v. *Clinique Laboratoires SNC* (Case C-315/92), [1994] E.C.R. I-317.

[638] See, for example, *Commission* v. *Denmark* (Case 302/86), [1988] E.C.R.4607, which related to laws requiring a proportion of imported re-usable containers of liquid beverages to be returned to manufacturers. Although, the Court found that the proportion of imported beverages in non-approved re-usable containers was set by these laws at too low a figure, i.e. disproportionate, it seemed willing to accept the utility of such laws.

[639] Including the Restrictive Trade Practices Act 1976, the Resale Prices Act 1976, and the Competition Act 1980.

[640] The office of Director of Fair Trading was abolished by s.2(2) of the Enterprise Act 2002.

(2) Conduct of undertakings which amounts to an abuse of a dominant position in a market and which may affect trade within the U.K. (Chapter II prohibition).

CHAPTER I

It prohibits agreements between undertakings, decisions by associations of undertakings (e.g. trade associations), and concerted practices which prevent, restrict or distort competition, or are intended to do so, and which may affect trade within the U.K. This prohibition applies to both formal and informal arrangements. Types of agreement caught under this prohibition are:

-agreeing to fix purchase or selling prices or other trading conditions;

-agreeing to limit or control production, markets, technical development or investment;

-agreeing to share markets or supply sources;

-agreeing to make contracts subject to unrelated conditions;

-agreeing to apply different trading conditions to equivalent transactions, thereby placing some parties at a competitive disadvantage.

There are certain agreements, which would not have any appreciable effect on competition and are not likely to be caught by the prohibition. Therefore, an agreement is unlikely to be considered as having an appreciable effect where the combined market share of the undertakings involved does not exceed 25%. However, agreements to fix prices, impose minimum resale prices or share markets will generally be capable of having an appreciable effect even where the undertakings' combined market share falls below 25%. An agreement which would otherwise fall within the scope of the prohibition may be exempted if it satisfies certain criteria. There are three types of exemption:[641]

-Individual Exemptions, which may be granted for individual agreements;

-Block Exemptions, which apply automatically to certain categories of agreement;

-Parallel Exemptions, which apply where an agreement is covered by an E.C. individual or block exemption under Article 81(3) (formerly Art.85) of the E.C. Treaty, or would be covered by an E.C. block exemption if the agreement had an effect on trade between member States of the European Union.

---

[641] In addition to these exemptions, there is a number of agreements which are excluded from the operation of Chapter I; see further Schedules 1-4 of the Competition Act 1998.

In addition, section 39 of the Act also provides a limited immunity from penalties for certain, non-price fixing, 'small agreements'. Breach of the Chapter I prohibition would render the agreement(s) void and the offending undertakings may be liable to financial penalties of up to 10% of their annual turnover in the U.K. In addition, undertakings which consider that they have been harmed may have a claim for damages in the Courts.[642]

CHAPTER II

This prohibition covers the abuse by one or more undertakings of a dominant position in the market. In particular it prohibits conduct, which amounts to abusive behaviour by a dominant undertaking.[643]

There is a two-stage test to be applied to this prohibition:

-the undertakings must be in a dominant[644] position, which will be largely determined by the extent to which they can act independently of their competitors and customers;

-the undertakings must be abusing that position.

---

[642] *Crehan* v. *Inntrepreneur Pub Co. CPC* [2004] EWCA Civ. 637; C leased a public house from D, under a lease which included a 'beer tie' term, i.e. to buy a minimum quantity of beer from D, and pay the price specified by D. C's business was in financial difficulties and he surrendered the lease, owing money to D in relation to unpaid purchases of beer. D claimed for these unpaid purchases and C counter-claimed that the terms of the lease, in particular the 'beer tie' provision, was in breach of Article 81 of the E.C. Treaty. The Court of Appeal awarded C damages as it found that the 'beer tie' provision infringed Article 81 and it did not fall within the Council Regulation 1984/83 ('the Block Exemption') an exemption relating to 'beer supply agreements'. It must be noted that in this case a Reference to the European Court of Justice was made, *inter alia*, on the issue of whether an individual has rights under Article 81 when he/she is party to the infringing agreement. This was in issue arising in English law, since parties of an illegal (void) agreement are not entitled to damages even if 'innocent'. The E.C.J. clearly stated that National Courts must safeguard the rights of individuals in relation to Articles 81 and 82, and that parties to such anti-competitive agreements could claim damages (Case C-453/99, O.J. C 317, 10/11/2001, p.4).

[643] It must be noted that Chapter II of the Act is supplemented by the Enterprise Act 2002, which deals in the main with mergers and cartel arrangements. The 2002 Act creates a cartel criminal offence which applies only to individuals. The penalties of the offence depend on the circumstances, which dictate its seriousness. These vary from five years' imprisonment or an unlimited fine or both, to six months' imprisonment or a limited fine or both. The Office of Fair Trading is given a number of powers in relation to market investigations. Mergers will, under the Act be tested on the basis of a 'substantial lessening of competition'. An investigation into a particular merger will now be 'triggered' if it leads to a combined market share of 25% or more, and/or if the total U.K. turnover of the target enterprise exceeds £70 million.

[644] Dominance is considered in terms of whether the undertaking concerned is able to behave to an appreciable extent independently of its competitors, customers and ultimately of its consumers; *United Brands Company and United Brands Continentaal B.V.* v. *Commission of the European Communities* (Case 27/76), [1978] ECR 207.

There are no exemptions provided for Chapter II prohibition.[645] The Office of Fair Trading would look at factors such as market share, and although these may vary from case to case, as a general rule an undertaking is unlikely to be considered dominant if it has a market share of less than 40%. Also the number and size of existing competitors as well as the potential for new competitors to enter the market would be considered.

Examples of specific type of conduct which is likely to be considered as abuse of a dominant position would include:

-imposing unfair purchase or selling prices;

-limiting production, markets or technical development to the prejudice of consumers;

-applying different trading conditions to equivalent transactions, thereby placing certain parties at a competitive disadvantage;

-attaching unrelated supplementary conditions to contracts.

RESTRICTIVE TRADING AGREEMENTS AND TREATY OF ROME

In addition to the U.K. statute mentioned above, there are also basic principles of E.C. competition law, which are applicable to individual commercial agreement. It must be borne in mind that these E.C. competition law principles have direct effect in the U.K. Furthermore, E.C. law takes precedence over, and is directly applicable to U.K. law,[646] and wherever there is a clash, E.C. law must prevail.[647]

Under Articles 81 and 82 (formerly 85 and 86 respectively) of the Treaty of Rome all agreements between firms which operate to prevent or restrict competition in the Market are void.

---

645 However, the Competition Act 1998 provides for some exclusions from the operation of Chapter II; for a list of these, see Schedules 1-4 of the Act.

646 Bearing in mind the similar provisions of the Competition Act 1998, *supra*, p.191, it will be seen that undertakings may be subject to both Articles 81 and 82 of the Treaty of Rome, as wells as Chapter I and Chapter II prohibitions under the Competition Act. For the relationship between E.C. and national competition law see further Council Regulation (EC) No.1/2003 of 16 December 2002 on the implementation of the rules on competition laid down in Articles 81 and 82 of the Treaty, O.J. L1, 04/01/2003, p.1.

647 Indeed, it may now be considered settled that European Community law is superior to all provisions of national law, whether legislative, administrative, jurisdictional, or constitutional; *Flaminio Costa* v. *ENEL* (Case 6/64), [1964] E.C.R.585; *Equal Opportunities Commission* v. *Secretary of State for Employment* [1994] 1 W.L.R.409; *R.* v. *Secretary of State for Transport, ex parte Factortame* (Case C-213/89), [1990] 3 C.M.L.R.867; *Wachauf* (Case 5/88), [1989] E.C.R.2609; *Internationale Handelsgesellschaft GmbH* v. *Einfuhr und Vorratsstelle fur Getreide und Futtermittel*, (Case 11/70), [1970] E.C.R.1125.

ARTICLE 81

In general the effect of Article 81 (formerly 86) is to prohibit any agreements, decisions or practices which have or may have an effect on trade between Member States. Such agreements, decisions or practices are void. It must be understood that the Article applies to all types of agreements, even oral ones.[648] The basic test is whether the relevant agreement affects considerably trade within the common market.[649]

However, this provision of Article 81 does not only apply to an agreement between two parties based in different E.C. countries, but also if (a) both parties are based in the same E.C. country, and (b) one party is based in a E.C. country and the other is not. It must be noted however, that the same Article allows the E.C. Commission to grant exemptions if the agreement is essentially pro-competitive, for example if it benefits consumers and is not unnecessarily restrictive.[650]

So, for example, Commission Regulation No.2790/1999 of 22 December 1999 on the application of Article 81(3) of the Treaty to categories of vertical agreements and concerted practices,[651] provides a block exemption from Article 81(1) where the undertakings involved are not at the same level of the market, i.e. do not compete, such as a manufacturer and a distributor, and the seller's/manufacturer's share of the relevant market is less than 30%, and the buyer's turnover does not exceed €100 million. Thus, on this basis an exclusive distributorship agreement might be feasible, provided that the terms of the agreement do not impede parallel trading.[652]

---

648 *SA Hercules Chemicals NV* v. *Commission* [1991] E.C.R. II-1711, C.F.I.

649 *Volkswagen A.G.* v. *Commission of the European Communities* (Case C-338/00), [2004] 4 C.M.L.R.7; Volkswagen was fined approximately £59m. for breach of Article 81(1), as it had entered into agreements with some of its Italian dealers whereby the dealers were prevented to sell V.W. cars to both consumers and dealers from other E.C. States. The fine took into account V.W.'s abuse of bargaining power and the number of years during which this malpractice was operated.

650 For example, by Commission Regulation 1475/95 of June 28, 1995, on the application of Art.81(3) of the E.C. Treaty to certain categories of motor vehicle distribution and servicing agreements, car dealership contracts are, subject to certain conditions, exempted from Article 81(1) of the E.C. Treaty.

651 O.J. L 336, 29/12/1999, p.21.

652 *Cf. Bundesverband der Arzneimittel-Importeure EV and the Commission of the European Communities* v. *Bayer AG* (Joined Cases C-2/01 P and C-3/01 P) [2004] E.T.M.R. 100 ECJ, where a particular drug was manufactured by Bayer, who sold it through their European distributors at considerably variable prices. In fact, the sale price of the drug in France and Spain was about 40% cheaper than in the U.K. Consequently, French and Spanish wholesalers exploited this price difference by ordering larger quantities of the drug from Bayer and exporting the surplus to the U.K. Bayer subsequently, adopted a policy whereby a quota was imposed on these wholesalers based on their sale figures of the previous year. The European Commission decided that this practice was an infringement of Article 81(1) since Bayer in effect imposed an export ban thus hindering parallel trading. However, the E.C.J. held that as the European Commission based its case on Article 81(1), an agreement by the wholesalers was

Furthermore, agreements between small undertakings are rarely capable of infringing Article 81, i.e. 'appreciably restricting competition' between E.C. countries.

For this reason the Commission has published a Notice on Agreements of Minor Importance,[653] which in a nutshell, states that agreements between undertakings will 'not appreciably restrict competition'[654] if either:

(a) the aggregate market share of the undertakings to the agreement does not exceed 10% on any of the relevant markets affected, and the undertakings involved are actual or potential competitors[655] on any of these markets; or

(b) the market share of each of the undertakings to the agreement does not exceed 15% of any of the relevant markets affected, and the undertakings involved are not actual or potential competitors on any of these markets.

Agency agreements are not generally within the scope of application of Article 81, because agent and principal are likely to be counted as one undertaking; Article 81 would not apply where the parties to an agreement cannot be described as two separate undertakings. For example Article 81 would generally not apply to an agreement between a parent and a subsidiary company.

However, it must be understood that the determinant factor in such cases is, similar to English law, the degree of control exercised by the principal/parent company over the agent/subsidiary.[656]

Article 81 may be considered under three headings:

Impeding Parallel Trading within E.C. Countries

This may be illustrated by the *Consten and Grundig* case.[657] Grundig set up a network of exclusive distributors for its products throughout the Community and appointed a French firm, Consten to be its exclusive distributor in France.

---

also required, which, the E.C.J. thought the Commission had failed to show it existed. The wholesalers' continuation of selling the drug was not adequate evidence that they had acquiesced to Bayer's practice.

653 O.J. C 368/13, 22/12/2001. This notice replaces the Notice on agreements of minor importance published in O.J. C 372, 09/12/1997.

654 This factor must be distinguished from 'appreciably affecting trade'. If this is the criterion, then according to the Annex to Commission Recommendation 96/280/E.C., O.J. L 107, 30/04/1996, a small undertakings are: (i) those with fewer than 250 employees, and either (ii) have an annual turnover up to €40m, or (iii) have an annual balance sheet total up to €27m.

655 As to what is 'actual or potential competitor', see paragraph 9 of the Commission's notice 'Guidelines on the applicability of Article 81 of the E.C. Treaty to horizontal cooperation agreements', O.J. C 3, 06/01/2001.

656 *Viho Europe BV* v. *Commission* (Case C-73/95P), [1996] E.C.R. I-5457.

657 *Consten S.A. and Grundig-Verkaufs GmbH* v. *E.C. Commission* (Cases 56 and 58/64), [1966] E.C.R.299.

Consten, in common with all other Grundig distributors was not permitted to sell either directly or indirectly outside France, and, to make certain that none of the other distributors violated Consten's exclusive territorial rights, Consten was permitted to register the trade mark 'GINT' (which stands for Grundig International) as its French trade mark. A third party imported Grundig products into France and Consten brought an action against the importer for infringement of trade mark. The case went to the European Court of Justice and it was held that the purpose of the trade mark agreement between Grundig and Consten was to guarantee complete territorial protection to Consten in the sale of Grundig products in France. That agreement was prohibited by Article 85(1) (now 81(1)) as its purpose was to hamper, by partitioning the market, the importing into France of Grundig products by other firms and in these circumstances the agreement was void.

It is interesting that in this case the E.C.J. confirmed that the prohibition of Article 85(1) (now 81(1)) not only applies to 'horizontal agreements', but also to 'vertical agreements', i.e. where parties do not compete with each other as they operate at different levels of the market.[658]

Concerted Practices[659]

An illustration of this is to be seen in the *Dyestuffs* cartel case.[660] In this case the Commission's investigations were commenced on the basis of information which they received from trade organisations of industrial users. These investigations revealed that the ten major manufacturers of dyestuffs had made uniform, and for all practical purposes, simultaneous price increases between 1964 and 1967 on the sale of their goods. This price fixing agreement led to the imposition of fines on the companies involved.

The use of patent rights to restrict competition

An illustration of the attitude of the European Court on this issue is to be found in *Parke-Davis* v. *Probel*.[661]. Parke-Davis, was a company based in Detroit. It held certain Dutch patents for an antibiotic. Another company imported the drug into Holland without the permission of the patent holder, Parke-Davis, and they

---

[658] *Cf.* the more recent case of *Glaxo Group Ltd.* v. *Dowelhurst Ltd.* [2003] EWHC 110, where pharmaceutical products were re-packaged/re-labelled on being imported into the U.K. from other E.C. States. C, the trade mark proprietor, claimed trade mark infringement. It was held that there was an irrebuttable presumption that re-packaging the goods is prejudicial to that subject-matter. On the other hand this presumption did not apply to re-labelling of the goods. Therefore, C could prevent D from re-packaging the medicines but not from re-labelling them.

[659] It could be said that a concerted practice is conduct which takes the form of informal co-ordination between undertakings; *Suiker Unie* v. *Commission* (Cases 40-48, 50, 54-56, 111, 113-114/73), [1975] E.C.R.1663.

[660] *Imperial Chemical Industries Ltd.* v. *E.C. Commission (Dyestuffs)* (Case 48/69), [1972] E.C.R.619.

[661] *Parke Davis & Co.* v. *Probel and Centrafarm* (Case 24/67), [1968] E.C.R.55.

(Parke-Davis) brought an action against this other company for breach of the patent. It appeared that the defendant company had purchased the drug in Italy, where there was no patent protection in medicines, and had then imported it into Holland. Thus Parke-Davis had been unable to take out patents in Italy in order to protect their rights because there was a gap in Italian law as regards patents. In these circumstances Parke-Davis took the only action they could by suing the defendant company. The defendant company pleaded that the action was in breach of competition rules and the Dutch Court referred the matter to the E.C.J. The European Court recognised the existence of the patent rights and that the exercise of those rights to prevent goods being imported into Holland from a country where such patent rights did not exist was a wholly proper action and did not constitute a restriction to competition. Note however, that if the goods had been imported from another country where patent rights were in existence, an attempt to prevent their importation would probably have constituted an infringement of Article 82.

ARTICLE 82

In general this Article prohibits the abuse of a dominant position within the common market.[662] Here the activities of one undertaking could infringe the Articles, unlike Article 81 where it is necessary to have an agreement between undertakings.

Three requirements must be fulfilled in order to make Article 86 applicable. It must be shown that:

(a) a dominant position is held by some undertaking; and

(b) there has been an abuse of that domination; and

(c) the abuse has had an effect on trade between member states.

An interesting recent case, relating to 'loyalty rebates' may serve as an example of the way that the Article is applied in practice. In particular, the European Commission found[663] that Michelin, the vehicle-tyre manufacturer, had abused its dominant position, in breach of Article 82, in the French

[662] Thus in *Deutsche Post* (Case COMP/35.141), Decision 2001/354/EC, O.J. L 125, 05/05/2001, p.27, the Commission ruled that the German Post Office had infringed Article 82 between 1974 and 2000 by, *inter alia*, using revenue from its profitable letter-post monopoly to finance a strategy of below-cost selling in parcel services, which were open to competition. In respect of this and some other Article 82 infringements, the German Post Office was fined a sum equivalent to £14,500,000.

[663] *Michelin*, (Case COMP/E-2/36.041/PO), Decision 2002/405/EC, O.J. L 143, 31/05/2002, p.1.

markets of new replacement tyres and re-treaded tyres for heavy vehicles, between 1990 and 1998, by setting up a complex system of rebates, bonuses and tying arrangements whose purpose was to induce loyalty to Michelin's brand and to exclude other competitors from the market. The Commission imposed a fine of about £12 million, which took into account the long duration of Michelin's breach.[664]

However, it would seem that there is a difference to be drawn between discounts or commissions[665] to encourage loyalty, and discounts in relation to efficiencies, for example for large orders. The former are considered an abuse whereas the latter would not seem to be so.[666] It should also be noted that Article 82 would be relevant where a dominant undertaking's conduct, through mergers or take-overs, amounts to an abuse.[667]

Finally, it should be noted that Articles 28, 29, 81 and 82, do not as such alter the notion of rights (e.g. patent rights, ownership rights, etc.) which exist within a national jurisdiction; rather they affect the way in which such rights are exercised. Thus, Article 295 (formerly 222) states that the Treaty (of Rome) 'shall in no way prejudice the rules in Member States governing the system of property ownership'. Or again as it has been seen, Article 36 allows restrictions on imports. Cases such as *Deutsche Gremmophon* v. *Metro*[668] and *Parke, Davis* v. *Probel*[669] dictate that the owner of a right cannot prevent parallel

---

[664] The Commission's Decision was affirmed by the European Court of First Instance; *Manufacture Française Des Pneumatiques Michelin* v. *Commission of the European Communities* (Case T-203/01), [2004] 4 C.M.L.R.18, C.F.I.

[665] *Virgin/British Airways*, (Case IV/D-2/34.780), Decision 2000/74/EC, O.J. L 30, 04/02/2000, p.1; British Airways was found infringing Article 82 by operating various incentive and commission schemes for certain travel agents by rewarding loyalty to such agents, and discriminating between travel agents, thus partitioning the U.K. market. A fine was imposed of approximately £4 million. This also seems to be the case under different jurisdictions, e.g. in 2005 Japan's Fair Trade Commission found that Intel, the microprocessor manufacturer, violated competition rules by offering rebates to five PC makers on the condition that they agreed not to purchase or limit purchases of chips made by AMD or other rivals.

[666] *NV Nederlandsche Banden Industrie Michelin* v. *Commission of the European Communities* (Case 322/81), [1983] E.C.R.3461.

[667] *Europemballage Corporation and Continental Can Company Inc.* v. *Commission* (Case 6/72), [1973] E.C.R.215; X was an American company producing packing materials such as fish tins, meat tins, and in 1969 it (X) took control of company Y which was the largest German producer of packaging. In 1970 X acquired a majority holding of company Z which was one of the few leading European (Dutch) manufacturer of packing materials. In the opinion of the E. Commission the situation arising from this concentration within the market of light packing in the North-West region of the Common Market constituted the necessary conditions for an abuse of dominant position within Article 82 (then 86). However, the finding of the Commission was set aside by the European Court on a technical ground that the E. Commission had failed to define which market was abused, whether it was that of meat tins, fish tins etc. However, the important point is that the Court stressed that Article 82 would have been infringed on a definition of the market abused so that the mergers would have been void.

[668] *Deutsche Gremmophon* v. *Metro* (Case 78/70), [1971] E.C.R.487.

[669] *Parke Davis & Co.* v. *Probel and Centrafarm* (Case 24/67), [1968] E.C.R.55.

imports of products sold by himself, his agent or his licensee in another E.C. State.

In simple words, Articles 81 and 28 recognise the legitimate existence of a right, as it is conceived/understood in each Member State, and this is the reason the Articles contain exceptions to the prohibitions they impose. In the case of Article 81, as we have seen, a right, such as a patent right in the U.K., may be granted an exemption from the Commission, if its exercise is essentially pro-competitive, for example if it benefits consumers and is not unnecessarily restrictive. Or an exclusive distribution agreement would not be void under Article 81 provided that only two parties are involved, and the terms of the agreement do not impede parallel trading; Regulation 1983/83 of the E.C. Commission.

This is what is meant by Article 295 (formerly 222), i.e. that the Treaty does not prejudice the rules in Member States governing the system of property ownership. It seems therefore that a distinction is drawn between the existence of such rights and their exercise; the 'philosophy' being that:

(a) although the existence of such rights is recognised,

(b) if the enforcement of their exercise becomes or is 'illegal', which means contrary to the aim and provisions of the Articles,[670] then

(c) there is an infringement of competition Community Law, and therefore such right cannot be enforced/exercised.

[670] *Cf. Intel Corporation* v. *VIA Technologies Inc and others* [2002] EWHC 1159 (Ch.); the proprietor of an intellectual property right had the right to refuse to license, but the refusal might be an abuse if, amongst other circumstances, a manufacturer decided no longer to produce spare parts for a model which was still in wide circulation. It might also be an abuse if reliance on the right prevented the appearance of a new product, which was not offered by the holder of the right and for which there was a consumer demand, and there was no justification for the refusal of the licence, and the holder of the right reserved to itself the market in the product by denying access to the material which was indispensable to the creation of the product. However, the refusal to license would be abusive conduct only in exceptional circumstances.

CHAPTER 9

INTRODUCTION TO F.O.B. AND C.I.F. SALES

Certain special clauses have been used over the years in sales where delivery has involved carriage by sea. These clauses have given rise to certain main types of contract, the major terms of which have become largely standardised. The more important quotations in exporting are C.I.F. (Cost, Insurance, Freight) and F.O.B. (Free On Board), although variations of these terms of export contract exist, such as C.FR. (Cost and Freight), EX.W. (Ex-Works), etc.

Under a **C.I.F.** (*port of destination*) contract of sale, the seller provides the goods, engages cargo space on the vessel, pays freight to the buyer's port which is normal, for example, C.I.F. Singapore, insures the goods on behalf of the buyer against normal marine and fire risk to that port and pays all charges incidental in getting the goods onto the vessel. The seller is liable for any loss or damage before the goods reach the ship.

F.O.B. (*port of shipment*) implies that the duty of the seller is to present the goods to the port/airport and see they are actually placed on board the vessel/aircraft which the buyer provides. The seller meets all charges incidental to placing the goods on the ship/aircraft such as collection, handling, insurance, but once the goods are on board and he has obtained receipt for the goods, the exporter's (seller's) responsibilities cease. Thereafter, the buyer pays all the charges. Thus, the buyer or his agent would insure the goods from the sea port or airport of departure to destination and pays the freight.

Under an **Ex-Works** (*named place*) contract it is the duty of the buyer to take delivery of the goods at the works or store of the seller or other named place as the case may be. The property and risk usually pass when the buyer takes delivery. These sales are almost always of unascertained goods, the appropriation taking place when the goods are selected or handed over at the works or store.

C.FR. (*port of destination*), is another cargo delivery term under which the seller pays the cost and freight necessary to convey the goods from the port of shipment to the port of destination. The buyer will be responsible for any damage or loss to the goods when the goods pass the ship's rail at the port of shipment and for the unloading costs. The seller bears the costs of freight from the port of shipment to the port of destination including cost of packing, and loading in port of departure.

An **F.A.S.** (*port of shipment*) 'free alongside ship' contract is one in which the goods are delivered alongside the ship free of expense to the buyer. Thereafter, charges incurred are to be met by him (buyer).

INCOTERMS

In a sale of goods contract is important that there must be no ambiguity in the interpretation by either party of the delivery terms quoted particularly in the area of cost and expenses. If such problems arise, much good will is lost, the exporter (seller) could lose the prospect of a repeat order in a competitive market and in addition costly litigation could arise. It is essential, therefore, that buyer/seller agree on the terms of delivery and their interpretation. Such a situation could be overcome by quoting the provisions of INCOTERMS.

In order to overcome any difficulties in interpreting the chief delivery terms used in foreign trade contracts, a set of international rules have been agreed by the member countries of the International Chamber of Commerce (I.C.C.). These rules eliminate the possibility of varied interpretation of the same terms in the same countries.

If the buyer/seller wish to use these rules, it must be specified in the contract that it is governed by the provisions of 'INCOTERMS 2000'.

F.O.B. CONTRACTS

The main characteristics of this type of contract have been mentioned above. The goods must be delivered on board by the seller, free of expense to the purchaser, and they are not at the buyer's risk until actually delivered on board, when the property in them passes to him. So it may be said that in this type of contract (F.O.B.) risk and transfer of property pass simultaneously.[671]

The buyer on the other hand, must name a ship or authorise the seller to select one. The seller cannot sue for the price until the goods are actually loaded, and if his inability to load was caused by the buyer's failure to name

[671] Although the effect of s.19 in the case of specific or ascertained goods should not be ignored. Where bills of lading are issued under an F.O.B. or F.A.S. contract, and are marked 'to the order' of the seller, the intention of the parties, in the absence of any other provisions, would be that no property would pass to the buyer/holder of the bill of lading until other conditions, such as payment, have been satisfied; *Transpacific Eternity SA* v. *Kanematsu Corp. (The Antares III)* [2002] 1 Lloyd's Rep.233.

an effective ship, his only remedy lies in damages, not an action for the price.[672] Section 32(3) of the Sale of Goods Act 1979 provides that, unless otherwise agreed, where the goods are sent by the seller to the buyer by a route involving sea transit, under circumstances in which it is usual to insure, the seller must give such notice to the buyer as may enable him (the buyer) to insure them during their sea transit, and, if the seller fails to do so, the goods shall be deemed to be at his (seller's) risk during such sea transit. Thus delivery to the carrier will not necessarily pass the risk in F.O.B. contracts as a rule. Nowadays under what is called an F.O.B. contract with additional services, the seller often makes the contract of carriage.[673] It must be reasonable in terms of the nature of the goods and other circumstances. If not and the goods are lost or damaged in the course of transit, the buyer may decline to treat the delivery to the carrier as a delivery to himself or may hold the seller responsible in damages.[674]

The duties of the parties to an F.O.B. contract expressly subject to the INCOTERMS may be summed up as follows:

The Seller must

-Provide the goods and the invoice.

-Obtain at his risk and expense any export licence[675] and carry out all customs formalities.

-Deliver the goods on board the named vessel[676] and port of shipment,[677] both of which will have been named by the buyer, and within the stipulated period.[678]

---

[672] *Petraco (Bermuda)* v. *Petromed International S.A.* [1988] 2 Lloyd's Rep.357, C.A.

[673] The three most common variants of F.O.B. contracts have been distinguished by the Court of Appeal in *the El Amria and El Minia* [1982] 2 Lloyd's Rep.28, in the following terms: 'In *Pyrene & Go* v. *Scindia Steam Navigation Co.* Mr. justice Devlin instanced three types of fob contract. In the first, or classic type, the buyer nominates the ship and he seller puts the goods on board for account of the buyer, procuring a bill of lading. The seller is then a party to the contract of carriage and if he has taken the bill of lading to his order, the only contract of carriage to which the buyer can become a party is that contained in the bill of lading which is endorsed to him by the seller. The second is a variant of the first, in that the seller arranges for the ship to come on the berth, but the legal incidents are the same. The third is where the seller puts the goods on board, takes a mate's receipt and gives this to the buyer or his agent who then takes a bill of lading. In this latter type the buyer is a party to the contract of carriage *ab initio'*. Notwithstanding these variants, the basic concepts such as delivery, property and risk remain common to each.

[674] Section 32(2), Sale of Goods Act 1979 (as amended).

[675] The standard of duty required by the seller is to use his best endeavours and failure to do so may operate to frustrate the contract; *Pagnan SpA* v. *Tradax Ocean Transportation SA* [1987] 2 Lloyd's Rep.342, where a 'force majeure' clause found in a standard trade contract, GAFTA, the Grain and Feed Trade Association, was held to protect the sellers in breaking a special condition in relation to the provision of an export licence.

[676] *Cargill U.K. Ltd.* v. *Continental U.K. Ltd.* [1989] 2 Lloyd's Rep.290, C.A.

-Bear all risks of loss of or damage to the goods until the goods have passed the ship's rail at the named port of shipment.[679]

-Pay all costs relating to the goods until the goods have passed the ship's rail; e.g. costs of customs formalities.

-Give the buyer sufficient notice that the goods have been delivered on board.

-Provide the buyer with the usual document in proof of delivery, as described above.

-Provide at his own expense packaging[680] and mark the goods appropriately.

-Render the buyer every assistance in obtaining any document or equivalent electronic messages, which the buyer may require for the importation of the goods.

The buyer must

-Pay the price.[681]

-Contract at his own expense for the carriage of the goods from the named port of shipment.

-Take delivery of the goods.

-Bear all risks of loss or damage to the goods from the time they have passed the ship's rail at loading port.

[677] The port of delivery in an F.O.B. contract has been held to be a condition; *Petrograde Inc.* v. *Stinnes GmbH* [1995] 1 Lloyd's Rep.142.

[678] An F.O.B. seller would normally be entitled to treat the contract as repudiated if the buyer fails to nominate a ship within the stipulated time, or if no express stipulation as to time is provided, then within a reasonable time; *Olearia Tirrena SpA* v. *NV Algemeene Oliehandel (The Osterbek)* [1973] 2 Lloyd's Rep.86, C.A.

[679] *Pyrene & Co* v. *Scindia Navigation Co* [1954] 2 Q.B.402.

[680] The goods must comply with the contractual description, quality and quantity and must be sufficiently packed to withstand the rigours of the voyage; *Mash & Murrell* v. *Emmanuel* [1962] 1 All E.R.77, the sellers, in Cyprus, agreed to sell potatoes to buyers, in England. The potatoes were in good condition when loaded, but rotten when they arrived at destination. It was held that although the potatoes were fit when loaded, they were not fit to travel to England. Hence the sellers were in breach of an implied condition that the goods would be merchantable.

[681] The buyer must also fulfil any arrangements made for the method of payment and failure to do so is a repudiatory breach, for example failure by the buyer to set up a letter of credit facility in favour of the seller when required under the contract, would amount to such a breach; *Transpetrol Ltd* v. *Transol Olieprodukten Nederland BV* [1989] 1 Lloyd's Rep.309. Note that in the absence of agreement to the contrary, the seller can demand payment in exchange for the documents since the delivery obligation in s.28 of the Sale of Goods Act 1979 (as amended) states that payment and delivery are concurrent conditions. In other words the seller's obligation under s.28 is deemed to be satisfied by the furnishing of the documents.

-Pay all costs relating to the goods from the time they have passed the ship's rail at the port of shipment.

-Give the seller sufficient notice of the vessel name,[682] loading point[683] and required delivery time.[684]

-Pay the costs of pre-shipment inspection except when mandated by the authorities of the country of export.

-Pay all costs and charges incurred in obtaining the documents or equivalent electronic messages and reimburse those incurred by the seller in rendering his assistance.

C.I.F. CONTRACTS

DUTIES OF THE SELLER

-To ship or procure goods of the description contained in the contract under a contract of affreightment which will ensure the delivery of the goods at the destination contemplated in the contract. As mentioned previously undertakings in the contract as to time and place of shipment are nearly always treated as conditions.[685]

[682] The nomination must be made and communicated to the seller within a reasonable period to allow the seller sufficient time to complete the loading by the end of the shipping period; *Bunge & Co.* v. *Tradax England* [1975] 2 Lloyd's Rep.235. Furthermore, the nominated vessel must comply with port restrictions of each one of the load ports listed in the contract, otherwise the seller is entitled to reject the buyer's nomination; *Richco International Ltd.* v. *Bunge & Co. Ltd. (The New Prosper)* [1991] 2 Lloyd's Rep.93.

[683] The delivery point is the port of shipment, usually designated by the buyer in the contract of sale. Failure on the part of the buyer to nominate the port of shipment when specified in the contract' or alternatively failure to notify the seller of the nomination by an agreed date, may amount to a breach of condition precedent; *Gill & Duffus* v. *Societe Pour l'Exportation des Sucres SA* [1985] 1 Lloyd's Rep.621.

[684] A date or period of shipment for the goods will normally be specified. Until the buyer has made an effective nomination of the date of shipment, the seller's obligation to have the goods ready to load at the port does not arise; *J.& J. Cunningham Ltd.* v. *Robert A Munro & Co Ltd.* (1922) 13 Ll. L. Rep.216. Unless the contract provides that the buyer's nomination is final, he is not confined to the single nomination and may substitute an earlier nomination with a subsequent one provided that the substitute nomination is made in time: see *Cargill U.K. Ltd.* v. *Continental U.K. Ltd.* [1989] 2 Lloyd's Rep.290, C.A. If the buyer substitutes one nomination for another one, the seller's expenses incurred by reason of the substitution are his own loss in the absence of an express or implied contractual stipulation to the contrary.

[685] Thus, in *Aruna Mills* v. *Dhanrajmal Gobindram* [1968] 1 Lloyd's Rep.304, a contract for sale of cotton provided for a variation in price if the prevailing rate of exchange should vary between the contract date and the date when the price was payable. The sellers, in breach of contract, failed to ship the cotton until 27th June, 1966, although the last permitted date for shipment was 31st May, 1966. The rupee was devalued on 6th June, 1966, and the buyers paid the additional price on receipt of the shipping document which were received after

-To arrange for insurance which will be available to the buyer.

-To make out an invoice for the goods.

-To tender the documents to the buyer in exchange for the price, so that the buyer will know the amount of the freight he must pay, and so that he can obtain delivery of the goods if they arrive, or recover for their loss if they are lost on the voyage.

INCOTERMS 2000, provide a slightly different set of duties and obligations for the seller and buyer under a C.I.F. contract. These could be summarised as follows:

The Seller must

-Provide the goods[686] and the invoice, in accordance with the contract of sale.

-Obtain at his own risk and expense any export licence and carry out all customs formalities necessary for the exportation of the goods.

-Contract on usual terms at his own expense for the carriage of the goods to the named port of destination.

-Obtain at his own expense cargo insurance as required by the contract,[687] and provide the buyer with insurance policy or other evidence of insurance cover.

-Deliver the goods on board the vessel at the port of shipment on the date or within the period stipulated.

-Bear all risks of loss of or damage to the goods until they have passed the ship's rail at the port of shipment.

6th June, 1966. They (buyers) sued to recover that additional price by way of damages for late shipment, alleging that if the goods had been shipped on or before 31st May, 1966, they would have received the shipping documents and made payment on or before 5th June, 1966, i.e. before devaluation. It was held that the loss due to the devaluation was not too remote, for the parties had contemplated it as likely to result from late shipment.

686 It must be noted that the C.I.F. seller, in the absence of a specific term in the contract of sale, need not actually ship goods. He may, for instance, purchase goods afloat; *Wildhandel* v. *Tucker & Cross* [1975] 2 Lloyd's Rep.240.

687 Unless the cargo insurance cover is specified in the sale contract, the seller is only required to conclude and produce an ordinary policy of insurance current in the particular trade; *E. Clement Horst Company* v. *Biddell Brothers* [1912] A.C.18, H.L.; *Groom* v. *Barber* [1915] 1 K.B.316, D sold to C 100 bales of cloth on C.I.F. terms. The goods were shipped and insured under a policy which did not cover war risks. There was no custom of the trade that the seller should insure against war risks. The ship carrying the goods was sunk by a German cruiser. It was held that C was bound to pay the price on tender of the shipping documents. If the goods are lost from a peril not covered by the ordinary policy of insurance current in trade, the buyer must nevertheless pay the full price on delivery of the documents.

-Pay the freight and costs of loading the goods on board and any charges for unloading at the port of discharge, and the costs of customs formalities necessary for exportation.

-Give the buyer sufficient notice that the goods have been delivered on board the vessel.[688]

-Provide the buyer without delay with the usual transport document for the agreed port of destination.

-Provide at his own expense packaging and mark the goods appropriately.

-Render the buyer every assistance in obtaining any documents or equivalent electronic messages required for the importation of the goods.

The Buyer must

-Pay the price as provided in the contract of sale.

-Obtain any import licence and carry out all customs formalities for the importation of the goods.

-Accept delivery of the goods when they have been delivered and receive them from the carrier at the named port of destination.

-Bear all risks of loss of or damage to the goods from the time the goods have passed the ship's rail at the port of shipment.

-Whenever he is entitled to determine the time for shipping the goods and/or the port of destination, give the seller sufficient notice thereof.

-Accept the transport document.

-Pay the costs of any pre-shipment inspection, except when mandated by the authorities of the country of exportation.

-Pay all costs and charges incurred in obtaining the documents or equivalent electronic messages and reimburse the seller in rendering his assistance.

688 This is normally done, in the case of unascertained goods, by the seller tendering to the buyer a 'notice of appropriation', as agreed in their sale contract. The giving of a valid notice of appropriation narrows the contract description to a particular parcel or parcels of goods being carried in a named vessel under a bill of lading of a given date. It may, but will not necessarily, convert the contract into one for specific goods, depending on whether the bill of lading relates to an unseparated part of a larger bulk cargo; *Waren Import Gesellschaft Krohn & Co.* v. *Alfred C. Toepfer (The Vladimir Ilich)* 1 Lloyd's Rep.322.

-Provide the seller, upon request, with the necessary information for procuring insurance.

REFUSAL OF BUYER TO ACCEPT GOODS

In a C.I.F. contract the buyer or his agent may repudiate the contract by:

a) refusing to accept the documents if they do not conform with the contract; and

b) rejecting the goods on delivery if following inspection they do not comply with the contract.

The buyer loses the right to reject documents once they have been accepted and paid.[689] Once the buyer has accepted the documents he may only reject the goods[690] for any non-conformity which was not apparent on the face of the documents. If the defect is apparent the buyer is taken to have waived his right to reject the goods or he may be estopped.

In general, however, by accepting the documents the buyer is not taken to have accepted the goods.[691] Once a buyer rejects the documents or the goods he can recover from the seller damages for non-delivery.[692]

PASSING OF THE RISK

As a general rule, the risk passes when the goods are shipped. The buyer will still have to pay for the goods if they are lost on the voyage.[693] Note however, that although the risk passes when the goods are shipped, the property in the goods is not transferred to the buyer until the seller transfers the documents to the buyer and the latter has paid for them. Therefore, it appears that a C.I.F. contract is a 'sale of documents', since it is the delivery of these documents that

---

[689] *Panchaud Frères S.A.* v. *Etablissements General Grain Co.* [1970] 1 Lloyd's Rep.53, under a C.I.F. contract of sale the bill of lading stated that the goods had been shipped on 31st July 1965, whereas the certificate of quality suggested that the goods had been shipped between 10th and 12th of August 1965. The question was whether the buyers by taking up the documents and paying for them were precluded from complaining of the defect in the documents. The Court stated that if a buyer's conduct is such as to lead the other party to believe that he is not relying on that ground, he cannot afterwards set it up as a ground of rejection.

[690] Of course, a buyer can reject the goods for breach of any of the terms implied by ss.12-15 of the Sale of Goods Act 1979 (as amended).

[691] *Kwei Tek Chao* v. *British Traders and Shippers Ltd.* [1954] 2 Q.B.459.

[692] See *supra*, p.177, s.51, Sale of Goods Act 1979 (as amended).

[693] *E. Clement Horst Company* v. *Biddell Brothers* [1912] A.C.18, H.L.

transfers the property to the buyer.[694] In order to simplify the above mentioned process involved in a C.I.F. contract, consider the following examples:

S, agrees to sell to B some goods, under a C.I.F. contract. S has to fulfil the above mentioned four duties, i.e. (1) to ship/procure goods of the contract description, at the port of shipment, within the time named in the contract and to contract for their carriage; (2) to arrange for insurance which will be available to the buyer; (3) to tender the documents to the buyer in exchange for the price.

1. If the contract does not provide for a particular time of delivery then a reasonable time will be assumed.

2. As mentioned earlier, risk of loss or damage to the goods passes when the goods are shipped. Assume that S ships the goods. Therefore, the risk has passed to B and he will have to bear any loss or damage that might happen to the goods.

3. However, as mentioned above, the property in the goods (i.e. ownership) does not pass to B until S has transferred the documents (e.g. bill of lading, invoice, etc.) to him![695] Therefore, one may anticipate the situation where the goods have been shipped, as in the example, but the documents have not been transferred. In other words, the buyer (B) has not got ownership of the goods, but nevertheless, the risk of the goods being lost or damaged in transit is for him (B) to bear! However, bear in mind that the buyer (B) has the benefit of the insurance. Under such circumstances it could be said that there is a conditional appropriation of the goods to the contract which will not become unconditional until the buyer (B) takes up the documents and pays for them. This is the reason why it was mentioned earlier in this chapter that a C.I.F. contract is effectively a 'sale of documents'; because it is the delivery of those documents which transfers the property to the buyer.[696]

---

[694] *Manbre Saccharine Co. Ltd.* v. *Corn Products Co Ltd.* [1919] 1 K.B.198, D sold quantities of starch and syrup to C. Subsequently, the ship carrying the goods was lost. Two days later D tendered the documents for payment and the C refused to take up the documents or pay. It was held that C were bound to take up the documents and pay the price. Risk normally passed to the buyer upon shipment. In a C.I.F. contract the transfer of the documents transfers to the buyer the right to the goods or, in the case where goods are lost or damaged, rights to compensation from the shipper or insurer.

[695] *The Kronprinsessan Margereta* [1921] A.C.486, the sellers sold and shipped coffee on F.O.B. terms to a number of buyers. Subsequently, they obtained bills of lading to the buyers' order but retained them until payment was arranged. It was held that property did not pass as the sellers, by taking out the bills in the buyers' names, could not demand possession without the buyers' endorsement. Equally, the buyers could not obtain possession until they received the bills. Thus, although the bills were taken out to the order of the buyers, this did not necessarily show an intention to pass property.

[696] Such title however, is defeasible; *Kwei Tek Chao* v. *British Traders and Shippers Ltd.* [1954] 2 Q.B.459, under a contract of sale of goods, delivery to be made in Hong Kong,

4. In the above example of a C.I.F. contract, let us assume that the documents arrive and are delivered to the buyer (B). However, he (B) suspects that the goods he ordered have been damaged/or are not up to his expectations, and therefore, he decides to wait until the goods have arrived (so that he can inspect them) and pay for them after inspecting them. It must be remembered that he is not entitled to take this action; he must pay the agreed price within a reasonable time after tender of the documents; he is not entitled to withhold payment until he has examined the goods.[697]

OTHER DELIVERY TERMS

'Payment on arrival', and such clauses are considered ambiguous and their meaning has to be ascertained from the intention of the parties. The parties may have intended that the arrival of the goods shall be a condition for the payment of the price. In this case it would seem that the contract is not a C.I.F. contract.[698]

As a concluding comment of this chapter on INCOTERMS, it must be borne in mind that pure inclusion of delivery terms, for example, of C.I.F. subject to INCOTERMS 2000, would not suffice for such sale contract to be treated as such.

Any term in the sale contract whereby the particular INCOTERMS' meaning is varied, would be capable of turning such delivery term to

---

property in the goods passed to the buyers when they paid in exchange for the bills of lading. Subsequently, however, it was discovered that the goods had been shipped outside shipment period, and the bills of lading had been forged without the seller's knowledge. It was held that the buyers were entitled to reject the goods, the title of which was defeasible.

[697] *E. Clement Horst Company* v. *Biddell Brothers* [1912] A.C.18, H.L.

[698] *Ginzberg* v. *Barrow Haematite Steel Co and McKellar* [1966] 1 Lloyd's Rep.343; C.I.F. contract for sale of goods, whereby payment was to be made upon tender of the shipping documents ('cash against documents'). The goods arrived before the documents and to assist the buyers to obtain possession, the sellers sent a delivery note, which enabled the buyers to take possession. Subsequently, the buyers went into receivership without having paid. Receiver claimed that the 'cash against documents' variation changed the contract to 'ex-ship', sellers claimed conversion. It was held that property had not passed. Sellers did not intend to depart from CIF but merely to expedite delivery. Furthermore, where the contract is 'cash against documents', the inference is that no property passes until the price has been paid. Similarly, in *Comptoir d'Achat et de Vente du Boerenbond Belge SA* v. *Luis de Ridder Limitada (The Julia)* [1949] A.C.293, H.L., under a C.I.F. Antwerp contract, the sellers were liable for the condition of the goods upon arrival and provided for payment against presentation of a delivery order. The documents were presented to the buyer who paid for the goods. The cargo was never delivered however, because of the German occupation of Belgium, and the ship was diverted to Lisbon and the goods were sold there. The buyer claimed a refund of the price. The sellers claimed that under a C.I.F. contract property passed upon payment against the documents. It was held that the buyer was entitled to a refund. This was not a C.I.F. contract in substance. The documents gave the buyer no property right in the goods entitling him to deal with them while afloat. In addition the fact that the seller undertook liability for the goods until delivery indicated that this was an 'ex-ship' contract. Hence, the sellers had not performed and a refund was ordered.

something completely different to that understood by the parties when they concluded the sale contract.[699]

[699] The Court of Appeal has held that words such as 'insurance to be effected by buyers' contained in C.F.R./C.& F. contracts were not merely declaratory but amounted to a contractual obligation on the buyer; *Reinhart Co.* v. *Joshua Hoyle & Sons Ltd.* [1961] 1 Lloyd's Rep.346. In *Leigh and Sillivan Ltd.* v. *Aliakmon Shipping Co. Ltd. (The Aliakmon)* [1986] 2 All E.R.145, H.L., there was a sale contract on C.& F. terms. After shipment of the goods, a variation of the contract was negotiated whereby the sellers indorsed the bill of lading to the buyer, whereby the buyers were able to take possession of the goods and store them as agents for the sellers. The sellers reserved property in the goods until they were paid. Although the rest of the facts and the issue of negligence are not relevant for the topic under consideration, it should be noted that in effect the C.& F. contract the parties had entered, as a result of these variations, was considered by the House of Lords not to give the rights that normally buyers in C.& F. contracts would enjoy. The two variations, namely, the reservation of property in the goods by the sellers until payment, and the way the bill of lading made them sellers' agents, had turned the C.& F. contract to a different one altogether. *The Parchim* [1918] A.C.157, where the price quoted by the seller was C.& F. and included provisions whereby (i) the buyer would bear the costs of insurance and any variations in the freight charges, and (ii) if the ship was lost after part of the goods had been loaded, the contract was to be cancelled (as to the balance of the goods). It was held the contract not a C.I.F., but had more characteristics of an extended F.O.B. See also *Law & Bonar Ltd.* v. *British American Tobacco Company* [1916] 2 K.B.605, where the term used was 'C.I.F. Smyrna - seller's risk until actual delivery'.

CHAPTER 10

EXPORT FINANCE

BILLS OF EXCHANGE & CHEQUES

NEGOTIABILITY

The concept of a 'negotiable' instrument is very important in overseas trade. Among instruments now legally recognised as negotiable are Bills of Exchange, Promissory Notes, Cheques, Exchequer Bills, Bank Notes, Dividend Warrants, Share Warrants, Banker's Circular Notes, Debentures payable to Bearer.

Post Office Orders, Money Orders, and Share Certificates and Transfers are not negotiable. Nor are letters of credit.

Negotiability is the property that some business instruments have of transferring a good title to the receiver of them irrespective of the title of the giver, provided that the receiver takes them in good faith, for value.

DEFINITION

Section 3(1) of the Bills of Exchange Act 1882, defines a Bill of Exchange as follows:

> 'A bill of exchange is an unconditional order in writing, addressed by one person to another, signed by the person giving it, requiring the person to whom it is addressed to pay on demand or at a fixed or determinable future time a sum certain in money to or to the order of a specified person, or to bearer.'

Every word of this definition is important, for an instrument is not a Bill of Exchange unless it fulfils every description given in the legal definition.

Cheques are bills of exchange, but remember the following differences:

a) A cheque is payable on demand.

b) The drawee is always a bank.

c) There is no indication on the face of a cheque as to the date on which it is payable.

The usual form of a bill does not differ materially from the following:

£84.00	297 London Wall, London, E.C.2 1st *January*, 200...

Thirty days after date [*or* On Demand] pay *X* or Order [*or* Bearer] the sum of *Eighty-four* pounds for value received.

Y.

To ***Z***,
87b Chancery Lane,
London, W.C.2.

Diagram 9: Form of Bill of Exchange (inland)

In the above specimen, **Y** is the '**drawer**' of the bill; **Z** is the '**drawee**'; and **X** is the '**payee**'. If the **drawee** (Z) agrees to pay the bill on the due date, he (Z) '**accepts**', that is, he (Z) writes the word 'Accepted' and his (Z) signature across the face of the bill. He (Z) is then termed the '**acceptor**'. Until he (Z) does this he is not a party to the bill, and is in no way liable thereon.

It is possible to explore the definition with reference to the above specimen bill of exchange. The essentials of a bill are therefore that:

(1) It must be an 'order in writing'. It can be seen in the specimen that the bill is in writing, and it tells Z (the drawee) to pay £84.

(2) The order must be 'unconditional', i.e., there must be no conditions attached to the making of the payment. As in the example, there are no conditions attached to the payment.

(3) It must be 'addressed by one person to another'. Again it can be seen that the order is addressed to Z (the drawee) from Y (the drawer). The drawer (Y) and drawee (Z) are usually different person, e.g. the customer (drawer) and a bank (drawee) but they may be the same person. The commonest example is a banker's draft.

(4) It must require payment to be made to a specified person or his order, or to bearer. Payment may be made to X and Y, as where X and Y are partners. Furthermore, a cheque may be payable in the in the alternative, i.e. pay X or Y.

(5) If the order is not to pay on demand, the time of payment must be fixed or determinable. In the example above, the order is not to pay on demand but at a fixed or determinable future time, because it says 'thirty days after date'. That is 30 days after 1st January 200..., i.e. the bill is payable on 31st January 200...

(6) It must order payment of a certain sum of money only. The main relevance in practice of this is where the words and figures on a cheque are different (s.9(2)). In such a case the words prevail and are taken to be the sum payable. In practice, however, bankers usually return such cheques with the comment 'words and figures differ'.

(7) It must be signed by the drawer (Y). A 'signature' is not defined in the Bills of Exchange Act 1882. However, the writing may be in ink or in pencil, and may be printed in whole or in part.

It must be understood from the outset that no one is liable on a bill unless he is a party to it and that a party to a bill is the drawer, acceptor or indorser, that is someone who has signed or authorised the signing of on his behalf, of the bill in one of those capacities. The payee and drawee of a bill are sometimes loosely called 'parties'. They do not become parties unless and until they sign as indorser and acceptor respectively.

Impersonal payee

Cheques made payable to impersonal payees such as 'Cash or order', 'Wages or order', had often been regarded as payable to bearer. But in *North & South* v. *Macbeth*[700] it was held that an instrument so expressed does not fall within the definition of a bill because it does not order payment to a 'person'.

Fictitious payee

If the payee is a fictitious, or non-existing person, the bill is treated as being payable to bearer. Following a number of case decisions,[701] the 'test' applicable in order to discover whether a payee is fictitious or not was enhanced to include the following factors:

a) if the drawer intends that an existing person whose name is inserted as payee shall actually be paid, the payee is not 'fictitious';
b) if the drawer does not so intend, then the payee is 'fictitious';
c) if the payee does not exist, then he is 'fictitious'.

Payee blank

An instrument made payable to '______order,' the blank not being filled in so as to specify a payee, is not a legal bill of exchange, but it will be construed as payable to the order of the drawer, and if the drawer endorses it, it becomes a valid bill of exchange.[702]

---

[700] *North & South Wales Bank* v. *Macbeth* [1908] A.C.137, H.L.

[701] *Bank of England* v. *Vagliano Bros.* [1891] A.C.107, H.L.; *Clutton* v. *George Attenborough & Son* [1897] A.C.90, H.L.;, *Vinden* v. *Hughes* [1905] 1 K.B.795.

[702] *Chamberlain* v. *Young* [1893] 2 Q.B.206, C.A.

Time of payment

A bill is payable at a 'determinable future time' within the meaning of the Act when it is expressed to be payable at a fixed period after date or at a fixed period after the occurrence of a specified event which is certain to happen, though the time of happening may be uncertain!

For instance, a bill payable seven days after the death of X would be a valid bill, as the specified event is bound to happen, and therefore the 'future time' is 'determinable'.

But a bill payable seven days after the marriage of X would not be valid, as although the event may happen, yet it may not, and thus there is no certainty. The marriage spoken of is a possibility.[703]

Finally, where a bill is payable at a fixed period after date, after sight, or after the happening of a specified event, the time of payment is determined by excluding the day from which the time is to begin to run and by including the day of payment.[704]

Negotiation of a bill

Negotiation is a transfer of a bill from X to Y in such a way as to make Y the holder (s.31).

Acceptance

Acceptance is the 'signification by the drawee of his assent to the order of the drawer' (s17(1)). It must be noted that presentation for acceptance is not necessary, but it is advisable that a bill should be presented for acceptance as soon as possible. The reason for such suggestion, is that if acceptance is refused, the parties to the bill, other than the drawee, become immediately liable (even though the bill has not yet matured), while if the bill is accepted, it becomes a more valuable security, by reason of the fact that the drawee, who has now become the acceptor, has acknowledged his liability upon it.

Furthermore, the wrongful omission of an agent to present a bill for acceptance would render him liable to his principal for any loss resulting from his neglect.

Restrictive endorsements

A restrictive endorsement makes the endorsee a holder, but for certain limited or restricted purposes only.[705] There are two types of restrictive endorsements:

i) Where further negotiation is prohibited, i.e. 'pay X only'.

ii) Where negotiation is permitted but with mere authority to deal as directed.

---

703 *Korea Exchange Bank* v. *Debenhams (Central Buying) Ltd.* [1979] 1 Lloyd's Rep.100.

704 Section 14(2), Bills of Exchange Act 1882.

705 Section 35(1), Bills of Exchange Act 1882.

For example, X, the payee of a bill/cheque for £600, owes £1,000 to Y, an overseas supplier, and he (X) wants to endorse the cheque to Y's agent, A, who is in England but he (X) wishes to make it clear that A is not the beneficial owner of the cheque/bill. In such a case, X can endorse the cheque/bill by stating 'Pay A for the account of Y'. A therefore, can obtain payment but must then account to Y, though A cannot transfer the bill/cheque.

Dishonour of a bill

When a bill is presented for acceptance, the drawee should accept it. If he refuses to do so, claiming perhaps that he has not authorised the bill to be drawn and knows nothing about it, the bill is dishonoured by non-acceptance.

A bill is dishonoured by non-payment when it is duly presented for payment and payment is refused or cannot be obtained.[706] Usually, when a bill is dishonoured by non-payment, an immediate right of recourse against the drawer and endorsers accrues to the holder, but in order to preserve this right the holder must give notice of dishonour to those parties.[707]

Thus, if a bill is presented for payment on the due date, and the acceptor refuses to pay it, then the bill is dishonoured by non-payment. It is now necessary for the holder to take certain action to protect himself. He must give notice of dishonour to the drawer and all other endorsers of the bill. In practice he usually gives notice of the dishonour to the person from whom he obtained the bill, who gives notice to the person from whom he obtained it and so forth, until the drawer is found. Eventually the drawer must honour it, and he will bring an action against the acceptor.

Thus, if on a cheque B is the drawer and C is the payee. C has negotiated the cheque to D, D to E, and E to F. Suppose that F is the holder at the time of dishonour and that he gives notice to E and to C but not to D. The result would be that F could claim on E and C because he gave notice. E could claim on C by reason of being a prior endorser who had a right of recourse against C. Finally, endorsers subsequent to F can also claim on E and C by reason of F's notice to them being subsequent holders. Furthermore, D can sue C because he is a prior endorser who has a right of recourse against C.

Holder of the bill

A holder of a bill is not necessarily the person who is legally entitled to it. Thus, a thief who steals a bearer cheque is a person in possession and therefore a holder, though obviously he has no title to the cheque and cannot sue upon it. However, if he delivers it to X who takes it in good faith and for value, then X will get a good title. If however, X knows of the theft and is not in good faith then his title is no better that the thief's. This arises because where there is a

[706] Section 47(1), Bills of Exchange Act 1882.

[707] Section 47(2), Bills of Exchange Act 1882.

'defect' on the cheque as where it has been stolen or obtained by fraud, then no one can sue upon it and obtain its face value, unless he has taken it without knowledge of previous defects and in good faith.

Finally, where X sells goods to Y a debt comes into being when the contract is made, so that when X decides to pay Y by cheque/bill the cheque is based on a previous or past debt or liability and is therefore for past consideration, which according to the basic elements of the law of contract, is not good consideration.

Does this mean that X and Y have not a simple contract, but all there is between them is a gratuitous promise? Do they need to 'seal' the contract? Section 27(1)(b) of the Bills of Exchange Act 1822 answers these questions by providing that a form of past consideration is enough.

Section 27(1)(a) furthermore provides that any consideration sufficient to support a simple contract will support a bill of exchange. This is the section under the Act (s.27) that most text books refer to and classify it as 'holder for value'. This is simply because what is required for a person to be termed as a holder for value, is consideration, in the context of the Act.

Holder in due course

Section 29(1) provides that a holder in due course is a holder who has taken a cheque, complete and regular on the face of it, under the following conditions:

-that he became the holder of it before it was overdue and without notice that it had been previously dishonoured if such was the fact;

-that he took the cheque in good faith and for value; and

-that at the time that the cheque was negotiated to him he had no notice of any defect in the title of the person who negotiated it to him.

Therefore, it could be said that the Act requires a person to have fulfilled the following six requirements, in order to become a holder in due course:

i. That the bill will be complete and regular on the face of it; and
ii. That he took it before it was overdue; and
iii. in good faith; and
iv. for value; and
v. without notice of any defect in title of the person who endorsed it over to him; and
vi. without notice of any previous dishonour of the bill.

If a cheque drawn in favour of X has been negotiated by X to Y as a result of fraud or misrepresentation or duress or undue influence on Y's part or for an illegal consideration, there is a 'defect' on the bill.

Suppose that Y negotiates it for value to Z. Ordinarily, Z will be a holder for value, but because there is a 'defect' on the cheque Z can only take it free from the defect in the title of Y and successfully sue on it if he is a holder in due course, which means amongst other things that he (Z) took it without notice of any defect in the title of Y. However, thanks to s.29, if it is established that Z is a holder in due course (i.e. to show that the holder for value of the bill is either a holder in due course as defined under s.29(1), or a person who has taken the bill through a holder in due course), then the defect is said to 'cured' and Z can sue the various parties to the cheque for its full face value.

In other words, it could be said that when a bill is negotiated to a holder in due course, he obtains a good title to it, notwithstanding any defect in the title of his transferor or previous holders.

'Notice' means actual, though not formal notice, that is to say, either knowledge of the facts, or a suspicion of something wrong, combined with a wilful disregard of the means of knowledge. Therefore, it comes without saying that an original payee of a bill is not a holder in due course, as the bill has not been negotiated to him.[708]

Defective title: when the person who negotiates the bill has obtained the bill, by fraud, duress, or force and fear, or other unlawful means, or an illegal consideration, or when he negotiates it in breach of faith, or under such circumstances as amount to a fraud.

'A holder in due course is a holder': This implies that no-one can be holder in due course after forgery of an essential signature.

'Bill, complete and regular on the face of it': If the bill is not complete, then no-one who takes it can be a holder in due course. Thus, a person who takes an instrument, even though he may have authority to complete it, cannot be a holder in due course. If the bill is not regular on the face of it then again no-one can be a holder in due course. For example, a bill marked 'Not Negotiable' or 'Not Transferable' is not regular on the face of it although quite valid.

'Before it was overdue': If a bill is due and payable on 31st October then, on and after 1st November it is overdue and anyone taking the bill then cannot be a holder in due course though he may be a holder for value.

'Without notice that it had previously been dishonoured if such was the fact': Although this provision of the Act might appear at first unnecessary, since if a bill had been dishonoured it would be overdue, note that this is not always true. If, for example, a bill is drawn on 1st October payable three months after

---

[708] *R.E. Jones Ltd.* v. *Waring & Gillow Ltd.* [1926] A.C.670, H.L.

date it is due on 1st January. Yet a holder might present it for acceptance on 15th October and find acceptance refused by the drawee. This would be dishonour of the bill by non-acceptance, yet the bill would still be current and not overdue. A person taking such bill with the knowledge that it has already been dishonoured in this way cannot be a holder in due course.

Liability of acceptor: The acceptor of a bill, by accepting it, undertakes that:

(a) He will pay it according to the tenor of his acceptance.

(b) He is precluded from denying to a holder in due course:

  i The existence of the drawer, the genuineness of his signature, and his capacity and authority to draw the bill;

  ii In the case of a bill payable to drawer's order, the then capacity of the drawer to indorse, but not the genuineness of validity of his indorsement;

  iii In the case of a bill payable to the order of a third person, the existence of the payee and his then capacity to indorse, but not the genuineness or validity of his endorsement.

Subsection (2)(b) means that the acceptor cannot refuse payment to a holder in due course on the excuse that (i) the drawer does not exist, or (ii) the drawer's signature is a forgery, or (iii) the drawer had no capacity or authority to draw the bill.

Liability of the drawer: The drawer is responsible for payment should the bill be dishonoured by the drawee (or acceptor).[709] Before the bill is accepted he is primarily liable for payment; after acceptance, the acceptor takes on the primary liability and the drawer becomes second in the order of liability or, in other words, becomes surety for the acceptor. If the drawer is called upon by a holder in due course to pay the bill, he cannot escape liability merely because the payee does not exist or has no capacity to indorse.

Liability of the indorser: The indorser is responsible to all who became parties subsequent to himself and also to the holder. He agrees to pay the bill, should the drawee (or acceptor) dishonour it. Furthermore, his (indorser's) indorsement acts as a guarantee to any subsequent holder in due course that all the indorsements prior to his own are genuine. Where the drawer's signature is forged the possessor of the bill has the rights of a holder in due course against all indorsers.

In the case of a forged indorsement the possessor of the bill has the rights of a holder in due course, though no actual title to the bill, against all parties who

[709] Section 55, Bills of Exchange Act 1882.

indorsed subsequent to the forgery. All this could be illustrated by the following example:

A draws a bill payable to B. B transfers it to C by indorsement. The bill is stolen from C by Z. Z forges C's signature to a special indorsement and transfers the bill to D. By further indorsements the bill passes to E and thence to F. Under s.24, F has no title to the bill since he is not a holder, the bill being payable to C. A and B will not recognise anyone else but C as having any right to the bill. C, in his turn, can compel F to restore the bill to him or pay him its equivalent. F, consequently, would be in a very poor position but for this section which says that those who indorsed the bill after the forgery (D and E) guarantee the genuineness of all indorsements prior to their own, which includes the forgery purporting to be C's indorsement. In this case they cannot escape their liability that they undertake in subsection (2)(a). Thus, F can recover from E and E from D. D the victim of the forgery will bear the loss unless he can recover from Z, the forger.

Forgery

Where a signature to a bill is forged or placed on the bill without the authority of the person whose signature it purports to be, such signature is wholly inoperative and no right can be acquired thereunder. Therefore a forged indorsement on an order bill would give no title to a transferee; he is not a holder in due course, even though he took the bill for value and with no knowledge of the forgery, as the bill has not been negotiated to him, negotiation requiring indorsement (which means a *valid* indorsement) and delivery.

The following example will clarify the issue of the effects of a forged or unauthorised endorsement:

A cheque is drawn by X in favour of C and endorsed by C to D. It is then stolen from D by a thief who forges D's endorsement and negotiates the cheque to E who endorses it to F, who endorses it to G. G has no knowledge of the forgery and in all respects complies with the definition of a holder in due course (s.29). G has no title to the cheque because it rests on a forgery.

i) He (G) cannot sue D or C

ii) He (G) has rights against E or F by virtue of section 55(2) which provides that an endorser gives a 'guarantee' to the transferee with regard to the validity of a cheque. This means that when E endorsed the cheque to F he impliedly guaranteed that it was a valid cheque and the signatures of the drawer and previous endorsers were valid signatures. F made a guarantee to the same effect when he endorsed the cheque to G.

Claused bills

Sometimes bills are 'claused' with phrases, which require the drawee to pay more than the actual value of the bill. The reasons why these 'claused' bills were introduced are:

a) In order to throw the burden of any exchange risk on to the foreign drawee, so that the U.K. drawer received the full sterling amount due to him.

b) To enable the drawer to provide for the payment of interest by the drawee, in order to compensate the drawer for the time taken for the drawee's payment to reach him.

c) A clause was often helpful in permitting the banker to act as an arbiter in deciding what rate of exchange to use when the drawee paid in local currency.

An 'exchange clause' may be defined as a clause included in the wording of a bill, which fixes the method of arriving at the rate of exchange to be used when the drawee pays the bill.

Inland and Foreign bills

An inland bill is a bill which is or on the face of it purports to be (i) both drawn and payable within the British Islands, or (ii) drawn within the British Islands upon some person resident therein.[710] Any other bill is a foreign bill.

Documentary bills

Where a bill has attached to it the bill of lading, invoice, and policy of insurance relating to the goods against which it is drawn, so that they are available in case the bill is not honoured, it is termed a Documentary Bill.

The bill of lading constitutes the title to the goods, and, to enable the drawee/buyer to obtain the goods which he has purchased, arrangements are made whereby the documents are handed to him against either his acceptance or his payment of the bill, the method adopted depending on his credit and standing. The bill is generally marked accordingly, i.e. 'Documents to be surrendered on Acceptance' known as a 'D/A' bill, or 'Documents to be surrendered on Payment' known as a 'D/P' bill, as the case may be. The documents are attached to the bill in the first place by the drawer/seller, when he has shipped the relative goods. A banker who purchases or discounts the bill retains the documents as security, and, through his correspondents abroad, collects the bill when due.

In simple words, the seller would normally arrange for the presentation of the documents by a bank which would be under (his) instructions not to part with the

[710] Section 4(1), Bills of Exchange Act 1882.

documents except against payment or acceptance. It would be this collecting bank which presents the documents to the buyer and which would receive payment, to be remitted to the seller.

When bills of exchange are to be passed to a bank for collection, as described above, the process is usually controlled by the Uniform Rules for Collections published by the International Chamber of Commerce (1995, publication number 522). The term 'collections' refers to the handling by banks of documents (financial documents or commercial documents, or both) in order to obtain payment or acceptance, or to deliver documents against payment or acceptance. The term 'documents' is applied to two types of remittances:

i) 'clean' remittances and

ii) 'documentary' remittances.

A clean remittance is simply a bill of exchange or similar document, which is not supported by any other document. The holder of this bill passes it to the bank for collection in the normal course of events as the due date approaches, and the bank has only this simple duty to perform.

With 'documentary' bills there are other duties involved, such as handing over the documents against payment or acceptance.

CHEQUES

After looking at bills of exchange, we continue with a brief examination of cheques and the basic duties of bankers and customers. For all intends and purposes a cheque is a bill of exchange drawn on a banker and payable on demand.[711]

1. The banker must obey his customer's mandate

A bank has no right to debit a customer's account for the amount of a cheque on which the customer's signature has been forged because the bank has then no mandate from the customer to pay. However, the customer may be estopped in some cases from denying the validity of his signature and in these circumstances the bank may debit his account even on the basis of a cheque on which the customer's signature was forged.[712]

---

[711] Section 73, Bills of Exchange Act 1882.

[712] Thus in *Greenwood* v. *Martins Bank Ltd.* [1933] A.C.51, H.L., X opened an account (joint) with bank Z, in the names of X and Y, his wife. Cheques drawn on this account were to bear the signatures of them both, i.e. X and Y. Later on X opened a further account with bank Z in his own name, i.e. X, though his wife kept the pass books and cheque books in respect of both accounts. Few months later, X asked his wife to give him a cheque, saying he wanted to draw

Furthermore, note that if a bank pays a cheque on which the signature of its customer as drawer has been forged the bank can sue the person to whom payment was made for restitution of the amount paid out, for the money with which payment was made was the property of the bank.

It should also be noted that the bank has no right to debit a customer's account where the mandate requires two signatures and only one signature in fact has been used.[713]

Finally, note that where one joint account-holder, say A, forges the signature of the other, say B, the bank in effect agrees with both, i.e. A and B, jointly that:

(a) it would honour cheques signed by them both and

(b) with A separately that it would not honour cheques unless signed by him, and

(c) with B separately that it would not honour cheques unless signed by him.

This in effect means that where the bank honours a cheque on which B has forged A's signature, A should be able to sue the bank because it is in breach of the separate agreement with him. Therefore, joint account-holders have separate actions against the bank.[714]

2. A banker must honour his customer's cheques

The general rule is that a bank is bound to honour its customer's cheques to the extent that the customer is in credit or to the extent of any agreed overdraft.

If a cheque is 'referred to drawer' although the customer is in funds or has an agreed overdraft the matter is treated as follows:

(a) If the customer is in business or practice in a profession, it is assumed that his credit-worthiness has been affected and damages will be awarded without proof of actual loss.[715]

£20 from his own account. His wife then told him that there was no money in the bank, and that she had used it to help her sister who was involved in legal proceedings over property. He (X) asked her(Y) who had forged his signature but she would not say. However, she did ask him not to inform the bank of the forgeries until her sister's case was over. X complied with this request for the next 10 months. Then he (X) discovered that there were no legal proceedings instituted by his wife's sister and that his wife had been deceiving him. He (X) told his wife that he intended to go to the bank (Z) and reveal her forgeries, but before he actually made the visit to the bank she (Y) shot herself. X claimed £410 from the bank (Z) on the grounds that this sum had been paid out of his own account and the joint account by means of forged cheques. The bank (Z) pleaded ratification, adoption or estoppel. It was held that there could be no ratification or adoption in this sort of case, but the essential elements of estoppel were present. X's failure to inform the bank (Z) was a representation that the cheques were good.

713 *B. Liggett (Liverpool) Ltd.* v. *Barclays Bank Ltd.* [1928] 1 K.B.48.

714 *Jackson* v. *White and Midland Bank* [1967] 2 Lloyd's Rep.68; *Catlin* v. *Cyprus Finance Corp. (London) Ltd.* [1983] Q.B.759.

715 *Wilson* v. *United Counties Bank Limited* [1920] A.C.102, H.L.

(b) Where the customer is not in trade or practising a profession damage to credit is not assumed and nominal damages will be awarded unless a particular loss is proved as where, for example, the customer can show that a particular creditor has refused to do business with him again.[716]

The bank's duty to honour cheques ceases on the customer cancelling payment. In this connection it should be noted that notice to the bank must be actual, not constructive.[717] A bank which overlooks its customer's instructions to stop payment of a cheque and consequently pays the cheque when it has been presented, can recover the money from the payee because it has been paid under a mistake of fact.[718]

3. Banker's duty to observe secrecy

A bank must not disclose the financial affairs of a customer. This is based on an implied term in the contract between the banker and his customer, and continues even after the account is closed.[719]

However, there are four exceptions: (a) where disclosure is required by law,[720] (b) where there is a public duty to disclose, e.g. where information is given to the police to protect the public against crime, (c) where disclosure is required in the interest of the bank, e.g. where the bank is suing to recover an overdraft, (d) where the customer gives permission, e.g. where a corporate customer of the bank gives the bank permission to disclose the state of its account to the company's auditors.

4. Banker's duty to collect cheques paid in by a customer

A bank is under a duty to collect for its customer's account cheques paid in by the customer. The bank then acts as a collecting bank and has certain protections if its customer has a defective title to the cheque.

MISCELLANEOUS POINTS ON CHEQUES

Where a cheque contains an addition of the words 'and Co.' or any abbreviation thereof (e.g. 'A/C Payee only', 'Not negotiable', 'Barclays Bank plc.') between two parallel transverse lines, the cheque is said to be *crossed* generally. Such a cheque will only be payable by the bank on which it is drawn through another bank, and not over the counter.

---

716 *Gibbons* v. *Westminster Bank Ltd.* [1939] 2 K.B.882.

717 *Curtice* v. *London City & Midland Bank Ltd.* [1908] 1 K.B.293.

718 *Barclays Bank Ltd.* v. *W.J. Simms Son and Cooke (Southern) Ltd.* [1979] 3 All E.R.522.

719 *Tournier* v. *National Provincial and Union Bank of England* [1924] 1 K.B.461, C.A.

720 For example, under the Taxes Management Act 1970 (as amended).

It is therefore a hindrance for someone who obtains the cheque wrongly because he could only obtain payment through a bank and the loss may be discovered meanwhile and the cheque stopped. In addition, collection through a bank may help trace a thief. If the words used are 'Not negotiable' then no other person apart from the previous holder can claim to have a better title. Even where a person satisfies the definition of a holder in due course such person will not take the cheque free from defects.

The crossing 'A/C Payee' or 'account payee' makes the cheque non-transferable, and is only valid as between the parties thereto.[721]

THE UNIFORM CUSTOMS AND PRACTICE FOR DOCUMENTARY CREDITS

This is a standardised code of practice formulated by the International Chamber of Commerce regarding the processing of Documentary credits. These Rules, regulate the implementation and operation of the documentary credit, and are published by the International Chamber of Commerce (I.C.C.). The current (1994) edition of the Rules, is referred to as 'U.C.P.500'.

An important point to remember is that these rules do not apply to a credit unless they are expressly incorporated therein. The parties to a documentary credit arrangement are:

1) The applicant for the credit; this is usually the buyer under the contract of sale. The instructions given by the buyer to his bank should reflect the contract of sale. Such instructions must be strictly complied with by the bank.
2) The beneficiary; under a documentary credit, this is the seller.
3) The issuing bank; this is the buyer's bank, i.e. is the bank which receives instructions by the buyer. As soon as this bank receives these instructions, it will issue notice to the seller as to the opening of the credit and its terms. Thus, it is referred to as the issuing bank.
4) The correspondent bank; this may play the role of either (a) the adviser, i.e. merely to advise the beneficiary of the terms of the credit, or (b) the confirmer, i.e. by giving the beneficiary an undertaking/confirmation that it will make payment if the correct documents are tendered to it.

LETTERS OF CREDIT

A Documentary Letter of Credit is an instrument by which a bank undertakes to pay the seller (exporter) for his goods providing he complies with the conditions

[721] Section 81A, Bills of Exchange Act 1882, inserted by s.1(1) of the Cheques Act 1992.

laid down in the credit. Whilst ensuring that the exporter receives payment for his goods it also gives the buyer (importer) the confirmation that he will not have to part with his money until he is presented with documents evidencing that the stipulated conditions have been fulfilled. The credit specifies when payment is to be made. Usually this is either when the documents are presented to the paying bank, or at some future date, usually within 180 days of receipt of the documents by the paying bank. Such a method of payment is common in export sales contracts. Overall it is a letter issued by a bank authorising credit to a correspondent.

The buyer's (importer's) bank (issuing bank) undertakes, or authorises its correspondent bank in the seller's (exporter's) country, to pay the seller (exporter) a sum of money (normally the invoice price of the goods) against presentation of shipping documents which are independent of the sales contract. It is a mandatory contract and completely independent of the sales contract. It is concerned only with documents and not the goods to which the documents refer.

TYPES OF DOCUMENTARY CREDIT

The usual form of these credits is the 'irrevocable' credit, which means that it cannot be cancelled or amended without the agreement of the beneficiary (the seller/exporter) and all other parties. Such a credit, opened by a reputable bank, means that the exporter/seller can rely on payment being made as soon as he has shipped the goods and produced the documents called for in accordance with the terms of the credit.[722]

The security provided by an irrevocable credit may be further enhanced if the bank in the exporter's/seller's country (advising bank) is requested by the buyer's/importer's bank (issuing bank) to add its 'confirmation'. The exporter/seller then has a 'confirmed irrevocable credit' and he need look no further than his own local bank for payment.

Finally, a credit may be irrevocable without being confirmed, but a confirmed credit is always irrevocable.

Another type of credit is the 'transferable' one, which is usually found when the seller (the first beneficiary) is not the manufacturer/original supplier of the goods, so that in effect the sale is performed by someone other than the seller. The credit is established in favour of the seller (prime beneficiary), and authorises the advising bank, i.e. the bank in the seller's/exporter's country, to accept instructions from the prime beneficiary to make the credit available, to one or more parties (second beneficiaries). The credit is then advised to the second beneficiary in the terms and conditions of the original, except that the

[722] Article 6c of U.C.P.500 suggests that a letter of credit would be presumed to be irrevocable unless it is clearly indicated otherwise.

amount and unit price are reduced and the shipment and expiry dates shortened. In simple words, when the credit is transferred, a second beneficiary steps into the shoes of the original first beneficiary, and he is entitled and bound to perform the obligations of the first beneficiary, but by using his own shipping documents. A documentary credit can be transferable only if it is expressly designated as such by the issuing bank.

Companies with surplus liquidity in one currency may wish to obtain funds in another currency, for investment or expansion, by employing their own surplus without conversion or incurring increased interest costs by borrowing unmatched funds. This may be arranged by means of a parallel, or 'back to back', loan or credit. In such a situation a form of financing whereby money borrowed in one country or currency is covered by the lending of an equivalent amount in another. Back to back credits arise in circumstances similar to those of the transferable credit and particularly where the supplier as well as the buyer is overseas.

'Revolving credits' arise where there are shipments in a series at intervals and the parties wish the programme to proceed without interruption. Accordingly a credit is established for a certain sum and quantity of goods with a provision that, when a shipment has been made and documents presented and paid, the credit automatically becomes available as the documents are presented for subsequent payment to the exporter/seller for the goods.

Another type of letter of credit is what is known as 'Red clause' credit. This allows the seller/beneficiary to obtain an advance on the price before the goods are shipped, which is conditional upon the presentation of documents such as a warehouse receipt.[723] Consequently, the buyer takes a risk in that he would be liable to reimburse the issuing bank even if the seller disappears with the amount advanced.

A letter of credit will set out in detail a description of the goods, price per unit and packing, name and address of the beneficiary, the voyage, that is port of shipment and port of destination, whether the price is F.O.B., C.FR. or C.I.F., and whether part shipments and transhipment are allowed. In some cases, the ship will be nominated. Details of insurance, if C.I.F. and the risks to be covered will also be shown. The credit will specify a latest date for shipment and an

---

[723] The 'dangers' of such arrangements can be seen in *Bank Melli Iran* v. *Barclays Bank (Dominion Colonial & Overseas)* [1951] 2 Lloyd's Rep.367; a confirmed credit authorised D (confirming bank) to effect payment of £40,000 representing the value of 100 new Chevrolet trucks against a delivery order, an invoice, an insurance policy, and a certificate of the U.S. Government. The invoice and certificate against which payment had been made by D described the trucks as 'in new condition' and 'new, good', respectively. The certificate did not purport to relate to any specific trucks. After D had paid £40,000, C (issuing bank) authorised D to make an increase in respect of part of the trucks shipped, authorised a representative to make a survey of the trucks, and attempted to negotiate a settlement with the U.S. authorities. It was held that although the documents against which the £40,000 payment had been made were not in accordance with D's mandate, the subsequent acts of C amounted to ratification/retrospective acceptance, and therefore, C had to reimburse D.

expiry date, which is the latest date for presentation of documents. The basic documents which are usually called for are:

1. **Invoice**: U.C.P.500 requires that this is made out in the name of the applicant for the credit/buyer.[724] The amount must not exceed the credit amount. If terms such as 'about' or '*circa*' are used, a tolerance of 10% is allowed. The description of the goods on the invoice and the packing must be exact and agree with the credit. An essential part of the description is the marks and numbers on the packages.

2. **Transport Document**: This is the document which indicates that loading on board or dispatch or taking into charge of the goods has occurred. Usually, this document would be a bill of lading, without which the buyer will not be able to obtain delivery from the shipping company. If the buyer has specifically requested the seller to tender a bill of lading, then U.C.P 500 require such bills of lading must be 'clean', that is, bearing no superimposed clauses derogatory to the condition of the goods such 'inadequate packing', 'used drums', 'on deck', etc. Unless the credit has specifically permitted the circumstances contained in the clause, the negotiating bank will call for an indemnity. The bills of lading must show the goods to be 'on board', as 'received for shipment' bills of lading are not generally acceptable under U.C.P 500. However, if the buyer has not specifically requested the seller to tender a bill of lading, then any other transport document fulfilling the requirements of U.C.P. 500, e.g. 'received for shipment' bill of lading, will be adequate.

3. **Insurance Policy**: The document must be as stated in the credit and issued by an insurance company or its agent. Cover notes issued by brokers are not acceptable.[725] The details on the policy must match those on the bills of lading/transport document. It must also be in the same currency as the credit and endorsed in blank. The amount covered should be at least the invoice amount.

SHORT-CIRCUITING OF LETTER OF CREDIT

Where the parties to the contract of sale have arranged for payment by a letter of credit, they must abide by such agreement and cannot short-circuit the credit by making direct claims connected with the payment of the price against each other. Thus, if there is an agreement to make payment under a

---

[724] Article 37a(ii), U.C.P.500.

[725] Article 34c, U.C.P.500. Insurance certificates are also not acceptable since they do not clearly determine the full terms of the buyer's cover; *Diamond Alkali Export Corp.* v. *Bourgeois* [1921] 3 K.B.443.

documentary credit, then the seller does not have the right to present the documents to the buyer direct.[726] Sometimes however, the short-circuiting of the letter of credit arrangement may be admissible.

For example, if the bank whom the parties have interposed as intermediary becomes insolvent, the seller normally can claim the price from the buyer directly, making a direct tender of documents to the latter. The implied condition is discharged by the insolvency of the intermediary.

AUTONOMY OF THE LETTER OF CREDIT

The contract of international sale is independent of the functions/workings of a letter of credit, and consequently it is said that as the issuing and advising banks are not involved in the commercial transaction of the sale, a letter of credit is autonomous.[727] It follows, that if the bank makes payment against conforming documents then it is entitled to be reimbursed by the credit applicant/buyer. The banks have therefore an obligation to pay 'irrespective of any dispute there may be between the parties as to whether the goods are up to contract or not'.[728]

It must be noted that although there is no reference in the U.C.P. to the existence of any exceptions to the principle of the autonomy of credit, exceptions do exist and are recognised by English law. For example, fraud, illegality, mistake, or frustration in the sale contract may affect the letter of credit.

Two possibilities exist in respect of fraud:

- Where it is clearly established to the satisfaction of the bank that a fraud has occurred, but there is no evidence before the bank which shows that the beneficiary (the seller) knew of the fraud, then the bank must pay.[729] Thus, in

[726] *Soproma SpA* v. *Marine & Animal By-Products Corporation* [1966] 1 Lloyd's Rep.367.

[727] 'Credits, by their nature, are separate transactions from the sales or other contract(s) on which they are based and banks are in no way concerned with or bound by such contract(s), even if any reference whatsoever to such contract(s) is included in the Credit.', Article 3a, U.C.P. 500. *Czarnikow-Rionda Sugar Trading Inc.* v. *Standard Bank London Ltd.* [1999] 2 Lloyd's Rep.187, the beneficiary (seller) presented the documents for payment to the confirming bank. Before maturity of credit, C, the buyer, sought an injunction to restraint D, the issuing bank, from reimbursing the confirming bank on the basis that C, the buyer, had been induced into entering the contract with the beneficiary (seller) by fraud. It was held that fraud in the underlying sale contract was not enough. It must be clearly shown that D, the issuing bank, is aware of the fraud before payment was made. The letter of credit must be isolated from the disputes between traders.

[728] *Per* Jenkins, L.J., in *Malas (Hamazeh) & Sons* v. *British Imex Industries Ltd.* [1958] 2 Q.B.127, 129.

[729] It would not be sufficient if the bank had some reasonable suspicion in relation to the beneficiary; *Society of Lloyd's* v. *Canadian Imperial Bank of Commerce* [1993] 2 Lloyd's Rep.579. An issuing bank has no obligation to question or investigate the genuineness of documents which appear on their face to comply with the terms of the credit, either under

the *United City Merchants* case[730] the bills of lading showed as date of shipment 15 December 1976, which was the latest date of shipment required by the credit, but the goods were, in fact, loaded a day later, which was out of time. The Royal Bank of Canada, which had confirmed the credit, became very wary of this because in the first tender of the bills of lading the date was blanked out and the date of 15 December 1976 was superimposed, but later, before the expiry of the credit, a second tender of unamended bills of lading was made which showed the date of 15 December 1976. The documents were thus correct on their face. The false date was inserted by an employee of the loading brokers and the sellers knew nothing about it. It was held that the bank was obliged to pay, in spite of its knowledge of the 'fraud', since not only the bank and the buyers, but also the sellers were deceived by the fraud of the third party.

-Where the bank has positive proof that a fraud has been committed and that the beneficiary (the seller) knew of this fraud, then the bank must not honour its obligation under the credit. Such a case may arise, for example, where the beneficiary (seller) himself tenders documents which, to his knowledge,[731] are false or if somebody else does so with his knowledge or connivance.

A letter of credit would also be affected by illegality of the sale contract, i.e. the bank may refuse payment.[732] Furthermore, this would be the case where

general principles or under U.C.P.500; *Montrod Ltd.* v. *Grundkotter Fleischvertriebs GmbH* [2002] 3 All E.R. 697.

730 *United City Merchants (Investments)* v. *Royal Bank of Canada* [1983] 1 A.C.168.

731 *Rafsanjan Pistachio Producers Co-operation* v. *Bank Leumi (U.K.) plc.* [1992] 1 Lloyd's Rep.513.

732 This view was supported by Staughton, L.J., 'there must be cases when illegality can affect a letter of credit. Take for example a contract for the sale of arms to Iraq, at a time when such a sale is illegal. The contract provides for the opening of a letter of credit, to operate on presentation of a bill of lading for 1,000 Kalashnikov rifles to be carried to the port of Basra. I do not suppose that a court would give judgment for the beneficiary against the bank in such a case. Would illegality, like fraud, have to be clearly established and known to the bank before it could operate as a defence, or a ground for restraining payment by the bank? That is not an altogether easy question, but I am inclined to think that it would.', in *Group Josi Re* v. *Walbrook Insurance Co. Ltd.* [1996] 1 Lloyd's Rep.345, 362. In this case C entered into a number of (re-insurance) contracts with D who acted through their agents. C further opened letters of credit in favour of D which provided for payment on presentation of debit notes. Later C claimed that the contracts were void because of their own illegality in carrying on an insurance business without statutory authorisation. C therefore applied for injunctions preventing the D and their agent from presenting documents for payment under the letters of credit. The Court of Appeal held that performance of the (re-insurance) contracts by C was not illegal. More recently the Commercial Court clearly stated that not only English law would not enforce a letter of credit which relates to an illegal underlying transaction, but also where the illegal purpose of the underlying contract was unlawful under the law of a foreign friendly state, and even if it was not unlawful in English law; *Mahonia Ltd.* v. *J.P. Morgan Chase Bank (No.1)* [2003] 2 Lloyd's Rep.911. See also, *Sirius International Insurance Co. Ltd.* v. *FAI General Insurance Ltd.* [2004] 1 All E.R.308. In *Montrod Ltd.* v. *Grundkotter Fleischvertriebs GmbH* [2002] 3 All E.R. 697, the Court of Appeal suggested that it might be possible for the conduct of a beneficiary in connection with the creation or presentation of a document forged

fraudulent misrepresentation[733] is made by the applicant (buyer), and the beneficiary (seller) is participating in the fraud.[734]

It is sufficient to note that if due to a fundamental/operative mistake the letter of credit is rendered void,[735] then the bank may be able to withhold payment to the beneficiary even after conforming documents have been tendered.

Finally, if a frustrating event prevents the bank to make payment, or indeed prevents the sale contract to proceed, e.g. government action, then the bank would be justified in not making payment.[736]

It could therefore be concluded that although it is the wider belief that a letter of credit is autonomous from the sale contract, there are more than a couple of exceptions applicable to this general rule.

THE DOCTRINE OF STRICT COMPLIANCE

As it is known, in a commercial transaction the buyer's bank operates the documentary credit as the buyer's agent. If the bank exceeds its principal's, i.e. buyer's, instructions, then according to the law of agency, it would have acted without authority. Consequently the loss would fall on the bank in question.

The doctrine of strict compliance dictates that a bank will refuse documents tendered by a seller, if such documents are not strictly compliant to the instructions.[737]

If the documents are correct and the bank delays in making payment against them, it may find itself liable in damages to the seller.[738]

---

by a third party, while not amounting to fraud, to be of such a character as to disentitle the beneficiary to payment. These cases clearly contribute to the erosion of the doctrine of autonomy of documentary credits.

733 As to fraudulent misrepresentation, see *supra*, p.92.

734 *Rafsanjan Pistachio Producers Co-operation* v. *Bank Leumi (U.K.) plc.* [1992] 1 Lloyd's Rep.513.

735 As to mistake, see *supra*, p.94.

736 As to frustration, see *supra*, p.147. For full consideration of these exceptions to the principle of autonomy, see Professor Goode in 'Abstract Payment Undertakings', Chapter 9 of P. Crane and J. Stapleton, *Essays for Patrick Atiyah* (1991), at pp.225-234.

737 *Equitable Trust Co. of New York* v. *Dawson Partners Ltd.* (1927) 27 Ll. L. Rep.49, H.L.; D agreed to buy goods from a seller, payment to be made by letter of credit. The credit called for, *inter alia*, 'a certificate of quality to be issued by experts'. The seller tendered a certificate of quality issued by a single expert. Furthermore, payment to the seller was made by the advising bank. However, when the certificate was tendered to D (buyer) he refused to pay on the grounds of non-compliance with the credit. The Court found in favour of D (buyer). See also *Seaconsar Far East Ltd.* v. *Bank Markazi Jomhouri Islami Iran* [1999] 1 Lloyd's Rep.36, C.A.

738 *Ozalid Group* v. *African Continental Bank* [1979] 2 Lloyd's Rep.231; payment was to have been made on 5th October but was not made until 12th December, even though the documents were correct. It was held that the beneficiary (seller) was entitled to damages for the

Strictly speaking, the law would justify a bank in rejecting documents evidencing a short shipment of 0.06%, as not complying with the terms of the credit.[739] However, U.C.P.500 allow for some margin of error:

a) a tolerance of 5% more or less would be permitted if the credit does not stipulate otherwise;[740]

b) if the words 'about', 'approximately', or 'circa' are used in connection with the quantity the permitted tolerance would be 10%.[741]

Obviously the above would not applicable in case the quantity is stipulated as a number of packing units or individual items; it would be preposterous to permit this in, for example container transport.

Besides stating an expiry date for presentation of documents, credits should also stipulate a specified period of time after the issuing of the bills of lading within which the documents must be presented for payment. If such period is not stipulated in the credit, banks will refuse documents presented to them later than 21 days after the issuance of the bills of lading.[742]

Also, Article 37c provides that the description of the goods contained in the commercial invoice must correspond with that required by the letter of credit. However, the same Article provides that in documents other than the commercial invoice the goods may be described in general terms not inconsistent with the description of the goods in the credit.[743] Indeed, the general view is that documents should be in apparent compliance, and there is no need for the bank to go further than checking this to be case.[744]

---

unjustifiable delay in making payment. However, if the bank involved in the letter of credit has exercised reasonable care to ascertain that the documents comply with the terms of the credit, then it would not be liable for the form, sufficiency, accuracy, genuineness, falsification or legal effect of any such documents; Article 15, U.C.P.500.

739 *Soproma SpA* v. *Marine & Animal By-Products Corporation* [1966] 1 Lloyd's Rep.367; the sellers agreed to sell certain quantity of Chilean fish fullmeal under a letter of credit. The credit required documents showing, *inter alia*, that the fish fullmeal contained a minimum 70% protein content. The protein content was actually 69.7%, and it was held that the bank was entitled to reject the documents. See also *Moralice (London) Ltd.* v. *E.D.& F. Man* [1954] 2 Lloyd's Rep.525, where it was held, *inter alia*, that a bank was entitled to reject the documents, as the *de minimis* rule did not apply where payment was to be made against documents in accordance with a letter of credit.

740 Article 39b, U.C.P.500.

741 Article 39a, U.C.P.500.

742 Article 43a, U.C.P.500.

743 *Banque de l'Indochine et de Suez S.A.* v. *J.H. Rayner (Mincing Lane) Ltd.* [1983] Q.B.711.

744 *Credit Industriel et Commercial* v. *China Merchants Bank* [2002] 2 All E.R. (Comm.) 427; the packing list and the invoice submitted to the bank were not apparently discrepant. However, when D calculated by reference to the packing list the percentage of some cargo parcels did not tally, e.g. one parcel was 38.64% whilst the commercial invoice recorded a percentage of 40%. The Court found that the documents, in view of Articles 13(a), 21, and 37(c) were not

Furthermore, banks would generally be entitled to reject documents in certain circumstances, since:

> '... it is quite impossible to suggest that a banker is to be affected with knowledge of the customs and customary terms of every one of the thousands of trades for whose dealings he may issue a letter of credit'.[745]

In conclusion, it could be said that:

> '... the requirement of strict compliance is not equivalent to a test of exact literal compliance in all circumstances as regards all documents. To some extent, therefore, the banker must exercise his own judgment whether the requirement is satisfied by the documents presented to him'.[746]

Original Document

After a long line of cases[747] which attempted to draw some general rules on different type of documents encompassed by the expression, the I.C.C. in 1999 published a policy statement, in order to assist banks dealing with documents. In this statement[748] I.C.C. recognises the presumption of an automated or computerised document should be in favour of its being an original, unless the document itself indicates otherwise.

Following this statement, a recent case[749] which came before the Courts on this issue, indicated that I.C.C.'s policy decision would be taken into

---

discrepant. In other words D, who checked the documents, was not required to embark on the calculations relied upon.

745 *Per* Mackinnon, L.J., in *J.H. Rayner & Co. Ltd.* v. *Hambro's Bank Ltd.* [1943] K.B.37, 41.

746 *Per* Evans, L.J., in *Kredietbank Antwerp* v. *Midland Bank plc.* [1999] 1 All E.R.801, 806.

747 *United Bank Ltd.* v. *Banque Nationale de Paris* [1992] 2 S.L.R.64, H. Ct. of Singapore; *Beyene* v. *Irving Trust Co. Ltd.* (1985) 762 Fed.Rep. 2d 4, U.S. Second Circuit Court of Appeals; *Kredietbank Antwerp* v. *Midland Bank plc.* [1999] 1 All E.R.801.

748 Relating to Art.20(b) of U.C.P.500 which states: 'Unless otherwise stipulated in the Credit, banks will also accept as an original document(s), a document(s) produced or appearing to have been produced: by reprographic, automated or computerised systems, as carbon copies; provided that it is marked as original and, where necessary, appears to be signed. A document may be signed by handwriting, by facsimile signature, by perforated signature, by stamp, by symbol, or by any other mechanical or electronic method of authentication.'

749 *Credit Industriel et Commercial* v. *China Merchants Bank* [2002] 2 All E.R. (Comm.) 427; among the issues contended by D, was that the various certificates produced by the beneficiary (seller) had to be treated as copies since they were not marked as originals. The particular certificates had all the difficulties associated with the recognition of documents, e.g. ink signatures and rubber stamps appeared on their face, but there was no way of determining whether they were produced by computer printers, or otherwise. The Court stated, *inter alia*, that it was entirely legitimate for the I.C.C. to seek to resolve any ambiguities/difficulties of interpretation of U.C.P.500, and cited with approval I.C.C.'s policy decision. Furthermore, it

consideration in resolving disputes relating to the originality of documents submitted to a bank.

OTHER METHODS OF PAYMENT

SIGHT PAYMENT

This type of credit is usually used when the seller does not allow any period of credit to the buyer. It is a credit which provides for payment of a sight bill of exchange drawn on the issuing bank, or some other bank when presented with the specified documents.

FACTORING

This is an American idea which was introduced to the U.K. in the 1970s. The underlying function of the factoring service is the maintenance of the supplier's sales ledger. It provides an administration service based on the copy invoices received from the supplier. It does not make sales or even raise invoices at the time of delivery of the goods. These functions are performed by the supplier against the background of the factor's credit approval. The factoring of export sales provides a comprehensive package of export services to short term exporters. Generally speaking, factoring would involve a company which administers the sale ledger and collects payments on behalf of an exporter/seller once the goods have been shipped. In practice, the supplier of goods or services who has raised an invoice would 'sell' the debt to a 'factor' at a discount, i.e. the supplier will not get payment of 100% of the invoice value. The balance, less a service charge, would be paid by the 'factor' once he collects the full invoice payment from the purchaser or recipient. Nowadays, it would appear that more and more businesses use factoring.[750]

FORFEITING

This is a method of international trade finance involving the discounting of bank-guaranteed overseas trade bills or notes. It has no recourse to the

found that the words of Art.20(b) 'or appearing to have been produced' would render the particular certificates as originals.

[750] This seems to be evident by the increase in the work of the Association of British Factors and Discounters (A.B.F.D.), where, for example, between 1991-92 there was a 15% growth in factoring and invoice discounting in the U.K. It would seem that this trend continues to-date; in 2003 a 12% annual growth in factoring was reported by the Factors and Discounters Association.

exporter/seller as he surrenders or relinquishes his rights in return for cash payment from the forfeiter. In such circumstances the seller/exporter agrees to surrender his rights to claims for payment on goods or services which have been delivered to the buyer/importer. Any type of trade debt can be forfeited, i.e. surrendered for cash, but the most common is trade payee, bills of exchange accepted by the buyer/importer or promissory notes from the buyer/importer. A forfeiter can provide finance for any type and duration of trade transaction but usually credit is provided for the export of capital goods which require finance for periods of between three and seven years.

Open Account

Under this scheme, the exporter/seller issues his promissory note to the bank for the invoice value of the goods exported/sold and falling due for payment in any one month. The bank advances the face value of the promissory note at once and the note must be paid at maturity whether or not the proceeds of the invoice have been received.

In other words, an open account is an agreement whereby the seller/exporter agrees to despatch the goods to the buyer/importer on the understanding that he will pay for the goods after he has received them, usually on a monthly basis.

This method of arranging payment, carries, however, considerable risk since the buyer/importer may withhold or delay payment, or the transfer of funds might be delayed as a result of exchange control regulations in his country.

There are various ways in which the buyer/importer can send money to the seller under open account and the seller/exporter may wish to stipulate the method to be used, e.g. Bankers draft, Buyer's cheque, etc. Overall open account business is transacted on credit terms where no security in forms of Bills of Exchange or Promissory Notes is obtained from the buyer/importer. This is a most popular method of payment within the E.C.[751] and the most common method of payment is by cheque, banker's draft, and telegraphic transfer.

[751] This is because despite the risk attached to such method, exporters/sellers can obtain credit insurance.

CHAPTER 11

INSURANCE LAW

1. LLOYD'S AND THE MARKET

Since the origins of marine insurance can be traced to the mercantile practices in London during the 16th century, it is not surprising that the development of marine insurance as a business took place in London so that, by the middle of the 17th century many financiers were specialising in the underwriting of marine adventures. Nevertheless, each underwriter acted strictly on his own, using his personal fortune and resources to back the outcome of the adventures he chose to underwrite. These underwriters eventually formed the community which founded Lloyd's and many of their traditional practices exist today. The London market contains many Insurance Companies but it was much later that the Company market as we know it came into existence and adopted many of the usages and customs of Lloyd's.

LLOYD'S

The 17th century underwriter was a person of sound financial reputation. His personal fortune had to be adequate to meet his commitments and his integrity had to be beyond reproach. Consequently, there was little documentation involved in underwriting transactions. Details of the cover required were written on a slip of paper and the underwriter simply entered the amount he was prepared to underwrite and initialled it.

At first, transactions would be negotiated in the private residence of the underwriter but, as business grew, this method became inconvenient and, following the practice of the day, the underwriter would spend his time in one or other of the many coffee houses which were becoming popular as meeting places in London in the 17th century.

Edward Lloyd owned such a coffee house which was situated in Tower Street close to the Pool of London. At the time the Pool, that part of the Thames just below London Bridge, was the part of the river where all ships visiting London moored to discharge and load cargoes. Due to its proximity to the river and the world of shipping, the coffee house became a favourite meeting place for underwriters and their associates, and was soon well known as the centre for marine insurance. Edward Lloyd was quick to realise the advantage of a reputation which would attract custom and so went out of his way to encourage association of underwriters on his premises. He provided his patrons with writing materials and set up a rostrum in one corner of the coffee house. From this rostrum a boy, called the Kidney, would make announcements of importance to the customers. To increase the facilities he had to offer, Lloyd published a news sheet in 1696 in which he included details of shipping movements and other matters of interest.

Lloyds of London is an association of insurers specialising in the insurance of marine and similar risks. The Corporation of Lloyd's of today is an organisation/institution which provides facilities to the underwriters to carry out their insurance business. It is important to note that the Corporation of Lloyd's does not underwrite insurance contracts but merely provides facilities for its members to conduct their own business. Following the traditions of Lloyd's each underwriting member is responsible up to his full personal fortune to meet his commitments.

The London Company Market

The first major steps towards establishing a Company market took place in 1720 when, following a campaign launched in 1717 by men with marine interests and a discontent for Lloyd's system, two Companies 'The London Assurance' and 'The Royal Exchange' were incorporated by Royal Charter and for the next 100 years or so these two Corporations held a monopoly of the London Company market in marine insurance.

The insurance company of today is a Joint Stock Company with a liability limited to its assets as declared to the Department of Trade and Industry. It must be remembered that the Lloyd's Underwriter has no such limit of liability. The Company may be part of a group of Companies or it may stand by itself. The majority of Companies each have a board of directors which appoints an underwriter to accept business on behalf of the Company. The title 'underwriter' is given out of courtesy for the Company Underwriter does not, in fact, have any personal liability for the risks he writes. He is a salaried employee of the Company, and it is the Company which is liable for the commitments undertaken by the Underwriter.

Apart from these differences, the Company and Lloyd's Markets work very well together using similar systems. Several Companies have underwriting rooms in Lloyd's building and others are situated in the same area of London, thus providing a compact market for the broker on his daily rounds.

The Insurance Broker

An insurance broker is usually an agent of the assured who effects policies of insurance but is paid by the insurer. The insurance broker fills a very important role in marine insurance practice. His knowledge of insurance and the insurance market available is invaluable to his client.

A broker, in general is not entrusted with the possession or control of the goods, nor with the documents of title thereto. Furthermore, insurance brokers are held personally and solely responsible to the insurer for payment of the premium. Therefore, it is recognised that insurance brokers have a lien on the policy document for any general balance due to them.[752]

It is a distinct advantage to the underwriters at Lloyd's that the public is not admitted to negotiate the insurance cover. Instead, a member of the public must employ the intermediary of a Lloyd's broker and the underwriter finds he is negotiating with a person well versed in the laws, customs and practices of marine insurance.

Not all brokers are Lloyd's brokers but any other broker may engage the services of a Lloyd's broker to place business at Lloyd's for him. Before admission to Lloyd's the broker, wishing to become a Lloyd's broker, has to satisfy the Committee of Lloyd's that he is a suitable and satisfactory person to become an authorised Lloyd's broker. Once admitted, he describes himself as such by using the term 'and at Lloyd's' on his notepaper and on the name plate identifying his premises. He is issued with a 'ticket' authorising him to enter the Lloyd's building, upon payment of the necessary subscription, and he may arrange for employees to represent him in the actual negotiations.

The first step is to meet with a broker and indicate clearly the type and extent of cover required. The broker will put together a form and then, if dealing with Lloyds, transfer all essential details to a document known as 'the slip'. He will then approach an underwriting agent whom he knows to be an expert in the type of insurance sought. This agent will enter on the slip the extent of cover he is prepared to meet, the premium and then initials it. This is called 'writing a line' (presenting the slip is an 'offer' and writing a line is an 'acceptance'). This process is then repeated with different agents until the entire risk is covered.

The slip is then taken to the signing office at Lloyds where it is signed. The insured is then advised of the successful cover, by the broker, on a document called the Memorandum. This document is essentially a cover note and should, by custom, be sent to the insured so that he can check the terms of his cover.

Where insurance cover is sought from an insurance company, the position of the broker is somewhat different. Such a broker must maintain links with the various companies specialising in the field so as to find the most competitive premium rate for their client's particular needs.

---

[752] Sections 53 and 54, Marine Insurance Act 1906.

2. THE CONTRACT OF INSURANCE

A contract of insurance comes into being when one party, say X, makes an offer and the other party, say Y, makes a valid acceptance. A better definition, however, would be that where:

> ' ... one party (the insurer) undertakes for a consideration to pay money to or for the benefit of the other party (the assured) upon the happening of an event which is uncertain, either as to whether it has or will occur at all, or as to the time of its occurrence, where the object of the assured is to provide against loss or to compensate for prejudice caused by the event ... '[753]

The premium may consist of a lump sum or of periodical payments. The instrument evidencing the contract is called a 'policy' of insurance. The insurer in marine insurance is usually termed an 'underwriter'.

In most cases, the would-be insured fills in a proposal form inviting the insurer to cover him for certain risks, and when the insurer accepts this proposal, the contract of insurance comes into being.

While writing is essential in the case of marine insurance, since oral evidence of its existence is not admissible in case of dispute, there is no legal necessity in other cases, and if the insurer accepted the proposal and a premium without qualification, he would probably be held bound after a reasonable time had elapsed.

There are five main principles of insurance law:

(a) insurable interest,

(b) utmost good faith,

(c) indemnity,

(d) subrogation, and

(e) proximate cause.

These will be briefly considered next, as they apply to cargo insurance business transactions.

[753] Per Templeman, J., in *Department of Trade and Industry* v. *St. Christopher Motorists Association Ltd.* [1974] 1 Lloyd's Rep.17, 20. It seems that three elements are required in a contract of insurance: (i) the contract must provide that the assured will become entitled to something on the occurrence of some event, (ii) the event must be one which involves some element of uncertainty, and (iii) the assured must have an insurable interest in the subject-matter of the contract; *Medical Defence Union* v. *Department of Trade* [1979] 1 Lloyd's Rep.499.

(a) Insurable Interest

The essential feature of an insurance contract is that a physical object is exposed to perils and that the assured stands in some relation, recognised by law, to that object, in consequence of which he either benefits by its preservation, or is prejudiced by its loss or mishap to it.[754]

In simple words, the assured must have something to lose and something to gain from the successful transportation or non-arrival of the insured property. It follows that if the assured has no interest in that object he cannot be prejudiced by its loss and there is nothing to reimburse. This is called an insurable interest, and it is absolutely necessary to exist in relation to the assured. Without such interest, the policy would be no better than a gaming policy, and being contrary to public policy therefore is considered void.[755]

Interest is not confined to rights in the nature of property or arising out of contract, e.g. a shareholder in a submarine cable company has an insurable interest in the successful laying of a cable, although he has no property in the cable.[756]

Master and crew,[757] mortgagor and mortgagee,[758] and insurer,[759] are some examples of persons who may have an insurable interest in a 'marine adventure'.[760]

Any interest may be insured which is dependent on the safety of the subject matter exposed to the risks insured against, provided in all cases that at the time of the loss it is an interest legal or equitable.[761]

Thus, where a charterer pays freight in advance to a shipowner, for the carriage of his goods, from one port to another, such money is usually non-returnable, even if the goods are lost and never arrive at their destination. Such charterer has got an insurable interest in the money paid since he may lose it, if the goods are lost. But the shipowner has no such interest in the freight, since earning it does not depend on the successful completion of the adventure.[762] However, where the charterer agrees to pay freight upon delivery of the goods at destination, then it is the shipowner who has an insurable interest in earning the freight, i.e. in the safe arrival of the goods at destination.[763]

---

754 Section 5(2), Marine Insurance Act 1906.

755 Section 4, Marine Insurance Act 1906.

756 *Wilson* v. *Jones* (1866-67) L.R. 2 Ex.139.

757 In respect of their wages; section 11, Marine Insurance Act 1906.

758 Sections 14(1) and 14(2), respectively; Marine Insurance Act 1906.

759 Section 9(1), Marine Insurance Act 1906.

760 A 'marine adventure' exists where, *inter alia*, 'any ship goods or other moveables are exposed to maritime perils'; section 3(2)(a) Marine Insurance Act 1906.

761 *Moran Galloway & Co.* v. *Uzielli* [1905] 2 K.B.555.

762 *Manfield* v. *Maitland* (1821) 4 B.& Ald.582.

763 *Weir & Co.* v. *Girvin & Co.* [1899] 1 Q.B.193.

Finally, a difference between marine and non-marine insurance is that in the former, insurable interest must exist at the time of the loss,[764] whereas with non-marine it must exist at the time of conclusion of the contract.

(b) THE PROPOSAL - *UBERRIMAE FIDE*

When an insurer issues a blank proposal form he is not making an offer of insurance even if premium rates are quoted on the form. The blank proposal form is an invitation to treat.

The duty of the proposer to make full disclosure of all material facts means that he must scrutinise the proposal form with great care. Neglect to do this may mean that, if the insurer accepts the proposal and the loss actually occurs, the insured may find that the insurer can avoid the contract and have no liability beyond the return of the premiums paid.[765]

As mentioned above, the contract of insurance is normally preceded by a proposal form, the answers to which are more than representations, namely warranties. It is important to note that in insurance law warranties are treated as equivalent to conditions in any other type of contract, and therefore, as a general rule a breach of condition gives rise to the right to repudiate.[766]

As mentioned above, the insured must disclose all material facts. The line between what is a material disclosure and what is immaterial is not always easy to draw.

Furthermore, it should be noted that a contract of insurance is *uberrimae fidei*, i.e. a contract based on the principle of utmost good faith. Thus either party may avoid a contract of insurance if he can establish that the other party failed to disclose a material fact or made a misrepresentation, even if innocent, of such a fact.[767] This means that the insurer cannot, for example, take advantage of a misstatement if he is really aware or ought to be aware of the true facts of the case.[768] The insured must disclose every material circumstance which is known

---

[764] *Moran, Galloway & Co.* v. *Uzielli* [1905] 2 K.B.555.

[765] Section 18(1), Marine Insurance Act 1906. *Roselodge Ltd. (formerly Rose Diamond Products Ltd.)* v. *Castle* [1966] 2 Lloyd's Rep.113.

[766] Thus, not putting forward an accurate and complete claims record would amount to non-disclosure; *Container Transport International Inc. and Reliance Group Inc.* v. *Oceanus Mutual Underwriting Association (Bermuda) Ltd.* [1984] 1 Lloyd's Rep.476, C.A. *Dawsons Ltd.* v. *Bonnin* [1922] 2 A.C.413, H.L., where it was held that the inaccuracy of the answer (in the proposal form) as to the place at which the lorry to be insured would be garaged, entitled the insurers to avoid liability on the score of breach of warranty; it made no difference that the answer was not material in the sense of affecting the rate of premium or that the inaccuracy was purely innocent and inadvertent.

[767] Section 17, Marine Insurance Act 1906.

[768] If the description of the property is substantially correct, and a more accurate statement would not have varied the premium, the error is not material; *Universal Non Tariff Fire Insurance Co, Re* (1874-75) L.R. 19 Eq. 485.

to him, and he is deemed to know every circumstance which, in the ordinary course of business, ought to be known to him. A circumstance is material if it would influence the judgment of a prudent insurer in fixing the premium, or determining whether he will take the risk.[769] However, in the absence of inquiry by the insurer, the insured need not disclose any circumstance:[770]

(a) which diminishes the risk;

(b) which is known or presumed to be known to the insurer;[771]

(c) regarding matters of law;

(d) which is superfluous to disclose because it is already covered by an express or implied warranty, e.g. a policy for burglary insurance may be subject to a warranty that a certain form of lock be fitted, but it is superfluous to disclose whether they are or are not fitted since the policy operates only if they are;

(e) which the insurer's representative fails to notice on a survey (provided there is no concealment).

It is a question of fact whether a circumstance which is not disclosed is material or not.[772] The duty of disclosure continues throughout the negotiations, and where circumstances alter, previous statements should be corrected. Furthermore, it would seem that this duty continues even after the conclusion of the contract.[773]

---

[769] Section 18(2), Marine Insurance Act 1906. 'To prove the materiality of an undisclosed circumstance, the insurer must satisfy the Court on a balance of probability - by evidence or from the nature of the undisclosed circumstance itself - that the judgment, in this sense, of a prudent insurer would have been influenced if the circumstances in question had been disclosed. The word "influenced" means that the disclosure is one which would have had an impact on the formation of his opinion and on his decision-making process', *per* Phillips, J., in *Inversiones Manria S.A.* v. *Sphere Drake Insurance Co. Plc. Malvern Insurance Co. Ltd. and Niagara Fire Insurance Co. Inc, (The Dora)* [1989] 1 Lloyd's Rep.69, 87.

[770] Section 18(3), Marine Insurance Act 1906.

[771] Such as the presumption of insurer's knowledge that a war was imminent, or that there have recently been disturbances in the area where the goods are to be carried; *Planché* v. *Fletcher* (1779) 1 Doug. K.B.251; *Bolivia Republic* v. *Indemnity Mutual Marine Assurance Co. Ltd.* (1908) 99 L.T.394, K.B.D.

[772] Section 18(4), Marine Insurance Act 1906. *Ionides* v. *Pender* (1873-74) L.R. 9 Q.B. 531, assured insured cargo for about £2,500 whereas the cargo's real value was about £900. This fact was not disclosed to insurers who were held to be entitled to avoid liability for the overvalued cargo. This was because in practice underwriters take into consideration whether the over-valuation is so great as to make the risk speculative.

[773] *Black King Shipping Corp.* v. *Massie (The Litsion Pride)* [1985] 1 Lloyd's Rep.437; good faith was held to apply to the requirement to give notice to the insurers under the war risk trading warranties and to the making of claims. However, it seems as if this post-contractual duty of utmost good faith means that the parties are obliged to refrain from a deliberate act or omission intended to deceive or concealment of 'material' facts. It does not apply to all facts deliberately misrepresented which do not affect a valid claim under the policy; *K/S Merc-Scandia XXXXII* v. *Lloyd's Underwriters (The Mercandian Continent)* [2001] 2 Lloyd's

(c) INDEMNITY

Ideally, the purpose of any form of insurance is to replace that which has been lost. Obviously, it is not practicable to expect the insurer to replace an object which is lost (despite the wording used in insurance policies). Therefore, any recompense must be of a monetary nature and this system of reimbursement is called 'indemnifying'.

A contract of insurance is a contract of indemnity, i.e. what the insured can recover is measured by the extent of his pecuniary, i.e. monetary, loss. It is a contract to compensate for the loss or damage in terms of the value of the insured goods. The amount insured as agreed between the insurer and the assured forms the basis of indemnity.[774]

(d) SUBROGATION

This is the transfer of the assured's rights of recovery to the insurer, and occurs upon the happening of a loss (either total or partial) of the subject-matter insured. For example, if you do not insure your house, and loss/damage occurs to it due to another person's negligent act, then you would be entitled to take legal action to recover from the wrong-doer for your loss/damage. If you are insured, then this right of recovery may be transferred to the insurer, who in turn can recover your loss from the wrong-doer. This transfer of recovery rights is called subrogation in insurance law.

There is a difference in marine insurance law, in that the insurer is only subrogated these rights upon payment to the assured.[775] This is not the case in non-marine insurance law where the insurer acquires subrogation rights immediately the assured has such rights of recovery. By this method, the insurer may be able to recover much of the payment he has made to the insured. Should he recover more, the excess is returned to the insured.[776]

Rep.563, C.A. Contrast s.18(1), Marine Insurance Act 1906, which states that the assured is under a duty to disclose all material facts 'before the contract is concluded'. Attempts to extend the principle of utmost good faith to the conduct of insurance litigation have also not been fertile; *Agapitos* v. *Agnew (The Aegeon) (No.1)* [2002] 2 Lloyd's Rep.42, C.A.

[774] *Goole and Hull Steam Towing Co. Ltd.* v. *Ocean Marine Insurance Co. Ltd.* (1927) 29 Ll. L. Rep.242, K.B.D.

[775] Sections 79(1) and (2), Marine Insurance Act 1906.

[776] *Yorkshire Insurance Co. Ltd.* v. *Nisbet Shipping Co. Ltd.* [1962] 2 Q.B.330, the insured vessel became a total loss following a collision with another vessel. The insurers paid the full sum insured to the insured (about £70,000) and the insured successfully sued the other vessel's owners. However, due to devaluation of the Pound (£) the insured owners actually recovered the equivalent of about £120,000, and repaid the insurers the £70,000. The insurers-claimants sued the insured for the £50,000, but were unsuccessful, as the Court held that they were not entitled to recover more than they had paid.

(e) PROXIMATE CAUSE

This simply means that a claim only becomes payable if the risk covered by the policy was the proximate (direct) cause of the loss.[777] Most 'standard' insurance policies covering ships and cargoes provide that the insurer is liable for any loss 'proximately caused' by specified/named perils which are normally referred to as 'perils insured against'. So the question in any insurance claim would be whether the loss or damage to the subject-matter of insurance, e.g. goods, was directly/proximately caused by a peril insured against.

For example, where following a collision one of the cargo carrying vessels put to port for repairs and her cargo is discharged and subsequently reloaded, resulting in deterioration of the vessel's goods through delay, the proximate cause of such damage (deterioration) could be said to be the delay and not the collision.[778]

THE INSURANCE POLICY

Once the broker has got the proposal, he will accumulate the facts of the insurance to be effected and will set these down on a piece of stiff card. This document is termed the 'slip' and it occupies a very important position in the negotiation of a marine insurance contract.[779]

The slip is used to obtain the agreement of one or many insurers to underwrite the insurance. The number of insurers anticipated depends on the monetary value of the subject-matter of the insurance and the amount of cover required.

Having prepared his slip, the broker will select the section of the market in which he anticipates the type of risk involved will be readily acceptable. Many insurers specialise in particular types of insurance and thereby achieve considerable knowledge of the peculiarities of such risks. This specialist underwriter is known in the market as a 'Lead' or 'Leader' and it is part of a broker's duty to know the recognised market 'Leads'.

The broker takes his slip to the 'Lead' and negotiates the insurance contract with him. This practice of negotiation is called 'broking', and it is at this point that the rate of premium is decided. The 'Lead' agrees the rate with the broker and impresses his Syndicate line stamp on the slip (if he is at Lloyd's). Within the line stamp the underwriter will insert his 'line'. His 'line' is the amount or

---

[777] Section 55(1), Marine Insurance Act 1906.

[778] *Pink* v. *Fleming* (1890) 25 Q.B.D.396. *Cf. Leyland Shipping Co.* v. *Norwich Union Fire Insurance Society Ltd.* [1918] A.C.350.

[779] The 'slip' is considered to be the complete and final contract between parties fixing the terms of the contract and the premium; *Ionides* v. *Pacific Fire and Marine Insurance Co.* (1871) L.R. 6 Q.B. 674.

percentage of the risk that the underwriter is prepared to accept on behalf of his Syndicate. The impression of a line stamp on the slip has the same effect as if the underwriter had initialled the slip. At this point the contract is concluded between the 'Lead' and the assured. The broker offers the slip to other insurers, until the required percentage of cover has been reached.

The initialling of the slip by an underwriter is deemed to be the acceptance of the contract, thus providing direct evidence as to the conclusion of the contract.[780] However, until the contract is embodied in a policy the 'slip' is only evidence of an intended contract and is binding in honour only.[781]

Once the policy is actually issued the slip does have a degree of importance in that it may be used in evidence for certain purposes, e.g. the date of the conclusion of the contract.

Thus the slip may be produced in evidence in order to rectify mistakes which may have appeared on the policy. Section 89 of the Marine Insurance Act 1906 specifically permits the slip to be used in legal proceedings once there is a properly issued policy. Therefore, no action against the insurer can be brought by the insured until the policy is issued, i.e. the slip cannot be sued upon.

The policy is not the contract but merely written evidence of it. Nevertheless, a Court will regard it as containing the expressed intentions of the parties in the absence of proof to the contrary. The policy contains the general conditions governing the insurance, commonly endorsed on the back, and where a policy continues from year to year, variations maybe incorporated by means of endorsement slips which are stuck on the back of the policy.

Policies of insurance may be classified into **(a)** valued, and **(b)** unvalued.

(a) Valued policy: is one which specifies the agreed value of the subject matter insured. It can usually be recognised by the use of the term 'so valued' after the details of the subject-matter insured or the term 'valued at' preceding the specified value. The value in the policy is deemed to be conclusive of the insurable value, as between the insurer and the assured, where there is no fraud, whether or not it is the true value. One must not confuse 'Insured Value'

---

[780] *Eagle Star Insurance Co. Ltd.* v. *Spratt* [1971] 2 Lloyd's Rep.116, C.A.

[781] Section 22, Marine Insurance Act 1906. *Commercial Union Assurance Co. Ltd.* v. *Niger Co. Ltd.* (1922) 13 Ll. L. Rep.75, H.L.; a policy insuring goods from the U.K. to Africa and from Africa to the U.K. was effected in January 1916. The goods were stored at port (Burutu) because of difficulties in obtaining shipping space and consequently a lot of other goods accumulated in that port, after the date of the policy. It was held that the insurers could not rely on non-disclosure of the accumulation of the goods for once the insurance contract was concluded, no further disclosure was necessary. Contrast the view of the Court of Appeal that the presentation of the slip by the broker constitutes the offer and the writing of each line constitutes an acceptance of this offer by the underwriter, in *General Re-Insurance Corp.* v. *Forsakringsaktiebolaget Fennia Patria* [1983] 2 Lloyd's Rep.287, 288. On this premise it would seem that each line written on a slip gives rise to a binding contract, and the underwriter is bound by his line; *General Accident Fire & Life Assurance Corp. Ltd.* v. *Tanter (The Zephyr)* [1985] 2 Lloyd's Rep.529, C.A.

with 'Sum Insured'. The 'Insured Value' is the amount specified in the policy as the value of the insured property, whereas the 'Sum Insured' is the total amount of the subscriptions of the insurers in the policy.[782] Where the property is insured for its full value both the sum insured and the insured value will be identical. This is usually the case in cargo insurance so that the policy will show for example, '£2,000 on merchandise so valued'.

(b) Unvalued policy: is one which does not specify any 'value' but leaves this to be determined if and when a claim arises. An unvalued policy merely states the maximum amount which the assured would be able to recover. The insurable value of the goods is the prime cost of the goods, plus expenses incidental to shipping and the charges of insurance.

Depending on the type of risk one wishes to insure and the particular requirements of the business, there are certain variations on the cover provided by current insurance policies.

Floating policy: this is a cargo policy with a sum insured sufficient to accommodate a large number of shipments for a single assured. Subject to a limit on any one vessel, each shipment is covered automatically as it goes forward. The sum insured is reduced by each declaration until the amount has been exhausted. A deposit premium paid at inception is adjusted on expiry of the policy to provide the correct premium. A certificate is issued for each shipment. In other words, a floating policy is a contract of insurance the terms of which are described generally, and it leaves for other particulars, such as the name of the ship, to be declared at a later time, i.e. when shipment takes place.

Open cover: this has become the most common and most popular form of insurance used in the export trade. It is quite similar to a floating policy. In particular, the assured is likewise bound to declare all individual shipments effected thereunder. However, unlike the floating policy, where the assured receives a formal policy document, under open cover no formal policy is issued. This is because the open cover is not an insurance policy but is a document by which the underwriter undertakes subsequently to issue specific policies within the terms of the cover. The open cover may be limited in time or may be permanent while a 'floating policy' is normally limited to 12 months.

---

[782] It must be noted, however, that purely stating in a proposal form that this is the 'sum insured' does not imply that this would be a valued policy. Instead, the intention of the parties would be adduced by the surrounding circumstances and the contract as a whole; *Kyzuna Investments Ltd.* v. *Ocean Marine Mutual Insurance Association (Europe)* [2000] 1 Lloyd's Rep.505, where the insurance proposal form stated a specific sum to be insured, the proposal was accompanied by a valuation certificate which was required by the underwriters, and the policy stated the proposed sum as 'sum insured'. It was held that this was, nevertheless, an unvalued policy.

Blanket policies: Such policies usually provide that the assured need not advise the insurer of the individual shipments, as in the case of open cover and floating policies, but a lump sum premium, instead of a premium at several rates, shall cover all shipments.

INSTITUTE CARGO CLAUSES

The current insurance policy and clauses were introduced in the 80s. This form of insurance policy is known as *Lloyd's Marine Policy* and the cargo clauses are described as *Institute Cargo Clauses* A, B and C. In addition to these three sets of cargo clauses, there are various other clauses such as the *Institute War Clauses (Cargo)* and the *Institute Strikes Clauses (Cargo)*.

INSTITUTE CARGO CLAUSES A, B AND C

Risks covered : Institute Cargo Clauses A cover all risks of loss or damage to the subject-matter insured, whereas Clauses B and C only cover risks which are specifically referred to. The exporter who, in order to save on the premium, does not wish to insure under Clauses A but prefers to insure under Clauses B or C, should make sure that the specific risks to which his cargo may be exposed are expressly covered, and also are not excluded by the provisions of Clauses B and C. In particular, the three Institute Cargo Clauses, i.e. A, B and C each contain:

(1) a Risks clause;

(2) a General Average[783] clause; and

(3) a Transit clause.

1. Risks Clause

This is a different Clause in each of the sets, since the cover provided is different between A, B and C. As it will be seen, the widest cover is provided by the Institute Cargo Clauses (A), whereas set (C) restricts cover to the effects of major fortuities, e.g. fire, collision, etc.

Institute Cargo Clauses (A) define the cover provided by this insurance in Clause 1 as follows:

> 'This insurance covers all risks of loss of or damage to the subject-matter insured except as provided in Clauses 4, 5, 6 and 7 below.'

[783] As to the law of general average, see *infra*, p.258.

The meaning of the words 'all risks' is wide, and it must be noted that it is sufficient for the assured/insured to show that the loss was caused by a casualty or something accidental without proving the exact nature of the casualty or accident which caused the loss.[784] Furthermore, because this type of insurance policy covers 'all risks', as opposed to the type of policies where risks of a specified class or classes, such as a motor policy (e.g. third party, fire and theft), the insured/assured discharges his special onus of proof when he has proved that the loss was caused by some event covered by the general expression, and he is not bound to go further and prove the exact nature of the accident or casualty which, in fact, occasioned his loss. Thus, in one case,[785] X had insured a consignment of bleached sponges with Y, on an 'all risks' policy, for a voyage from N. York to London. The sponges were tightly packed in wooden cases. X found that they were damaged, and claimed against Y. He (X) alleged that the goods were stained by water, dirt, paint and other substances penetrating the cases. Y, on the other hand, maintained that the damage was due to normal transit risks of dust and dirt combined with the atmospheric pressure. X's action succeeded since he (X) was able to show that the loss was, on the balance of probabilities, due to an abnormal peril, and the damage to the sponges was due to an extraneous and accidental cause.

Institute Cargo Clauses (B) state in Clause 1 that the policy covers:

(a) loss of or damage to the cargo reasonably attributable to
   1 fire or explosion;
   2 the vessel or craft being stranded, grounded, sunk or capsized;
   3 the overturning or derailment of a land conveyance;
   4 the collision or contact of the vessel, craft or conveyance with any external object other than water;
   5 the discharge of the cargo at a port of distress; and
   6 **earthquake, volcanic eruption or lightning**.

(b) the loss of or damage to the cargo caused by
   1 general average sacrifice;
   2 jettison or **washing overboard**, and
   3 **the entry of sea, lake or river water into the vessel, craft, hold, conveyance, container, liftvan, or place of storage**.

(c) **the total loss of any package lost overboard or dropped whilst loading on to or unloading from the vessel or craft**.

The above highlighted risks are not covered by the Institute Cargo Clauses (C).

---

[784] *British and Foreign Marine Insurance Co Ltd.* v. *Gaunt* [1921] 2 A.C.41.

[785] *Theodorou v. Chester* [1951] 1 Lloyd's Rep.204, K.B.D.

Institute Cargo Clauses (C) state in Clause 1 that the policy covers:

(a) loss of or damage to the cargo reasonably attributable to
  1 fire or explosion;
  2 the vessel or craft being stranded, grounded, sunk or capsized;
  3 the overturning or derailment of a land conveyance;
  4 the collision or contract of the vessel, craft or conveyance with any external object other than water; and
  5 the discharge of the cargo at a port of distress.

(b) the loss of or damage to the cargo caused by
  1 general average sacrifice;
  2 jettison.

2. General Average Clause

Clause 2 states that the policy covers general average and salvage charges, adjusted or determined according to the contract of affreightment and/or the governing law and practice, incurred to avoid or in connection with the avoidance of loss from any cause except those causes which are excluded.

3. The Transit Clause

The effect of this clause, which is present in Institute Cargo Clauses A, B and C, is to extend the sea voyage to include the risks whilst the goods are transported from the inland warehouse or place of storage to the time of loading, as well as the risks from the time of discharge to the delivery at the final warehouse or place of storage at the named destination. Therefore, an assured can, under this clause, for example, insure a consignment of goods from Manchester to Paris, provided these places are named in the policy as the commencement and destination of the transit.

Under the Transit Clause, the goods are covered from the time they leave the warehouse at the place named in the policy for the commencement of the transit and continue to be covered until they are delivered to the final warehouse at the destination named in the policy or another warehouse, whether prior to or at the destination named in the policy, but the policy provides an overriding time limit of 60 days after the completion of discharge overside the overseas vessel at the final port of discharge; on the expiration of that time limit cover ceases even though the goods may not have reached a warehouse. If before the expiration of the 60 days after discharge the goods are forwarded to a destination other than that named in the insurance, the cover terminates when the transit begins. The 60 days' cover is very valuable for the assured/insured if, for some reason, the goods cannot proceed to the warehouse, for instance, because the buyer has not paid the import duties, and the assured/insured cannot dispose of them quickly.

The principle underlying these provisions is that the assured/insured shall be covered until he or a buyer from him can reasonably be expected to have made further insurance arrangements for the goods. If under the contract of carriage the goods are unloaded at a place other than the contemplated place of destination, due to circumstances beyond the control of the assured/insured, they continue to be insured until they are forwarded to the agreed or another destination and have arrived at the final warehouse, or until they are sold and delivered. The word 'warehouse' has to be given its ordinary and natural meaning.

Risks not Covered

Clauses 4, 5, 6 and 7 are exclusion clauses. Clause 4 is the General Exclusion Clause and, it is present in Institute Cargo Clauses A, B and C.

Clause 4.1 excludes 'loss damage or expense attributable to wilful misconduct of the Assured.' Wilful misconduct is essentially a question of fact.[786]

Clause 4.2 excludes 'ordinary leakage, ordinary loss in weight or volume, or ordinary wear and tear of the subject-matter insured.'

'Ordinary' refers to the normal transit losses such as the nature of the goods or the loads exerted on them. When the ordinary leakage of one cargo damages a second cargo, the assured in respect of the second cargo can only recover if he is insured under Cargo Clauses A, but not if his insurance is based upon Clauses B or C only.

Clause 4.3 excludes 'loss or damage or expense caused by insufficiency or unsuitability of packing or preparation of the subject-matter insured'.

The question of whether packing is suitable or sufficient is often determined according to what is customary and reasonable in a particular trade. Where the packing is such that the cargo cannot withstand the usual conditions appertaining to a particular voyage, the assured cannot recover for any loss or damage caused or for any expenses incurred in replacing inadequate packing. Loss of, or

---

[786] '...misconduct to which the will is party as contradistinguished from accident, and is far beyond any negligence, even gross or culpable negligence, and involves that a person wilfully misconducts himself who knows and appreciates that it is wrong conduct on his part in the existing circumstances to do, or to fail or omit to do (as the case may be), a particular thing, and yet intentionally does, or fails or omits to do it, or persists in the act, failure, or omission regardless of consequences', *per* Lord Alverstone, C.J., in *Forder* v. *Great Western Railway Co.* [1905] 2 K.B.532, 535. See further *infra*, footnote 872. Section 55(2)(a) of the Marine Insurance Act 1906, also excludes insurer's liability for any loss attributable to the wilful misconduct of the insured.

damage to, the contents of a container will not be covered where such is loaded by the insured/assured or his servants prior to or after the attachment of the insurance.

This exclusion will not apply, however, when the stowing takes place after the attachment of the insurance and without the assured or his servants being involved.

Clause 4.4 excludes 'loss damage or expense caused by inherent vice or nature of the subject-matter insured.'

This exclusion clause covers situations where the goods insured are damaged or destroyed by an internal development (*inherent vice*). As an example, spontaneous combustion may occur within one cargo damaging a second cargo. The owner of the first cargo cannot recover where the spontaneous combustion is the result of inherent vice, such as may be the case in a cargo of grain, but the owner of the second cargo can recover for his own loss under Clauses A, B or C since the risk of loss or damage due to fire explosion is covered.

Clause 4.5 excludes 'loss damage or expense proximately caused by delay even though the delay be caused by a risk insured against.'

Therefore, although under the Transit Clause the insurance will remain valid where a delay is beyond the control of the assured/insured, the assured/insured will not be protected in respect of any damage which is proximately caused by that delay. However, in the case of a general average act which causes a delay, the assured/insured is entitled to recover his proportion of any expenses incurred during the period of the delay, such as, for example, his contribution to the wages of the crew.

Clause 4.6 excludes 'loss damage or expense arising from insolvency or financial default of the owners managers charterers or operators of the vessel'

If due to financial difficulties, the carrier has to stop short at a port, the insurer will not have to pay the forwarding expenses incurred by the assured/insured. Note that Clause 12 is applicable only to expenses incurred where a voyage is terminated as a result of the peril insured against.

Clause 4.7 of the Institute Cargo Clauses B and C is an additional exclusion not found in A, and provides that the insurance cover will not cover 'deliberate damage to or deliberate destruction of the subject matter insured or any part thereof by the wrongful act of any person or persons'.

Clause 6 is the War Exclusion Clause and is present in Cargo Clauses A, B and C. Deletion of this Clause will mean that war risks are covered in Clauses A, but not in Clauses B or C, since such perils are not present in the risks clause. Where an assured/insured requires war risk cover, he should ask for the addition of the Institute War Clauses.

Clause 7 is the Strikes Exclusion Clause and is present in all three Institute Cargo Clauses. Deletion of this Clause will enable an assured/insured to recover for such risks where he is insured under Clauses A, since in Clauses B and C the peril is not within the specific risks covered. Where an assured/insured specifically wants cover for strikes and other labour disturbances, he should require the addition of the Institute Strikes Clauses.

INSTITUTE WAR CLAUSES (CARGO)

Clause 1 of this set of Clauses states that the insurance covers loss or damage to the cargo caused by:

1.1 war civil war revolution rebellion insurrection, or civil strife arising therefrom, or any hostile act by or against a belligerent power;

1.2 capture seizure arrest restraint or detainment, arising from risks covered under 1.1 above, and the consequences thereof or any attempt thereat;

1.3 derelict mines torpedoes bombs or other derelict weapons of war.

Clause 2 states that the insurance covers general average and salvage charges, adjusted or determined according to the contract of affreightment and/or governing law and practice, incurred to avoid or in connection with the avoidance of a risk mentioned above.

INSTITUTE STRIKES CLAUSES (CARGO)

Clause 1 states that the insurance covers with specified exceptions, loss of or damage to the cargo caused by:

1 strikers, locked-out workmen or persons taking part in labour disturbances;

2 any terrorist or any person acting from a political motive.

Clause 2 states that the insurance covers general average and salvage charges, adjusted or determined according to the contract of affreightment and/or governing law and practice, incurred to avoid or in connection with the avoidance of a risk mentioned above.

AVIATION INSURANCE

Air transport operators have a legal liability towards (a) the general public, (b) passengers, and (c) consignors. Insurance cover for liabilities (a) and (b) is beyond the scope of this book. Firstly, it should be noted that so far as legal aviation insurance principles are concerned, these are similar to the ones applicable to marine insurance, e.g. insurable interest. Lloyd's and the company market use the same basic policy form for aircraft hull and liability business. An indemnity of an insured against the sums he may become legally liable to pay, i.e. freight liability, is not usually covered in the standard aircraft policy. Such cover may however, be obtained by endorsement, thus covering any or all of the following three types of risk/liabilities: (a) handler's liability, (b) freight forwarder's liability, and (c) freight all risks. War, hi-jacking and similar risks may also be insured, as are strikes, on a separate policy. These risks are normally excluded from the ordinary type of policy. Various factors are considered when effecting aviation insurance such as geographical limits, and general market conditions.

CHAPTER 12

CARRIAGE OF GOODS BY SEA

INTRODUCTION

The party responsible for shipping the goods is the 'shipper' or 'consignor'. This would usually be the seller. The 'consignee' is usually the buyer and is the person named as consignee in the bill of lading. The term 'indorsee'/'endorsee' means a subsequent buyer, i.e. a person who buys the goods by an indorsement made by the buyer/consignee on the bill of lading and the delivery of the bill of lading from the consignee to him (indorsee). Either of them may be entitled to delivery of the goods by the 'carrier' (shipowner). The shipper (seller) frequently employs a 'forwarding agent' and the shipowner (carrier) a 'loading broker'. The forwarding agent usually has to ascertain the date and place of sailing, obtain a space and fill in the bills of lading indicating the name of the consignee (buyer), or person to whom the goods are to be delivered (indorsee).

Once the shipper (seller) or his agent (forwarding agent) becomes aware of the sailing schedules of a particular trade, through some form of advertisement, he communicates with the shipowner (carrier) with a view to booking cargo space on the vessel or container. Provided satisfactory arrangements have been concluded, the shipper (or his forwarding agent) forwards the cargo. At this stage, it is important to note that the shipper (seller) always makes the offer by forwarding the consignment, whilst the shipowner (carrier) either accepts or refuses it.

Furthermore, it is the shipper's duty, or that of his agent, to supply details of the consignment; normally this is done by completing the shipping company's form of bill of lading, and the shipping company then signs the number of copies requested.

The goods are signed for by the vessel's chief officer (chief mate), and this receipt (mate's receipt) is exchanged for the bill of lading. If the cargo is in good condition, no endorsement will be made on the document (bill of lading). Conversely, if the goods are damaged or a portion of the consignment is missing, the document will be suitably endorsed by the master or his agent.

Bills of lading are usually drawn in sets of three or four, one copy being retained by the consignor (shipper), one by the master of the ship (shipowner), and one sent on in advance of the goods to the consignee (buyer), if a fourth exists, then is sent to the consignee later in case the first is lost or delayed. As a rule any rights in relation to possession and/or title to the goods passes with this third bill of lading.

Where the shipper had sold the goods under a letter of credit established through a bank, or when he wishes to obtain payment of his invoice before the consignee obtains the goods, he will pass the full set of original bills to his bank, who will in due course arrange presentation to the consignee against payment. The shipowner or his agent at the port of destination will require one original bill of lading to be presented to him before the goods are handed over. Furthermore, he will normally require payment of any freight due ('freight collect'), should this not have been paid at the port of shipment. When one of a set of bills of lading has been presented to the shipping company, the other bills in the set lose their value.

In the event of the bill of lading being lost or delayed in transit, the shipping company will allow delivery of the goods to the person claiming to be the consignee, if he gives a letter of indemnity; this is normally countersigned by a bank, and 'insures' in effect the shipping company against any liability should another person eventually come along with the actual bill of lading.

BAILMENT

Before we consider the legal aspects of bills of lading and the Hague-Visby Rules, it is important to briefly mention 'bailment'.

In effect, a bailment is the delivery of goods by one person to another for a particular purpose, and once this purpose is fulfilled the goods must be returned from the bailee, the person to whom the goods are entrusted, to the bailor, the owner or person entitled to the goods bailed.

In this sense, delivery means the transferring of possession, and the bailor need not do this voluntarily. The taking of possession is considered to create an assumption of responsibility for the safe keeping of the goods.[787]

The extent of this responsibility varies according to the extent of benefit derived by each party. Hence, where both parties may be said to benefit equally, an ordinary degree of care and skill is required, but where the bailee benefits comparatively little, his responsibility is reduced whereas if he receives the majority of benefit his responsibility is correspondingly greater.

However, it should be noted that this is the common law position and, if a contract exists, as normally does in the case of carriage of goods, the parties are at liberty to vary this position within the contract. From the above, it must be plain that there is no single rule for bailment. A carrier would normally be considered to be the bailee of the goods entrusted to him. Indeed, the very

[787] *Nugent* v. *Smith* (1875-76) L.R. 1 C.P.D.423.

contract of carriage of goods would be clear evidence of this fact. The bailee may only redeliver the goods or chattels to the bailor and is not permitted to redeliver to anyone else even if apparently showing title. Should a dispute arise, the bailee should 'interplead'.[788] A bailee who fails to return the goods as required may be sued in tort or if applicable, in contract.[789]

COMMON AND PRIVATE CARRIER

A common carrier is one who is engaged in the trade of carrying goods as a regular business, and who hold himself out as ready to carry for any who may wish to employ him.[790]

Where a person, while inviting all to employ him, reserved to himself the right to accept or reject offers of goods for carriage, it was held not to be a common carrier.[791] It is a question of fact whether a person is a common carrier or not.[792]

The characteristics of a common carrier may be summed up as follows:

(1) Is bound to take any goods brought to him if he has room for them and they are suitable.[793] The latter means that the goods are properly packed and their destination is the same as the one that the carrier usually travels.

---

[788] If a person finds himself exposed to claims of two opposite parties, each requiring him to pay or to deliver certain goods, and he is unable to comply with such demands because he has reasonable doubts relating to which one of them is the rightful claimant, then such person may proceed for relief by 'interpleading'.

[789] Even if he exercised reasonable care; *Shaw* v. *Symmons* [1917] 1 K.B.799. Thus where a carrier parts with cargo without presentation of bills of lading, the cargo owners are entitled to claim in bailment despite the transfer of contractual rights to third party; *East West Corp.* v. *DKBS 1912* [2003] 1 Lloyd's Rep.239.

[790] Common carriers could be taxi companies; *Mizenchuk* v. *Thompson and Nash Taxi and U-Drive Co.* [1948] 1 D.L.R.136.

[791] Bailhache, J., said, *inter alia*, that 'to make a man a common carrier he must carry as a public employment; he must carry for all indifferently; he must hold himself out as ready to carry for hire as a business and not as a casual occupation', in *Belfast Ropework Co. Ltd.* v. *Bushell* [1918] 1 K.B.210, 212. In this case D was a haulage contractor who carried sugar from Liverpool to Manchester. At Manchester D invited offers of goods of all kinds for carriage to Liverpool and other places, at charges varying with the state of his business. These offers he accepted or rejected according to the rate, route, and class of goods. D concluded a contract for C's goods from Manchester to Liverpool, and C's goods were damaged by fire during the carriage without D's negligence. It was held that since he reserved to himself the right of accepting or rejecting offers of goods for carriage from Manchester to Liverpool he was not a common carrier of such goods and consequently not liable. *Cf. A. Siohn & Company Ltd. and Academy Garments (Wigan) Ltd.* v. *R. H. Hagland & Son (Transport) Ltd.* [1976] 2 Lloyd's Rep.428, where it was stated by the Court that a common carrier does not lose his legal character because he limits the class of goods he is prepared to carry or the routes or areas over which he is ready to operate.

[792] *Webster (EJ)* v. *Dickson (F) Transport* [1969] 1 Lloyd's Rep.89.

[793] *Johnson* v. *Midland Railway* (1849) 18 L.J.Ex.366.

(2) He must charge only at a reasonable rate for carrying the goods, and he must not impose unreasonable conditions.[794]

Liability of Common Carriers: For any breach of the above characteristics a common carrier could be sued for damages. Furthermore, a common carrier is absolutely responsible to the owner of the goods carried for any loss or damage to them. Absolutely, means irrespectively of negligence.[795]

However, if such loss or damage is caused by (1) an act of God,[796] or (2) an act to the Queen's enemies,[797] or (3) an inherent vice[798] in the goods, or (4) the negligence of the owner of the goods, or (5) in the case of carriage by sea, a general average sacrifice, then the common carrier would not be liable for such loss or damage.

Finally, please note that if a person is not a common carrier, then his liability will be[799] only that of a bailee.

GENERAL AVERAGE

In maritime and marine insurance law, the word 'average' simply means the partial loss of maritime property. The expression 'particular average' means a partial loss which must be borne by the maritime property which suffered it. However, there are instances where an average, i.e. a partial loss of maritime property, may be borne not only by the maritime property which suffered it, but also by other maritime properties involved in the same sea-voyage. Therefore, such partial loss, average, would be termed as 'general'.

During a sea-voyage, the master of the ship has very wide powers of action in time of peril, and at such times he may, if necessary, sacrifice property or incur

---

794 *Garton* v. *Bristol and ExeterRailway Co.* (1861) 30 L.J.Q.B.273.

795 *A. Siohn & Co. Ltd.* v. *RH Hagland & Son (Transport) Ltd.* [1976] 2 Lloyd's Rep.428

796 An Act of God would seem to include any accident arising without human intervention, which could not be reasonably foreseen and avoided; *Nugent* v. *Smith* (1875-76) L.R. 1 C.P.D.423.

797 This exception seems to cover acts done by public enemies; *Russell* v. *Niemann* (1864) 34 L.J. C.P.10.

798 Examples of inherent vice are spontaneous combustion, disease, decay or fermentation 'Vice' means the '...sort of vice which by its internal development tends to the destruction or the injury of the animal or thing to be carried'; *per* Willes, J., in *Blower* v. *Great Western Railway Co.* (1872) L.R. 7 C.P.655, 662. Inherent vice is the risk of deterioration of goods shipped as a result of their natural behaviour in the ordinary course of the contemplated voyage without the intervention of any fortuitous external accident or casualty; *G.m.b.H. Mainz K.G.* v. *White* [1983] 1 Lloyd's Rep.122. *TM Noten BV* v. *Paul Charles Harding* [1990] 2 Lloyd's Rep.283; *Cf. Bird's Cigarette Manufacturing Co. Ltd.* v. *Rouse* (1924) 19 Ll. L. Rep.301. See s.55(2)(c), Marine Insurance Act 1906.

799 To exercise a degree of care and skill; *Nugent* v. *Smith* (1875-76) L.R. 1 C.P.D.423.

expense for the general safety.[800] It would be unfair that the owner of the particular property should bear the whole of the loss thus incurred for the general benefit, and the loss is therefore apportioned or adjusted rateably between all the parties interested. Such a loss is termed a general average sacrifice or expenditure.

Where ship and cargo are exposed to a common danger and some part of the cargo or of the ship is intentionally sacrificed, or extra expenditure is incurred, to avert that danger, such loss or expense will be the subject of a general average contribution. It will be apportioned between ship and cargo in proportion to their salved values. For example, assume a ship, which has run aground. If it stays aground then an approaching storm may break the ship up on the rocks and all the ship and the cargo would be lost. To pull the ship back into deep water the engines may have to be used so severely that they are damaged. The shipowner can subsequently ask for a contribution from the cargo owners to make good this damage. Note, however, that only the loss which was voluntarily incurred for the common safety may be claimed for. In this example the damage incurred by the ship going aground is not a general average situation, only the financial sacrifices subsequently necessary to get her out of danger.

Although the idea is simple in theory, in a real situation the practical application of it can be complicated. Supposing shipper X has a general average loss of £1,000. The shipowner appoints an average adjuster who has to establish the total cost of the ship and cargo which is say £3,000,000. Shipper Y whose cargo was not damaged but assessed to have a value of £3,000 would be asked to contribute:

$$\text{£}3{,}000 \times \frac{\text{£}1{,}000}{\text{£}3{,}000{,}000}$$

or £1 as his (Y's) proportion of the general average payment. This does of course take time to calculate, it may sometimes take years.

The shipowner is responsible for collecting all these contributions, so before he loses his (possessory) lien on the cargo he may therefore ask his agents at the various discharging ports to collect a general average deposit or bond from the consignees before releasing the cargo. Thus, the duty of seeing that the person injured by the sacrifice obtains contribution is on the shipowner.[801]

Note that in the absence of agreement, the law of the port where the adventure ends is to be applied in adjusting the various contributions.

Very commonly a clause is inserted in the contract incorporating the York-Antwerp Rules, which are a standard set of rules relating to general average. The name 'York-Antwerp' is derived from the places where conferences were held which brought the Rules into existence. For a sacrifice or expenditure to be the

---

800 See agency of necessity, *supra*, p.136.

801 *Morrison Steamship Co. Ltd.* v. *Greystoke Castle (Cargo Owners)* [1947] A.C.265.

subject of general average contribution the following conditions must be fulfilled:

There must be a danger common to the whole adventure
The danger must be, in fact, a real one, not merely imagined to exist by the master, however reasonable such fear may be. Furthermore, the fact that a part of the cargo has already been discharged will not preclude the owners of the rest, under all circumstances, from claiming a general average contribution from the shipowner.[802]

The sacrifice or expenditure must be real and intentional
Where the thing abandoned is already lost, there is no real sacrifice, and consequently no claim for contribution, e.g. cutting away a mast which is already virtually useless.[803]

The sacrifice or expenditure must be necessary
Generally the duty of deciding whether a sacrifice or expenditure is necessary rests with the master of the ship.[804]

The danger must not be the fault of the person claiming contribution
In order to prevent a person recovering general average contribution on the ground that he was at fault, the fault must be something which constitutes an actionable wrong. Accordingly, a shipowner cannot claim a general average contribution where, for example, he allowed a vessel to sail with smoke in her holds or the cargo had not been properly stowed.[805]

The property must have been actually benefited by the sacrifice
If the general average act has been successful but consequently, owing to new causes, ship and cargo are lost, no contribution is due.[806] Where there is a general average act, the property concerned must in fact come through the adventure, otherwise there will be no benefit to the person who owns such property. This can be more easily understood if one remembers that the fund from which the contribution to the general average act is made is based on the

---

802 *Whitecross Wire & Iron Co. Ltd.* v. *Savill* (1822) 8 Q.B.D.653, C.A.; where most of the cargo had been discharged and a fire broke out on the ship. The remainder of the cargo was damaged by water used in putting out the fire. It was held that the shipowner must contribute in respect of this damage.

803 *Shepherd* v. *Kottgen* (1877) 37 L.T.618.

804 *Papayanni & Jerinica* v. *Grampian Steamship Co. Ltd.* (1896) 12 T.L.R.540.

805 The issue to consider is whether the party claiming contribution 'has by his own fault, occasioned the peril which immediately gave rise to the claim', *per* Watson, L.J., in *Strang Steel & Co.* v. *A. Scott & Co.* (1889) 14 A.C.601, 608. U.S.A. law on the point is similar; *United States* v. *Eastmount Shipping Corp.* (1974) A.M.C.1183, cargo owners not liable to contribute where unseaworthiness was a proximate cause of the general average act.

806 *Chellew* v. *The Royal Commission on Sugar Supply* [1922] 126 L.T.103.

value of the property saved at the end of the adventure. Therefore, there may be a general average act after which the entire of the adventure may be lost, in which case, there will be no case for a general average contribution, since there will be no fund out of which such contributions may be made.

Only direct losses are recoverable

Only losses which are the direct consequence of the general average act are allowed as general average. Thus, loss of market, caused by delay due to a general average act, would not be considered to be a direct loss, and therefore, it cannot be recovered.

CHARTER-PARTIES

There are two types of contract of carriage by sea: (i) contracts evidenced by bills of lading, and (ii) contracts contained in charter-parties. The former type of carriage contracts are mainly regulated by legislation and is considered later in this part.[807] A charter-party is a contract whereby the shipowner, or the person having the right to make an agreement for the ship, agrees to carry goods by water or to furnish a ship for such purpose, in return for a sum of money called the freight. Hence, we have the all embracing expression of 'contract of affreightment',[808] which simply means a contract for payment for the carriage of goods. In so far as charter-parties are concerned, they be classified into three main categories:[809]

(1) A time charterparty, which is a contract whereby the 'lessor' (the shipowner) places a fully equipped and manned ship at the disposal of the 'lessee' (the time charterer) for an agreed period of time for a consideration called 'hire' payable at specified intervals during the term of the charter.

(2) A voyage charterparty, which is a contract whereby the 'lessor' (the shipowner) places all (or part) of the carrying capacity of a ship at the disposal of the 'lessee' (the voyage charterer) for the transport of goods agreed upon, on one or more voyages, for a consideration called 'freight' based on the quantity of cargo carried.

---

[807] See Hague-Visby Rules 1968, *infra*, p.271.

[808] The expression 'charter-party' probably derives from the Latin *carta partita*, i.e. divide document, which referred to the practice of writing the contract on a sheet and tearing it in two. Thus, the existence of the contract was established by bringing the two halves together. The word 'affreightment' probably comes from the Dutch word 'urecht' which means a reward for the carriage.

[809] This is not an exhaustive list since in practice there are numerous 'hybrid' types of charter-parties such as 'consecutive voyage', 'slot', 'space', 'bareboat'/'demise' charters.

(3) A demise charter-party, which is a contract by which the 'lessor' (shipowner) places a ship in the hands of the 'lessee' (the demise charterer) over a long period of time, who assumes full possession and control, including paying and controlling the master and the crew.

Charter-parties are mainly governed by the rules of common law, and thus the shipowner may, by agreement with the charterer, modify his normal liability as a carrier. As the principles of law governing a simple contract are applicable to charter-parties, there is no need for special forms, nor does a charter-party need to be in writing.[810] However, until the parties have reached clear agreement on all essential terms, 'there is no contract'.[811] Thus, bills of lading issued under charter-parties are governed by the charter-party.[812]

However, where the charterer, having obtained a bill of lading by the shipowner, subsequently transfers it to a third party, e.g. an buyer/indorsee, then a new contract of carriage comes into existence between the shipowner and the third party transferee which is governed not by the charter-party but by the terms of the bill of lading.[813]

SEAWORTHINESS

Where goods are carried under a charter-party at common law there is an absolute duty upon the shipowner to supply a seaworthy ship. Such duty has

[810] *Lidgett* v. *Williams* (1845) 14 L.J. Ch.459.

[811] Per Blackburn, L.J., *Rossiter* v. *Miller* (1878) 3 A.C.1124, 1151.

[812] Unless the shipowner and the charterer have agreed that such bills of lading will vary the terms of the charter-party; *The Jocelyne* [1977] 2 Lloyd's Rep.121.

[813] This is a general rule, and it is possible that the bill of lading incorporates the terms of the charter-party, in which case, depending on the particular charter-party terms incorporated, the charter-party terms may bind such third party transferee; *President of India* v *Metcalfe Shipping Co. Ltd. (The Dunelmia)* [1970] 2 Q.B.289, where the bills of lading were endorsed to by the sellers to the charterers and the bills stipulated 'Freight payable by the charterers as per charterparty' and 'all conditions and exceptions as per charterparty' but did not incorporate the charter-party's arbitration clause. A dispute arose between charterers and shipowners over an alleged short delivery on discharge. The charterers sought to refer it to arbitration but the shipowners claimed that the matter was governed by the bills, which excluded arbitration. It was held by the Court of Appeal that the charter-party was *prima facie* the contract governing relations between the parties, unless expressly or impliedly altered by them; here the bills of lading had had no impact on the charterparty; so the arbitration clause in the charter-party remained effective. In *Miramar Maritime Corp.* v. *Holborn Oil Trading (The Miramar)* [1984] A.C.676, a tanker voyage charterparty in the standard form known as 'Exxonvoy 1969' was concluded, and the bill of lading purported to incorporate all the terms of the charter including a demurrage clause rendering the charterers liable for demurrage. The shipowners claimed that the demurrage clause thereby incorporated into the bill of lading rendered the consignees of the cargo, as holders of the bill of lading, directly liable for the demurrage incurred. It was held that on the true construction of the bill of lading it was the intention of the parties to the bill of lading contract that the charterers alone should be liable for demurrage.

been considered by the Courts to be an intermediate/innominate term in nature, which means that breach of it only justifies rescission if it leads, or amounts, to a serious failure in performance.[814]

Furthermore, this is referred as an absolute duty because it does not depend on fault,[815] but purely on the question of whether the vessel has that degree of fitness which an ordinary careful and prudent owner would require his vessel to have at the commencement of her voyage having regard to all the probable circumstances of it,[816] and where the vessel is to call at various ports during the agreed voyage she must be seaworthy when she leaves each one of these ports.[817]

Seaworthiness means the ship is fit in design, structure, condition and equipment to encounter the ordinary perils of the voyage.[818] She must have a competent master and a competent[819] and sufficient crew.[820] Seaworthiness in this context includes cargoworthines, for example that the ship is fit in her holds,[821] she has all necessary certificates/documents to carry the particular goods,[822] etc. Finally, section 39(4) of the Marine Insurance Act defines seaworthiness as follows:

> 'A ship is deemed to be seaworthy when she is reasonably fit in all respects to encounter the ordinary perils of the sea of the adventure insured.'

DEVIATION

Where goods are carried under a charter-party, the shipowner undertakes that the ship shall proceed on the agreed voyage without departure from her proper course. Where this is not defined, the proper course is the normal trade route.[823]

---

814 *Hong Kong Fir Shipping Co. Ltd.* v. *Kawasaki Kisen Kaisha Ltd.* [1962] 2 Q.B.26, C.A.

815 The shipowner undertakes responsibility for any defects even if these are not discoverable by careful examination; *Steel* v. *State Line Steamship Co.* (1877-78) L.R. 3 App. Cas.72, H.L.

816 *Per* Channell, J., in *McFadden* v. *Blue Star Line* [1905] 1 K.B.697, 706.

817 For example, if the vessel fails to take on sufficient fuel to the next port of call, she would be unseaworthy; *The Vortigern* [1899] P.140, C.A.

818 *Owners of Cargo Laden on Makedonia* v. *Makedonia Owners (The Makedonia)* [1962] 2 All E.R.614.

819 See for example, *Moore* v. *Lunn* (1922) 11 Ll. L. Rep.86, vessel unseworthy due to a drunken master and an unqualified engineer.

820 *Robin Hood Flour Mills Ltd* v. *N.M. Paterson & Sons Ltd., (The Farrandoc)* [1967] 2 Lloyd's Rep.276 (Exchequer Court of Canada).

821 *Rowson* v. *Atlantic Transport* [1903] 2 K.B.666, vessel's faulty refrigeration.

822 *Cheikh Boutros Selim El-Khoury* v. *Ceylon Shipping Lines, Ltd., (The Madeleine)* [1967] 2 Lloyd's Rep.224, vessel not possessing deratisation certificate from health authorities, held vessel not fitted for ordinary cargo service.

823 *Reardon Smith Line Ltd.* v. *Black Sea & Baltic General Insurance Co. Ltd.* [1939] A.C.562, H.L.

To constitute an unjustifiable deviation the departure from the contractual voyage must be the result of a deliberate act on the part of the owner or the ship's officers. Consequently there will be no breach of this obligation if the vessel is blown off course during a storm, or is set on a wrong course as the result of the illness of its navigation officer or reliance on a defective compass.[824]

A departure from the proper route is justified at common law in the following cases:

(i) To save human life or to communicate with a vessel in distress in case lives may be in danger.[825]

(ii) To avoid danger to the ship or cargo. The risks may arise from natural causes such as storms, ice or fog, or they may involve political factors such as the outbreak of war, or the fear of capture by pirates.[826] Deviation may be justified even if resulting from the initial unseaworthiness of the vessel.[827]

(iii) Where there is an express clause in the carriage contract permitting deviation for specified reasons. A clause permitting the towing or assisting other vessels is common, while a liberty is often given to call in at intermediate ports at the shipowner's discretion.[828]

Finally, it would seem[829] that a shipowner who deviates (unjustifiably), would be liable in a similar, but not identical, fashion, to that of a common carrier, i.e. being strictly liable for the goods.

He would therefore only be able to rely on the exceptions of (1) act of God, (2) act of the Queen's enemies, (3) inherent vice in the goods, (4) the negligence of the owner of the goods, provided the shipowner can show that the loss or damage to the goods would have happened if the deviation had not occurred.[830]

---

[824] *Rio Tinto Co. Ltd.* v. *Seed Shipping Co. Ltd.* (1926) 24 Ll. L. Rep.316.

[825] But deviation is not justified to save property; *Scaramanga & Co.* v. *Stamp* (1879-80) L.R. 5 C.P.D.295, where a ship deviated to assist a vessel, and agreed to give her a tow. While towing the distressed vessel, she ran aground and was lost. It was held, *inter alia*, that the deviation to save the ship was not justified.

[826] *The Teutonia* (1871-73) L.R. 4 P.C. 171.

[827] *Kish* v. *Taylor* [1912] A.C.604, H.L.

[828] However, such liberty clauses are strictly construed by the Courts *Glynn* v. *Margetson & Co.* [1893] A.C.351, H.L.

[829] This area of law is not without difficulties. For example, it is not clear whether a deviating shipowner can rely on exclusion clauses for loss or damage to the goods which occurred before the deviation. In fact, even the proposition put forward here that a deviating shipowner's position changes to that of a common carrier, has not been made satisfactorily clear by the Courts, e.g. see the view of Fletcher Moulton, L.J., in *Joseph Thorley Ltd.* v. *Orchis Steamship Co. Ltd.* [1907] 1 K.B.660, 669.

[830] *Morrison & Co. Ltd.* v. *Shaw Savill & Albion Co. Ltd.* [1916] 2 K.B.783, C.A.

BILLS OF LADING

A bill of lading has been defined as a receipt for goods shipped on board a ship, signed by the person (or his agent) who contracts to carry them, and stating the terms on which the goods were delivered to and received by the ship. The principal purpose of the bill of lading is to enable the owner of the goods to dispose of them rapidly although the goods are not in his hands but are in the custody of a carrier. When goods are on the high seas in transit from, say, London to New York, and the bill of lading has been forwarded to the buyer in New York and the buyer thus has become the holder of the goods, the bill of lading representing the goods enables the buyer to pledge the goods with his bank in New York or to resell them to a re-purchaser in Singapore.

FUNCTIONS OF BILLS OF LADING

A bill of lading serves three functions:

(1) It is a document of title to the goods, once they are shipped;

(2) It is evidence of the contract which has been entered into between the shipper of the goods and the shipowner;

(3) It is a receipt for the goods delivered to the shipowner/carrier.

(1) As it has been mentioned, the principal purpose of the bill of lading is to enable the person entitled to the goods represented by the bill to dispose of the goods while they are in transit. By mercantile custom, possession of the bill is in many respects equivalent to possession of the goods and the transfer of the bill of lading has normally the same effect as the delivery of the goods themselves.
Without a bill of lading delivery of the goods cannot normally be obtained. Therefore, it enables the consignee to dispose of the goods by indorsement and delivery of the bill of lading.[831]
Two points should be noted in this connection:

a) The transfer of the bill of lading is merely deemed to operate as a symbolic transfer of possession of the goods, but not necessarily as a transfer of the property in them. The transfer of the bill passes such rights in the goods as

[831] Thus, in *E. Clement Horst Company* v. *Biddell Brothers* [1912] A.C.18, H.L., a contract was made for the sale of hops to be shipped from the U.S.A. to the U.K. C.I.F. net cash. The buyer refused to pay for the goods until they were actually delivered. It was held that possession of the bill of lading is in law equivalent to possession of the goods, and that under a C.I.F. contract, the seller is entitled to payment on shipping the goods and tendering to the buyer the documents of title.

the parties intend to pass.[832] Thus, where the consignee or indorsee of the bill is the agent of the shipper at the port of destination, it is evident that the parties, by transferring the bill of lading, intend only to pass the right to claim delivery of the goods from the carrier upon arrival of the goods, but not the property in them. Where the seller of goods transfers the bill of lading to the buyer, as he is bound to do in case of a C.I.F. sale, it depends again on the intention of the parties whether the property passes by transfer of the bill of lading or remains in the seller. As far as English law and specific or ascertained goods are concerned, this is in accordance with the fundamental rules laid down by sections 16 and 17 of the Sale of Goods Act 1979 (as amended),[833] which, it should be noted, apply irrespectively of whether the goods sold are represented by a bill of lading or not.

b) Only a person holding a bill of lading is entitled to claim delivery of the goods from the carrier. The carrier is protected if he delivers the goods to the holder of the first original bill presented to him. The bill of lading retains its character of document of title until the contract of carriage by sea is discharged by delivery of the goods against the bill, and the carrier is not responsible for wrongful delivery of the goods against the bill unless he knows of the defect in the title of the holder. If the carrier delivers the goods to a person who is not the holder of the bill of lading, he does so at his peril.[834] Finally in the event of the bill of lading being lost or delayed,

[832] The transfer of a bill of lading transfers only such proprietary interest as the parties intend; *Sewell* v. *Burdick* [1884] 10 App.Cas.74, H.L., a shipper indorsed the bill of lading in blank to the bank as security for a loan. The carrier enforced his lien over the goods and auctioned them in order to recover freight. However, the auction's proceeds were insufficient to meet the freight, and hence the carrier brought an action against the bank as holder and indorsee of the bill of lading. It was held that as the relationship between the shipper and the bank was not one of sale, no property had passed through the indorsement of the bill of lading, therefore the carrier was prevented from taking action against the bank. *Cf. Lickbarrow* v. *Mason* (1793) 126 E.R.511, H.L., goods had been bought by B, by a blank indorsement of a bill of lading. B sold the goods to C, who paid for them, and had the bill of lading transferred by B's indorsement. Then B became bankrupt without having paid S, his seller. S sold the goods to D who obtained possession when the ship arrived. C claimed that he had title to the goods. It was held that since the bill of lading was delivered to B, the buyer, who had indorsed it for valuable consideration to a third party who acted in good faith, i.e. C, the property in the goods passed to that third party, i.e. C. Hence, the property was transferred with the documents to C, and S, the original seller, had no title to transfer to D.

[833] See *supra*, pp.160 and 158 respectively.

[834] *Per* Denning, M.R., in *Sze Hai Tong Bank* v. *Rambler Cycle Co. Ltd.* [1959] 2 Lloyd's Rep.114, 120. A carrier is entitled to refuse to deliver the goods without production of the bill of lading, even if the person requesting delivery is entitled to receive them; *Truck & Spares Ltd.* v. *Maritime Agencies (Southampton) Ltd.* [1951] 2 All E.R.982, a number of trucks and spares were sold to a buyer in Canada. When the goods arrived, the buyer had no bills of lading because due to debts owed by the seller to the carrier, the seller had not received one, i.e. the carrier kept the bill of lading. It was held that the bill of lading must be produced to make a good title to the goods.

the carrier will allow delivery of the goods to the person claiming to be the consignee, if he gives a letter of indemnity, countersigned by a bank.

(2) A bill of lading is evidence of the contract of carriage, though not the contract itself, which has been entered into between the shipper of the goods and the shipowner before the bill of lading is signed.[835] This is better understood if one realises that bills of lading are issued only when the ship actually sails from the port of loading. Therefore, it could be said that the bill of lading is a memorandum of the contract of carriage, repeating in detail the terms of the contract which was in fact concluded prior to the signing of the bill.

(3) The bill of lading, being a receipt of the shipowner for the goods, contains a description of the goods. This description is perhaps the most vital part of the whole bill because the intended indorsee of the bill, who wishes to buy the goods by having the bill indorsed to him, normally has no opportunity of verifying the representation of the buyer as to their quantity and quality by examining them, and parts with the purchase price in reliance upon the shipowner's description of the goods in the bill of lading.

THE DATE OF THE BILL OF LADING

The correct dating of the bill of lading is a matter of considerable importance. In the case of a 'shipped' bill this is the date when the goods are taken on board and in the case of a 'received for shipment' bill is the date when they are taken into the charge of the carrier. If a 'received for shipment' bill is noted 'shipped', the date of shipment of the goods is that of the notation, i.e. when the goods were actually shipped, and not that of the receipt of the goods by the carrier. Where the loading extends over several days, the bill should be dated when the loading is completed but there may be a trade custom admitting the insertion of the date when the loading commences.[836] The date of the bill of lading is material in three legal relationships: in the contract of carriage, in the contract of sale, and in relation to the banks if payment is arranged under a letter of credit.

---

[835] *Owners of Cargo Lately Laden on Board the Ardennes* v. *Owners of the Ardennes (The Ardennes)* [1951] 1 K.B.55; an oral contract of carriage was made between the shipper and the carrier. It was agreed that the ship should go directly to London in order to avoid an expected rise in import tax. However, the bill of lading subsequently issued allowed for deviation from the agreed route. In the event, the ship called at some other ports, and she arrived in London after the tax increase. It was held that as between shipper and carrier, a bill of lading is a receipt for the goods and excellent evidence of the terms of carriage but not the contract itself. The carriers were bound by the oral contract made.

[836] *Rudolph A Oetker* v. *IFA Internationale Frachtagentur AG (The Almak)* [1985] 1 Lloyd's Rep.557.

As to the contract of carriage, the shipper is entitled to demand that the bill of lading should be dated correctly. If the carrier (i.e. master or another agent of the carrier) negligently misdates the bill, he would be liable in damages, provided that the shipper can prove that he has suffered a loss as the result of the misdating, but the position may be different if the misdating is due to want of care on the part of the shipper.

The date of the bill of lading may also be relevant in the contract of sale. In one case the contract provided that the bill should be dated December and/or January of a particular year. The bill was dated February but the goods were actually shipped in January. The buyers rejected the bills and the Court held that the rejection was justified.[837]

Where payment is arranged under a letter of credit, the credit often states a date for shipment and, apart from this date, every credit states invariably an expiry date. Here the date of the bill of lading is important. An issuer of a bill of lading, who deliberately backdates it in order to bring it within the shipment time, acts fraudulently,[838] and as far as the issue of the bill is concerned, there is no difference between the case where he has forged the bill and where he has deliberately backdated it.

However, note that in the hands of an innocent person, the fraudulently backdated bill is valid.[839]

---

[837] *Procter & Gamble Philippine Manufacturing Corp.* v. *Kurt A. Becher GmbH & Co.* [1988] 2 Lloyd's Rep.21, C.A.

[838] *Standard Chartered Bank* v. *Pakistan National Shipping Corporation and Others (No.2)* [2003] 1 Lloyd's Rep.227, H.L.; here the shipper company, through its director, agreed with the shipowners that backdated bills of lading will be issued, in order to bring the shipment within the time limit of shipper's letter of credit. Indeed, the company presented the bill of lading and other documents along with a letter by the company's director stating that the submitted documents were all those required by the credit. However, some of the documents were rejected as discrepant and re-submitted after the date for the negotiation of the credit had passed. Despite this late presentation, C, the confirming bank, paid the shipper/beneficiary and sought to be reimbursed by the issuing bank. The issuing bank was unaware of the backdating of the bill of lading, but rejected some of the documents due to discrepancies which C had not noticed. C sued the shipper/beneficiary and the shipowners for deceit. It was held that the shipper/beneficiary company's director could be held personally liable for fraudulent misrepresentation. So that C could pursue the claim against either the shipper/beneficiary company and/or its director personally. One of the interesting issues raised by the shipper/beneficiary's director was that, should he be found personally liable for fraudulent misrepresentation, the claim should be reduced as a consequence of C's contributory negligence (i.e. paying despite late presentation). However, the Court held that a reduction due to contributory negligence in any damages for fraudulent misrepresentation was not appropriate.

[839] Such innocent party may, nevertheless, have a valid claim for any losses suffered as a result; *Finlay* v. *Kwik Hoo Tong* [1929] 1 K.B.400, the bill of lading had inaccurately stated that shipment had taken place within shipment period. The buyers accepted the documents without notice of the fact that the goods had been shipped outside this shipment period. Subsequently, the buyers entered into several sub-contracts, and some of their sub-purchasers refused to take delivery alleging that the goods did not meet their contractual description, i.e. shipment period. It was held that the failure to tender genuine documents had deprived the buyers of their right of rejection which, in the circumstances (of a falling market), they would have exercised.

TYPES OF BILLS OF LADING AND OTHER SIMILAR DOCUMENTS

Shipped bill of lading: The shipper can demand that the shipowner supplies bills of lading proving that the goods have been actually shipped. For this reason most bill of lading forms are already printed as shipped bills and commence with the wording 'Shipped in apparent good order and condition'. It confirms the goods are actually on board the vessel. This is the most satisfactory type of receipt, and the shipper prefers such a bill as there is no doubt the goods being on board and consequent dispute on this point will not arise with the bankers or consignee, thereby facilitating earliest financial settlement of the export sale.

Received for Shipment bill of lading: This type is used more in the U.S.A. and in container transport. This arises where the word 'shipped' does not appear on the bill of lading. It merely confirms that the goods have been handed over to the shipowner and are in his custody. The cargo may be in his dock, warehouse, transit shed, or even inland. The bill has therefore not the same meaning as a 'Shipped' bill and the buyer under a C.I.F. contract need not accept such a bill for ultimate financial settlement through the bank unless provision has been made in the contract. Forwarding agents should avoid handling 'Received for Shipment' bills for their clients unless special circumstances require it.

Through bill of lading: These are used for door-to-door container cargo where several different modes of transport may be involved. In such cases it would be very complicated and more expensive if the shipper had to arrange on-carriage himself by employing an agent at the point of transhipment. Shipping companies therefore issue bills of lading which cover the whole transit and the shipper deals only with the first carrier. This type of bill enables a through rate to be quoted and is growing in popularity with the development of containerisation.

Transhipment bill of lading: This type is issued usually by shipping companies when there is no direct service between two ports, but when the shipowner is prepared to tranship the cargo at an intermediate port at his expense.

Groupage bills of lading: Forwarding agents are permitted to 'group' together particular compatible consignments from individual consignors to various consignees, situated usually in the same destination country/area, and despatch them as one consignment. The shipowner issues a groupage bill of lading to the forwarding agent who will issue to the individual shippers a Certificate of

---

Therefore the buyers were awarded damages to reflect the difference between the contract price and market price.

Shipment sometimes called 'House bill of lading'. At the destination, another agent working in close liaison with the agent forwarding the cargo will break bulk the consignment and distribute the goods to the various consignees. This practice is on the increase, usually involving the use of containers and particularly evident in the deep sea container services. The main reasons for this 'popularity' are: (a) lower insurance premiums, (b) less risk of damage and pilferage, (c) transit times are shorter, and (d) lower rates for the principals.

Clean/Unclaused bills of lading: Each bill of lading states 'in apparent good order and condition', which of course refers to the cargo. If this statement is not modified by the master (shipowner), the bill of lading is regarded as 'clean' or 'unclaused'. By issuing clean bills of lading the shipowner admits his full liability of the cargo described in the bill under the law and his contract. This type is much favoured by banks for financial settlement purposes.

Claused/'dirty'/'unclean' bills of lading: If the master (shipowner) does not agree with any of the statements made in the bill of lading he will add a clause to this effect, thereby causing the bill of lading to be termed as 'unclean', 'foul', or 'claused'. This type of bill of lading is usually unacceptable to a bank. Although this is an obvious and necessary precaution for the shipowner to take it may create problems for the shipper/exporter. Very often the foreign importer pays the exporter by a letter of credit which is passed from his bank to the exporter's bank. The exporter can, therefore, expect payment on presenting the bill of lading to his bank. This payment can usually only be made, however, if the bill of lading is clear. If the bill is dirty there may be considerable delay in payment. This, in turn, causes the shipper to ask the shipowner for clean bills of lading even offering him a letter of indemnity by which he offers to accept the shipowner's liability for claims made against him for damaged cargo. However, as the bill of lading is a transferable document, such letters are illegal as the bill could be sold without the purchaser being aware of the existence of such a letter. Nevertheless because of the financial problems that can arise for the shipper they are still sometimes used.

Negotiable bills of lading: If the words 'or his or their assigns' are contained in the bill of lading, it is negotiable. There are, however, variations in this terminology, for example the word 'bearer' may be inserted in the preamble to the phrase.

'Stale' bills of lading: The expression 'stale bill of lading' is used in banking practice. A bank which is instructed by, or on behalf of, a buyer to make finance available under a letter of credit upon presentation, by the seller, of a bill of lading (and of other documents) might feel obliged, in order to safeguard the interest of its principal, to reject the bill as being 'stale'. By that is meant that the bill, though conforming in all respects with the requirements of the credit, is presented so late that, as the result of the delay in its presentation, the consignee might become involved in legal or practical complications or might have to pay additional costs, e.g. for the warehousing of goods. The Uniform Customs and Practice for Documentary Credits provide that transport documents must be presented within a specified time after issuance and that, if no time is specified, banks may refuse documents if presented to them later than 21 days after issuance of the bill of lading or other transport document.

HAGUE-VISBY RULES 1968

As mentioned earlier, there are two types of contract of carriage by sea; (i) contracts evidenced by bills of lading, and (ii) contracts contained in charter-parties.

Charter-parties are of little interest to the 'average' exporter, since the quantity of his shipments is not normally such that the hire of a whole ship would be a viable proposition.

Contracts of carriage evidenced by bills of lading are to a large measure regulated by statute law, in particular by the Carriage of Goods by Sea Act 1971 (giving the Hague-Visby Rules force of law in the U.K.), which effectively restrains the shipowner from introducing exemptions from his liability beyond those admitted by the standard Rules relating to bills of lading, i.e. the Hague-Visby Rules, appended to the 1971 Act.

Although the clauses contained in a bill of lading represent the terms of agreement between the shipper and the carrier, the shipper has little discretion in the negotiation of these terms. The terms of the contract which he concludes are fixed in advance, and his position is not unlike that of a railway passenger who buys a ticket. The shipper, like the railway passenger, is protected by Act of Parliament against abuse of the greater bargaining power of the other party. As far as the shipper is concerned, this protection is contained in the Carriage of Goods by Sea Acts of 1971 and 1992.

The Carriage of Goods by Sea Act, 1971, came into force in June, 1977. The Act together with the Carriage of Goods by Sea Act 1992 govern the liabilities and rights relating to carriers under bills of lading as well as to other documents of title. The more important points to remember, in connection with the application of this (1971) Act are:

1. It only applies to 'outwards' bills of lading, i.e. from a British port, or Northern Ireland port, the port of destination is immaterial. In particular, Article

X provides that the Act will apply to every bill of lading relating to the carriage of goods between ports in two different States if:

a) the bill of lading is issued in a Contracting State; or

b) the carriage is from a port in a Contracting State; or

c) the contract contained in or evidenced by the bill of lading provides that these Rules or legislation of any State giving effect to them are to govern the contract.

2. The Act does not apply to the transportation of live animals, and deck cargo which is carried on deck in pursuance of the contract of carriage. But where cargo is carried on deck without specific agreement between the parties as to the carriage on deck, and no statement appears on the face of the bill of lading that goods carried on deck are in fact so carried, the carriage is subject to the Rules.

3. It applies both to shipments under bills of lading and those under 'any similar documents of title'. Therefore, it applies to a receipt which is a non-negotiable document, if it expressly states that the contract for the carriage of goods by sea contained in or evidenced by it shall be governed by the Act/Hague-Visby Rules, as if the receipt were a bill of lading. Thus, a forwarder's receipt (or a liner waybill, or data freight receipt) such as a House bill of lading or container receipt would be subject to the Act, if so endorsed.

The bill of lading, under the Act, provides *prima facie* evidence of receipt by the carrier of the goods, i.e. identification of cargo marks, condition of cargo, number of packages and their weight, and it further provides conclusive evidence when the cargo has been transferred to a party acting in good faith.

4. The responsibilities of the carrier in respect of the safety of the goods entrusted to his care are described in the Act as follows:

'1) The carrier shall be bound, before and at the beginning of the voyage, to exercise due diligence to -

a) Make the ship seaworthy.

b) Properly man, equip and supply the ship.

c) Make the holds, refrigerating and cool chambers, and all other parts of the ship in which goods are carried, fit and safe for their reception, carriage and preservation.

2) Subject to the provision of Article IV, the carrier shall properly and carefully load, handle, stow, carry, keep, care for and discharge the goods carried. (Article III rule 1)'

The principle underlying these provisions is that the shipowner is only liable if acting negligently. Seaworthiness within the meaning of the above Article, includes cargo-worthiness (Article III rule 1(c)); consequently the vessel is unseaworthy if its condition before loading the cargo constitutes a major and permanent obstacle to the completion of the contract voyage.

Thus, a vessel will be unseaworthy if before loading it is infested with insects and for this reason the discharge of the cargo is prohibited by the authorities at the port of destination.[840] Also, the vessel would be unseaworthy if it is provided with navigational charts which are out of date,[841] or is manned by an incompetent crew.[842] The obligation of the carrier to use due diligence in the cases stated in the above Article is not limited to his personal diligence, but he is also liable if servants and agents in his employment fail to act with due diligence.[843]

However, it must be noted that under the Act the carrier only need exercise due diligence rather than actually provide a seaworthy ship, so that the emphasis is on due diligence rather than actual seaworthiness. In simpler terms, it might be possible that a ship is unseaworthy, but as the carrier exercised due diligence, he is not liable for the loss!

5. The Act permits the carrier to be discharged from all liability in respect of goods unless legal proceedings for loss/damage to cargo were started within one year of delivery of the cargo or the date when they should have been delivered.[844] Therefore, generally speaking, the Act, puts a time-bar to claims made after the expiration of one year.[845] The Act, also provides that a notice of loss or damage must be given in writing to the carrier or his agent at the port of

---

840 *Empresa Cubana Importadora de Alimentos Alimport* v. *Iasmos Shipping Co. SA (The Good Friend)* [1984] 2 Lloyd's Rep.586.

841 *Grand Champion Tankers Ltd.* v. *Norpipe A/S (The Marion)* [1984] A.C.563, H.L.

842 *Papera Traders Co. Ltd.* v. *Hyundai Merchant Marine Co. Ltd. (The Eurasian Dream)* [2002] 1 Lloyd's Rep.719.

843 *Riverstone Meat Co. Pty Ltd.* v. *Lancashire Shipping Co. Ltd. (The Muncaster Castle)* [1961] A.C.807, H.L.

844 The test of whether 'suit' has validly commenced does not seem to be whether the correct claimant commenced proceedings before a competent Court against the correct defendant, within the one year limit of the Rules; *Thyssen Inc.* v. *Calypso Shipping Corp. SA* [2000] 2 Lloyd's Rep.243, where under a charter-party governed by English law and the Hague Rules and containing a London arbitration clause, the cargo owners, in breach of the arbitration clause, commenced an action for damage to their goods, in the U.S.A. Their action in the U.S.A. stayed, and they subsequently wished to commence an arbitration claim. The carrier sought to rely on the time bar in the second set of proceedings. It was held, that as the cargo owners' action in the U.S.A. stayed by reason of the breach of the arbitration clause, no suit had been brought within the year. Therefore, the arbitration proceedings were time-barred.

845 It must be noted however, that this time limit only applies for suits brought by the cargo owners against the carrier. If the contract of carriage, evidenced by a bill of lading, is subject to English law, then the carrier has got six years to take action against the cargo owners for breach of contract, as prescribed by the Limitation Act 1980.

discharge, and if the damage to the goods is not apparent, then this time is extended to three days.

6. Finally, the Act provides that unless the value of lost or damaged goods has been declared by the shipper before shipment and inserted in the bill of lading, neither the carrier nor the ship will be or become liable for any loss or damage to the goods in an amount exceeding 666.67 (Special Drawing Rights) units of account per package, or 2 (S.D.R.s) units of account per kilogramme of gross weight of the goods (lost or damaged), whichever is the higher. The unit of account is a Special Drawing Right (S.D.R.) as defined by the International Monetary Fund (I.M.F.).[846] The Act also confirms that the maximum liability does not apply if the damage resulted from an act or omission of the carrier done with intent to cause damage, or recklessly and with knowledge that damage would probably result.[847]

Excepted Perils

The Act also contains, in Article IV(2), a list of 17 matters in respect of loss or damage arising or resulting from which the carrier's liability is exempted.[848] The burden of proof rests upon the shipowner. He has to prove that the goods were lost without his fault, and if he wants to rely on one or more of these exceptions in order to exempt his liability, i.e. that the damage or loss of the cargo is due to one of the exempted perils, he has to establish this fact also. Note that risks which the shipper has to bear under the contract of carriage should be covered by his marine insurance policy.

As it has been mentioned earlier in this Chapter a bill of lading is a receipt for the goods shipped and contains certain admissions as to their quantity and condition when put on board; i.e. it is a formal receipt by the shipowner acknowledging that goods of the stated species, quantity and condition are

[846] The S.D.R. is an International monetary unit credited by the International Monetary Fund from a composite of several currencies.

[847] Article IV, rule 5(e), Hague-Visby Rules 1968.

[848] These exemptions are: (a) Act, neglect, or default of the master, mariner, pilot, or the servants of the carrier in the navigation or in the management of the ship; (b) Fire, unless caused by the actual fault or privity of the carrier; (c) Perils, dangers and accidents of the sea or other navigable waters; (d) Act of God; (e) Act of war; (f) Act of public enemies; (g) Arrest or restraint of princes, rulers or people, or seizure under legal process; (h) Quarantine restrictions; (i) Act or omission of the shipper or owner of the goods, his agent or representative; (j) Strikes or lockouts or stoppage or restraint of labour from whatever cause, whether partial or general; (k) Riots and civil commotions; (l) Saving or attempting to save life or property at sea; (m) Wastage in bulk of weight or any other loss or damage arising from inherent defect, quality or vice of the goods; (n) Insufficiency of packing; (o) Insufficiency or inadequacy of marks; (p) Latent defects not discoverable by due diligence; (q) Any other cause arising without the actual fault or privity of the carrier, or without the fault or neglect of the agents or servants of the carrier.

shipped to a stated destination in a certain ship, or at least received in the custody of the shipowner for the purposes of shipment.

DESCRIPTION OF THE GOODS IN THE BILL OF LADING

The Carriage of Goods by Sea Act 1971, provides that the shipper is entitled to demand that the bill of lading which the owner is obliged to issue to him should contain certain leading marks and other particulars.

When the shipowner affirms that the goods received are in 'apparent good order and condition', he issues a 'clean' bill. The words 'in apparent good order and condition' denote that 'apparently, and so far as met the eye, and externally [the goods] were placed in good order on board this ship' but the statement does not extend to qualities of the goods 'which were not apparent to reasonable inspection having regard to the circumstances of loading'.[849]

The shipowner who gives a clean bill does not promise to deliver goods 'in apparent good order and condition' to the consignee, and may prove that the goods were damaged subsequent to the issue of the bill by an excepted peril, but he is prevented ('estopped') from denying that he received the goods in apparent good order and condition and cannot escape liability by alleging that an excepted peril existed prior to the issue of the clean bill, e.g. insufficient packing. This estoppel operates only in favour of a consignee/indorsee who relies on the statement in the bill that goods were in apparent good order and condition.[850]

The shipper is deemed to have guaranteed to the carrier the accuracy of the marks, number, quantity and weight as furnished by him, and the shipper has to indemnify the carrier against loss or damage arising from inaccuracies in such particulars. However, note that the right of the carrier to be indemnified by the shipper in these circumstances cannot be pleaded by the carrier in defence against a consignee who tries to hold him responsible.

A bill of lading issued under the Carriage of Goods by Sea Act 1971 is *prima facie* evidence of the receipt of the goods by the carrier as described in accordance with Article III of the Act. This provision applies to 'shipped' and 'received' bills alike. Furthermore, the Act provides that the bill shall be conclusive evidence regarding those particulars in the hands of a third party

---

[849] *National Petroleum Co.* v. *Owners of the Athelviscount* (1934) 48 Ll. L. Rep.164; where the Court clearly stated that 'condition' in this context means external and apparent condition and not 'quality' which is not usually apparent to an unskilled person. Furthermore, it was stated that bills of lading containing the statement 'weight, quantity and quality unknown' do not constitute any representation as to quality of the goods shipped.

[850] 'A statement that the goods were supplied in good order and condition estops the shipowner as against the person presenting the bill of lading to get delivery of the goods from proving that the goods were not in apparent good order and condition when shipped', *per* Branson, J., in *National Petroleum Co.* v. *Owners of the Athelviscount* (1934) 48 Ll. L. Rep.164, 170.

acting in good faith. Such a third party, it is thought, would be the consignee, to whom the bill is transferred, and an indorsee.

Finally, a shipper warrants that the goods are fit for carriage in the ordinary way. Furthermore, the shipper warrants not only that the goods will not cause physical injury or damage to ship/other cargo, but also that the goods can be discharged without delay due to import restrictions or prohibitions.

However, the shipper will not be liable under the warranty if he duly informs the shipowner of the nature of the goods or if the shipowner knows, or ought to know, that they are dangerous or that delay in the discharge may be encountered.

CARRIAGE OF GOODS BY SEA: RIGHT TO SUE

Before 1992, it was the case that the carrier could have been sued by any consignee or indorsee provided:

(a) the document was a bill of lading,

(b) the holder of the bill of lading was a consignee or indorsee, and

(c) property in the goods had passed to the holder of the bill of lading by way of indorsement or consignment.

Therefore, an indorsee or consignee could sue the carrier for breaches of the contract of carriage even if such breaches occurred before the bill of lading had been transferred to him.[851] However, problems arose with this arrangement, which may be highlighted by the following simple example.

X, the seller/shipper, ships 5,000 tons bulk cargo and sells 1,000 tons of it to Y, the buyer/consignee. As the 1,000 tons out of 5,000 are considered to be unascertained goods, the property in the goods will pass once they become ascertained.[852] In such a situation the property in the goods would not pass before the goods are discharged from the vessel. If Y received no goods then it is obvious that one of the above mentioned three requirement would not be fulfilled, and therefore, Y would not be in a position to sue the carrier.[853]

Other problems also arose as a result of the Bills of Lading Act 1855, which are beyond the scope of this Chapter, and as a result the Carriage of Goods by Sea Act 1992 was enacted, repealing the Bills of Lading Act 1855.

The main philosophy behind the 1992 Act is that a bill of lading holder can sue the carrier in contract for loss or damage to the goods covered by the bill of lading, irrespectively of whether property in the goods has passed to the holder. Furthermore, it should be noted that the Carriage of Goods by Sea Act 1992 now

851 *Monarch Steamship Co. Ltd.* v *A/B Karlshamns Oljefabriker* [1949] A.C.196, H.L.

852 Section 16, Sale of Goods Act 1979 (as amended).

853 See *The Delfini* [1990] 1 Lloyd's Rep.252.

covers sea waybills and ship's delivery orders.[854] The following is a summary of section 2(1) of the Carriage of Goods by Sea Act 1992, on the persons entitled to sue the carrier:

(1) the holder of a bill of lading; i.e. consignee or indorsee or whoever is in possession of the bill.

(2) the person to whom delivery of the goods to which a sea waybill relates is to be made by the carrier in accordance with that contract.

(3) the person to whom delivery of the goods is to be made in accordance with the undertaking contained in a ship's delivery order.

HAMBURG RULES 1978

The Hamburg Rules was an attempt by the United Nations, through U.N.C.T.A.D., to counter what was seen by many states as the excessive protection from liability of the carrier. The Rules came into force in November 1992, one year after the 20th ratification. They deal with the same area as the Hague-Visby Rules and are very similar in structure.

However, there are differences, some of great importance, making a brief consideration of the Rules necessary at this point. This is because the very nature of the construction of these Rules means that they could apply even when the carriage is from a non-contracting State, e.g. a Hague-Visby Rules State, but the cargo is to be discharged in a contracting State, i.e. Hamburg Rules State.[855] The Hamburg Rules are seen as much more favourable to the shipper than the carrier, which explains why major maritime States, i.e. countries with a significant ship tonnage, have not ratified them.

Article 2 deals with the application of the Rules, and provides:

'1. The provisions of this Convention are applicable to all contracts of carriage by sea between two different States, if:

(a) the port of loading as provided for in the contract of carriage by sea is located in a Contracting State, or

(b) the port of discharge as provided for in the contract of carriage by sea is located in a Contracting State, or

(c) one of the optional ports of discharge provided for in the contract of carriage by sea is the actual port of discharge and such port is located in a Contracting State, or

[854] Section 1(3), Carriage of Goods by Sea Act 1992.

[855] Article 2(1)(b), Hamburg Rules 1978.

(d) the bill of lading or other document evidencing the contract of carriage by sea is issued in a Contracting State, or

(e) the bill of lading or other document evidencing the contract of carriage by sea provides that the provisions of this Convention or the legislation of any State giving effect to them are to govern the contract.'

It is clear therefore, that the Hamburg Rules can apply to a voyage because of the country in which the port of discharge is located. This is very significant because it can have the consequence that a carrying voyage can be subject to two inconsistent, and as we will see incompatible, regimes. For example, if cargo is loaded in the U.K. where the Hague-Visby Rules are mandatory in their application and is to be discharged at Egypt, a Hamburg Rules contracting State, it is clear that there would be a clear conflict which in practice may depend on where (which country) the Court in which any claims are brought is situated. A U.K. Court would likely treat the contract as being subject to the Hague-Visby Rules, whereas an Egyptian Court would likely treat it as subject to the Hamburg Rules. The commercial implications of this are therefore substantial.

Similarly to the Hague-Visby Rules, the Hamburg Rules exclude bills of lading issued under charter-parties, except where such bills of lading are transferred to a third party.[856] However, the Rules apply to the carriage of deck cargo,[857] live animals,[858] and to all 'contracts of carriage by sea'.[859]

Article 4 of the Rules deals with the period of responsibility, and extends the 'tackle to tackle' rule of the Hague-Visby Rules to the time the carrier takes responsibility for the goods at the port of loading until they are handed over at the port of discharge. In effect the Rules make the carrier liable for loss or damage to the goods if it occurred when they were in his charge. This could render the carrier liable even if the loss or damage occurs in the port.

Unlike the Hague-Visby Rules there is no list of exemptions, and therefore, all the shipper has to do is show that the damage occurred while the goods were in the carrier's charge. The only defence available to the carrier under the Hamburg Rules is if he can show that 'he, his servants or agents took all measures that could reasonably be required to avoid the occurrence and its consequences'.[860]

---

856 Article 2(3), Hamburg Rules 1978.

857 Provided such carriage has been agreed or it is in accordance to the usage of the particular trade; Article 9(1), Hamburg Rules 1978.

858 Article 5(5), Hamburg Rules 1978.

859 This means 'any contract whereby the carrier undertakes against payment of freight to carry goods by sea from one port to another'; Article 1(6), Hamburg Rules 1978.

860 Article 5(1), Hamburg Rules 1978.

Given the above mentioned provisions, it is not surprising that no requirement of 'due diligence' is included in the Rules; it is in the carrier's interest to ensure that his vessel is seaworthy, particularly, as all the shipper needs to show is that the loss or damage occurred whilst the goods were in the charge of the carrier.

The Rules permit the carrier to be discharged from all liability in respect of goods unless legal proceedings for loss/damage to cargo were started within two years.[861] Therefore, generally speaking, the Rules, put a time-bar to claims made after the expiration of two years. The Rules further provide that a notice of loss or damage must be given in writing to the carrier at the port of discharge at the time or on the next working day following delivery of the goods,[862] and if the damage to the goods is not apparent, then this time is extended to fifteen 'consecutive' days after delivery.[863]

The Rules provide that the carrier's liability for loss or damage to goods is limited to 835 S.D.R.s (Special Drawing Rights) per package or other shipping unit or 2.5 S.D.R.s per kilogram of gross weight of the goods lost or damaged, whichever is the higher.[864]

Similarly to the Hague-Visby Rule, the Hamburg Rules also confirm that the maximum liability does not apply if the loss, damage, or delay, resulted from an act or omission of the carrier done with intent to cause damage, or recklessly and with knowledge that damage would probably result.[865]

---

[861] Article 20(1), Hamburg Rules 1978.

[862] Article 19(1), Hamburg Rules 1978.

[863] Article 19(2), Hamburg Rules 1978.

[864] Article 6(1)(a), Hamburg Rules 1978.

[865] Article 8(1), Hamburg Rules 1978.

CHAPTER 13

CARRIAGE OF GOODS BY ROAD

CONVENTION ON THE CONTRACT FOR THE INTERNATIONAL CARRIAGE OF GOODS BY ROAD (C.M.R.)

The provisions of the International Convention concerning the carriage of goods by road (C.M.R.) 1956 were notified and enacted in the U.K. by the Carriage of Goods by Road Act 1965, which came into force in 1967. The 1956 Convention was amended by the 1978 Protocol. It represents an attempt by the principal European nations to regulate the responsibilities and liabilities of carriers engaged in the international distribution of goods by road.

SCOPE AND APPLICATION

The Convention applies to all international carriage of goods by road in vehicles for reward, when the place of taking over the goods and the place for delivery, as specified in the contract, are situated in two different countries of which at least one is a Contracting Party, i.e. a State which has accepted the Convention.

The provision of Article 1 of the convention therefore, can be summed up as follows:

(a) there must be a contract of carriage for reward;

(b) this contract must be one for the carriage of goods;

(c) the carriage must be made by road;

(d) the contract must have international status.

The Act/Convention does not apply to traffic between the U.K. and the Republic of Ireland. Further, the C.M.R. does not apply:

(i) to carriage performed under an international postal Convention;

(ii) to funeral consignments; or

(iii) to furniture removal.

It should be observed that the Convention continues to apply provided the goods are not unloaded from the vehicle when it continues its journey by sea or some other means of transport.[866] Thus, the C.M.R. applies in the cases in which a container, particularly a groupage container, is taken by road on a trailer or similar vehicle from a contracting country to another country.

But if the loss, damage or delay has occurred during the carriage by the other means of transport and was not caused by an act or omission of the carrier by road, the liability of the carrier by road is determined not by the C.M.R. but by the applicable international Convention; if there is no such Convention, the C.M.R. applies.

Thus, in a case,[867] the question arose as to whether damage suffered by the cargo during its loading on board ship was governed by the C.M.R. or by the Hague Rules, which then applied to the carriage by sea. The cargo was to be transported from the U.K. to Denmark on a trailer. As the cargo was loaded on board the ship, it struck the bulkhead of the ship and was damaged. The trailer had already passed the outward ramp of the vessel and crossed the line of the stern. It was held that the carriage by road had ceased, although the trailer and its load had not been secured in the ship, and that the damage was governed by the Hague Rules. If in this case the damage had occurred before the trailer crossed the ship's rail, the C.M.R. would probably have applied.

THE CONSIGNMENT NOTE

The contract of carriage is evidenced by a C.M.R. consignment note, containing the following, which is not deemed to be an exhaustive account of all the details required:

[866] Article 2. *Quantum Corp. Inc.* v. *Plane Trucking Ltd.* [2003] 1 All ER.873, C.A.; C sent a consignment of hard disk drives from Singapore to Ireland. The consignment was issued with a master air waybill by an agent of D, the airline, which recorded that the goods were to be carried in two stages, first by air from Singapore to Paris and thence by road to Dublin on a service arranged through D. By clause 6.3.2 of its terms, D had the right to substitute some other means of transport on either leg. In the course of being carried by road the consignment was stolen. D accepted liability, but alleged that it was entitled to rely upon its contractual limitation of liability. C contended that the Paris to Dublin leg of the shipment was governed by the C.M.R. Convention which would, in the instant case, have overridden D's terms and provided for a more generous limit on liability. Article 1(1) of the C.M.R. provided for its application to every contract for the international carriage of goods by road. The Court of Appeal state, *inter alia*, that the place of taking over and delivery of the goods, for the purposes of Article 1(1), was the start and end of the contractually provided or permitted road leg. The fact that D, the airline, in the instant case could have elected to substitute a method of carriage other than road between Paris and Dublin was not relevant since the mere inclusion of such an option in a contract could not sensibly be decisive as to the application of the C.M.R. Therefore, the contract between the parties was for carriage by road within Article 1(1) of C.M.R. in relation to the road leg from Paris to Dublin and that D's own terms, to the extent that they limited its liability, were overridden, i.e. the C.M.R. limitation applied.

[867] *Thermo Engineers Ltd and Anhydro A/S* v. *Ferrymasters Ltd.* [1981] 1 W.L.R.1470.

1) date and the place where it is made out;
2) the names and addresses of the sender, the carrier and the consignee; the place and date of taking over the goods, and the place designated for delivery;
3) the ordinary description of the nature of the goods and the method of packing and, in the case of dangerous goods, their generally recognised description;
4) the number of packages and their special marks and numbers;
5) the gross weight of the goods or their quantity otherwise expressed;
6) charges relating to the carriage;
7) the requisite instructions for customs and other formalities;
8) and a statement that the carriage is subject to the provisions of the Convention.

Article 6 sets out at length all the particulars necessary. The consignment note has to be made out in three original copies signed by the sender and the carrier. The first copy is handed to the sender, the second accompanies the goods, and the third is retained by the carrier.

When goods are carried in different vehicles or are divided into different lots the seller or the carrier is entitled to require a separate consignment note for each vehicle or each kind or lot of goods. The consignment note is not a negotiable instrument, nor a document of title.

SUCCESSIVE CARRIERS

The C.M.R. provides that if the carriage by road is governed by a single contract but performed by successive road carriers, each shall be responsible for the performance of the whole operation, the second and each successive carrier becoming a party to the contract of carriage, under the terms of the consignment note, but, legal proceedings in respect of liability for loss, damage or delay may only be brought against the first carrier, the last carrier or the carrier who was in control of the goods when the event which caused the loss, damage or delay occurred, but several carriers may be sued at the same time.[868]

In the case of successive carriers the one responsible for the loss or damage is, as between the carriers, solely liable for compensation but if it cannot be ascertained to which carrier liability is attributable, the compensation has to

868 Article 34.

be borne by them proportionally. If one of the carriers is insolvent, the share of compensation due from him has to be paid by the other carriers in proportion to the share of the payment for the carriage due to them.[869]

Finally, note that if a person has contracted to carry the goods to their destination by a single contract but does not take the goods into charge himself and arranges for them to be delivered directly to the actual carrier to whom he has sub-contracted the job, he is nevertheless the first carrier and the actual carrier is the successive carrier.

If, on the other hand, a person undertakes (contracts) to procure carriage, i.e. to act as a forwarder, then C.M.R. does not apply to him.

LIABILITY OF THE CARRIER

The carrier is liable for the total or partial loss of the goods and for damage occurring between the time when he takes over the goods and the time of delivery, as well as for delay in the delivery. But the carrier is relieved of liability if the loss, damage or delay was caused:

(a) by the wrongful act or neglect of the claimant; or

(b) by the instructions of the claimant given otherwise than as the result of a wrongful act or neglect on the part of the carrier; or

(c) by inherent vice of the goods; or

(d) through circumstances which the carrier could not avoid and the consequences of which he was unable to prevent.

If the carrier wishes to rely on the fourth of these, it is not sufficient for him to show that he did not act negligently; he has to show that the loss could not be avoided. Thus, in one case,[870] the carrier, who was driving a consignment of shoes from Milan to England, parked the lorry in an unguarded lorry park in Milan in order for him and his assistant to have a meal. The only guarded lorry park was two hours away and to drive there would have involved breaching the driving period regulations. The alarm on the lorry was left on but thieves managed to by-pass it and to steal the lorry and its load. The carrier was held liable to the owner of the shoes because the loss was avoidable; he and his assistant could have taken turns to guard the lorry.

The carrier cannot rely on any of the relieving events if the loss, damage or delay is caused by the defective condition of the vehicle. In addition, the

---

[869] Article 38.

[870] *Michael Galley Footwear Ltd (In Liquidation)* v. *Iaboni* [1982] 2 All E.R.200.

C.M.R. contains a catalogue of special risks which relieve the carrier from liability. Thus, the carrier discharges the onus of proof if it can be shown that the loss can be attributed to:

(1) Permitted use of open unsheeted vehicles.

(2) Improper packing, marking and numbering.

(3) Handling operations undertaken by the cargo owner.

(4) Nature of the goods, i.e. ordinary leakage, breakage, etc.

(5) Carriage of livestock.

The fact that the goods have not been delivered within 30 days following the expiry of the agreed time limit or, if no time limit has been agreed, within 60 days from the time when the carrier took over the goods, shall be conclusive evidence of the loss of the goods.[871]

The compensation which the carrier is liable to pay in respect of total or partial loss of the goods is subject to a maximum limitation of liability. It is 8.33 S.D.R.s per kilogramme of gross weight short; in addition, the carrier has to refund in full the carriage charges incurred, Customs duties and other charges incurred in respect of the carriage of the goods.

In the case of delay, the measure of damages is limited to the carriage charges if the claimant can prove that he has suffered damage to that amount. It must be noted, however, that by Article 29(1) the above limits of liability would not be available to a carrier who is guilty of wilful misconduct. Wilful misconduct is:

> '...misconduct to which the will is party as contradistinguished from accident, and is far beyond any negligence, even gross or culpable negligence, and involves that a person wilfully misconducts himself who knows and appreciates that it is wrong conduct on his part in the existing circumstances to do, or to fail or omit to do (as the case may be), a particular thing, and yet intentionally does, or fails or omits to do it, or persists in the act, failure, or omission regardless of consequences.'[872]

---

[871] Article 20(1).

[872] *Per* Lord Alverstone, C.J., *Forder* v. *Great Western Railway Co.* [1905] 2 K.B.532, 535. This definition was cited with approval *in Texas Instruments Ltd.* v. *Nason (Europe) Ltd.* [1991] 1 Lloyd's Rep.146, 153. In *Laceys (Wholesale) Footwear Ltd.* v *Bowler International Freight Ltd.* [1997] 2 Lloyd's Rep.369, C.A., D were employed by C to transport a consignment of shoes from Spain to England. The Spanish driver reported to an office in Slough, where he was instructed to deliver the shoes only to L's premises in London. On reaching L's premises in London, however, the driver was persuaded to divert to an industrial estate and load the goods into an unmarked vehicle, which was subsequently reported stolen. D, contrary to C's express instructions, had neglected to insure the consignment. C were awarded damages on the grounds of B's wilful misconduct. for wilful misconduct to be established, it was necessary first to

Finally, Article 41(1) states that any stipulation which would directly or indirectly derogate from the provisions of the convention shall be null and void.[873]

TIME LIMITS

If the consignee takes delivery of the goods and does not in the case of apparent loss or damage, at the time of delivery, or in the case of loss or damage which is not apparent, within seven days of delivery,[874] send the carrier a notice of reservations, giving a general indication of the loss or damage, the fact of taking delivery is *prima facie* evidence that he received the goods in the condition described in the consignment note.

In the case where a person intends to claim for compensation in respect of delay in delivery, he should send a reservation in writing to the carrier within 21 days from the time that the goods were placed at the disposal of the consignee.[875] The period of limitation for bringing an action arising out of the carriage under the C.M.R. is one year.

ROAD HAULAGE ASSOCIATION

The normal terms of contracts of carriage by road include those of the Road Haulage Association. The most recent revision of contract terms for the carriage of goods by road, recommended to the members of the Association, are the 'Road Haulage Association Conditions of Carriage 1998'. The section covering liability for loss and damage under the above is given below:

'Subject to these Conditions the Carrier shall be liable for:

> physical loss, mis-delivery of or damage to any other goods comprising the Consignment unless the same has arisen from, and the Carrier has used reasonable care to minimise the effects of:
>
> *(i)* act of God;

consider what conduct was expected of someone entrusted with the property of another and then determine whether that person's acts or omissions were so far outside the range of what was to be expected that it could properly be considered misconduct. The Court considered that the combination of deliberate disregard of express instructions with the fact that D, who was entrusted with goods, knew that loss or damage might result from his actions but nevertheless deliberately took a risk when it was unreasonable to do so, could be construed as acting with reckless carelessness, and hence wilful misconduct.

873 *Quantum Corp. Inc.* v. *Plane Trucking Ltd.* [2003] 1 All ER.873, C.A.

874 Article 30(1).

875 Articles 30(3) and (4).

(ii) any consequences of war, invasion, act of foreign enemy, hostilities (whether war or not), civil war, rebellion, insurrection, military or usurped power or confiscation, requisition, or destruction of or damage to property by or under the order of any government or public or local authority;

(iii) seizure or forfeiture under legal process;

(iv) error, act, omission, mis-statement or misrepresentation by the customer or other owner of the goods or by servants or agents of either of them;

(v) inherent liability to wastage in bulk or weight, latent defect or inherent defect, vice or natural deterioration of goods;

(vi) insufficient or improper packing;

(vii) insufficient or improper labelling or addressing;

(viii) riots, civil commotion, strike, lockout, general or partial stoppage or restraint of labour from whatever cause;

(ix) consignee not taking or accepting delivery within a reasonable time after the Consignment has been tendered.

The Carrier shall not in any circumstances be liable for loss or damage arising after transit is deemed to have ended ..... whether or not caused or contributed to directly or indirectly by any act, omission, neglect, default or other wrongdoing on the part of the Carrier, its servants, agents or sub-contractors.

The Carrier shall not in any circumstances be liable in respect of a Consignment where there has been fraud on the part of the Customer or the owner, or the servants or agents of either, in respect of that Consignment, unless the fraud has been contributed by the complicity of the Carrier or of any servant of the Carrier acting in the course of his employment.'

Where loss, mis-delivery or damage is sustained to the consignment liability is limited to £1,300 per tonne or the value of the goods lost, whichever is the lowest. Notice of claim for loss, damage, or non-delivery should be made within seven days of termination of transit, and for any other loss within twenty-eight days. Claims must be made within one year of the date when transit commenced.

CHAPTER 14

CARRIAGE OF GOODS BY AIR

INTRODUCTION

The air law relating to the carriage of goods has reached a considerable measure of international uniformity. The U.K. legislation applicable to such carriage consists of the Carriage by Air Act 1932, 1961 and 1962.

These Acts gave effect to a Convention for 'the Unification of certain rules relating to International Carriage by Air' which was signed in Warsaw in 1929, and the 1955 Hague Protocol amendment.

The Warsaw Convention regulated the legal liabilities and relationships between carriers by air on the one hand, and passengers as well as cargo consignors and consignees on the other.

This was followed by a further convention supplementing,[876] as well as a number of Protocols amending,[877] the Warsaw Convention and its Hague Protocol[878] (referred to as the 'amended' Warsaw Convention).

However, the most recent, and perhaps most successful,[879] convention is the 'Convention for the Unification of Certain Rules Relating to International Carriage by Air', signed at Montreal on 28th May 1999.

In so far as the U.K. is concerned, the amended Warsaw Convention with the Montreal Protocol No.4 was the law applying to international carriage of goods by air until 27 June 2004. Since then, the Montreal Convention 1999 is

---

876 Convention Supplementary to the Warsaw Convention, for unification of certain rules relating to international carriage by Air performed by a person other than the contracting carrier, Guadalajara, September 18, 1961.

877 Protocol to amend the Warsaw Convention, Guatemala City, March 8, 1961: This dealt with carriage of passengers and their baggage but not cargo or mail. The Montreal Additional Protocols 1975: These three Protocols replaced the old unit of liability with Special Drawing Rights (S.D.R.). They applied the changes to the original Warsaw convention, the Hague Protocol, and the Guadalajara convention, respectively. The Montreal Protocol No.4: This dealt with cargo provisions, e.g. airway bill, of the Warsaw convention as amended by the Hague Protocol.

878 It must be noted that in addition to the various conventions and protocols, there have been numerous 'inter-carrier' agreements, i.e. agreements whereby air carriers tried to amend, or in a few cases denounce, the existing applicable legal regimes. For example, the Montreal Inter-carrier Agreement 1966.

879 Over fifty-four countries, including the U.S.A. and all E.C. Member States have ratified the Convention.

the legal regime applicable.[880] Therefore, it would appear that there are four possible legal regimes, in so far as carriage by air is concerned:

(1) carriage governed by the original Warsaw Convention, 1929 as amended by the Hague Protocol ('the Warsaw Convention');
(2) carriage governed by 'the Warsaw Convention' as amended by the 1975 Montreal Protocol No.4 ('the amended Warsaw Convention');
(3) carriage governed by the Convention known as 'the Montreal Convention 1999' ('the Montreal Convention'); and
(4) non-Convention carriage.

Having some knowledge of the basic system of liability and the general application of these regimes is necessary. Therefore, what follows is a brief description of the basic system of liability under carriage by air, followed by an account of the circumstances under which each regime applies.

BASIC SYSTEM OF LIABILITY

The carrier of goods by air is automatically liable for destruction or loss of, or damage to, or delay of cargo if it occurs during the carriage by air. The carrier has the right to use specified defences if he can, but he cannot contract out of liability or for a lower limit of liability. In return for this liability the carrier can rely on the benefit of maximum limits for his liability. The maximum limits of the air carrier's liability are:

Under the Warsaw Convention:

(i) 250 gold francs[881] per kilogramme; or
(ii) the value declared by the shipper.

[880] This Convention has been approved on behalf of the European Union, by Council Decision 2001/539/EC, 'on the conclusion by the European Community of the Convention for the Unification of Certain Rules for International Carriage by Air ("the Montreal Convention")', (O.J. 2001 L 194, 18/07/2001, p.38). This 1999 Convention in effect supersedes the Warsaw Convention and subsequent related provisions. The Carriage by Air Acts (Application of Provisions) Order 2004, (S.I.2004, No.1999), brought the Montreal 1999 Convention into force in the U.K. Amendments to the Carriage by Air Act 1961 were made by the Carriage by Air Acts (Implementation of the Montreal Convention 1999) Order 2002 (S.I.2002, No.263).

[881] The 'gold franc' referred to is a 'diplomatic' unit of currency, not an actual coin in commercial use, weighing 10/31 of a gramme and being of millesimal finess 900. The Carriage by Air (Sterling Equivalents) Order 1996, (S.I.1996, No.244), came into force in February 1996, and introduced the Sterling equivalents for expressing the limitation figures contained in the First Schedule (containing the Warsaw Convention 1929, and the amended Warsaw Convention 1975; 250 francs are £15.89, 5,000 francs £317.71, 125,000 francs £7942.79, and 250,000 francs £15,885.58.

Under the amended Warsaw Convention:

(i) 17 S.D.R.s[882] per kilogramme; or

(ii) the value declared by the shipper.

Under the Montreal Convention:[883]

(i) 17 S.D.R.s per kilogramme; or

(ii) the value declared by the shipper.[884]

The carrier loses the benefit of the above limits in the event of wilful misconduct. However, it must be noted that under the Montreal Convention no such defence exists in so far as loss/damage or delay is concerned, so it could be said that in this case the limitation of the carrier's liability is 'unbreakable'.[885]

An interesting point to note on Article 22(4) of the Montreal Convention is that when calculating the limit of liability for loss/damage/delay to goods, not only the weight of the package/packages is to be taken into account, but also the weight other packages covered by the same air waybill/receipt, if such loss/damage/delay affects the value of such other packages. This is an addition to bring the Convention up to date with legal developments in this area.[886]

Similarly to the Hague-Visby Rules, receipt of cargo by the person entitled to delivery without complaint (notice of loss/damage) is *prima facie* evidence of delivery in good condition. The right to claim for loss, damage or delay to the goods is time-barred if brought after the expiration of two years from the

---

882 The S.D.R. (special drawing rights) is an International monetary unit credited by the International Monetary Fund from a composite of several currencies.

883 It must be noted that under Article 23 the limits of liability are to be reviewed by each member State of the convention at five-year intervals. The Article also contains a list of factors to be taken into account when determining the reviewed liability figures.

884 There are also limits for (i) damage caused by delay to passengers of 4,150 S.D.R.s (Art.22(1)), and (ii) loss, damage or delay of baggage of 1,000 S.D.R.s (Art.22(2)).

885 In the Montreal Convention this 'test' is only applicable to the loss/damage or delay to baggage (Art.22(2)), and to damage caused by delay to passengers (Art.22(1)).

886 See for example, *Applied Implants Technology Ltd.* v. *Lufthansa Cargo AG* [2000] 2 Lloyd's Rep.46, where a carriage was subject to the original Warsaw Convention. C claimed damages against D for damage caused to part of a machine contained in one of the packages carried by D (all packages included in one airway bill). Under the amended Convention the weight of the damaged package or the combined weight of all packages covered under one air waybill was to be taken into account. However, D contended that the value of the remaining packages had not been affected since the damage to one part had not permanently affected the value of the remaining parts. Further, D suggested that C could replace the damaged machinery part without delay. It was held that the important point in the carriage with regards to this provision was the end of the carriage by air in which the damage was sustained. In the circumstances the damage caused the remaining parts of the machine to be worthless until the damaged part had been replaced. Furthermore, the ability of a claimant to mitigate its loss by obtaining a replacement part speedily would not affect the limitation of liability.

date of actual or expected arrival at destination, or the date on which carriage stopped.

'Carriage by air' comprises of the whole period during which the cargo is in the charge of the carrier, whether in an airport for the purpose of loading, delivery or transhipment of air cargo. Therefore, any damage is presumed to have taken place during the carriage by air, subject to contrary proof.

Finally, it must noted that none of the Conventions define 'aircraft'.

CARRIER'S DEFENCES

The carrier is not liable if he proves either:

(1) in so far as the Warsaw and amended Warsaw Conventions are concerned, that the carrier and his servants and agents have taken all necessary measures to avoid the damage or that it was impossible for him or them to take such measures. However, under the Montreal Convention this defence is only available[887] against a claim for delay; or

(2) if the carrier proves that the damage was caused by the negligence of the injured person.[888]

In addition, the carrier would not be liable if the loss/damage to the cargo was caused by:

(1) Inherent defect, quality or vice of that cargo; or

(2) defective packing of that cargo performed by person other than the carrier or its servants or agents; or

(3) an act of war or an armed conflict;

(4) an act of public authority carried out in connection with the entry, exit or transit of the cargo.

Claims in connection to luggage or goods may only be brought by the consignor against the first carrier, or the consignee against the last, whilst each, i.e. consignor and consignee, may take action against the actual carrier who performed that part of the carriage during which the loss, damage or delay occurred.

Servants and agents of the carrier acting within the scope of their employment can claim the benefit of the limits of liability applicable to the carrier.

[887] Article 19, Montreal Convention, 1999.

[888] However, this defence is not a complete one, but reflects the principle of contributory negligence, i.e. that the claimant contributed to his loss or damage. Hence, in English law, such provision would rarely 'exonerate' the defendants from liability.

APPLICATION OF THE LEGAL REGIMES

The Warsaw Convention

When, according to the contract between the parties, the places of departure and destination are located either:

- in the territories of two State parties to the original Convention; or
- in the territory of a single such State with an agreed stopping place anywhere outside that State.

The document of carriage is called the **air consignment note** (A.C.N.). This is not a document of title, but it is *prima facie* evidence of the conclusion of the contract, receipt of the goods, the conditions of carriage, the weight, dimensions, packing and number of goods.

It comes in three original parts; one is for the carrier (signed by the consignor); the second is for the consignee (signed by the consignor and accompanies the goods); the third is signed by the carrier and handed to the consignor after the goods have been accepted for carriage.

In cases of damage complaints must be made in writing to the carrier immediately after receipt of the goods, or not later than 7 days after receipt. In cases of delay, the complaint must be put in writing within 14 days from the date on which the goods were delivered.

The Amended Warsaw Convention and the Montreal Convention

When, according to the agreement between the parties, the places of departure and destination are located either:

- in the territories of two States both of which are parties to the Convention; or
- in the territory of a single State party to the Convention with an agreed stopping place anywhere outside that State.

If the place of departure is in the territory of a State party to the amended Warsaw Convention whilst the place of destination is in the territory of a State which is not only a party to the Warsaw Convention but has also become a party to the amended Warsaw Convention, then the only obligations which bind both of the States concerned are those contained in the Warsaw Convention.[889]

[889] The same would seem to be position under the Montreal Convention; Article 55. *Cf. Philippson and Others Appellants* v. *Imperial Airways, Limited* [1939] A.C.332, H.L., where it was held, *inter alia*, that a State (Belgium) which had only signed the (Warsaw) Convention was a 'High Contracting Party'.

The document of carriage is called an **air waybill** (A.W.B.). The Montreal Convention, however, states that alternatively any means which preserves the information prescribed in Article 5 would be acceptable.

Most of the provisions applicable for the air consignment note, mentioned above, apply also to the air waybill. Upon discovery of damage to the goods, complaint must be made in writing to the carrier immediately after delivery, or not later than 14 days after delivery. In the case of delay, the complaint must be put in writing within 21 days.

Under the Montreal Convention, the 'person entitled to delivery' of the goods must put his complaint in writing to the carrier immediately after discovery of damages, and at the latest within 14 days from the date of receipt. In the case of delay, the complaint must be made in writing within 21 days.[890]

The Non-Convention Rules

When the carriage of cargo is governed neither by the original nor by the amended Convention, and there is no agreed stopping place in another State then, whatever the place of departure, no part of the carriage would, as a matter of law, be governed by either of the Conventions, and in an action before the English courts the carriage would be governed by the non-Convention rules.

JURISDICTION

All three regimes (Warsaw, amended Warsaw, and Montreal) allow a suit to be brought against a carrier in the country:

(1) of its incorporation; or

(2) of its principal place of business; or

(3) where the ticket was purchased; or

(4) of destination of the passenger.

One notable difference, however, in the Montreal Convention is Article 33(2), which allows for claims for death or injury of passengers to be brought in the country(ies) of the passengers' principal and permanent residence, provided the carrier provides service to such country(ies), and the carrier conducts business in such country(ies).

[890] Article 31(2), Montreal Convention, 1999.

	HAGUE-VISBY RULES	HAMBURG RULES	C.M.R.	WARSAW CONVENTION	AMENDED WARSAW CONVENTION	MONTREAL CONVENTION
RELEVANT ACTS	Carriage of Goods by Sea 1971	N/A	Carriage of Goods by Road 1965	Carriage by Air Act 1932	Carriage by Air Act 1962	Carriage by Air Act 1961 (as amended)
APPLICATION	- Bill of Lading is issued in a contracting state, **OR** - Carriage is from a contracting state, **OR** - Bill of Lading provides so	- Port of loading in a contracting state, **OR** - Port of discharge in a contracting state **OR** - Relevant document is issued in a contracting state, **OR** - Relevant document provides so	- The place of departure and destination are in two different states; **AND** - At least one of those states is a contracting party	- The place of departure and destination are in two states parties to the convention; **OR** - The place of departure and destination are in one state party to the convention, and there is an agreed stopping place anywhere outside that state		
RELEVANT DOCUMENT	Bill of Lading **OR** Any Similar Document of Title	Bill of lading **OR** Any other Document Evidencing the Contract of Carriage by Sea	Consignment Note (set of 3)	Air Consignment Note (acn) (set of 3)	Air Waybill (awb) (set of 3)	Air Waybill **OR** Any other cargo receipt
CARRIER'S LIABILITY	Loss/Damage	Loss/Damage/Delay	Loss/Damage/Delay	Loss/Damage/Delay	Loss/Damage/Delay	Loss/Damage/Delay
NOTICE OF CLAIM (In writing)	Loss/Damage - Apparent immediately - Non-apparent 3 days	Loss/Damage - Apparent working day after delivery - Non-apparent 15 consecutive days Delay 60 Consecutive days	Loss/Damage - Apparent immediately - Non-apparent 7 days Delay 21 days	Loss/Damage - Apparent immediately - Non-apparent 7 days Delay 14 days	Loss/Damage - Apparent immediately - Non-apparent 14 days Delay 21 days	Loss/Damage - Apparent immediately - Non-Apparent 14 days Delay 21 days
TIME BAR	1 year	2 years	1 year	2 years	2 years	2 years
LIMITATION OF LIABILITY	Carrier not liable in excess of: 666.67 SDRs/package; **OR** 2 S.D.R.s/kilogramme of gross weight of the goods lost/damaged, whichever is the higher	Carrier not liable in excess of: 835 SDRs/package; **OR** 2.5 SDRs/kilogramme of gross weight of the goods lost/damaged, whichever is the higher	Carrier not liable in excess of: 8.33 SDRs/kilogramme of gross weight short	Carrier not liable in excess of: 250 gold francs/kilogramme **OR** the value declared and agreed by the shipper	Carrier not liable in excess of: 17 SDRs/kilogramme **OR** the value declared and agreed by the shipper	Carrier not liable in excess of: 17 SDRs/kilogramme **OR** the value declared and agreed by the shipper

Table 3: Conventions for Carriage of Goods

INDEX

A

absolute interest 23
abuse of a dominant position 198
acceptance by post 80
acceptance of bill of exchange 216
acceptance of goods 174
acceptance of offer 78
action *in personam* 30
action *in rem* 30
actual authority 134
actus reus 32
additional judge 11
ademption 23
administrators 27
advance disclosure 52
advance information 52
advertisements 23
agency agreements and E.C. law 148
agency by ratification 137
agency creation 133
agency of necessity 136
agency termination 147
agent 129
agent's authority 134
agent's capacity 129
agent's duties 139
agent's rights 141
agents' classification 129
air consignment note 293
air waybill 294
all risks 249
allocation 47
alteration of will 26
anticipatory breach 114
apparent authority 135
appellant 18
applicable law 120, 126
appropriation 161, 201, 207
arbitration 14
arrestable 51
Article 28 189
Article 30 190
Article 81 195
Article 82 198
artificial person 86
attestation 23
attorney, power of 130
Attorney-General 10, 12, 41
autonomy, letter of credit 230
average adjuster 259

B

back to back credit 228
bail 51, 52, 54, 55, 56, 58
bailee 256, 258
bailment 256
bailor 256
battle of the forms 79
bearer 270
beneficiary 23, 227
bequest 23
bilateral mistake 94
bilateral offer 76
bill of exchange 213
bill of lading 265
binding in honour only 83
binding precedents 14
blanket insurance policy 248
block exemption 192, 195
bought as seen 154
breach of contract 103
breach of warranty of authority 144
broker 131
broking 245
but for test 70
buyer's remedies 177

C

c.fr. 201
c.i.f. 205
C.M.R. 281
C.M.R. consignment note 282
capacity 85, 152
carriage of goods by air 292
carriage of goods by road 281
carriage of goods by sea 255
carrier 255
case reporting 17
cash or order 215
chain of causation 70
characteristic performance 121
charging order on land 48
charter-parties 261
chattels 30
cheques 213

C

chose in action 30
chose in possession 30
circuit judges 11
civil law 2
claimant 46
claused bill of lading 270
claused bills of exchange 222
clean bill of lading 229, 270, 275
clean remittances 223
codicil 23
collections 223
committal proceedings 57
committee stage 20
common carrier 257
common law 2
community sentences 61
companies 86
compensation award 39
compensation orders 61
Competition Act 1998 191
competition law 189
condition 100
confirmed letter of credit 227
consideration 81
consideration, past 81
consignee 255
consignor 255
constitutional conventions 21
constructive dismissal 38
contempt of court 12
contingent gift 23
contra proferentem 182
contract by deed 75
contract of insurance 240
contracts evidenced by writing 75
contracts in writing 75
contributory negligence 72
conversion 66
corporate veil 86
counsel 41
counter-offer 79
County Courts 6
Court of Appeal 9
cross-examination 48
Crown Court 9
Crown Prosecution Service 41
current account clause 166
current Court system 4
current legal system 17
custodial sentences 61

D

debt 48
defamation 68
defence statement 53
del credere agent 130
delegated legislation 18
demonstrative 24
deposition 57
description 110
determinable future time 216
deviation 263
devise 23
directions 47
director of public prosecutions 42
dirty bill of lading 270
disclosure 47
distributor 132
divisible contracts 111, 173, 118
documentary bills 223
domestic arbitration agreement 16
double actionability 127
drawee 214
drawer 214
due diligence 273
duress by threats 35
duress of circumstances 35
duty of care 69

E

economic duress 90
either way trialable offence 50
employment law 36
Employment Rights Act 1996 37
employment tribunals 7
endorsee 255
entire contracts 111, 173
equitable and beneficial ownership 165
European directives 19
European regulations 19
ex parte 44
ex turpi 72
examination in chief 53
exchange clause 222
exclusive distributor 132
exclusive licence 132

E

executor 27
executrix 27
exemption clauses 179
export distributor 133
express terms 98

F

f.a.s. 202
f.o.b. 201
factoring 235
factors 131
Family Reform Act 1969 85
fast track allocation 47
fictitious payee 215
firm 87
first reading 20
fitness for particular purpose 156
floating policy 247, 247
forfeiting 235
forum 120, 126, 128
forwarding agent 255
fountain of justice 4
fraud 16, 92, 231
fraudulent trading 87
free movement of goods 189
freezing orders 107
freight collect 256
frustration 115, 147
future time 216

G

garneshee order 48
general average 258
general criminal defences 34
grant of representation 27
green paper 20
gross misconduct 38
groupage bill of lading 269
guardian *ad litem* 86

H

Hague-Visby Rules 1968 271
Hamburg Rules 1978 277
High Court 7
holder for value 218
holder in due course 218
horizontal agreements 197
house bill of lading 270
House of Lords 10

I

implied terms 98
implied warranty of authority 144
in apparent good order 270, 275
inadequate packing 229
inchoate offences 33
INCOTERMS 202
indemnifying 244
indemnity 244
independent contractors 71
indictable offence 17, 43, 49
indictment 49
indorsee of bill of lading 255
inherent vice 252, 258
injunctions 44, 107
innominate term 102
Institute Cargo Clauses 248
insurable interest 241
insurance law 237
insured value 246
intention to form legal relations 83
inter partes 45
inter praesentes 96
interim order 44
interlocutory 42, 44
interplead 257
inter-vivos 31
intestacy 26
intestate 23
invitation to treat 77
irrevocable letter of credit 227

J

judge-made law 21
judges 10
judgment in default 46
Judgments Regulation 128
judicial office 10
judicial precedent 2
jurisdiction 8, 107, 107, 120, 128, 199
jurisdiction clauses 121
juristic person 86
jury 9, 49, 55, 59, 60, 68
justice of the peace 6

J

justices in eyre 3
justices of the Supreme Court 5

K

King, The 17
King's Bench Court 4
King's Court 3
King's Grand Council 3

L

lapse 24
laying of an information 51
legacy 24
legal burden 32
legality 87
letter before action 45
letters of credit 226
liability of carrier by air 290
liability of carrier by road 284
liens 131, 142, 259, 176
life interest 24
limitation of actions 42, 108
liquidated damages 104
loading broker 255
Lord High Chancellor 10
loyalty rebates 198

M

Magistrates Court 5
mandatory requirements 191
Mareva injunction 107
marine adventure 241
material circumstance 243
material facts 243
means enquiry form 52
mens rea 32
Mental Health Act 1983 85
Mental Health Act 2005 85
mercantile agent 131
merchantable quality 155
minors 85
misrepresentation 91
mistake 94
mode of trial hearing 54
money judgment 48
Montreal Convention 1999 289
multi-track allocation 47

N

necessaries 85
necessary goods or services 85
negligence 68
negotiability 213
nemo dat 168
next friend 86
non est factum 94, 180
nuisance 67

O

offer 76
offer, revocation 78
offeree 76
offeror/offerer 76
officious bystander 98
open cover 247
ostensible authority 135
overruling 14

P

particulars of claim 45
partnership 87
past consideration 81
per incuriam 14
personal representatives 27
persuasive precedents 14
plaintiff 46
plea and directions hearing 59
postal rule 80
private carrier 257
private nuisance 67
privity of contract 181
Privy Council 9
procedure in Crown Court 58
promissory estoppel 82
property in English law 29
proximate cause 245
public nuisance 67

Q

quantum meruit 113, 118

R

ratio decidendi 14
received for shipment 269
red clause credit 228
redundancy 39

R

remedies for breach of contract 104
rescission 107
reservation of title clauses 164
reversing 14
revocation of will 26
right of disposal 163
rights of agent 141
road haulage association 286
Romalpa clauses 163, 164, 167

S

S.D.R. (Special Drawing Right) 274
sale by description 153
sale by sample 157
Sale of Goods Act 1979 151
satisfactory quality of goods 155
seller's remedies 174
sequestration 12
serious arrestable offence 50
setting-down 47
shipped bill of lading 269
simple contract 75
small claims track 7, 47
Societas Europea 86
sources of Constitutional law 21
sources of English law 18
specialties 75
specific goods 158
specific performance 107
stale bill of lading 270
stipendiary magistrate 6
stoppage in transit 176
strict compliance 232
subject to contract 83
subrogation 244
subsequent authority 137
sum insured 247
summary offences 17, 44, 49
summary procedure 44, 52, 54, 58

T

termination of agency 147
terms of a contract 97
testate 23
third party debt order 48
through bill of lading 269
torts 63
transfer of property 157
transfer of title by non-owners 168
transferable credit 227
transhipment bill of lading 269
transit clause 250
trespass 63
trial bundle 48
tribunals 7

U

U.C.P. 500 (1994) 226
U.T.C.C. Regulations 1999 188
unascertained goods 160
undisclosed principal 143, 145
undue influence 90
unenforceable contract 83
Unfair Contract Terms Act 1977 183
unfair dismissal 38
unilateral offer 76
unliquidated damages 105
unnamed principal 144
unvalued insurance policy 247
utmost good faith 242

V

validity of wills 25
valued insurance policy 246
vicarious liability 70
vitiating factors 85
void contract 75, 84
voidable contract 83
volenti 72

W

warranties 101, 102, 103, 112, 153
wilful misconduct 251, 285
wills 22
writ of sequestration 12
wrongful dismissal 37
wrongful trading 87

Y

York-Antwerp Rules 259
youth courts 6